THE HISTORY
OF [LOWER]
CALIFORNIA

THE HISTORY OF [LOWER] CALIFORNIA

By

Don Francisco Javier Clavigero, S.J.

TRANSLATED FROM THE ITALIAN BY
SARA E. LAKE
EDITED BY A. A. GRAY

Reprinted from the Stanford University Press edition of 1937

MANESSIER PUBLISHING COMPANY
Box 5517, Riverside, California 92507

Library of Congress Catalog Card Number 79-150156
Standard Book Number 910950-03-2
Manessier Publishing Company
Box 5517, Riverside, Calif. 92507
© 1971 by Hugh Manessier   All Rights Reserved
Printed in the United States of America
by the A-to-Z Printing Company
Riverside, California

Copyright 1937 by the Board of Trustees of the Leland Stanford Junior University. Copyright renewed 1965 by Sara E. Lake. Reprinted (1971) by arrangement with Stanford University Press. New introductory material and new photographs and captions appearing in this reprint Copyright 1971 by Hugh Manessier.

Contents

Illustrations vii

Editor's Preface xi

Acknowledgments xv

Introduction To This Reprint xvii

Half Title Page, Original Stanford Edition xxvii

Frontispiece xxviii

Title Page, Original Stanford Edition xxix

Translator's Preface xxxiii

Table of Contents, Original Stanford Edition xlvii

Appendix 387

Index 397

Other Scholarly Reprints About Baja California And The Pacific Coast

THE CENTRAL DESERT OF BAJA CALIFORNIA:
Demography and Ecology
by Homer Aschmann

LC 66-29636   SBN 910950-01-6

LOWER CALIFORNIA AND ITS NATURAL RESOURCES
by Edward W. Nelson

LC 66-24189   SBN 910950-00-8

MARINE MAMMALS AND THE AMERICAN WHALE FISHERY
by Charles M. Scammon

LC 68-56382   SBN 910950-02-4

Illustrations

FOLLOWING PAGE 34

Fig. 1 — The *pitahaya dulce* or *tammia* (*Lemaireocereus Thurberi*), an unusually large specimen.

Fig. 2a — The *pitahaya agria* or *tajua* (*Machaerocereus gummosus*). In sites near the west coast of Baja California it has this low-growing form as described by Clavigero.

Fig. 2b — The *pitahaya agria* showing its characteristic growth form in the interior of the peninsula.

Fig. 3a — Fruit of the *pitahaya agria*. Note the extreme thorniness matching Clavigero's description.

Fig. 3b — A clump of *viznaga* (*Echinocactus peninsulae*).

Fig. 4 — The *cardón* (*Pachycereus Pringlei*). This is the largest species of cactus in the world.

FOLLOWING PAGE 36

Fig. 5 — The *garambullo* or *gkakil* (*Lophocereus Schottii*)

Fig. 6 — Fruits on the upper stems of a *garambullo*.

FOLLOWING PAGE 38

Fig. 7 — *Opuntia* sp. or *a*, one of the platyopuntias native to Baja California.

Fig. 8 — *Ficus Palmeri* or *anaba*. The name *zalate* is still used locally along with *higuera cimarrona* or wild fig.

Fig. 9 — *Ficus Palmeri*. The roots characteristically drape themselves over the rocks of a canyon side.

Fig. 10 — *Opuntia cholla*. There are many species of cylindropuntias growing in the peninsula. Clavigero (*v.i.* pp. 56-57) indicates that they were regarded as noxious weeds rather than as bearers of useful fruit.

FOLLOWING PAGE 50

Fig. 11 — *Agave deserti* or *mescal* with many clumps in bloom. This small species of the interior of the peninsula seems to have been the preferred food source. Clumps of *viznaga* and platyopuntias are scattered on the hillside.

Fig. 12 — *Palo blanco* (*Lysiloma candida*) or *gkokio*. The bark, purplish-brown beneath the white skin, has excellent tanning properties.

FOLLOWING PAGE 56

Fig. 13 — A stand of *cirio (Idria columnaris)* or *milapa*. The bizarre plants are present only in the northern part of the Jesuit area of Baja California.

Fig. 14 — A plant association near the northern limits of Jesuit missionization. The thick trunked trees are *Pachycormus discolor* (elephant tree). *Cirio, cardón,* and some cylindropuntias are also present.

FOLLOWING PAGE 170

Fig. 15a — The mission church at Loreto. This photograph was taken in 1949 early in the modern refitting of the church.

Fig. 15b — The refitted mission church in Loreto.

Fig. 16a — Interior of the nave of the mission church at Loreto early in its refitting period. The details of the masonry work in the massive walls indicate several reconstructions, but some of the structure dates from Jesuit times.

Fig. 16b — Remnant of the chapel at San Juan Londó. This site was designated a mission only for a short time, and then it became a subsidiary *pueblo de visita* of Loreto.

Fig. 17 — The mission church and part of the modern village of San Javier Viggé. A carved inscription bears the date 1758 so the building is clearly of Jesuit construction and is their greatest architectural monument in Baja California.

Fig. 18a — Looking north over the village of San Javier from the roof of the mission church.

Fig. 18b — Interior of the church at San Javier.

FOLLOWING PAGE 210

Fig. 19 — The mission site at Santa Rosalía Mulegé looking north. The church is built on an Indian settlement site and stands on an outcrop of a sill of volcanic rock that forces to the surface the ground water of an extensive drainage basin, forming the oasis of Mulegé. The modern concrete dam replaces one constructed early in the mission period.

Fig. 20 — The mission church at Mulegé. The period of construction of this building complex is not known, but part at least must date from Jesuit times. It has had a resident priest most of the time since 1905 and so has received some maintenance.

FOLLOWING PAGE 256

Fig. 21 — The mission church at San Luis Gonzaga. The building must be of Jesuit construction since the mission was abandoned shortly after the Jesuit expulsion. Father Baegert is given credit for building it. During the late nineteenth century, when San Luis Gonzaga was a regional trading center, the facade was refinished.

Fig. 22 — Rear view of the mission church at San Luis Gonzaga.

FOLLOWING PAGE 262

Fig. 23 – San Ignacio, the central settlement and the mission church surrounded by date gardens and vineyards.

Fig. 24 – The mission church at San Ignacio. Although the mission was operated by the Jesuits for nearly 40 years, the imposing church was built under the administration of the Dominicans during the 1780s.

FOLLOWING PAGE 330

Fig. 25 – The mission church at Santa Gertrudis. It is likely that this stone structure dates from Dominican rather than Jesuit times.

Fig. 26a – The site of Mission San Borja, looking west. Local residents say that the adobe ruins on the near side of the stone church include the Franciscan church; they may, however, be of Jesuit origin. The stone buildings were constructed by the Dominicans.

Fig. 26b – The mission church at San Borja. This is the most northerly of the stone missions.

FOLLOWING PAGE 364

Fig. 27 – Ruins of the mission church at Santa Maria. This was the last and most northerly of the Jesuit missions. At its rugged and barren site it never prospered. The extant ruins are almost certainly of Franciscan or Dominican construction since the Jesuits occupied the site only a little more than a year.

Fig. 28 – Ruins of the mission church at San Fernando Velicatá (Guiricata). The site was discovered by the Jesuit Father Link and selected for a mission, but the expulsion intervened. The Franciscan Father Serra founded the mission in 1768, but the building probably was built by the Dominicans.

Although all of the illustrations listed above are new, and did not appear in the original Stanford edition of 1937, it was agreed by those concerned with the production of this reprint that the illustrations would be more useful if they were placed throughout the text rather than at the front of the reprint. However, the original pagination has been retained on all pages with arabic numerals; new roman numerals have been assigned at the front of the book. In the Stanford edition, a gray screen was added to the map provided by the Huntington Library. In this reprint, that screen has been omitted to provide greater clarity.

Mrs. Sara E. Lake, from a photograph taken at the time she was translating Clavigero's work.

About the Authors of this Translation...

*E*very good book enriches mankind; surely Clavigero's *Storia della California* justifies the space it takes on any Baja California bookshelf. With this widely-acclaimed translation, Sara E. Lake has accomplished far more than necessary to bring us a better understanding, in English, of this fascinating historical era. Even before she had finished translating the original volume, Mrs. Lake knew that additional notes were needed in many places throughout the text. This information, much of which was written in Italian, Spanish, and Latin, was obtained from various libraries in the United States and also in Mexico. Even now, some 34 years after publication, the dedication and scholarship which must have been required to produce this translation still seem astonishing. The interesting and unusual circumstances which made it possible deserve some comment as this first reprinting is prepared for a wider audience.

Just as Clavigero capitalized on his knowledge of many languages when he originally wrote *Storia della California*, Sara Lake has also used her command of languages to advantage in writing the English translation. Her early life was spent in Mexico with relatives. In answer to my inquiry, she wrote in part: "Mexico, because of its climate, was good for my frail health at the time. I grew up bilingual; I came here and entered the University of California, where I received my degree. My teaching vacations were nearly always spent in Mexico, studying and painting. Very definitely, the time I spent there enriched my life linguistically, historically, and artistically, for all of which I am very grateful."

Sara Lake taught Spanish and Italian in the Berkeley High School for many years; she is also conversant with French, Portuguese, and Latin. At the time of her retirement, she was Chairman of the Modern Language Department. In addition to her regular duties, she made translations in several languages for Dr. H. E. Bolton of Bancroft Library and, through him, became very much interested in the Jesuits. She translated the Italian and Latin manuscripts for his book, *Rim of Christendom*, for which Bolton was knighted by the last king of Italy.

Sara Lake's account of her initial interest in Clavigero's work is quoted from one of her letters: "I have always been interested in the colonial history of Mexico and own some old Spanish and Italian books, among the latter an original copy of Clavigero's *Storia della California* published posthumously in 1789 in Venice. When I could find no English translation for it I wrote to the Library of Congress in Washington to find out if there might be other copies. At that time they wrote that there were 8 known copies and named the libraries where they were. That made my copy the 9th and so I decided to translate it about 1932. It seemed a pity that such important information was not more widely available."

She began working on the Italian version early in 1933, and before the end of that year had completed typing the translation. Then the search for information for the footnotes was begun; more than another year passed before the basic footnote materials could be compiled.

It was at this time that the significant contributions of Mr. A. A. Gray began to affect the final form of the work. He was chairman of the History Department in the Berkeley High School, and was deeply interested in California history. He had written a textbook for high schools titled *History of California* which was published in 1934. Sara Lake had translated a number of Spanish articles into English for him, and so it was natural that she would turn to him for the editing of her notes. In addition to editing her notes, he also added others pertaining to that period, which he located in English during his research.

On her annual trips to Mexico prior to publication, Sara Lake had searched for a painting of Clavigero. She felt strongly that there must be a portrait of the second-best educated man of his time in Mexico. She wrote: "I finally found it in the Museo Nacional de Mexico, knew it was he because it had a scroll with his name, place of birth plus place and date of death. When the Director of the Museum learned why I wanted a photograph he very graciously had one made for me. It is reproduced in the Stanford publication."

After I wrote to Mrs. Lake, asking if there was some financial aid provided to assist in the completion of such a large book, she replied that there was some, but not a large amount. "I gave some of my own money to see it published," she wrote, "so that the work of these selfless men might be further known."

It is interesting to speculate whether Clavigero's classic work would be available in English today, if Sara Lake and A. A. Gray had not been so determined to perform their dedicated work. It seems apparent that both were inspired by the monumental efforts of the Jesuits in Baja California as well as by Clavigero's labors in Italy.

Mrs. Lake has asked only that the one error which appeared in the 1937 edition be corrected in this reprint. In the original Stanford edition, both Lake and Gray were listed as translators. Mrs. Lake was solely responsible for the translation. Mr. Gray's contribution in editing her notes and adding others of his own was most important too; his work materially enhanced Mrs. Lake's translation. It seems obvious that their combination of talents makes this edition in English even more useful than Clavigero's remarkable original work.

Mr. Gray died in 1957. Mrs. Lake now lives in Berkeley, California. Clavigero finished his work on *Storia della California* in 1786, several years before it was finally published. Now, almost two centuries later, this first reprinting of his work in English is offered for your enjoyment. Perhaps Clavigero, if he could, would join with us in hoping that this volume will provide not only pleasure but a better understanding of Baja California's most important historical period, and of the men who changed the destiny of that arid but unforgettable peninsula.

Hugh Manessier

Acknowledgments

I am grateful to Homer Aschmann for writing most of the new introductory material which appears in this reprint. We have now worked together on a number of books, and his assistance and advice have always been valued highly. My appreciation is also extended to Eben, Jim, and Francis Dale; these three brothers operate the A-to-Z Printing Company where this book was printed.

The encouragement and assistance of Dr. George E. Lindsay, director of The California Academy of Sciences, has been most useful in the preparation of this reprint. His suggestion that we include additional pictures of many of the plants and missions which Clavigero describes in the text was most welcome. Many of the new illustrations which appear in this book were provided by Dr. Lindsay. His suggestions and assistance have improved each reprint we have prepared on Baja California and the Pacific Coast.

My most cordial thanks are also extended to the translator of this book, Mrs. Sara E. Lake. Her cooperation and kindness in providing valuable background information has permitted me to include in this reprint the biographical material about her and about Mr. A. A. Gray, the editor.

Finally, a personal "thank you" to Mrs. Alfrida Classon, Miss Mae Classon, and to Mr. and Mrs. E. L. Manessier. Their unfailing encouragement over the years is difficult to acknowledge adequately, but it remains an ever-pleasant memory.

Hugh Manessier

Introduction To The Reprinted Edition

Of the three major histories of Jesuit missionary activities in Baja California, Clavigero's *Storia della California* is the third and last to be written. Like the earliest, the effort by Miguel Venegas[1] and his posthumous collaborator Andrés Marcos Burriel,[2] it was the work of a professional Jesuit historian who had never visited the peninsula. Though it lacks the immediacy of observation that Baegert's[3] work contains, it shows the author's access to and skilled utilization of official documents and other historical source materials. As a record of events it probably cannot be superseded.

The Jesuit chapter in the history of Baja California that began with Kino's tentative ventures under Admiral Atondo at La Paz and San Bruno in 1683-85, and was firmly established

---

(1) "Empressas Apostólicas de los P. P. Missioneros de la Compañía de Jesús de la Provincia de Nueva España Obradas en la Conquista de Californias, debida y Consagradas al Patrocinio de María Santíssima, Conquistadora de Nuevas Gentes en su Sagrada Imagen de Loreto. Historiadas por el Padre Miguel Venegas de la Misma Compañía de Jesús. Se acabó esta Historia en Sabbado 7 de Noviembre de 1739." A beautiful copy of this manuscript is in the Bancroft Library, Berkeley, California; other copies are in the library of the Real Academia de la Historia in Madrid and that of Mariano Cuevas S.J. in Mexico City as well as an incomplete one in the Huntington Library, San Marino, California.

(2) Miguel Venegas and Andrés Marcos Burriel, *Noticia de la California y de su conquista temporal y espiritual hasta el tiempo presente. Sacada de la historia manuscrita, Formada en Mexico año de 1739 por el Padre Miguel Venegas. de la Compañía de Jesús; y de otras Noticias y Relaciones antiguas y modernas*, 3 vols. Madrid 1757. Although he left Venegas' name alone on the title page, Burriel made major additions to and deletions from the original manuscript work.

(3) Johann Jakob Baegert, *Nachrichten von der Amerikanischen Halbinsel Californien: mit einem zweyfachen Anhang falscher Nachrichten*. Mannheim, 1772. Translated with introduction and notes as *Observations in Lower California* by M. M. Brandenburg and Carl L. Baumann, Berkeley, 1952.

under Salvatierra at Loreto in 1697, was terminated completely in 1768. Although the missions founded and explorations accomplished would be exploited by other religious orders and the Spanish government, the surviving Jesuit missonaries could never return to the fields of their labors. The only monument that they could construct and behold as they ended their lives in enforced retirement in Italy or Germany was a history of their deeds and those of their predecessors in the Company of Jesus. Seldom can an historical sequence be bounded so sharply. With the expulsion of the Jesuits a new set of actors with new policies and significantly different goals would dominate Baja California's long decline and modern recovery.

Probably to a greater degree than in any of the other areas of missionary activity in the New World, the Jesuits dominated what went on in Baja California. The isolation of the region meant that it did not protect a vulnerable frontier as did the Pimería Alta of Sonora nor was it a zone of contention between established colonial powers as were Florida and Paraguay. The basic unproductiveness of the land meant that secular pressures for settlement and economic development were weak. Interest in pearling and the silver mines of Santa Ana are basically transient exceptions. Almost to the end of the Jesuit period it is likely that without the zeal of the missionaries, there would have been no effort by Europeans to maintain permanent occupation of the peninsula. Although the Jesuits did negotiate some sharing of their once absolute authority with secular officials following the Indian revolts of the 1730's, they held nearly complete temporal as well as spiritual power until the end of their stay. Realities of life on the peninsula meant that erection of the City of God had to yield priority to a struggle for survival. The Jesuit mission did survive, and it was able to accomplish a thorough exposure to Christianity of an Indian population that was so distant culturally and economically from the missionaries that it seemed perversely resistant and recalcitrant.

It seems needless to question the conclusion that expulsion of the Jesuits from the Spanish Empire was a decision of high national policy made in Madrid. It probably could not have been affected by any changes in activities or policies carried on by the Order in California or even in New Spain. On the other hand, by 1768 British, Russian and French interests in the Northeast Pacific regions had given California a new strategic importance. The active and expensive intervention by the Spanish Crown, initiated by its visitor-general José de Gálvez, that promoted rapid expansion northward into Alta California was a logical geopolitical move at that time. It just happened to coincide with expulsion of the Jesuits from the Americas. By 1768 the time was past when the California missions could be considered primarily and simply the product of evangelical zeal applied to some of the world's most impoverished inhabitants.

Francisco Javier Clavigero S. J. was an established historian and man of letters by the time he was expelled from Mexico and found refuge in Cesena and later Bologna in Italy. With neither teaching nor pastoral responsibilities he could concentrate on historical study, and his great four volume work on the ancient history of Mexico[4] was his major product. One remains somewhat puzzled why a now established scholar would shift from a broad subject of wide interest and appeal to the detailed investigation of a minor and peripheral province, one that he had never even visited, for the concluding work of his life.

The completeness and self-contained character of the history noted above must have been a factor in turning his interest to California. The extreme poverty and apparent cultural backwardness of the Indians of Baja California also made them very special. The idea of bringing Christianity to these, the lowliest of God's children, was a sustaining and inspiring force for both the Jesuits and their Franciscan and Dominican successors, and Clavigero was vulnerable to the same influence. Curiously, though his *History of Mexico* was a highly creditable, even innovative work, its importance today is small. The author was temporally too far from the scene and was completely dependent on interpreting the contemporary chronicles, though he did make use of Indian linguistic evidence. Modern students prefer to go directly to the original sources. The *Storia della California*, however, retains its value as a basic document. Clavigero in Italy had access to letters, reports, and diaries, some of which are no longer to be found, and he could consult, directly or by correspondence, with missionaries who had served

---

(4) *Storia antica del Messico*, Cesena, 1780-1781.

in California. He thus had access to data that would never again be available, and his synthesis of them becomes a primary and invaluable source. We may wish that he had been more careful to note his sources and the precise times and places where certain observations on the natural history of Baja California and on its aboriginal inhabitants were made, but his statements often are all the knowledge we have.

By paying a modest pension to each of the Jesuits exiled in the Papal States in Italy[5] the Spanish Crown exercised some control over the ability of the Jesuits to protest their expulsion. As a native of Mexico Clavigero had special reasons to resent his exile, but his account of the actual expulsion from the California Peninsula is remarkably spare and objective, much more so than that of Baegert who wrote in Germany much closer to the time of the event.[6] Fear of reprisals on his fellow exiles has been suggested by modern Jesuit writers as a reason for this reserve,[7] but it is more likely that as a mature historian he recognized that a calm recital of conditions and events would have greater impact than would complaints about injustices. Modern Jesuit historians tend to show less restraint.[8]

One returns to the question of why the excellent English translation by Lake and Gray here presented is of such value that students of Baja California are pleased to see it returned to print and availability. Modern historians, beginning with Bancroft[9] and continuing through Englehardt and Dunne, have exploited Clavigero's work thoroughly, quoting it extensively. Their access to documents unavailable to Clavigero has made it possible to amend and elaborate the historical narrative, and, more significantly, the Jesuit mission to California can be placed in clearer context in respect to historical currents in the

(5) One hundred and fifty florins a year according to Baegert, *Observations in Lower California*, p. 198.

(6) ibid, pp. 165-172.

(7) Zephyrin Engelhardt, *Missions and Missionaries of California*, Vol. 1, Lower California, Santa Barbara 1929, p. 314; Ernest J. Burrus, "Jesuit Exiles, Precursors of Mexican Independence," *Mid-America*, Vol. 36 (July, 1954), p. 162-163.

(8) Peter Masten Dunne, *Black Robes in California*, University of California Press, Berkeley and Los Angeles, 1952.

(9) Hubert Howe Bancroft, *Works*, Vol. 15, *History of the North Mexican States and Texas, Vol. 1. 1531-1800*, San Francisco, 1886.

outer world. To a considerable degree, however, Clavigero's record of what went on from 1739, the effective completion date for Venegas' *Noticias*, to 1768 remains our primary source of information. The narrative flows, tells a coherent story, and gives the reader confidence in the accuracy and historical judgment of the author.

With the recent rise of interest in Baja California some of the important manuscripts Clavigero utilized have been identified and published. Examples are some of Linck's letters and the diary of his exploration northward in the peninsula in 1766,[10] and an anonymous account (I believe it to be by Fernando Consag) of natural history and ethnography of the central portion of the peninsula.[11] One cannot fail to be impressed by how incisively and accurately these materials were exploited to make their contribution to the chronicle. It is also clear that not all of Clavigero's manuscript sources are now available. The diary of Consag's 1753 exploration in the desolate and rugged spine of the peninsula that led to the discovery of the springs at Calamajué has not been found, and there are many similar gaps in the surviving documentary record that only Clavigero's narrative fills.

Perhaps of greatest value are discussions of the Indian inhabitants and their cultures. Not only in the introductory section that is expressly devoted to the subject do these appear, but revealing remarks and anecdotes are found in the historical sections of the work, especially in accounts of explorations and in those of the establishment of each of the several missions. In my own efforts to reconstruct the culture of the extinct Indians of the central portion of the peninsula,[12] basic information was found in Clavigero's work that is available nowhere else. Future students will no doubt wish to return to the original source. Of special importance are data concerning

(10) Ernest J. Burrus, *Wenceslaus Linck's Diary of his 1766 Expedition to Northern Baja California*, Dawson's, Los Angeles. 1966; _____, *Wenceslaus Linck's Reports and Letters 1762-1778*, Dawson's, Los Angeles. 1967.

(11) Homer Aschmann, *The Natural and Human History of Baja California from Manuscripts by Jesuit Missionaries*, Dawson's, Los Angeles. 1966.

(12) Homer Aschmann, *The Central Desert of Baja California: Demography and Ecology*. Ibero-Americana 42, Berkeley and Los Angeles, 1959. Reprinted by Manessier, Riverside, California. 1967; _____, "Historical Sources for a Contact Ethnography of Baja California," *California Historical Society Quarterly*, Vol. 44 (June, 1965), pp. 99-121.

Indians who lived north of San Ignacio, an area that was essentially unknown when Venegas completed his report. It cannot be denied that Clavigero's failure to cite Indians of specific tribes or localities as possessing particular customs or culture elements reduces the utility of this information. The student can use two correctives. A definite location is indicated when mention of a custom occurs in an account of an exploration that led to the founding of a mission. Also, a custom mentioned by Clavigero but not by Venegas can with considerable confidence be associated with the north central part of the peninsula.

No historian is without a point of view, certainly not a Jesuit. In his account there will be some features or events he chooses to emphasize and some that he subdues or even suppresses. Emphasis on the dedication, ability, and self-sacrifice of the missionaries is fully expected, and objective examination of their achievements would indicate only a very modest need to discount it. There are two areas, however, in which Clavigero and his predecessors Venegas and Burriel seem to have been less than willing to publish all the information that was available to them. One concerns the demographic history of the missionized Indian populations. From the *libros de missiones* that still survive we can be sure that each mission kept careful track of baptisms, marriages, and burials among its neophytes. Clavigero does not conceal the fact that there was a tremendous decline in the aboriginal population following missionization, especially in the south, and he submits a crude census of the missions at the time of expulsion. He recognizes as well that epidemic disease was a major cause of population decline, but devotes only a little speculation as to the reasons for its virulence (*v.i.* pp. 366-369). It is almost certain that series of censuses could have been made at all or most of the missions; perhaps they were. They would be of great theoretical value today. Baegert does make a guess at the pre-mission Indian population of Baja California.[13] Clavigero does not, though he had access to more information. Curiously, modern studies

---

(13) Baegert, *Observations in Lower California,* p. 54.

suggest that Baegert's estimate of 40,000 to 50,000 was remarkably accurate.[14] Census-type records are much more complete for the Franciscan and Dominican periods than for the Jesuit period, though it is hard to believe that the Jesuits knew less about their charges than did their successors. The stronger secular pressures on the later missionaries are probably causative. It might be suggested that the Jesuits were not interested in counting people, though the quality of the mission record books indicates otherwise. More likely, the decline of the Indian populations under their tutelage was a serious embarrassment. While it was not ignored it was not a subject to dwell on.

The other downgraded topic is the economic potential of Baja California. The pearl fisheries of the Gulf of California had been known to the world for centuries, and they are treated at some length. Precious metals, a resource of transcendant importance and interest in New Spain, are given remarkably little attention. Only the silver mines of Santa Ana and San Antonio are mentioned at all (*v.i.* pp. 24-32, 346-349), and the reference is to the poverty of the mines as well as pressure on food supplies and demoralization of the Indians caused by mining activity. From Santa Gertrudis northward there are a number of mineralized districts of which Calmallí is perhaps the most important. It is hard to imagine the Jesuits, many of whom had extensive backgrounds in natural history, not recognizing a district that in the late nineteenth century supported thousands of miners and prospectors.[15] Clavigero is definitely more interested in discussing base materials such as salt and sulfur, evidently feeling that their exploitation was unlikely to provoke immigration and the accompanying disruptions in the missionary control of the Indians. Just at the end of the Jesuit period some members of the Order felt that their position in Baja California would be strengthened if the peninsula could be made to yield wealth rather than expenses to the crown. Father Burriel, writing from Madrid to Juan de Armesto in Mexico City in 1760, definitely requested data

(14) Sherburne F. Cook, *The Extent and Significance of Disease Among the Indians of Baja California* 1697-1773, Ibero-Americana 12, Berkeley, 1937; Aschmann, *The Central Desert of Baja California,* pp. 145-180.

(15) George F. Deasy and Peter Gerhard, "Settlements in Baja California 1768-1930." *Geographical Review,* Vol. 34 (October, 1944), pp. 574-586.

on economic potential of the peninsula.[16] Clearly Clavigero took a different attitude toward economic development.

Finally, a comment on the Lake translation may be appropriate. In the more than thirty years that it has been available students have found the rendition from the original Italian highly satisfactory. It is distinctly superior to the extant Spanish translations. Though today we know Clavigero's sources better and would be able to amend and add to the notes, the thorough annotations by Lake and Gray are of great worth. The original edition, published with a limited number of copies by the Stanford University Press, went out of print in 1945 and quickly became a rare book. The scarcity of this basic document has for decades been a handicap to students of the history of Baja California.

Homer Aschmann

---

(16) The manuscript letter is in the Huntington Library, San Marino, California (HM22243). cf. Aschmann, *Natural and Human History of Baja California*, pp. 18-22.

THE HISTORY
OF [LOWER]
CALIFORNIA

Courtesy of the National Museum of Mexico City

FRANCISCO XAVIER CLAVIGERO

THE HISTORY OF [LOWER] CALIFORNIA

By

Don Francisco Javier Clavigero, S.J.

TRANSLATED FROM THE
ITALIAN AND EDITED
BY SARA E. LAKE AND
A. A. GRAY

STANFORD UNIVERSITY PRESS
STANFORD UNIVERSITY, CALIFORNIA
LONDON: HUMPHREY MILFORD
OXFORD UNIVERSITY PRESS

STANFORD UNIVERSITY PRESS
STANFORD UNIVERSITY, CALIFORNIA

LONDON: HUMPHREY MILFORD
OXFORD UNIVERSITY PRESS

THE BAKER AND TAYLOR COMPANY
55 FIFTH AVENUE, NEW YORK

MARTINUS NIJHOFF
9 LANGE VOORHOUT, THE HAGUE

THE MARUZEN COMPANY
TOKYO, OSAKA, KYOTO, SENDAI

COPYRIGHT 1937 BY THE BOARD OF TRUSTEES
OF THE LELAND STANFORD JUNIOR UNIVERSITY

PRINTED AND BOUND IN THE UNITED STATES
OF AMERICA BY STANFORD UNIVERSITY PRESS

To those
whose interest in
the study of California history
and whose generosity made
possible the publication
of this book

⚜

TRANSLATORS' PREFACE

THE history of Lower (Baja) California is closely related to that of the state of California with which it was long identified and called simply "California." The first settlement in what is now the state, a settlement founded in 1769, was made possible by the supplies which were furnished by the Missions of that barren peninsula, and for many years afterward these Mission settlements continued to aid those founded in Upper (Alta) California, sending them food, church furniture, tools, seed, live stock, and other necessities of life. So dependent were these later settlements on those of Lower California and so closely were the two Californias related that it may be said that Lower California is the mother of the state of California.

The peninsula of Lower California has been of considerable interest to the people of the United States on several occasions. Our troops occupied this peninsula during the Mexican War, capturing La Paz in November 1847, after some severe fighting. At the close of this war when peace negotiations were being considered, President Polk planned that Lower California would be added to any land that might be ceded to us by Mexico. He suggested that five million dollars be paid for the country. Later the Secretary of State, James Buchanan, wrote to our peace commissioner, Nicholas P. Trist, "to secure to our citizens, in accordance with your original instructions," the entire peninsula. Buchanan, when he became President, continued his efforts to get possession of Lower California. When the French were in Mexico during the Civil War in the United States it was proposed that the United States lend Mexico twenty million dollars with which to drive France from her soil. As security for such a loan we hoped to get a first mortgage on Lower California, as well as on Chihuahua, Sinaloa, and Sonora. At the same time and for many years after the close of the Civil War various corporations in the United States attempted to colonize the peninsula and to develop the natural resources there. All these ventures failed, but they increased the interest of the American people in that country. Within the present century various proposals have been made, some of them in Congress, that our government should try to purchase the peninsula from Mexico, so far without effect.

The still earlier efforts of the Spanish government to colonize Lower California and the work of the missionaries there are told in a most fascinating style in this volume. Only thirty years after Columbus discovered the New World, in 1522, that brave and able *conquistador*, Hernán Cortés, after landing at Vera Cruz, fought his way westward across Mexico and founded the settlement of Zacatula on the west coast of Mexico. At intervals he sent out ships from there to explore the northern coast. In 1532 two ships were used for this purpose, but one was lost at sea, the crew of the other mutinied, and nothing was accomplished. Cortés then equipped two more ships, and in 1534 they left Acapulco, Mexico, to explore the unknown waters of the North. One ship, under command of Fortún Jiménez, made a landing at a place which he called La Paz, because he found the Indians at the place so peaceable. Jiménez had discovered the peninsula of Lower California, though he thought it to be an island. His impression of the Indians was wrong, for he and twenty of his crew were murdered there by them, only a few of his men escaping.

The next year Cortés himself set sail with three ships and landed at La Paz to plant a settlement. He named the "island" Santa Cruz. But supplies ran short, and Cortés was obliged to return to Mexico for food. On his return he found that twenty-three of his men whom he had left there had died of starvation, and he abandoned the colony in order to save the lives of the others. This failure did not discourage him, for in 1539 he sent out Francisco de Ulloa with three small ships to explore the Gulf of California. Ulloa, having reached the end of that body of water, concluded that the land that Jiménez had discovered was not an island. Yet the dissemination of geographical knowledge was so difficult in that day that nearly two centuries elapsed before the insular theory of the peninsula was abandoned by navigators.

Following the explorations of Cortés and Ulloa, the Spanish government sent out during the next century many successive and costly expeditions to subdue the Indians of Lower California and to found settlements there. All of these attempts ended in failure. After the Company of Jesus, a worldwide missionary society known commonly as the Jesuits, had repeatedly requested of the king of Spain permission to go to Lower California and convert the Indians to Christianity, they were at length allowed to undertake that difficult work.

This great missionary society is one of the many Catholic orders. It was founded in 1534 by Saint Ignatius Loyola, and its object was to propagate the Christian faith in the various countries of the world. It was not, however, until the seventeenth century that the society took the name of "Jesuits." When it was founded, the chief colonizing powers of the world were Spain and Portugal; and from these two countries went early scores of Jesuits into almost every land—India, China, South America, Mexico, and what are now Canada and the United States.

One of the most famous of the early Jesuit missionaries was Saint Francis Xavier. He went to Ceylon in 1542, and three years later he was working in Malacca. In 1549, with two companions and three Indian converts, he entered Japan to do missionary work, but since he was not welcome there he sailed for China. Before he arrived in China he died in 1552 on the island of St. Johns. His companions reached the mainland, where they established Missions. They may be regarded as the true founders of the Missions in the Orient.

During the years in which these missionaries were introducing Christianity in the Orient, others were founding Missions in South America and in Central America. Father Nombreza and five missionaries from Portugal went to Brazil in 1549. They met with remarkable success in converting the natives, although in 1579 Father Ignacio de Azevedo and thirty-nine of his men met death at the hands of the Indians while working among them. At the time of the subsequent

Jesuit expulsion in 1768 Brazil had been divided into missionary districts, and nearly five hundred Jesuits were stationed in the country. In Paraguay and in other provinces they founded scores of Missions and converted to Christianity a vast number of Indians.

Shortly after this religious order invaded South America, it had its priests working in Canada. Two French Jesuits, Fathers Biard and Masse, landed at Port Royal, Acadia, in 1611. Three years later they were taken prisoners by some English colonists who had arrived from Virginia and were sent to England. But other Jesuits from France soon arrived, and in 1635 they opened at Quebec a college with a few teachers from Paris who were "the most accomplished professors in France." For more than thirty years the French Jesuits built their Missions along the banks of the St. Lawrence River, around Hudson Bay, and southward to the Gulf of Mexico. After England took Canada from France in 1763, the work of the Jesuits rapidly declined in that country.

The first Jesuits to come to the English colonies in America arrived in 1634. They came with Cecilius Calvert, who founded Maryland as a home for the persecuted Catholics of England. Among the first settlers were five Jesuits who built Missions on the Potomac River. Some thirty years later the Puritans swept down from Massachusetts and exiled from the colony Father Andrew White, the leading Jesuit there, and sent him to England as a prisoner. During these years of religious quarreling the Jesuits were also working among the Indians of Florida. Missions were built north as far as the present state of Virginia. The natives were very hostile to the new religion, and several missionaries were murdered by them. Father Pedro Martínez was killed at St. Augustine in 1566, and some years later eight priests were murdered by the savages along the banks of the Rappahannock River.

In 1571 the first Jesuits arrived in Mexico and quickly spread throughout the main provinces of that country. Twenty years later they were working in Sinaloa. From there they advanced into Sonora; and when the order for expulsion came from the Spanish crown this province contained twenty-eight

Missions and seventy-two villages, having in all a population of more than forty thousand people. Following the founding of these Missions came the Spanish settlers to cultivate the land and to develop trade.

The success of the Jesuits in these Mexican provinces and the repeated failures of the Spanish government to subdue the Indians in Lower California induced the Company of Jesus to seek permission of the king of Spain to found Missions in that peninsula. The Jesuits were finally allowed to establish Missions in the peninsula and to try to civilize the natives of that barbarous land. This great favor was granted to Father Juan María Salvatierra, a contemporary of the great Father Eusebio Kino, who had previously visited that peninsula and whose work among the Indians of Sonora for twenty-four years gives him enduring fame.

It is believed by historians that it was principally the influence of Kino that inspired Salvatierra to seek the conversion of the savages of Lower California. And so, nearly two centuries after the unsuccessful attempts of Cortés and others to plant settlements in this country and after similar repeated and dismal failures on the part of the Spanish government, it remained for the Jesuits to accomplish that which the government had been unable to do. The ravages of an uncharted sea, the mutinies of sailors, and the savagery of the Indians which had brought quick disaster to many an expedition which was well financed by the royal treasury were overcome by the faithful Jesuit missionaries in the permanent occupation of that sun-baked and barren peninsula. They established there eighteen Missions, converted thousands of Indians to the Christian faith, collected them into villages, established ports of entry for the Manila galleons, built ships, cultivated the soil, raised live stock, established schools, taught the Indians self-government and the principles of Christianity, and laid the foundation for a permanent and a prosperous state.

The colorful story of this remarkable achievement is told in a most vivid and pleasing style in the volume written by Father Francisco Javier Clavigero, a contemporary historian and one of the most learned men in all Mexico. He was born in

Vera Cruz, Mexico, on September 9, 1731, being the youngest of eleven children. His father, a native of Leon, Spain, as a young man had come to Mexico after finishing his schooling in Paris. He entered the services of the state, served as alcalde (mayor) of Tetzuitlan, a small village in the present state of Vera Cruz, and later filled the same office in Jicayan in Misteca, a province on the western coast of Mexico. Young Clavigero's mother, a member of a distinguished Spanish family that had moved to Mexico, was a gifted musician. The boy's love for music was discovered early, and he was taught the rudiments of music by his talented mother.

Clavigero's education was carefully supervised by his parents. When a mere boy he attended the college of San Gerónimo in the city of Puebla, specializing in Latin and in literature. Later he became a student at San Ignacio College in the same city, and here he gave most of his time to the study of religious philosophy. His father was a skilled linguist, and before the boy had reached his majority he was able to write in several languages. He entered the Company of Jesus when seventeen years old, and began his novitiate in Tepotzotlán. He then perfected his study of languages and acquired a knowledge of Greek and Latin from a German Jesuit who was a teacher there. At the end of his three years' study in that city he enrolled in a Jesuit college in the city of Puebla. Clavigero's earliest interest was in natural philosophy. He developed a lifelong love for literature, but his special joy lay in the study of history.

After finishing his studies at Puebla, Clavigero became an instructor in the secular college of Ildefonso. But he was considered too radical in his educational theory and in his practice of teaching. He was removed from his position by Francisco Zevallos, the provincial of the Jesuits. Clavigero was then made an instructor in the college at Valladolid, and later in the one at Guadalajara.

In the meantime this vigorous, scholarly, and conscientious young man wrote several learned treatises that attracted the attention of scholars not only in Mexico but also in Europe. These productions were written in Latin. He translated many

French, Greek, Latin, and Hebrew works into Spanish, and it is said that a few years after his collegiate training he knew more than twenty languages and dialects. In all his early studies Clavigero was aided by the erudite Mexican antiquarian, Don Carlos Sigüenza y Góngora, considered to have been the most learned Mexican of his day. While a student at the College of San Pedro y San Pablo (Saint Peter and Saint Paul) in Mexico City, Clavigero, through the interest which Father José Rafael Campoi took in him, became acquainted with the large collection of valuable documents on the antiquities of Mexico which Góngora had in his library. It is probable that the boy's first great desire for knowledge came from a study of these documents.

As a college youth he astonished his fellow students by his mastery of languages and by his knowledge of philosophy and the sciences. Before he was seventeen years old he had completed all the courses of philosophy in the college and had written twelve theological treatises. In one day he defended twenty-four treatises on scholastic and canonical theology, a task sufficient for the most scholarly men then teaching in the colleges of Mexico.

After becoming a member of the Jesuit Order, Clavigero did not neglect his studies. Before reaching the age of thirty he had won for himself wide distinction as a linguist and as a thorough, careful, and fair historian. An indefatigable worker, he devoted himself as much to profane literature as to sacred history. By this time he had written, among his more scholarly treatises: *Ensayo de la historia de la Nueva España*,[1] *De las colonias de los Tlaxcaltecas*,[2] and *De los linages nobles de la Nueva España*.[3] He had also written in Spanish *Un diálogo entre Filaletes y Paleofila contra el argumento de authoridad en la Física*,[4] and *Cursus philosophicus diu in Americanis gymnasis desideratus*,[5] in Latin. Both of these were published

[1] *"An Essay on the History of New Spain."*
[2] *"About the Settlements of the Tlaxcaltecans."*
[3] *"Concerning the Noble Families of New Spain."*
[4] *"A Dialogue between Filaletes and Paleofila against the Arguments of the Worth of Physics."*
[5] *"A Philosophical Course Long Desired in American Schools."*

in Mexico in 1753. In the same year Clavigero wrote his six *villancicos* (religious works), entitled "Certámen Poético para la Noche de Navidad del año 1753,"[6] still in manuscript form in the library of the University of Mexico. These contributions were followed by *Cartas de San Francisco de Sales a los predicadores y confesores (traducidas del francés, con dos discursos sobre los abusos de los oradores de este siglo y sobre los confesores iliteratos);*[7] *Memorias edificantes,*[8] printed in Mexico in 1761; *Compendio de la vida de San Juan Nepomuceno*[9] and *Elogio de San Francisco Javier,*[10] both printed in 1762 in Mexico; and *Elogio de San Ignacio de Loyola, predicado a la Real Audiencia de Guadalajara,*[11] also printed in the same city in 1766.

Two years later King Charles III of Spain expelled the Jesuits from all the Mexican provinces. Clavigero was then thirty-six years old and ranked among the most scholarly of his order in Mexico. With other Jesuits he sailed from Vera Cruz for Italy in the small *paque bote* (mail boat), "Nuestra Señora del Rosario de Torrenteguí," by the way of Havana, Cuba. His brother Ignacio left Mexico on the same day but in a different boat.

These expelled Jesuits went to different European countries. Some returned to Spain, others to Germany, some to Austria; many took refuge in Italy. A few years after his arrival in Italy, Clavigero went to the city of Cesena, which had been set aside in that country by the Pope as an asylum for the exiled Jesuits. In this city Clavigero had opportunity to confer intimately with other learned Jesuits and to use their fine libraries. In a few years he moved to Bologna, where he founded a

[6] "A Poetic Contest for the Christmas Eve of 1753."
[7] *"Letters of Saint Francis de Sales to Preachers and Confessors (Translated from the French, with Two Discourses on the Abuses of the Illiterate Preachers and Confessors of This Age)."*
[8] *"Edifying Memoirs."*
[9] *"A Compendium of the Life of Saint John Nepomuceno."*
[10] *"A Eulogy of Saint Francis Xavier."*
[11] *"A Eulogy of Saint Ignatius de Loyola, Preached to the Royal Audiencia of Guadalajara."*

literary academy, which was called by his friends the House of Wisdom.

All the while he was collecting historical material relating to Mexico and seeking knowledge about that country from every possible source. He spent most of his time in the libraries in Bologna, Ferrara, Modena, Rome, Genoa, Venice, and Milan, searching for important documents dealing with the history of Mexico. He owned a considerable number of valuable manuscripts himself. And after he had classified all the material that he was able to study, and especially after *Recherches philosophiques sur les Américains*,[12] written by the Prussian author, Paw, had appeared, which Clavigero believed to be full of grievous mistakes about the Americas, he decided to write a history of Mexico. Within a few years his *Storia antica del Messico*[13] came from the press. He wrote it in Spanish but was obliged to translate it into official Italian (Tuscan), in which language it appeared, because of the opposition which King Charles III had to its being published in Spanish and by a Jesuit. This four-volume history, with maps and various engravings, dedicated to the University of Mexico, was published in Cesena, Italy, in 1780–1781.

This work immediately gave Clavigero wide distinction as a historian. He wrote fairly, accurately, and, above all, impartially; and contemporary writers, as well as those of recent years, have followed Clavigero closely. There were few sources dealing with the ancient history of Mexico which he did not use. He had an advantage over many men who attempt to write history, for he knew well many different languages and wrote in them with the same facility that he did in his native tongue. Also he had access to the many extensive records which the Jesuits had made of their long and intimate acquaintance with the natives of Mexico and with the customs and institutions of that country.

The year after the *History of Mexico* was published it was

---

[12] "*Philosophical Researches about the Americans.*"

[13] "*Ancient History of Mexico*," usually cited by Clavigero as *History of Mexico*.

translated into English by Charles Cullen of London, and in 1789 a German translation, based on the English version, appeared in Leipzig. William Richard of Virginia translated the history into English in three volumes in 1806, and the following year another English translation in three volumes appeared in London. A Spanish edition, edited by José Joaquín de Mora, was published later (1826) in London. Father Francisco Pablo Vásquez, a Franciscan friar, translated the Italian edition in 1844, and nine years later it was published by R. Navarro in Mexico City.

Shortly after completing his *History of Mexico*, Clavigero wrote (1782) his *Breve ragguaglio della prodigiosa e rinomata immagine della Madonna di Guadalupe del Messico*.[14] His intense application to his scholarly productions undermined his health. Disregarding his physical ills, he continued his work. He began to write an ecclesiastical history of Mexico, but his poor health prevented its completion.

In the meantime Clavigero's great ambition had been to write a history of Lower California, the barren country, known to him simply as California, in which the Jesuits had achieved such marked success in founding Missions and in Christianizing the Indians. The work of the Jesuits had been carried on for seventy years with great industry and under such suffering and hardship that it is doubtful if the pages of history record any greater sacrifices than those made by these men in reducing the savages there to a civilized mode of existence. Struggling with failing health and poverty, grappling with the huge task of gathering material for the undertaking, Clavigero finally completed his *Storia della California* in 1786. Before he could revise and carefully edit this history he died at Cesena, Italy, on April 2, 1787, after a painful and prolonged illness. With simple but solemn obsequies he was buried in the church of Santa Lucia in Cesena.

It is most unfortunate that no more is known of this great churchman and historian. We have searched in vain for more

---

[14] "*A Brief Comparison of the Marvellous and Famous Image of Our Lady of Guadalupe of Mexico.*"

concerning his life. It may be that tucked away in the archives of Mexico, or in Spain, or in the libraries in Italy are manuscripts that would tell us more about him. Spanish writers give him slight attention. Italian biographers neglect him, although he is the author of so many works in Tuscan Italian. Even Antonio Lombardi makes no mention of him in his *Storia della letteratura Italiana nel secolo XVIII*. To be sure, Father Agustín Castro wrote *Elogios del Padre Francisco Clavigero* in 1787; and one of the exiled Jesuits of Mexico, Father Juan Luis Maneiro, wrote and published in Latin a life of Clavigero at Bologna in 1789, a mere sketch but the fullest account that we have been able to find.

Two years after the death of Clavigero his brother Ignacio had the *Storia della California* published in Venice. He added to the book a preface which extolls his brother and praises his literary genius but tells little of his life. This preface has been omitted from this translation on account of its length and because it does not deal with the history of Lower California.

The *Storia della California* has twice been translated into Spanish, the later translation appearing in 1852. We can find no record that this history has ever been translated into any other language. Parts of this history, deriving from the Spanish translation, were printed in English in the *San Diego Herald* in 1858–1859. The present volume is a translation from the original Italian edition. This interesting and vivid history, the only history of Lower California from the time of the discovery of this peninsula to the expulsion of the Jesuits in 1768 (the *Noticia de la California* by Father Miguel Venegas ends in 1756), is here presented entire in English.

Clavigero divides his history into four parts. In Book One he deals with the physical features of the peninsula, with the flora and fauna of the country, and with the character, the customs, and the religious and social life of the various Indian tribes before and after they accepted Christianity. Book Two describes briefly the attempts to colonize the peninsula and the coming of the Jesuits, the great difficulties encountered by the missionaries and the founding of the first six Missions, the many and strict orders of King Philip V relating to the Missions, and the explorations and death of Father Eusebio Kino. Book Three contains an account of eight additional Missions and of the great work of Fathers Salvatierra, Piccolo, Ugarte, and other devout and self-sacrificing missionaries. Here the recital of the life of Brother Bravo shows the zeal and the labors of those who assisted in the work of civilizing the natives, and the fateful revolt of the Pericues, in which two Fathers were murdered and two Missions were destroyed, is vividly portrayed. Book Four tells of the continued interest of King Philip V in the affairs in California, and describes the many land explorations made to establish Missions farther north. Some of the outstanding men who labored so long in California are eulogized, and an account is given of the founding of the last four Missions and of the abandonment of others. The author then sketches the condition of Christianity as it was when the Jesuits were expelled from the peninsula, and he closes his fascinating story with a description of the government which was provided for the Indians and with a few pages telling about the departure of the Jesuits from the land in which they had labored for almost seventy years.

In the preparation of this brief biographical sketch of Clavigero, we have used the following sources: Maneiro, Juan Luis, *De vitis aliquot Mexicanorum* (Bologna, 1791–92); Beristain de Souza, José Mariano, *Biblioteca Hispano-Americana*, Vol. I Mexico, 1816); Sommervogel, Carlos, *Bibliothèque de la Compagnie de Jesús;* and Zelis, Rafael, *Catálogo de la Compañia de Jesús* (Mexico, 1871).

We are deeply indebted to the Bancroft Library of the University of California, to the Los Angeles City Library, to the Henry E. Huntington Library, San Marino, California, and to the Stanford University Library for placing at our disposal materials without which our editorial work would have been impossible. We also wish to thank Dr. John Thomas Howell, Mr. Joseph R. Slevin, and Mr. Howard Walton Clark of the California Academy of Sciences, and Mr. William F. Taylor of the Berkeley High School for their kindness in assisting us in editing those chapters dealing with the physical features and with the flora and fauna of Lower California.

Thanks are also due Dr. Herbert Eugene Bolton of the University of California for the guidance and encouragement given us as members of his several seminars.

S. E. L.
A. A. G.

BERKELEY, CALIFORNIA
January, 1937

TABLE OF CONTENTS

	PAGE
AUTHOR'S PREFACE	3

BOOK I

THE LOCATION, SOIL, CLIMATE, MINERALS, PLANTS, AND ANIMALS OF CALIFORNIA—THE CHARACTER, LIFE, RELIGION, AND CUSTOMS OF THE CALIFORNIANS BEFORE THEIR CONVERSION TO CHRISTIANITY

Chapter One. The Location and Name of California, Its Harbors, Capes, and Islands in Both Seas	15
Chapter Two. Soil and Climate	21
Chapter Three. Mountains, Stones, and Minerals	24
Chapter Four. Plants and Their Divisions	32
Chapter Five. Plants Native to California and Useful for Their Fruits	33
Chapter Six. Foreign Plants	42
Chapter Seven. Plants Useful for Their Leaves and Branches	46
Chapter Eight. Plants Useful for Their Trunks or Stalks	47
Chapter Nine. Plants Useful for Their Roots	53
Chapter Ten. Plants Useful for Their Juice or Gum	54
Chapter Eleven. Noxious and Grotesque Plants	55
Chapter Twelve. Insects	58
Chapter Thirteen. Reptiles	66
Chapter Fourteen. Fish	67
Chapter Fifteen. Birds	77
Chapter Sixteen. Quadrupeds	78
Chapter Seventeen. The Inhabitants, Their Language, Arithmetic, Year	84
Chapter Eighteen. The Origin and Character of the Californians	89
Chapter Nineteen. Arts, Meals, and Drinks	92
Chapter Twenty. Habitations, Clothing, Decoration, Household Goods	95
Chapter Twenty-One. Occupations	99
Chapter Twenty-Two. Holidays and Social Rank	101
Chapter Twenty-Three. Weddings	105
Chapter Twenty-Four. Religion and Dogma	107
Chapter Twenty-Five. Guamas, or Charlatans, and Their Power	112

BOOK II

ATTEMPTS OF THE CONQUEROR CORTÉS AND MANY OTHERS TO DISCOVER CALIFORNIA. THE INSISTENCE OF THE CATHOLIC MONARCHS ON THE ESTABLISHMENT OF SOME COLONIES THERE. THE ENTRY OF THE JESUITS TO THAT PENINSULA. THE DIFFICULTIES, NEEDS, AND OPPOSITION ENDURED BY THE MISSIONARIES. THE ESTABLISHMENT OF SIX MISSIONS UP TO 1711. THE STRICT ORDERS OF THE KING, PHILIP THE FIFTH, IN FAVOR OF THE MISSIONS. EXPEDITIONS, UNDERTAKINGS, AND THE DEATH OF FATHER KINO

	PAGE
Chapter One. The Attempts of the Conqueror Cortés to Discover California	119
Chapter Two. The Attempts of the Viceroy, Incited by Certain Accounts	124
Chapter Three. Expeditions Ordered by the Kings, Philip the Second and Philip the Third	127
Chapter Four. The Attempts Which Some Made at Their Own Expense. The Fabulous Voyage of Admiral Fonte	134
Chapter Five. New Orders and Attempts	136
Chapter Six. The Famous Expedition of Admiral Otondo	139
Chapter Seven. Other Unsuccessful Plans	146
Chapter Eight. The Zeal of Some Jesuits for the Conversion of California and Its Success	148
Chapter Nine. The Jesuits are Permitted to Go to the Conversion of California	154
Chapter Ten. The Peninsula Is Taken Possession of in the Name of the King. Father Salvatierra Establishes the Mission of Loreto. A Conspiracy of the Indians and the Victory of the Spaniards	157
Chapter Eleven. Rules and Regulations and Work of Father Salvatierra	162
Chapter Twelve. Father Piccolo, Missionary. A Letter from Father Salvatierra. The Labors of the Colonists. A Conspiracy against the Spaniards, and the Victory of the Latter	165
Chapter Thirteen. The Occupations of the Missionaries and the Lack of Provisions	168
Chapter Fourteen. The Loss of the Colony. The Missions of San Juan Bautista de Londò and San Javier de Viggè	170
Chapter Fifteen. The Misfortune of the Colony, for the Reparation of Which Father Salvatierra and Father Ugarte Vainly Asked the Government for Help	172

Chapter Sixteen. The Trip of Father Salvatierra to Supply the Colony. The Arrival of Father Juan de Ugarte in California. A Boatload of Provisions 178

Chapter Seventeen. The Appointment of Another Captain. The Transgressions of the Indians of Viggè 181

Chapter Eighteen. Father Ugarte Accepts the Mission of San Javier. His Extraordinary Zeal 182

Chapter Nineteen. The Penury of the Colonists. The Uprising and the Pacification of the Indians 188

Chapter Twenty. Royal Orders. Offers to Establish Missions. Two New Missionaries. The Trips of Fathers Salvatierra and Ugarte . . . 190

Chapter Twenty-One. The Festival of Corpus Christi. A Conspiracy and the Punishment of the Conspirators. The Kindness of the Missionaries toward Some Smugglers. The Scarcity of Provisions . . 193

Chapter Twenty-Two. Father Basalduá Goes to Mexico on Business of the Colony. The Orders of the King without Effect 195

Chapter Twenty-Three. Father Pedro de Ugarte, Missionary. A Conference. Father Salvatierra's Speech. The Determination 197

Chapter Twenty-Four. They Endeavor to Provide the Colony. The Voyage of Fathers Salvatierra and Pedro de Ugarte. The Dedication of the New Church of Loreto. A New Ordinance of the Presidio . 199

Chapter Twenty-Five. Father Salvatierra Goes to Mexico and Is Appointed Provincial. His Unsuccessful Visit and Petition to the Viceroy 202

Chapter Twenty-Six. Father Salvatierra Visits the Missions of California. Brother Bravo Is Employed in Them. Orders from the Provincial on Departing 206

Chapter Twenty-Seven. Father Pedro de Ugarte Establishes the Mission of Liguig 207

Chapter Twenty-Eight. Father Basalduá Establishes the Mission of Mulegè. Juan de Ugarte Is Entrusted with the Care of Three Missions 210

Chapter Twenty-Nine. The Unsuccessful Trips of Father Juan de Ugarte and Brother Bravo 212

Chapter Thirty. Father Salvatierra Renounces the Office of the Provincialship and Returns to California. The Mission of Comondù and Its Missionary, Father Mayorga 214

Chapter Thirty-One. The Misfortunes of the Colony. The Death of Father Kino. His Eulogy 216

BOOK III

THE ESTABLISHMENT OF EIGHT OTHER MISSIONS. NEW TASKS, HARDSHIPS, HOSTILE RESISTANCE, AND DANGERS. THE EXAMPLES OF SOME CATECHUMEN AND NEOPHYTES. THE DEATHS OF FATHERS SALVATIERRA, PÌCCOLO, UGARTE, AND MAYORGA. THE CONSPIRACY OF THE PERICÙES; TWO MISSIONARIES MURDERED; THE LOSS AND RE-ESTABLISHMENT OF SOME MISSIONS

	PAGE
Chapter One. The Lack of Vessels in the Colony. The Indians of Cadegomò and Kadakaaman Ask for Missionaries	225
Chapter Two. Father Salvatierra Vainly Attempts the Pacification of the Guaicuras and Continues Working, Although He Is Ill	227
Chapter Three. The Arrival of Father Tamaral in California. The Departure of Father Salvatierra for Mexico and His Death	228
Chapter Four. The Claims of Brother Bravo before the Government. The Tribunal Commands. A Storm in the Peninsula	230
Chapter Five. Father Sistiaga, Missionary. Father Tamaral Appointed to the Mission of Concepción	233
Chapter Six. The Plans of Father Ugarte	235
Chapter Seven. Brother Bravo Receives Sacred Orders and Is Made a Missionary. The Alférez of the Presidio Becomes a Jesuit	237
Chapter Eight. The Mission of La Paz and Its Missionary, Father Bravo	239
Chapter Nine. The Mission of Huasinapi, or Rather of Guadalupe, and Its Missionary, Father Helen	241
Chapter Ten. The Commands of the Viceroy Carried Out by the Missionaries	245
Chapter Eleven. The Undertaking of Father Ugarte and the Information Acquired with It	246
Chapter Twelve. The Prudent Zeal of the Missionaries in the Spread of the Gospel. The Mission of the Virgen de Los Dolores, and Its Missionary, Father Guillen	254
Chapter Thirteen. The Port of Las Palmas Is Allotted a New Mission, and Father Nàpoli Is Appointed to Guide It	256
Chapter Fourteen. Hostilities in La Paz. Father Nàpoli Moves His Mission and Names It Santiago Apóstol	259
Chapter Fifteen. The Mission of San Ignacio de Kadakaaman. Its Missionary, Father Luyando	260
Chapter Sixteen. The New Mission of San Ignacio Is Afflicted	264

Chapter Seventeen. The Progress of the Mission. The Fervor of a Gentile 268

Chapter Eighteen. The Misfortune of the Mission. The Determination Made and Its Success 271

Chapter Nineteen. The Deaths of Fathers Piccolo and Juan de Ugarte. The Condition of the Missions 275

Chapter Twenty. The Mission of San José del Cabo; Father Tamaral Is Appointed to It 277

Chapter Twenty-One. Father Taraval Reaches California. He Governs Other Missions, and He Establishes That of Santa Rosa 279

Chapter Twenty-Two. Indications of General Rebellion against the Missionaries. The Kindness and Singular Generosity of Father Tamaral toward Certain Navigators 284

Chapter Twenty-Three. Rebellion Breaks Out and Spreads through the Southern Part 287

Chapter Twenty-Four. The Glorious Deaths of Fathers Carranco and Tamaral. Their Corpses are Mutilated and Burned with the Church Furnishings 291

Chapter Twenty-Five. The Insurgents Try to Kill Father Taraval. They Attack the Neophytes of Santa Rosa. Father Guillen Vainly Informs the Viceroy about Everything 295

Chapter Twenty-Six. The Rebellion Continues. Measures Put into Effect to Check It 297

Chapter Twenty-Seven. Hostilities Shown the Ship from the Philippine Islands. The Captain Gives an Account of Them to the Viceroy. The Command of This Gentleman to the Governor of Sinaloa . . 300

Chapter Twenty-Eight. The Death of Father Mayorga. The Governor Follows the Advice of the Missionaries in His Operations, and Triumphs over the Conspirators 302

Chapter Twenty-Nine. The New Presidio Is Not Agreeable to the Intentions of the King. The Viceroy Revokes His Orders, Which Are Contrary to the Former 304

Chapter Thirty. The Four Destroyed Missions Are Restored. The Attempt on the Life of Father Wagner. The Punishment of the Guilty 305

Chapter Thirty-One. A New Rebellion of Some Tribes of the Pericùes. The Punishment of the Leaders Puts an End to the Disturbances of That Nation 308

BOOK IV

NEW ORDERS OF THE CATHOLIC KING IN FAVOR OF CALIFORNIA. TRIPS TO THE RED RIVER. THE EXTRAVAGANT CLAIMS AND DISTURBANCES OF THE PERICÙES. THE EULOGY OF SOME WORTHY MEN OF CALIFORNIA. THE ESTABLISHMENT OF THE LAST FOUR MISSIONS AND THE SUPPRESSION OF OTHERS. THE CONDITION OF THAT CHRISTIANITY IN 1767. THE SYSTEM OF GOVERNMENT OF THE MISSIONS AND PRESIDIOS. THE EXPULSION OF THE JESUIT MISSIONARIES

	PAGE
Chapter One. Philip the Fifth Consults His Council. Answers. The Cédula of the King. The Provincial Informs the King about the Missions of Sonora and California. The Cédula of Ferdinand the Sixth	313
Chapter Two. The Effect of the Cédula. The Command of the Provincial. The Trips of Fathers Consag and Sedelmayer	317
Chapter Three. The Misfortunes of the Missions of the South and the Decision Taken There. The Loss of Five Worthy Men of California and Their Eulogy. The New Governor of the Peninsula	319
Chapter Four. The Apostolic Trips of Father Consag. The Mission of Santa Gertrudis and Its Missionary, Father Retz	327
Chapter Five. The Difficulties Are Overcome Which Halted the Advance of the Missions toward the North. Father Consag Dies. His Eulogy	332
Chapter Six. The Lack and the Construction of Ships. The Death and the Eulogy of Brother Mugazabal	334
Chapter Seven. The Mission of San Francisco de Borja and Its Missionary, Father Link	338
Chapter Eight. The Mission of San Francisco de Borja Becomes Restless, and a Remedy is Applied There	342
Chapter Nine. The Death of Father Neumayer. The Voyage of Father Link	344
Chapter Ten. A New Calamity for the Southern Missions. The Iniquitous Claims and Complaints of the Pericùes	346
Chapter Eleven. The Unlawful Meeting of the Pericùes. The Outcome of Their Deliberations and Claims	351
Chapter Twelve. The Jesuits Solemnly Renounce the Missions and a Great Inheritance	355
Chapter Thirteen. Other Places Are Sought for the Establishment of New Missions, and This Commission is Entrusted to Father Link	357

Chapter Fourteen. The Mission of Calagnujuet and the Missionaries Appointed to It 360

Chapter Fifteen. The Mission Is Moved to Another Place with the Name of Santa María, and It Is the Last One that the Jesuits Establish in California 364

Chapter Sixteen. The Number and Location of All the Missions. The Number of Neophytes. The Number of Superiors Whom Each Missionary Had over Him. Visits Rare among the Missionaries . . 366

Chapter Seventeen. A Description of the Capital of Each Mission. How Time Was Distributed for the Neophytes. Their Fervor 369

Chapter Eighteen. The Expenses Which the Missionaries Incurred for the Welfare of the Missions. The Duties of the Two Procurators of California. The Rights and the Authority of the Captain . . . 373

Chapter Nineteen. Pearl Fishing Is Prohibited. The Distribution and the Duties of the Soldiers. The Authority of the Jesuits over Them. The Residence of the Captain in Loreto. The Exemplary Habits of That Village 377

Chapter Twenty. The Royal Order for the Expulsion of the Jesuits from Spanish Domains. Their Successors in the Missions of California 380

APPENDIX

Appendix A. Experiments and Observations Which Father Inamma, a German Jesuit Missionary in That Peninsula, Made on the Snakes of That Peninsula 389

Appendix B. The Lord's Prayer in Three Dialects 396

Index 399

THE HISTORY
OF [LOWER]
CALIFORNIA

Author's Preface

<small>✜✜</small>

ALTHOUGH California* from its discovery began to acquire fame for the abundance of pearls in the neighboring sea, there was no one in the last two centuries who might have undertaken to write the history of that peninsula, because its coasts were scarcely known and almost nothing was known of the customs of its inhabitants. In the present century, since the Jesuits explored the greatest part of the peninsula and established many Missions there, Father Miguel Venegas, a Mexican Jesuit, wrote its history in a bulky volume, availing himself of the letters of those missionaries, and especially of those of Fathers Salvatierra, Piccolo, and Ugarte, the most celebrated and the oldest missionaries; of the manuscript history of Sonora written by the indefatigable Father Kino; of the diary of the captain-governor of California, Don Estevan Rodríguez Lorenzo; of the reminiscences written by the erudite Father Sigismundo Taraval, and of other original documents which were in the archives of Mexico.

The manuscript of Father Venegas was sent to Madrid to Father Andrés Marcos Burriel, an erudite and industrious Jesuit of the province of Toledo and well known for his work on the ancient weights and measures of Toledo. Having given a better form to that history, and having polished it up and enriched it with new materials which were in part sent him from Mexico and which he took in part from the archives of Madrid

* [Clavigero of course refers to what is now known as Lower California. Hereafter Clavigero's original notes appear with their conventional indices, followed by the footnotes of the present editors in smaller type, numbered from 1 up in each Book.]

and from many authors, Venegas printed it in that city in the year 1757, dedicating it to the Catholic monarch, Ferdinand VI, in the name of the Mexican province. This work was published with the modest title of *Noticias de la California,* because that learned Spaniard did not believe that he had the materials necessary for a history. But the English translator, afterward imitated by the French and the Holland translators, entitled it *A Natural and Civil History of California,* in spite of there being in it nothing of natural history. Subsequently, Father Jacobo Begert, a German Jesuit who had been in California for seventeen years, wrote a new history of it in the German language and published it in Munich in 1772. Although we know that it had considerable approval there, we have not been able to make use of it for our history, because it has not reached our hands.

Not only the natural history but much other essential information is lacking in the Spanish edition; and there are, besides, not a few errors, although excusable ones. The acuteness of the abbés, Don Miguel del Barco and Don Lucas Ventura, men very familiar with California, and exact and sincere, endeavored to remedy this, as is known to all who are acquainted with them. The Abbé del Barco was a missionary there for thirty years, and visited all those Missions as a superior; and, although he is not a naturalist by profession nor did the important occupations of his ministry permit him to devote himself to the study of nature, nevertheless, being very fond of making such observations and being endowed with good judgment and the faculty of criticism, he could observe things in the space of so many years and afterward write sufficient to give an exact idea of the soil, climate, productions, and animals of California. The Abbé Ventura was also a missionary for eleven years at Loreto and procurator of all the Missions; and, for this reason, he was informed about all the affairs of the peninsula. Therefore they corrected the errors of the Spanish edition and added to it the essay on natural history and that information which it lacked, continuing the narration until the year 1768.

Since I believe that I perform a service to the public by presenting it with a true and exact history of California, I have availed myself of the said writings, omitting from the Spanish history all that which neither directly or indirectly belongs to the history of the peninsula. Although I have made use of all the information that I have acquired with my study and research, and although I have taken verbal reports from many persons worthy of credence who have been in California for many years, nevertheless it is very easy for the one who writes the history of a country in which he has never been to make a mistake. I have had this work revised by two persons who are most familiar with that country, and experience has taught me that this caution was not superfluous.

Therefore, if he who has devoted himself with every care to seeking the truth and has acquired so much information about the country of which he writes is exposed to being mistaken, what may probably be said about those who write without such painstaking attention and without such knowledge? What should be said, for example, about M. Paw, Dr. Robertson, and the other Europeans, who paint California with colors that do not suit her, daring to contradict the sincere description of those who have lived in that peninsula for so many years and who have observed it very attentively? Let it be enough to know that the geography of Lacroix has almost as many errors as lines regarding California; the *Geographical Portable Dictionary* of Vosgien has nine very notable errors in the brief article "California"; the *Recherches Philosophiques** of Paw, in a single page devoted to the peninsula, contain forty-eight falsehoods, patiently enumerated by me among simple mistakes, formal falsehoods, and rash calumnies. I should indeed annoy you very much, courteous reader, if I should wish to specify them all; but here are some for a sample.

I. The principal carnivorous animal which is known there (in California) is the cowardly tiger, similar to that of Canada. There are also bears and whole herds of bison. But unfortunately for M. de Paw, not a bear nor a bison has been seen in all the extent of that peninsula.

II. In 1690 a Spanish colonist had planted in California, in the vicinity of San Lucas, a small vineyard which did better

* M. de Paw, *Recherch. Philos. sur les Américains*, part 2.

than he expected. This attempt inspired the missionaries with the desire of having vineyards also; and one of them, named Piccolo, who was more inclined to botany and agriculture than to discussions on versatile and efficient grace, took upon himself to plant them; and they progressed in such a way that for forty-seven years afterward the Jesuits sold so much wine that they could supply all of Mexico and even put many barrels on the ships to the Philippine Islands, where they used it for masses. How many errors and falsehoods in such a few words! (1) In 1690 there was no Spanish colonist in California, nor was there one until after the entry of the Jesuits in 1697, and by no means in the vicinity of San Lucas, that is, in the southern part of that peninsula, which was not inhabited by any Spaniard until 1730, when Father Piccolo had already died. (2) However many efforts the missionaries made, never was there any vineyard in the southern part of California, either large or small, the fruit of which could give drinkable wine. (3) Father Piccolo never planted any vineyard, nor could M. de Paw find any man less suited to botany than that good Father. The first one who planted a vineyard there was Father Juan de Ugarte; but he was influenced not by the example of that imaginary Spaniard but because of having seen so many wild grapevines in the peninsula. (4) There was wine at only five or six Missions, and all that was made did not amount to one hundred casks, as I well know from the very ones who made it. Could this quantity have been sufficient to supply Mexico? (5) The missionaries of California never sold their wine, as is publicly known in that country. They used it for mass, the table, and the sick; and what was left over they sent as a gift to their benefactors or exchanged for those provisions which they received from Sinaloa and Sonora. (6) The navigators from the Philippine Islands never bought wine in California, nor is it known that a mass has been held in those islands with such wine, where they did not use, nor do they use, any other than that from Spain, sent them from Mexico at the expense of the king.

III. M. Anson was the first one who discovered by accident, at the end of 1744, that the Society of Jesus was then dangerously powerful in that corner of the world. Unlucky Spanish court, that in order to know about its interests in California needed to be informed by an English privateer who never was there! Unlucky monarchy, that was in a condition to fear a few old men confined to that corner of the world, accompanied by only sixty* soldiers and absolutely unprovided with artillery and fortifications! Unlucky Catholic king Ferdinand VI, who even after being enlightened by that privateer, continued until his death protecting the missionaries and helping the Missions with new favors! It is a pity that M. de Paw, in order to make evident the dangerous power of the Jesuits in California, had not created a king in it similar to the one which Carvallo created in Paraguay, giving him the name of Alexander, or Frederick, or another more royal one than that of Nicolás; that he had not transformed those miserable towns into strongly walled cities, and made at least seventy thousand soldiers out of those seventy, converting the rocks of California into men, after the example of Deucalion; he could have done this not only without any cost but, on the contrary, with profit, for in this way his *Recherches Philosophiques* would have had a better sale.

IV. In California many tribes of Indians who persevere in their barbarity have still continued this abuse (that of mutilating their members) and even today they cut some phalanges of their fingers at the death of their relatives. They commence with the extremities of a finger of each hand, and when these members are cut, they do the same afterward with the second finger, and they have an admirable secret for curing these wounds, which would be considered dangerous in Europe.† The talent of M. de Paw is certainly admirable for exaggerating, altering, and pretending facts which he turns to account. He read in the history of California written by Father Venegas that when any of those barbarians fell ill the *guama* (medicine man called to cure them), among other outlandish remedies, made an incision in the little finger of the daughter or sister of the patient so that the blood might drop on the body of the latter. He read this and nothing more in this history, but it was sufficient for him to affirm all that we have seen. In order to

* [Evidently a misprint since below, and later on, seventy is given.]
† *Recherch. Philos. sur les Américains*, part 5.

extract a little blood out of the incision on the little finger he made a mutilation of the phalanges of the fingers of both hands. What was done in illness to cure the patient he wished to be done at the deaths of relatives in sign of grief. What the *guama* practiced on only the daughter or the sister of the patient, he would have us understand that all the relatives of the deceased performed on themselves.

Just as M. de Paw has been the inventor of these dangerous wounds, he has also invented that admirable secret for curing them promptly which was unknown to the historian of California and even to the Californians themselves. He also makes those tribes of Californians, who persevere in their barbarity, still maintain this abuse, nothwithstanding the fact that the missionaries who lived in the countries containing those barbarians did not know it. These are some of the many falsehoods and errors which M. de Paw hazards when speaking of California. Then in regard to the gross calumnies against the respected memory of Father Salvatierra, a man venerated as a saint in California as well as in Mexico, and against other persons worthy of our esteem, we refer to public and well-known facts related in this history.

These same facts likewise give the lie to the assertions of Dr. Robertson. Although he praises the Jesuits for having reduced the barbarous Californians to civil life, he tries to prove, among other things, that the Jesuits themselves endeavored to discredit the climate and the soil of California in order to hide their designs and operations from the court; and he flatters himself with the fact that in the future, when the population is increased, that peninsula will not be counted among the barren and desolate deserts of the Spanish empire.[*] But let him say what he wished; California, in spite of his political prophecies, will always be one of the most unproductive and desolate districts of the Spanish empire, and its inhabitants will always be poor and miserable.

Two persons animated by the same spirit as Robertson in a certain writing use the words "very rich" in referring to

[*] *Storia d'America*, Tom. IV, lib. vii, pags. 116–117. Edit. of Florencia.

California. Indeed, it should be desired that they go there to enjoy those riches and to employ the zeal which they have displayed against the Jesuits in order to help those poor and abandoned nations.

Abbé Raynal, on the contrary, appears better informed about the affairs of California and talks about it with more sincerity. "It is impossible," he says, "that the nature of the soil and the temperature of the atmosphere should be the same in such a great space. Nevertheless, it may be said, generally speaking, that the air is too warm and dry, and the soil untillable, mountainous, covered with stones and sand, and consequently barren and little suitable for cultivation and for the raising of cattle."* Speaking of the entry of the Jesuits in that peninsula, he states as follows: "They attracted those savages whom they wished to civilize by taking them some little trifles which they liked, some food for them to sustain themselves, and some clothes that might please them. The hatred which those peoples professed for the Spanish name could not be overcome at these demonstrations of kindness. They reciprocated as much as their slight perception and their fickleness permitted. These defects were partly overcome by the priests, who devoted themselves to carrying out their project with the insistence and the constancy which were characteristic of their Order. They became carpenters, masons, weavers, and agriculturists; and by this means they succeeded in acquainting the natives with the principal arts and even inspiring affection in them to a certain degree. Afterward they gathered them together in succession, etc."

I should observe that this author was not so well informed on what he adds about the livelihood of the Californians. He states: "Whatever they may need they acquire with the pearls which they fish for in the gulf and with the wine which they sell to New Spain and to the ships from the Philippine Islands." Neither the one nor the other is true. The Californians who were accustomed to engage in fishing for pearls were very few; and the profit which they derived from it was also so small that it would not have been sufficient to supply their needs if the missionaries had not cared for their maintenance. As re-

* *Hist. Philos. et Polit.*, lib. 6°, c. 22.

gards the wine, they did not have even a single drop to sell. The missionaries, well knowing how strong the inclination is among the Americans toward drunkenness, were always very careful not to give their neophytes in California occasion to contract that vice, which was fortunately unknown to them.

I have gathered these errors here, courteous reader, to save you the annoyance of reading not a few notes which otherwise would have been necessary in this history. As for the rest, in order not to convert this preface into a defense, I have omitted the gross calumnies of Paw, Robertson, and other authors who are bitter against the missionaries of California, although it would have been very easy for me to refute them with authentic documents and demonstrative reasons. I could also have abstained from those eulogies of some missionaries which will be found in this work if the laws of history, justice toward them, and faithfulness toward the public had not exacted them; on the other hand, I certainly do not know how an impartial and sincere history of any country can be written without praising those to whom is due all the good that there is in it. If the Crucified Redeemer, who was previously unknown in California, is worshiped today in almost all of it, and if that peninsula in which only naked, wanton, and brutish savages were seen is now inhabited by well-instructed citizens of good habits; if at present there are churches erected to the honor of God, and very orderly towns where there was not even a cabin before; if that land, formerly uncultivated and covered with thickets, is now tilled and enriched by many new and useful plants—all is due to the indefatigable zeal, the active industry, and the great efforts of those missionaries who, animated and assisted by divine grace, introduced social life there, together with the Christian religion.

Let us then celebrate the memory of these very worthy men of religion and the state by means of those praises of which they made themselves deserving and which the peoples themselves whom they benefited render to them. And we make no effort to appraise the invectives of some Europeans who without blame are ignorant of or maliciously misrepresent the glorious accomplishments of those missionaries.

I should have nothing more to say, kind reader, if I were sure that the present history were to be read by you in these pages. But as many are content to read works which continue being published in summaries which journalists make of them, so I have warned you that those who trust similar extracts are frequently deceived by the unfaithfulness of the journalists themselves. I could cite very many examples of them to you; but that abridgment suffices which certain Florentine journalists made from Volume One of my *Storia del Messico* in their *Giornale Enciclopedico di letteratura Italiana e ultramontana*, *num.* IX (Italy, 1782). Here are some of those absurdities and calumnies which the said journalists attribute to me, without paying attention to their own reputations, so necessary to their principal intent of becoming rich at the cost of their subscribers. This becomes clear when I refer to the testimony of Cortés, as given by an eyewitness, and to that of other historians. I say on page 269 of my first volume that three or four hundred very orderly young noblemen who served the meal to King Moctezuma presented it before the king reached the table and then retired. The journalists have me say that 30,400 pages served him at the table. The difference is nothing less than thirty thousand.

On page 271 I say that among the halls of the principal palace of Moctezuma there was one so large that, according to what a dependable eyewitness asserts, three thousand men could be put in it. The journalists have me say that there was a hall so vast that it could contain 60,000 persons. The difference is nothing less than fifty-seven thousand. But if the journalists had not purposely constructed a hall capable of containing sixty thousand persons, how could the thirty thousand pages, imagined by them, have served the table in it?

When I speak of the table linen and the kitchen utensils of King Moctezuma, I say on page 269 (corroborated by the testimony of the other historians of Mexico) that none of these things was of use to him more than once, because then he gave them to some of the nobles; and I made the same statement about his clothing. But the journalists have me say that Moctezuma did not eat the same delicacy twice—the crassest absurdity, which never occurred to any of the historians of Mexico. Without doubt the Mexican cooks needed much creative faculty in order to vary the dishes so much; and a marvelous memory they had that they might bear in mind all the foods that had been presented to the king so that they might not present them again to him!

On page 286, speaking of several misfortunes which happened during the early years of the sixteenth century, I state that these and other calamities, together with the appearance of a comet which occurred at the same time, caused great consternation among all those peoples; and that Moctezuma, who was too superstitious to be able to see similar phenomena with indifference, consulted his astrologers about this, etc.; but the journalists have me state that the comet of 1507 appeared to foretell to the Mexicans their ruin—a thing that I have never said, nor am capable of saying.

On page 288 I state that it is not possible to divine the first origin of the very universal superstition which, according to the uniform testimony of all the historians of Mexico, existed among those peoples, about the future arrival of new peoples who were to take possession of those countries. And again the journalists assert that I exert myself to prove that the Evil One was the person who announced the said coming to these worshipers, only because I add that the Devil could conjecture it and foretell it to those peoples dedicated to his cult. Afterward the journalists explain themselves in these terms: "It is a pity that in this history so many examples of superstition and credulity are found, which perhaps obscure its merit." But this is a jest with which they would like to decorate their charitable calumnies.

The journalists have me state that the city of Mexico was founded in 1335, whereas I say many times, and even prove in a dissertation, that it was in 1325. Besides this, among the few names of persons, nations, and cities which they cite, twenty-two are misstated. Such is the summary which those journalists made of Volume One of my *Storia del Messico;* and such will probably be what they will make of this *Storia della California.*

BOOK I

THE LOCATION, SOIL, CLIMATE, MINERALS, PLANTS, AND ANIMALS OF CALIFORNIA—THE CHARACTER, LIFE, RELIGION, AND CUSTOMS OF THE CALIFORNIANS BEFORE THEIR CONVERSION TO CHRISTIANITY

Chapter One

THE LOCATION AND NAME OF CALIFORNIA, ITS HARBORS, CAPES, AND ISLANDS IN BOTH SEAS

CALIFORNIA is a peninsula of North America which is separated from the continent of New Spain[1] at the mouth of the Colorado River, or Red River, at 33° North latitude and 262° [West] longitude,[2] and terminates at the cape of San Lucas[3] at 22° 24' North latitude, and 268° longitude.* This cape is its southern terminus, the Red River is the eastern limit, and the harbor[4] of San Diego, situated at 33° North latitude and about 156° longitude, can be called its western limit. To the north and the northeast it borders on countries of barbarous nations little known on the coasts and not at all in the interior.[5] To the west it has the Pacific Sea and

---

* There is incredible variation among geographers about the geographical longitude of California. I base my opinion on the observations made by the Spanish astronomer, Mr. Vicente Dos, about whom mention is made in the Supplement to the *Official Report of Pèsaro* of November 13, 1790. He found a difference of 7 hours, 28 minutes, between the meridian of Paris and that of the village of San José, near the cape of San Lucas, from which is deduced the common longitude of the village mentioned, and consequently that of the cape of San Lucas, which is situated under the same meridian, is 268°.

---

[1] [Editors' notes numbered from 1 up.] New Spain, a name at that time applied to Mexico.

[2] Clavigero was wrong in his estimates. The early explorers and colonizers who came to the New World often made mistakes in reckoning the size and location of various places. The Colorado River flows into the Gulf of California a few miles south of 32° North latitude and 115° West longitude.

[3] It is 22° 24' North latitude and 109° 30' West longitude.

[4] This harbor is 32° 42' North latitude and 117° 14' West longitude.

[5] The Jesuits, who went to Italy after their expulsion from Mexico in 1768, rarely received any direct word relative to the continued expansion of

on the east the Gulf of California, already called the Red Sea because of its similarity to the Red Sea, and the Sea of Cortés, named in honor of the famous conqueror of Mexico, who had it discovered and who navigated it. The length of the peninsula is about ten degrees; but its width varies from thirty to seventy miles and more.[6]

The name "California" was applied to a single port in the beginning, but later it was extended to mean all the peninsula. Some geographers have even taken the liberty of comprising under this denomination New Mexico, the country of the Apaches,[7] and other northern regions very remote from the true California and which have nothing to do with it. The origin of this name is not known;[8] but it is believed that the conqueror,

---

the missionary work there. It is therefore not surprising that Clavigero did not know in 1786 that settlements had been made as far north as the bay of San Francisco and that much of the interior of the land just north of Lower California had been explored. By 1786 nine Missions had been founded by the Franciscans in what is now the state of California. Four presidios and two civic pueblos (San José in 1777, and Los Angeles in 1781) had also been established. Juan Bautista de Anza had led two expeditions overland from Sonora to California by way of the Colorado River. The great Indian apostle, Fray Francisco Garcés, had crossed into California from Sonora and had explored the central portion of the state northward nearly to Lake Tulare. Gabriel Moraga had crossed the coast mountains and penetrated the south-central valleys of the state. Two Franciscans, Silvestre Velez de Escalante and Francisco Dominguez, had traveled northwest from Santa Fé in 1776 and reached northern Utah.

[6] In some places the peninsula is more than one hundred miles wide. It is about eight hundred miles long.

[7] When the Spaniards conquered Mexico they found two types of Indian tribes—the "savages" and the "barbarians." In general the dividing line between the two ran near the twenty-first parallel. Those in the south were somewhat civilized and cultured, while those north of this line were savage and very warlike. The Apaches dwelt chiefly in the country bordering on the Rio Grande River, principally southwest of it. Some claim that they were the most cruel and bellicose tribe that inhabited the Southwest. Their long-continued wars upon the Spanish settlements, especially upon those in Sonora, greatly delayed the advance of the Spanish civilization toward Upper California.

[8] A scholarly discussion of the origin of the name "California" may be found in Charles E. Chapman, *A History of California: The Spanish Period*, chapter vi, and in the *University of California Publications in History*, Vol. IV, No. 4; see also *Grizzly Bear*, March 1916.

Cortés, who pretended to have some knowledge of Latin, named the harbor, where he put in, *Callida fornax,* because of the great heat which he felt there; and that either he himself or some one of the many persons who accompanied him formed the name "California" from these two words. If this conjecture be not true, it is at least credible.*†

The western coast on the Pacific Sea, beginning with the cape of San Lucas, goes toward the northwest and continues beyond the peninsula almost always in the same direction, perhaps as far as the most westerly extremity of America. The littoral lands of this part of California are usually arid, covered with barren sand, uninhabited, and lacking everything that is necessary for life, even firewood and water. Besides, there is scarcely a port in which ships can shelter themselves from the danger of the northwest winds, which prevail there. Boats, therefore, and other smaller craft can hardly put in on the coast without danger of going to pieces on the reefs because of the very heavy and violent swells of the sea.

* The famous corsair, Drake, called California "New Albion" in honor of his native land. Father Scherer, a German Jesuit, and M. de Fer, a French geographer, used the name "Carolina Island" to designate California, which name began to be used in the time of Charles II, King of Spain, when that peninsula was considered an island; but these and other names were soon forgotten and that given it by the conqueror, Cortés, prevailed.

† We shall add the opinion of the learned ex-Jesuit, Don José Campoi, on the etymology of the name "California," or "Californias," as others say. This Father believes that the said name is composed of the Spanish word *cala,* which means a small cove of the sea, and the Latin word *fornix,* which means arch, because there is a small cove at the cape of San Lucas on the western side of which there overhangs a rock pierced in such a way that in the upper part of that great opening is seen an arch formed so perfectly that it appears made by human skill. Therefore, Cortés, noticing that cove and arch, and understanding Latin, probably gave to that port the name "California" or *Cala-y-fornix,* speaking half-Spanish and half-Latin.

To these conjectures we could add a third one, composed of both, by saying that the name is derived from *cala,* as Campoi thinks, and *fornax,* as the author believes, because of the cove, and the heat which Cortés felt there, and that the latter might have called that place *Cala, y fornax.*

The best-known harbors of that coast are those of Marqués (Santiago), Magdalena, Año Nuevo, San Juan Nepomuceno, San Francisco, and San Diego; and farther on beyond the peninsula on the same coast is that of Monterey at 37° North latitude.[9] The capes of the same coast, after San Lucas, which is the most famous, are those of Morro Hermoso, Engaño, Año Nuevo, and Rey. The coast as far as 40° goes constantly toward the northwest; and from 40° to 42° it breaks toward the north, and from 42°, where Cape Mendocino is,[10] it takes its first direction toward the northwest again. At 43° is Cape Blanco de San Sebastián,[11] which was the limit of the discoveries made by the Spaniards up to 1770. In this year, or in the following one, they advanced, it is believed, as far as 55° and even to 58°; but we can say nothing of their discoveries,[12] since we have not seen the accounts of their trips.

The eastern coast on the Gulf begins at the cape of Porfía, more than thirty miles distant from that of San Lucas, and follows almost the same direction as the other. Between these two capes is the port of San Bernabé, where the ships from the Philippines are accustomed to put in. The harbors of the Gulf are those of Las Palmas, Cerralvo, La Paz, San Carlos, Loreto, San Bruno, Comondù, La Concepción, Los Ángeles, San Luis, La Visitación, and San Felipe de Jesús.[13] Between the ports of Cerralvo and La Paz there is a small peninsula which extends toward the north, and another is between the ports of Comondù and Concepción.

---

[9] It is 36° 31′ North latitude.

[10] Just north of the mouth of the Eel River, California. Its location was given at from 41° to 43° North by the early navigators.

[11] It is at latitude 42°. Clavigero undoubtedly followed the diary of Vizcaíno.

[12] In 1774 Juan Pérez, sent from Mexico by the viceroy Bucareli to look for foreign settlements, reached 55° on the northern coastline of Queen Charlotte Island. The following year Bruno Heceta went as far north as 57° 58′. These voyages gave Spain claim to the northwestern coast of North America.

[13] For the names of these harbors and of the capes mentioned above, Clavigero must have used the maps of Venegas. See Hubert Howe Bancroft, *History of the North Mexican States and Texas*, Vol. I, p. 471.

The capes of this coast, after that of Porfía, are those of Cerralvo, San Lorenzo, Púlpito, San Marcos, Vírgines, San Miguel, and San Gabriel. From 31°, and especially from 32°, the coast breaks toward the north, and it continues as far as the Red River, which is the terminus of the peninsula and the Gulf.

Descending from the mouth of this river toward the southeast is the coast of Pimería, Sonora, Ostimuri, Sinaloa, Culiacán, Chiametla, and Acaponeta (all provinces of New Spain)[14] until reaching Cape Corrientes, situated at 20° 20′ North latitude[15] and almost 270° [West] longitude. This cape and that of San Lucas form the opening of the gulf by which the gulf connects with the Pacific Sea. By following the same direction southeast from Cape Corrientes along the coasts of the dioceses of Nueva Galicia, Michoacán,[16] and Mexico, one reaches the port of Acapulco,[17] where the ships from the Philippine Islands go to unload.

In both seas of California there are innumerable islands, but for the most part they are small and deserted. The largest in the Gulf are those of Cerralvo,[18] Espíritu Santo,[19] San José,[20]

---

[14] The states of Sonora and Sinaloa now include this coastline.

[15] Latitude 20° 55′.

[16] The present states from Sinaloa south to Guerrero, on the coast of which is the port of Acapulco, are Nayarit, Jalisco, Colima, and Michoacán.

[17] Latitude 19° 13′. One of the largest and best harbors on the Pacific Coast. In this place were built many of the ships that first sailed along the coast. It was the chief harbor for the Manila galleons. The town of Acapulco has today a population of about 8,000. Hides, skins, cotton, coffee, copra, and sugar are among its principal exports.

[18] Located four miles southwest of the bay of La Paz. It is about fifteen miles long and four miles wide, being largely a desert and having few inhabitants and little fresh water. Formerly it was a good place for pearl fishing. It was discovered in 1535 by Cortés, and four years later Ulloa named it Santiago. It is noted for its dense growth of cactus and its many iguanas (*California Historical Society Quarterly*, Vol. III, p. 336).

[19] Near La Paz Bay. It is not so large as Cerralvo. It was also discovered by Cortés in 1535, and he named it San Miguel. Later it was known by the names of Las Perlas and San Cristóbal (*ibid.*, Vol. I, p. 94).

[20] Also near La Paz Bay. It is about sixteen miles long and seven miles wide, having a mammal fauna perhaps more intensive than any other island in the Gulf.

Carmen,[21] Ángel Custodio,[22] and Tiburón;[23] and in the Pacific Sea are those of Huamalguà,[24] Cerros or Montes,[25] Ceniza,[26] Pájaros,[27] and Santa Catalina,[28] of which something will be said when there is opportunity.

[21] About five miles from the mainland, just north of the bay of La Paz. This island is perhaps the best known of all those in the Gulf, because of its extensive salt beds. The salt lagoon is about a mile square, consisting of almost pure salt, which is completely shut off from the sea. Father Salvatierra thought this island contained "enough salt to supply the whole world" indefinitely. These salt beds have been worked for more than two hundred years, and today they show no signs of depletion. They are worked chiefly by English firms (*Proceedings of the California Academy of Sciences*, January 1923, p. 68). Salt is also found in Ojo de Liebre, on the island of San José, and in a few other places.

[22] The largest island on the coast of Lower California, being about forty miles long and ten miles wide. Some of its mountain peaks reach a height of four thousand feet. The island is noted for its large number of rattlesnakes, chiefly black rattlers.

[23] Thirty miles long and from fifteen to twenty miles wide. It was discovered by Alarcón in 1540, and named (Shark Island) from the large number of sharks which he saw there. This island is inhabited by the Seri Indians, a race of gigantic size and perhaps the most warlike and dangerous Indian tribe in North America. But they do not practice cannibalism, as is commonly believed (*United States Bureau of American Ethnology*, Vol. XVII, pp. 1–344; also *Proceedings of the California Academy of Sciences*, June 1923, p. 58).

[24] Meaning "Fog Island." When Father Taraval visited this island in 1737 he was surprised to see with what great ease the Indians killed the sea otter (Miguel Venegas, *Noticia de la California* [London, 1759], Vol. II, p. 113; also *Proceedings of the California Academy of Sciences*, Vol. II, p. 24).

[25] The largest island on the west coast of the peninsula. It is about twenty miles long and is some forty miles from the shore. It is volcanic in origin, and a mountain range, with several peaks nearly four thousand feet high, runs the entire length of the island. Ulloa discovered this island in 1539, and named it "La Isla de los Cedros," but later the name was changed to Cerros on account of its high peaks (George Davidson, *Early Voyages*, p. 174). Some good timber is found on this island, and also small quantities of gold and silver.

[26] Today called San Martín. Located at 30° 29', just north of the port of San Quintín.

[27] Off the coast south of Ensenada; small and barren.

[28] Discovered by Cabrillo, 1542. They are some twenty-five miles from Long Beach, and have an area of about eighty square miles. They are within the confines of Los Angeles County, but are owned largely by a few persons.

Chapter Two

SOIL AND CLIMATE

GENERALLY speaking, the appearance of California is unpleasant and rough. Its land is usually uneven, arid, especially rocky and sandy, lacking water, and covered with thorny plants where it is capable of producing vegetation; and where it is not, it is covered with immense heaps of stones and sand. The air is hot and dry and in both seas harmful to navigators, since it occasions a fatal scurvy[29] when they ascend to a certain latitude. Then the windstorms, which are sometimes felt, are so furious that they uproot trees and carry the miserable houses away with them. Rains are so scarce there that the Californians consider themselves fortunate if two or three heavy showers fall in the year.[30] Springs are very few and scanty.

In regard to the rivers, there is not one in all the extent of that peninsula, although the two small streams of Mulegè and San José del Cabo are honored with this name.[31] The latter empties into the port of San Bernabé; and the former, after a course of barely two miles, flows into the Gulf at 27°. All the rest are brooks or dry beds which, although dry nearly all year, have so much water when it rains and such a rapid course that they upset everything and carry desolation to the few fields which are there.

---

[29] Scurvy is not caused by any condition of the atmosphere.

[30] Sereno Watson reported that rain fell at Los Angeles Bay once in twenty-two months (*Proceedings of the American Academy of Sciences*, Vol. XXIV, p. 37). Father Link testified that he never saw rain fall at the Mission in San Borja on the peninsula during the seven years that he was stationed there (*University of California Publications in Geography*, Vol. II, No. 8, p. 272).

[31] The peninsula has numerous rivers, but owing to the scanty rainfall most of them are dry the year around. In the entire coastline of more than two thousand miles, only five rivers flow into the sea for the entire year. Only one of these, the Río Santo Domingo, has a constant flow for its full length. Perhaps no stream in the peninsula has a length of a hundred miles.

Although the Red River[32] is large, it can be of little use to the peninsula because the river is at the end of it and separated from it by high mountains. This river, although it rises in the unknown countries of the North, augments its waters greatly with the Gila, also a large river which unites with it[33] at 35°; from there the Red River flows toward the southwest as far as 34°. Here it takes its first direction again for half a day, or as far as its mouth,[34] which has a width of almost three miles and is obstructed by three small islands which divide the course of its waters. At this end of the Gulf larger boats cannot approach the mouth on account of the shallow water; nor can the smaller ones pass it on account of the very violent force of the current and the large trees which it is accustomed to bring down. Thus this river will not be useful for trading in California with the people who live on its two banks.

Near the mouth there are two lagoons of reddish water (from which the river takes its name) and of a caustic quality that is so severe that, by touching any part of the body, it raises blisters[35] immediately and occasions a great burning which does not go away for some days. It may be believed that this effect is caused by a certain bituminous mineral which is found in the depths of those lagoons and which has been observed by navigators on raising anchor. If the fogs were abundant they could act as a substitute for the lack of rains in California, as in Perú; but they are very scarce also.

Coming now to the particular regions of the peninsula, we shall find some diversity among them. In the southern part, from Cape San Lucas to 24°, it is not so rolling, nor are the springs so rare in the proximity of the mountains; but the coasts are very arid and the air there is very hot. The country of the

---

[32] The Colorado River, which the early Spanish explorers had great difficulty in ascending. Francisco de Ulloa was the first white man to enter (1539) the mouth of this river and follow up its course. The vast delta lands at its mouth are perhaps the richest agricultural portions of the peninsula. The Spaniards first called this river "Buena Guía" (Good Guide).

[33] The juncture of the two rivers is about 170 miles south of 35°.

[34] The Colorado River flows into the Gulf just below 32°.

[35] Probably caused by the intense heat of the sun rather than by any chemical effects of the water.

Guaicuras,[36] situated between 24° and 26°, is the least mountainous but at the same time the driest and the most barren of all California.[37] The lands of the Cochimìes,[38] which extend from 25°, in part, as far as 33°, are the most rolling and rocky; but from parallel 27° onward the atmosphere is more benign. Toward 30° it begins to feel cold, and it snows there; but the land, although less broken and stony, is very arid and barren as far as 32°. The appearance of the country changes at 32°, [beyond which] the land has a greater abundance of water and a more beautiful vegetation.

Father Kino, the celebrated missionary of Sonora, of whom we shall make frequent mention in this history, after he had forded the Red River between 34° and 35°, found beautiful flats abundant in water and covered with good grazing and luxuriant trees in the countries situated to the west of that river.[39] Those Spaniards said the same thing about the coast of the Pacific Sea, included between 34° and 43°, when they went to explore it at the command of the Catholic monarch at the beginning of the past century; but as these countries are outside of the peninsula and are not yet inhabited by Spaniards[40] they are indeed remote from our purpose.

---

[36] One of the Indian nations that inhabited the peninsula, to be described in detail later.

[37] This is only partly true, since the western section of this part of the country contains some high mountain ranges. The least mountainous region of the peninsula is the central part, extending from the great desert of Vizcaíno north to 31°. A continuous mountain range runs the entire length of the peninsula except at the bay of La Paz, where a great break occurs, a pass scarcely two hundred feet above the sea level and about fifteen miles wide. Just north and south of this interesting pass the mountains rise to a height of from 4,000 to 8,000 feet.

[38] Another Indian nation to be described presently.

[39] Kino probably went no farther north than 33°.

[40] See footnote 5 *supra*.

Chapter Three

MOUNTAINS, STONES, AND MINERALS

THE MOUNTAINS of California form two ranges which extend through all the length of the peninsula, leaving little flat land. That of the southern part occupies the middle at an equal distance from both seas; and in these mountains stones are so rare that it is necessary to use bricks for building. The range in the northern part is longer than the first; it approaches the Gulf more than the Pacific Sea, and its mountains are higher and more rugged, and so rocky that all who see them are astonished, since it seems that besides the universal deluge of water there was another special one of rocks in this peninsula.[41] There is a volcano among these mountains at 28°, so that this unhappy country might not be lacking such a feature. This volcano was discovered by the missionaries in 1746, but there has not been any eruption nor has it caused any earthquake[42] since the Spaniards have been living there.

It is inferred from the structure of those mountains that this peninsula was covered with the waters of the sea in ancient times.[43] Near Kadakaamang, an inland place situated at 28°,

---

[41] A large part of the peninsula is volcanic in origin, and this accounts for the rocky surface of so much of the land upon which the early missionaries made frequent comment. The great volcanic plateau which covers an area about twenty-five miles wide and three hundred miles long in the central portion of the peninsula, along the Pacific Coast, is perhaps the most barren section of the entire country. Hundreds of square miles are thickly covered by layers of lava rock. Many of the mountain peaks range over 8,000 feet, and La Providencia, which is the highest peak on the peninsula, rises to a height of more than 10,000 feet.

[42] Earthquakes are rather rare on the peninsula, although the section south of La Paz has been severely shaken at times. Loreto was completely ruined by an earthquake in 1717. The records of the padres frequently refer to slight quakes there.

[43] Scientists believe that formerly much of Lower California was submerged and that it was gradually raised to the outline of what it is today. The vast Vizcaíno Desert, located along the Pacific Coast in the central portion of the peninsula and extending eastward across the plateau of San Ignacio almost to the Gulf, contains unmistakable evidence that one day it was covered by water.

there is a mountain of argillaceous earth on which is seen a layer of sea shells which seems pasted with clay at a perpendicular height of more than two hundred feet. The thickness of this stratum is more than two feet, and it is situated horizontally almost at the middle of the height of the mountain.

In the mountains nine or ten miles distant from that place a great quantity of [fossil] oysters[44] is found. So excessively large are they that a missionary who had carried one which he had found to his house and had it weighed, without the cover or the animal which formerly lived in it, found that it weighed twenty-three Spanish pounds.[45] It was about a foot and a half in circumference, almost nine inches long and four wide, and very thick. In California, as in other places, they made a very good lime from these oysters. Near Mulegè,[46] a place situated at 27° North latitude and near the Gulf shore, there is a high mountain of very hard rock, which they use there for buildings. In any part of the mountain, whether they cut into the slope of the mountain or into its summit, shells are found embedded in even the innermost parts of the rock, and some cavities are seen which appear to have been occupied by marine bodies already consumed by time; this proves that the said mountain was formed within the sea.

Rocks of this kind are very common on all the coasts of the Gulf. At nine or ten miles from Loreto,[47] the small capital of the peninsula, in a place surrounded by lofty mountains, there is a little hill also formed by shells,[48] and another similar one

---

[44] Fossils of these huge oysters have been found occasionally in the southwestern part of the United States and in the state of California as far north as the valley of the San Joaquin River.

[45] Equal to 1.01 English pounds.

[46] The Mission of Santa Rosalía de Mulegé, founded in 1705 and located at 26° 50′ North latitude on the Mulegé River. The Mission site is now a village of some two thousand people, engaged chiefly in mining and fishing.

[47] Located at latitude 26°, and the first permanent settlement made (1697) on the peninsula. It was the first capital of California.

[48] This may have been a shellmound. From Alaska to the southern end of Lower California shellmounds are common. They simply represent the accumulation of debris from the natives' food, piled high from centuries of residence. They were not used especially as burial grounds, and were usually

near the Mission of San Luis[49] in a place more than thirty miles distant from the sea. If the many signs which are discovered there indicating eruptions of the volcano in former times together with the multitude of islands by which California is surrounded are added to these facts, it seems that one can have no doubt about the revolutions made by nature in that place. Besides it is manifest that the sea has decreased on both coasts of the peninsula. The Jesuit missionaries of Loreto observed that the waters had receded many paces on that coast in less than forty years; and this decrease is more noticeable on the shores of the western coast, for there all the space which is between the sea and the mountains is completely covered by littoral sand, in spite of the fact that in some places the mountains are more than thirty miles distant from the sea. Therefore, it is certain that California has greater width today than it had in the past centuries; and we can prophesy safely that this width will go on increasing in the future, and perhaps some of the many islands will be united with the peninsula.[50]

---

built where there was fresh water; they varied in size and shape. One of the largest and most noted shellmounds stood near Berkeley on the edge of the bay of San Francisco. It had a diameter of 310 feet, and rose to a height of thirty-two feet. Some years ago it was leveled, and a greater variety of shells and bones was found in it than in any other shellmound explored up to that time. In it were found not only shells of the oyster, mussel, clam, and other sea animals but the bones of the bear, beaver, deer, dog, duck, elk, gopher, rabbit, raccoon, sea lion, sea otter, seal, squirrel, turtle, whale, wildcat, wolf, and others not identified (*University of California Publications in American Archaeology and Ethnology*, Vol. VII, No. 1, p. 18). In the region of San Francisco Bay, extending north to within a few miles of Vallejo and south to Palo Alto, more than four hundred of these shellmounds have been located (*ibid.*, No. 4, p. 322). In this publication will be found a map locating these interesting mounds. Lower California has not yet been similarly investigated.

[49] San Luís Gonzaga, founded in 1737, some twenty-four miles from Loreto.

[50] Scientific investigation since Clavigero's time establishes, on the contrary, that several of the islands off the coast of Lower California were formerly connected to the mainland. The islands of Cedros, Espíritu Santo, Todos Santos, and Tres Marías are good examples of this change. Espíritu Santo seems to be merely the continuation of a point or cape of the mainland to which it is connected by a shallow submerged range of hills only a few feet under the surface of the sea. The Tres Marías Islands are likely of very recent origin. Not only the surface features of the peninsula but the varied

Among the rocks with which the mountains of California are filled there are flint, pumice stone, whetstone, crystals, gypsum, *tezontle*,[51] and other slightly useful ones. It is believed that there are marbles[52] in the northern part, but up to the present time this is not well ascertained. Rock crystal is found, as it is accustomed to be, in hexagonal pieces, in the district of the Mission of Santa Gertrudis,[53] under the 29° parallel. There is a great quantity of pumice stone in the vicinity of the volcano. Common gypsum is very abundant in many places, but in the little hill of the island of San Marcos,[54] situated[55] in the Gulf near the beach of Mulegè, is a peculiar crystallized gypsum in transparent pieces four to five feet in length, about a foot and a half around, and three or four fingers' breadth in thickness, which when calcined produces an excellent and very fine white powder. A missionary succeeded in making glass windows out of it such as those made of alabaster. In various places in California there are many quarries of *tezontle*, a rock much valued in the capital of Mexico, a description of which we gave in the *Ancient History* of that country. The inhabitants of this peninsula mention among the rocks *múcara* and *rizo*, two kinds of white coral which are cast on the beach by the waves of the Gulf and which are also used for making lime.

fauna and flora give clear evidence that Lower California was one day joined at the south to the mainland. The peninsula in remote times was evidently much wider than it is now.

[51] A rather soft, porous stone, which is easily cut and which was used in Mexico and in the peninsula for constructing permanent buildings.

[52] Little marble has ever been found in the peninsula or even north in the present state of California, which is so rich in other minerals.

[53] Founded July 15, 1752. A few years after the Franciscans took over the Missions on the peninsula (1768), this Mission had almost a thousand persons, of whom nearly one-half were boys and girls. Among the live stock were listed 113 head of cattle, 140 head of sheep, and 470 goats. This Mission is inland from the Gulf about twelve leagues, just north of 28° latitude. See Fray Francisco Palóu, *Historical Memoirs of New California*, translated and edited by Herbert Eugene Bolton, Vol. I, p. 204. Hereafter cited as Bolton, *Palóu*.

[54] About fifteen miles long, and the location of a large tannery where hides are cured from the large number of cattle killed at Santa Rosalía (*Proceedings of the California Academy of Sciences*, January 1923, p. 61).

[55] The island is north of 27° North latitude.

In sterile countries the aridity of the soil is often compensated for (at times) by the abundance and wealth of minerals, but in California it is not so. Until the present, no metals but gold[56] and silver[57] have been found in it and both in a small quantity. In the year 1748 a wealthy person,* who had become rich from pearl fishing,[58] began to work some silver mines in the

* Don Manuel de Ocio, previously a soldier in the presidio of Loreto, a discharged soldier of the militia, busied himself in fishing for pearls to such an extent that he became almost the absolute owner of that branch of commerce. He has been the only rich man of California.

---

[56] Some of the earliest explorers to reach the coast of California told stories about gold being in the country. When Drake landed just north of the bay of San Francisco in 1579, probably at the place which afterward was called Drake's Bay, one of his officers reported that he was told by Indians that gold could be found in the mountains. Similar reports were heard when the first Missions in the Californias were founded. Gold was found early in the peninsula of Lower California, and when the Franciscans took over the Missions there from the Jesuits in 1768 "over five thousand pesos" of gold and silver bullion were found in the Missions. See Bolton, *Palóu*, p. 65. During the Civil War there was a renewed activity in mining in the peninsula. Several mining companies were formed in San Francisco to operate in Lower California. One was capitalized at $100,000, others at $120,000 and $540,000, and another, advertised as owning "probably one of the most valuable mines in the Continent of America," at $640,000. Another large company organized in San Francisco promised to produce gold from the mines described by Clavigero. Little paying ore was found. It seems that the first gold found in any quantity in the peninsula was near Real del Castillo in 1870. Extensive placer mines were opened in 1889 at Santa Clara. Pockets yielding $50,000 or more were found. Today little effort is made to find gold deposits in that country. See pamphlets and prospectuses in the Bancroft Library, University of California.

[57] The companies mentioned above also mined for silver. Today there are small silver mines at Comondù, Loreto, Mulegè, Real del Castillo, San Borja, Santa Gertrudis, San Luís, and El Triunfo.

[58] One of the main industries of the peninsula from the very beginning. The survivors of the Jiménez expedition were the first men to carry to Mexico City information about pearls which they found in the Gulf. But the industry was not much developed until the middle of the nineteenth century. Most of the companies doing pearl fishing were foreign. One American company, in 1874, had exclusive privileges to fish for pearls from Cape San Lucas to the Colorado River; another had a monopoly of the west coast of the peninsula; and one company controlled pearl fishing from Acapulco to Guatemala. Some companies used five hundred or more divers. They wore rubber suits,

southern part toward 23° and continued for some years, going from one mine to another, without augmenting his capital greatly. Gold also has been found in these mountains, but in small amount. Other silver mines were discovered in a mountain called "Rosario," situated at about 28° 30', but working them will always be expensive because there is a lack of all necessities in that place, firewood and water included. In the district of Mulegè there is also a mountain of reddish clay which has veins of gold, according to the opinion of the well-informed. Be this as it may, what is certain is that it would be detrimental to the Californians if there should be anything in their peninsula which could attract wicked people, as those are accustomed to be who are occupied in extracting that precious metal from the bowels of the earth.

The other minerals of California which deserve some mention are sulphur, copperas,[59] ochre, and chalk. On the slope of the volcano is found a great quantity of pure, clean sulphur which anyone could gather without any work, because it is on the surface of the earth. There is some also at 28° on the beach of the Pacific Sea, and the place of its vein is recognized from the color of the soil, which is very different from all the rest. By digging there a little, one finds sulphur, although mixed with earth; but it is credible that it would be found as pure as that of the volcano if one should dig to greater depth.

with glass-fronted helmets, which were weighted with lead. Most of the oyster shells were taken to La Paz to be opened; often pearls of great value were found. In 1881 one was found that weighed twenty-eight carats and was sold in Paris for $10,000; two years later another was obtained that sold for $8,600. Indians were often cheated of their catch. A white man bought from an Indian an oval-shaped pearl in 1883 for ten dollars. It was of "a light sandy color, of surprizing luster and weighed 32 carats." It was sold in Paris for $5,500 (*United States Fish Commission*, 1891, No. 5, p. 94). Some of the most magnificent pearls worn by the queens of Europe came from the bay of Mulegè (P. L. Simmonds, *The Commercial Products of the Sea*, p. 420). For an excellent historical review of pearl fishing in the Gulf of California see an unpublished thesis by S. A. Mosk in the library of the University of California. In recent years the industry has yielded about a million dollars annually (Herman Schnitzler, *The Republic of Mexico*, p. 462).

[59] A French concern, the Boleo Mining Company, at Santa Rosalía, has been in operation there for more than fifty years. It mines about ten thousand tons of pure copper annually.

Copperas is found in small cuts in some damp places in the district of the Mission of Guadalupe,[60] and in other more northern territories. These crevices are probably formed from the sediment of the water, which is saturated with copperas on passing through its seams.

In that mountain of reddish clay situated near Mulegè and which is believed to contain gold, various veins of yellow ochre have been observed which the Indians used previously for painting their bodies. In this same mountain they have likewise found chalk, which is a kind of native ceruse, a very white mineral earth and quite similar to white lead. In California they use it for whitewashing buildings; but as it gives a whiteness so intense that it is dazzling, they soften it with glue. In Mexico they generally use it for polishing silverware.

In regard to salts, there are common salt, rock salt, and saltpeter. Since California is surrounded almost everywhere by the sea, it cannot fail to have good salt beds. In fact, there are many, but none comparable to that of the island of Carmen, situated in the Gulf at 26°, opposite the port of Loreto, from which it is twelve miles distant. This island, which has a circumference of forty miles, is entirely deserted, nor are there any animals supported on it except mice and snakes in great numbers. It has a rugged mountain in the western part; but the land of the eastern part is quite flat, and in this place is that salt bed, which, without contradiction, is one of the best in the universe.

It begins at a distance of a mile and a half from the sea, and it extends for so many miles that the end is not seen with the eyes; it appears to the observer as an immense plain covered with snow. Its salt is very white, crystallized, and pure, without a mixture of earth, or of other foreign bodies. Although it is not so hard as rock salt, it is broken with picks, and in this manner it is cut into square cakes of a size such that each laborer can carry one of them on his back. This work is carried on in

---

[60] Nuestra Señora de Guadalupe. It was richly endowed by Villapuente of Mexico City (see footnote 162, Book II, p. 191), and founded in April 1720. It is located a few miles northwest of La Paz, about equidistant between the ocean and the Gulf.

the first and last hours of the day, because at other times the reflection of the rays of the sun on it is so bright that it dazzles the workmen. Although all the merchantmen of Europe might go there to load salt from that salt bed, they never could exhaust it, not only because of its great size but principally because all that salt which is taken from it is reproduced at once. When not more than seven or eight days have passed after the quantity necessary for loading a boat has been dug out, the excavation is rapidly refilled with new salt.

If this salt bed were in some country of Europe, it would produce for the sovereign who possessed it a more considerable income than that of the famous mines of Williska[61] in Poland, in whose shadowy and terrible depth so many hundreds of slaves are buried to get out the salt; but in the Gulf of California it serves only to provide the few inhabitants of the peninsula. It would be much more useful, even in the place where God has put it, if it could excite the industry of the inhabitants of Sinaloa,[62] Culiacán,[63] and those other towns of that coast. Fish are very abundant and excellent there, as we shall mention later; and since men there have all the salt that is desired without any cost they could carry on a very lucrative trade in salted fish with the inland provinces of New Spain.

Two mines of rock salt have been discovered in the peninsula. One is on the coast of the Pacific Sea at 26°, and the other at 28°, which is on the plain belonging to the Mission of San Ignacio.[64] The salt which is extracted from them is similar in whiteness and purity to that of Carmen; but it is not so smooth and bright. There is pure saltpeter in the mountain of Rosario,

[61] A small town about twenty miles southeast of Krakow. Mines are still operated there.

[62] A town in the state of Sinaloa and founded by Guzmán. For a time it was the capital. It now has a population of 1,300.

[63] Founded by Guzmán in 1531. It is located about forty miles from the Gulf on the Sinaloa River, and has a population of about 15,000.

[64] Founded in 1725 by Father Juan Luyando, who endowed it with ten thousand pesos; three years later the Mission church was opened for services. It is located about midway between the ocean and the Gulf and is a few miles southwest of Santa Rosalía, one of the chief seaports on the eastern coast of the peninsula.

and it exists, mixed with earth, in various moist places. This is called *tequizquitl* by the Mexicans and *tequezquite* by the Spaniards of Mexico; it is rather aphronitrum and is accustomed to be used in New Spain, as in Egypt, for making lye for bleaching cloth, and for cooking vegetables, since they become softer and more tasty with this mineral.

Chapter Four
┼┼

PLANTS AND THEIR DIVISIONS

PERHAPS those fond of natural history might wish us to classify the plants of California. When we pass to the vegetable kingdom, according to some of the systems invented by the modern naturalists, the plants of the peninsula are not in such great numbers as to require a similar method; nor are the ideas which we have of them sufficient for us to follow it; consequently we shall make use of the same division which we have adopted in the *History of Mexico*, as being more suitable to the knowledge of all kinds of people.

Since vegetation is always in proportion to the quality of the land, in California those plants which crave a dry and gravelly soil, such as *pitaji*[65] and *opuntie*,[66] do very well. It has

[65] *Lemaireocereus thurberi*. The name "*pitahaya*" (Spanish), in Italian "*pitaja*," is used commonly throughout Mexico to describe the various fruits of the cacti of the Cereus family. It is thought that the name "Sinaloa" is derived from the two Indian words "*sina*" for *pitahaya* and "*lobala*" for "round" (*United States National Herbarium*, Vol. XXIII, p. 907). The fruit of this plant is either sweet or sour. It is red and about the size of a large English walnut. The pulp resembles that of the ripe watermelon (*Zoe*, II, 193).

[66] A plant common throughout Mexico and southwestern United States. Nopal is one of the many names given the subgenus *Platyopuntia*. In the United States the nopal is called the prickly pear, and the fruit is called "tuna." It is still one of the principal foods for many of the natives in certain parts of Mexico. A syrup (*miel de tuna*) is made from the fruit, and *tejuino* and *calonche* are beverages derived from it. For a discussion of *Una Nueva Plaga del Nopal*, see the report of Secretaría de Agricultura y Fomento, Mexico City, February–April, 1929, pp. 7–17. In Italian *pitajo* is the plant, and *pitaja* the fruit. The plural of *pitaja* is *pitaje*; the plural of *pitajo* is *pitaji*.

been observed that thorny plants abound there proportionally more than in other places and that those which are common to other countries are ordinarily smaller there, the trunk or stalk has less thickness, and the leaves are narrower. There are also many trees which are leafless and nude the greater part of the year, for which reason the heat of the sun is unendurable to travelers, who do not find shade where they can take a little rest. When it rains, those trees are covered with some foliage, but as soon as the rains cease they remain leafless again.

Among the plants of California, therefore, some are useful for their fruit, some for their leaves or branches, others for their trunk or stalk, others for their roots, and, finally, others for their juice or gum. There are also noxious and fantastic ones.

Chapter Five

PLANTS NATIVE TO CALIFORNIA AND USEFUL FOR THEIR FRUITS

IN THE class of plants useful for their fruits, there are many that are native to the soil and others that are foreign. Among the native plants, the *pitajo** deserves the first place because of its strange shape and because the wretched Californians have their principal crop and most delicious fruit from it. There are two kinds of *pitaji*, quite different from each other, not only because one gives sweet fruit and the other bitter-sweet but also because the two plants have different shapes.

The *pitajo* of the first species is very common in Mexico and

---

* The French call this plant spiny wax candle (*Cierge épineux*); but this name is suitable only for the first species, as will be seen by its description. We state the same about the name *organ*, which many Spaniards in America give to the plants of this species. In Mexico, where this plant is common, they call it *pitahayo*, and the fruit *pitahaya*. We shall make use of the name *pitajo* and *pitaja* as more adapted to the Italian language.

in other countries of America, but in no place does it thrive so well as in California. The trunk of this tree grows scarcely a foot from the earth. From it issue branches as thick as the arm of a man, ten, twelve, or more feet in height, set in a row, parallel, and upright, except in their origin, where the laterals have a curvature in proportion to their distance from those of the center. The branches have a green rind, which borders on yellow, and they are all furrowed with numerous grooves which extend in an upright line through all their length, about an inch in distance apart. Instead of leaves, which they lack absolutely, they are all armed with strong thorns, arranged after the fashion of stars and so closely set together that no part of the plant can be touched without wounding oneself. Under this rind there is about a finger's width of green and very juicy pulp, and within it a woody tube full of a whitish pith. These tubes burn well when dry and are used for torches.

Toward the end of the branches there appear beautiful white flowers spotted with bright red but without odor, and these flowers are succeeded by the fruit called *pitahayas* by the Spaniards, and *tammià*[67] or *dammià* by the California Cochimìes. This fruit is round, large as an average peach, and armed also with small thorns; at the beginning it is green, but on reaching maturity it turns red or yellow. The variety which has the red peel has a pulp of a beautiful blood color; and that with the yellow peel has white, yellow, or yellowish pulp. The peel is thick, but soft and easy to detach. The pulp is sweet, soft, cooling, and healthful. When the peel is removed, it is eaten together with the little seeds with which it is filled and which are somewhat similar to those of the fig, but smaller. The red *pitaje* stains the urine the color of blood, and for this reason strangers who eat it for the first time have been greatly worried, believing that they have broken some vein.

In the southern part of the peninsula the gathering of the sweet *pitaja* begins about the first of June and ends with the last of August; in the northern part it begins later and its greatest abundance is in August. When it rains a little more than usual

---

[67] The sweet *pitahayo* (*Lemaireocereus thurberi*).

Hugh Manessier

Fig. 1 – The *pitahaya dulce* or *tammia* (*Lemaireocereus Thurberi*), an unusually large specimen.

Homer Aschmann

Fig. 2a—The *pitahaya agria* or *tajua* (*Machaerocereus gummosus*). In sites near the west coast of Baja California it has this low-growing form as described by Clavigero.

George E. Lindsay

Fig. 2b—The *pitahaya agria* showing its characteristic growth form in the interior of the peninsula.

Hugh Manessier

Fig. 3a — Fruit of the *pitahaya agria*. Note the extreme thorniness matching Clavigero's description.

Fig. 3b — A clump of *viznaga (Echinocactus peninsulae)*.

Hugh Manessier

Hugh Manessier

Fig. 4 — The *cardón* (Pachycereus Pringlei). This is the largest species of cactus in the world.

the crop is very scarce or absolutely lacking, because there is no plant to which moisture is more harmful.

When the Californians wish to gather the crop, they use a rod or a cane on the end of which they firmly tie a slender bone arranged in the form of a hook for pulling the fruit from the plant, and a net is used to catch it in order to prevent its falling to the ground. From all that they have picked they remove the thorns with some straw or little stick, which is done easily when it is ripe, and they pare it to eat; and in this manner they go on gathering and eating until they satiate themselves. Then they carry the surplus to their homes. All the time that the gathering lasts they go every day through the hills and plains hunting for ripe *pitaje;* and this is the happiest season for them, as we shall mention later.

When the gathering of the sweet *pitaje* ends, there follows that of the bitter-sweet, called *tajuà* by the Cochimìes. This lasts during September and October, and when the year is abundant the fruit is picked in November also. The branches of these plants are also grooved, thorny, and leafless; but the grooves are coarser and the thorns larger, thicker, and stronger. They are not even upright and parallel like those of the *tammià* or *pitajo* with the sweet fruit. As soon as the branches leave the trunk they extend here and there without any order or symmetry, and, extending over the ground, they throw out roots, forming new plants, which are united with others; thickets result which are disagreeable to the sight and inaccessible to animals.

This plant is different from the first also with respect to the place where it grows, because the *tammià* bears well in any place in the hills or plains provided it is dry; while the *tajuà* is found only in the flat country near the beach and if it is found in the hills it is sometimes absolutely barren. The flower of the *tajuà* is vigorous, white, and red, and from four to five fingers' width in length. Its fruit, even more esteemed than that of the sweet *pitajo*, is spherical, the size of an orange, and armed also with thorns; and it is red inside and out. When it is ripe, it has a very pleasant bitter-sweet flavor and stains the urine blood color even more than the other. There are also some of these bitter-sweet *pitaje* in Mexico, but inferior in flavor to those of California.

The *gkakil*, or *garambullo*,[68] as the Spaniards call it, is the fruit of another plant with fleshy, grooved, leafless, and thorny branches, similar in form to those of the *pitajo;* but the plant of the *garambullo* is smaller, its grooves are broader, and its thorns are smaller and fewer. The fruit, although similar in shape to the *pitaja*, is much smaller, of a more vivid red, and very inferior in flavor. It comes earlier than the *pitaja* and is gone in less time.

The *cardón*,[69] thus called by the Spaniards in the peninsula, is a gigantic plant of the pulpy, grooved kind. Grooved, thorny, leafless, upright, and parallel branches, like those of the *pitajo*, grow from its thick trunk, but they are much taller and thicker. They grow to the height of even forty feet, and are thick (in proportion) and uniform from the trunk to their tips. Their structure is similar to that of the branches of the *pitajo;* and the rind is a most beautiful green color, but it has not so many thorns. This plant produces its fruit on the end of its branches; the fruit is pear shaped and has a yellow peel; and it contains a viscous liquid of a very bright red color and certain shining, black, spherical little seeds the size of those of a coriander.

These little seeds are the only useful things which the Californians obtain from this very large plant. In order to render them edible they extract the viscosity by means of the sun and

[68] From a tree-like cactus (*Cereus cochol*) found also from San Luis Potosí to Oaxaca, Mexico. This fruit is sold commonly in the markets there.

[69] In general "*cardón*" is a word commonly used to describe the giant cactus (*Cereus pringlei*). It is also frequently called "*cardón hecho*," or "*cardón barbón*." It is very abundant in the southern section of the peninsula, and is found as far north as San Quintín. The plant also grows extensively in Chihuahua, Colima, and Sonora. It sometimes reaches a height of fifty feet, and Father Baegert states that the natives on the peninsula climbed these "weak, trembling stems, sometimes thirty-six feet high," to scan the country to see game (*Report of the Smithsonian Institution*, 1864, p. 379). The Indians used the spines of this plant, which are sometimes two inches long, as fishhooks. Combs are made from the burr-like fruit, and the seeds are ground into flour for making cakes. The extensive growth of this plant near La Paz may have caused the early explorers to call the land the Isla de Cardón.

George E. Lindsay

Fig. 5 – The *garambullo* or *gkakil* (Lophocereus Schottii).

George E. Lindsay

Fig. 6 – Fruits on the upper stems of a *garambullo*.

fire. Afterward they toast them, to preserve them from decay and to be able to keep them. But the missionaries also found a way of making the branches very useful. They used to squeeze the juice out of a piece about two spans long, then they pounded it, and extracted the juice, which they boiled, removing the scum to a certain degree of condensation. This kind of balsam has been found very good for wounds and sores.

The thorny *viznaga*[70] is another kind of pulpous, grooved, leafless, thorny plant; but it is still stranger than all the rest of this class, since it lacks not only leaves but also branches; and it consists entirely of a pulpy, juicy, green, very thick trunk or stalk of the height of two, three, or four feet. Besides the small thorns with which it is armed everywhere, it has toward the end of the branch other very different ones. They are strong, of a bony substance, of four or five fingers' width in length, part white and part red, and with a small curvature at the point.

In New Spain these thorns are used for cleaning the teeth,* and in some Missions of California they use them instead of knitting needles, after having straightened the point and made the thickest part more slender. Among these thorns the *viznaga* produces its beautiful flowers, tinged with white, red, and yellow, which are succeeded by the fruit, much smaller than that of the *tammià*, and filled, like that of the *cardón*, with a viscous liquid and seeds, which the Californians eat after treating them as they do those of the *cardón*. In Mexico they make a good candy of the juicy pulp of this *viznaga*.

The *opuntia*, or *nopal*, a plant well known in Europe, is somewhat different from those which have been described to

---

* The Spaniards gave this plant the name of *viznaga* only because those bony thorns provided toothpicks like those of the true *viznaga*. As for the rest these two plants have no similarity to each other.

---

[70] Commonly known as the barrel cactus (*Echinocactus peninsulae*) because of its very large size. The spines of this plant were used by the early Mexicans in their religious services to draw blood from their bodies, and it therefore became sacred to *Mixcoath*, one of their gods. Fishhooks were made from the spines. It is also known by the Mexicans as *"teocomitl"* or *"tepenexcomitl."*

you, because their branches, although entirely leafless, have some resemblance to leaves, and they were commonly called *pencas,* or leaves. There are many kinds in California, all inferior to those of Mexico in size and quality of fruit. The Jesuit missionaries transplanted different kinds of Mexican *opuntias* there, which rooted well in that arid peninsula. The Californians eat not only the pulp but also the inner rind of the fruit; and in California, as well as in Mexico, the more tender leaves are eaten, baked, and stewed. The name which the Cochimìes give to the pear or fruit of the *opuntia* is only the single vowel "*a*."

It is truly remarkable that the plants of which we have spoken and others of which we shall speak later have more juice in the arid places than the other kinds of trees have in the damp places. But it is still more singular that they maintain themselves without any detriment, and with little or no dew, although ten months or more may pass without any rain, as is frequent in California. But I am persuaded that those plants are juicier because they transpire less; and they transpire less because they do not have leaves, since the leaves, as the naturalists believe with good reason, are the principal organs of transpiration of plants. Therefore, it may be conjectured that the Creator entirely denied leaves to those plants because he destined them to live in dry countries.

The plum of California (*ciruelo*[71] in Spain), is very different from the true plum, and it received this name from the Spaniards only through the similarity of the fruit. The tree is of medium height, and it has a whitish bark on trunk and branches and serrated leaves. Its branches extend horizontally more than seems fitting for the height of the tree. The fruit, although similar in its color and shape to the dark plum, is smaller, harsh to the taste, and good only to the palate of those wretched

---

[71] The tree of this fruit is called "*ciruelo*" (*Crytocorpa procers*). The tree blooms in April and May, and the fruit matures in August and September. The kernel tastes like the nut of the pistachio. This plum is perhaps the most widely distributed fruit in the southern section of the peninsula, and it is a universal food. Some have a tart or slightly turpentine taste (*Proceedings of the California Academy of Sciences,* Vol. V, p. 757).

Hugh Manessier

Fig. 7 — *Opuntia* sp. or *a,* one of the platyopuntias native to Baja California.

George E. Lindsay

Fig. 8 – *Ficus Palmeri* or *anaba*. The name *zalate* is still used locally along with *higuera cimarrona* or wild fig.

Fig. 9 – *Ficus Palmeri*. The roots characteristically drape themselves over the rocks of a canyon side.

George E. Lindsay

Fig. 10 — *Opuntia cholla*. There are many species of cylindropuntias growing in the peninsula. Clavigero (*v.i.* pp. 56-57) indicates that they were regarded as noxious weeds rather than as bearers of useful fruit.

Indians who are accustomed to eat whatever offers itself to them. But the kernel contained within the pit is very tasty and for that reason esteemed even by the Spaniards. This tree is characteristic of the southern part, and is found in no other place on the peninsula.

Anabà[72] is the name of a fruit similar to the fig and to the tree which produces it. The tree is large, and the bark of its trunk and branches is whitish like that of the fig tree. The fruit is similar in shape and color to the early fig of the fig tree, but it is smaller, less juicy, and without the very sweet flavor of our figs. Notwithstanding this, the Californians esteem it so much that when they receive news about an *anabà* with ripe fruit they go quickly to look for it in order to provide themselves with it, although it may be twelve or fifteen miles distant from where they live. As this tree usually grows among rocks, it inserts its roots into any crevice that it finds there, and where crevices are lacking it extends them over the rocks themselves. On this account the roots are generally broader than they are thick. The wood is absolutely useless. The *anabà* produces better fruit and grows larger in Mexico, where it is known by the name of *zalate*.

The *medesà*[73] is a large tree the trunk of which has a whitish green bark, and its leaves are fine and few. Its seed is similar to beans enclosed in small pods. This seed is very much valued by the Indians, who shell it and toast it in order to eat it afterward in the winter. Oxen readily eat the tender branches of this tree, but its wood is useful only for fuel. It does not bear fruit every year, and almost never bears in high altitude The Indians of Loreto call it *dipuà*.

The *asigandù*[74] is a leguminous shrub which grows near brooks and dry beds of streams. It has thorny branches and

[72] *Ficus palmeri*, the species undoubtedly described here. It is a fig grown widely in Mexico, and is frequently known by the name of *"coamichin"* or *"amate"* (*ibid.*, pp. 77–78).

[73] This tree seems to be the *Palo Verde* or *Palo de Púa* (*Cercidium torreyanum*). It is abundant south of La Paz (*United States National Herbarium*, Vol. XVI, p. 336).

[74] Probably an *Acacia* or a *Mimosa*, belonging undoubtedly to the family *Leguminoceae*.

bears seed a little larger than wheat in narrow pods from three to four fingers' width in length. As this seed is among the earliest to ripen and comes exactly at that time in which there is the greatest scarcity of provisions, the Indians use it, although it is really not edible. They eat it reduced to flour after they have roasted and ground it, as they do with other seeds. The stench which it emits when it is roasted is very disagreeable, as well as the breath of those who eat it, which is unendurable when they are gathered in the church or some other closed place at that season.

The *guisache*[75] (a name taken from the Mexican *huitzaxin*) is a leguminous shrub, thorny and narrow-leafed. The pods which it bears are not edible, but in California as well as in Mexico they use them for making writing ink by adding a certain quantity of copperas to them. Oxen readily eat the tender branches, but their flesh acquires a bad savor.

The *jojoba*[76] is one of the most valuable berries of California. The plant which produces it is a shrub which grows on the dry slopes of the mountains. Its leaves are oblong, notched, and smooth; they are the size of rose leaves, and a green color

---

[75] This species (*Acacia farnesiana*) seems to be the type described here. It grows throughout the tropical areas of the continent, often being called "*huisache*," "*quisache*," or "*huicachin*." In the southern part of the United States it is frequently called "*apopomax*" (*United States National Herbarium*, Vol. XXIII, pp. 351, 375, 379). The tree has many uses; the bark is used in tanning; from the gum glue is made; the seeds produce a good ink; a liquid extracted from the flowers is a remedy for headache and for dyspepsia; its dried leaves are commonly used to dress wounds; and live stock feed upon the green leaves. The natives probably used the glue from this plant to mend their broken pots.

[76] A plant (*Simmondsia californica*) widely distributed in northern Mexico and in southern California. The leaves and fruits are eaten readily by deer, goats, and sheep. The fruit is the color of a chestnut, and the Indians eat the seeds parched and raw. They make a drink, from grinding up the parched seeds and mixing the meal with the yolk of hard-boiled eggs, which is used instead of coffee. The seeds are composed of nearly fifty per cent oil, and even today the natives use this as a hair tonic. *Jojoba* is also known as "goatnut," "pignut," "wild hazel," "quinine nut," and "sheepnut." It is believed that Clavigero first described this plant and, of course, it has no medicinal value as a cure for cancer (*ibid.*, Vol. XXIII, pp. 654–55). See also *Proceedings of the California Academy of Sciences*, Vol. II, p. 21.

that shades into gray. The seed is an oblong berry, the size of the kernel of a hazel nut, red-brown outside, white inside, and of an oily but not disagreeable taste. This berry has become celebrated for its medicinal value, especially for curing the suppression of the urine arising from mucous concretions, for facilitating childbirth, and for wounds. The oil which is derived from it is an excellent remedy for cancer; and, on the other hand, as it has a good flavor, some in California are accustomed to use it in salads instead of olives. This plant does not bear every year but only when at least one heavy shower has fallen during the winter.

The *pimentilla*,[77] so named by the Spaniards because it is similar in shape and size to the common pepper, is the seed which is produced within certain berries of a little shrub the shoots of which are similar to the sprouts of the wild olive, although smaller. The Indians eat it readily, but they have little of it.

When it has rained more than usual in some parts of the peninsula, a grass called *teddà* grows up with many shoots, which reach about a foot in height and produce some ears which contain certain little seeds the size of anise seed. The Indians endeavor with great care to prevent the seed from ripening and becoming detached from the ear so that it may not fall on the ground. After having gathered it, they roast it and reduce it to flour for food.

The *tedeguà* is a plant that grows in various places on the peninsula, chiefly in the southern part, when it rains in the summer. Its stalk is about a finger in thickness; its leaves are large and somewhat like those of the mallow, but covered, like those of the thistle, with little stickers or hairs that prick when one touches it, causing much burning and raising blisters on the skin. Because of this the Spaniards in California call it "nettle," although it is very different in other respects from the true nettle. The nut which it produces has a good flavor and is similar to an almond, although less broad.

[77] Called "mangle" and "Negrito" in the state of Durango, and "Copulin manso" in the state of Vera Cruz (*United States National Herbarium*, Vol. XXIII, p. 709).

These are the principal plants, useful for their fruit, which California produced when the inhabitants of that miserable peninsula were entirely barbarous and savage. But the missionaries themselves who civilized them introduced into the peninsula, along with the Christian religion, gracious and good habits, and the cultivation of very many foreign plants which are better than the native ones of that country.

Chapter Six

FOREIGN PLANTS

AMONG the plants and fruit trees transplanted there from different places in Mexico some have done well and others have not. In the few places where water is not lacking and the soil is suitable for the respective vegetation, olives, lemons, oranges, peaches, pomegranates, fig trees, apple trees, guava trees, yellow sapota trees, grapevines, watermelons, muskmelons, squash, date palms, wheat, corn, rice, and various kinds of vegetables such as chick-peas, lentils, beans, and French beans have predominated, with the produce of which the great poverty of those peoples has been considerably relieved. Of all these plants none thrives so well as the fig tree and the grapevine. The ripe figs have an exquisite flavor.

The wine which the few vineyards there yield is excellent. There were also and still are wild grapevines; but they are smaller than the cultivated ones. Their racemes do not bear more than eight or ten sour grapes, which never succeed in ripening. Rice produces better in the southern part, where there is that quantity of water which this plant requires. In occasional places there are now *ahuacati*,[78] and in Loreto some coconut

---

[78] The avocado (*Persea gratissima*), better known as the "alligator pear." It is widely grown throughout Mexico and other tropical countries. In the various Mexican states it is known as "*aguacatello*," "*tonal*," "*ahute*," "*aguacate oloroso*," and simply as "*on*" (*ibid.*, p. 290). Recently an extensive acreage in southern California has been planted to this fruit, and the fruit growers and merchants now call it "Calavo."

palms which have produced well. Those peoples are provided likewise with Cayenne peppers, *gitomates,* and tomatoes, three kinds of vegetables that are much used and esteemed among the Americans. It has been observed that the climate of the peninsula is quite unfavorable to apples, pears, pineapples, cherimoyers,[79] and other delicate fruits of Mexico.

The places in which grain can be cultivated are certainly few; but in them the abundance of the harvests is not less to be wondered at than the strange method of cultivation. First, arable ground is sought which can be irrigated frequently either by the water of some spring near by or by the rain water reserved in some reservoir. The land is irrigated before it is plowed; and, after being plowed in the ordinary manner, furrows are made in it, not straight as is done ordinarily, but winding and undulating, so that the water, being delayed in them a longer time, will leave them a greater supply of moisture. When the furrows are made, the land is irrigated again, for it is almost always dry; and after it has been exposed to the air a little while it is sown.

Two men are employed for the sowing. One goes through the furrows making with the *coa* (a certain farming tool used by the ancient Mexicans) a few holes somewhat long but slightly deep, trying to make them two or three spans distant from each other and placing them on the sides of the furrow so as not to make one side face the other. The sower goes behind this workman with the grain which has been in water all the night before; he throws in each hole the number of seeds which the quality of the soil demands, and then with his foot he covers them lightly with the soil. If the soil is of good quality and rested, or at least manured, they do not put more than four or five seeds in each hole; but if it is not they throw in even ten or twelve. They try to keep the grains separated, for which purpose they make the holes more or less large according to the quality of the land. As soon as the plant sprouts

---

[79] Often spelled "chirimoya" (*annona cherimolia*). It is widely distributed in most American tropical countries, being seen perhaps more in the state of Guanajuato than in any other Mexican state (Schnitzler, *op. cit.,* p. 88).

they irrigate the land again; and they continue doing it weekly unless the soil has some moisture of its own, which rarely happens.

Each grain sown usually throws out fifteen, twenty, and even thirty reeds, and each reed bears a head; but if the soil be fertile six or eight smaller heads grow on each reed around the principal head. The harvest is in proportion to this fertility. When the land is inferior, it renders forty, fifty, and sixty *moggia*[80] for one. If it is moderately good and well cultivated, it yields eighty, one hundred, and one hundred and twenty; but if the land is superior soil, although it may not be well worked and suitably manured, they are accustomed to have a yield of two hundred and even three hundred and more *moggia* for one. A respectable missionary,[81] worthy of credence because of his well-known sincerity and to whom we are indebted for almost all the materials of this essay about natural history, relates in his manuscripts that, after he had sown eight and one-half *moggia* of grain in a field of the Mission of San Francisco Javier,[82] he harvested two hundred and six fanegas,* that is, two thousand four hundred and seventy-two *moggia*; consequently that field yielded three hundred and twenty-nine for one, in spite of the fact, as related by the missionary himself, that one part of the field was bad land and that the most of the harvest came from a large bend of superior land which composed about a third of the sowing.

This grain, which produces various heads on each reed, is for this reason called *espiguin*. It is somewhat thick and bearded, and makes good bread, although not comparable to that which is made from *candial*, which is a larger wheat, although less

---

* The fanega is a measure of dry weight which contains twelve *moggia*, called *almues* or *celemines* by the Spaniards.

[80] A dry measure in Italy which varies widely, being about five English bushels.

[81] Probably Father Miguel Barco or Father Lucas Ventura, whose manuscript histories were used by Clavigero (Bancroft, *History of the North Mexican States and Texas*, Vol. I, p. 282).

[82] See footnote 145, p. 172.

thick and with a smaller beard. Each reed of this variety produces only one head, but yet it yields as much or more than the other, because it shoots forth many more reeds. In spite of this, little of it is sown in California, since it is much more subject to the blight known there as well as in Mexico by the Mexican name of *chahuiztle.*

Nor is this the only danger to which grain is exposed in the peninsula. It has other more harmful enemies there such as *tuze*,[83] squirrels, birds, and especially locusts. On the other hand, the water itself which is used to germinate the seeds produces among them an abundance of clover which, having robbed the wheat of moisture, makes it dry up and necessitates weeding frequently.

The crops of corn are not so abundant, in proportion, as those of wheat, because corn needs more water, which is very scarce in California. Notwithstanding, it ordinarily yields two hundred, two hundred and fifty, and at times four hundred *moggia* for one. When the yield does not reach one hundred, the harvest is considered wretched. Just as the wheat is exposed to the blight, so corn is exposed to a certain kind of dew. This consists of a clear liquid, sweet and viscous, which appears on the leaves in such abundance that when it drops on the ground it leaves a stain on it. I do not doubt but that this liquid is the juice of the plant itself drawn outside of it by the excessive heat which expands its fibers too much. Losing that substance which is very necessary for its life, it soon withers and dries up.

In view of what we have said, it should not be wondered at that in spite of the small population of California and the extraordinary multiplication of those grains it is necessary in order to provide themselves with grain to have recourse to Sinaloa and other countries of New Spain. In the peninsula the tillable lands are few, the water is very scarce, and the obstacles which must be overcome to succeed in raising a crop are many.

[83] The pocket gopher, which has cheek pouches opening on each side of (not into) the mouth.

Chapter Seven

PLANTS USEFUL FOR THEIR LEAVES AND BRANCHES

THE PLANTS useful for their leaves and branches are few. Near dry stream beds and reservoirs sage is abundant, and also reed and corn flags, the stalks and roots of which the Californians eat willingly; and with the leaves they make mats, since they have been taught to do so. Purslane abounds when it rains in the summer, but the Indians eat only its seed. *Estafiate*,[84] or the wormwood of the Mexicans, grows freely in the cultivated fields; but if clover grows there, as it is accustomed to do, it chokes the wormwood as well as the wheat.

The wild marjoram of California does not resemble the true, except a little in the odor; as for the rest, it is a bush which grows on the dry plains and reaches the height of almost four feet. Its leaves are small and of a beautiful green; they are used instead of the true marjoram for seasoning foods. It is said that the flesh of cattle which are fed on it is very savory. Tobacco[85] grows wild in various places on the peninsula, and the Indians use it for smoking.

The Jesuits[86] introduced into the peninsula lettuce, cabbage, endive, and other similar plants, which have done well in those places where they are cultivated.

---

[84] *Artemisia filifolia*, found throughout western United States and commonly known as sagebrush.

[85] A plant native to the Western Hemisphere. It was introduced into England by Sir Francis Drake.

[86] A religious order founded in Europe in 1534 by Ignatius Loyola. It soon spread throughout the world. The Order founded the first Mission in Lower California.

Chapter Eight

PLANTS USEFUL FOR THEIR TRUNKS OR STALKS

OF THE TREES which furnish wood for building and working, or at least firewood, there are *guaribi*, pines, evergreen oaks, palms, arbutus trees, poplars, and a few others. Among those plants whose stalk serves for eating or which are put to other uses, are mescal, *batamoti*, *nombò*, and a few others.

The *guaribo*[87] is the largest tree in California. It is so similar to the poplar in appearance that at first sight it cannot be distinguished from it; but the poplar is very different in the quality of its wood, while that of the *guaribo* is excellent for making beams and is used in all kinds of work. The misfortune is that this tree exists in only a few rugged and almost inaccessible places. The same thing is true also with the pines in the southern part.

The red palms of the mountains are esteemed there for their reddish and strong wood; but the latter is so slender that it has scarcely eight fingers' width in diameter; so that in order to get beams out of the palm it is necessary to make use of its entire trunk with its bark, which is of a gray color, as in the other palms. Besides the coconut and the date palms, there are two other kinds of palms: one is of white wood, less strong than the red, and more easily gnawed; and the other has scarcely two or three fingers' width of solid wood underneath the bark, and within this is a light and spongy pith of four fingers' width in diameter.

Before the Spaniards entered California there were many beautiful palm groves in it, because the Indians did not make use of them. But after they learned, through contact with the inhabitants of Sinaloa, to eat the sprouts of the palms, and after the Spaniards began to take wood from them for building, some

---

[87] *Guaribo* (*Populus monticola*) is apparently the type of tree here described.

of the palm groves were destroyed. The sprouts make a delicious meal for the Indians as well as for the Spaniards, but at the same time, such a food is costly, because the palms dry up as soon as the sprouts are cut.

There are two kinds of acacias in the peninsula, differing in the size of the tree and in the quality of their seed. The one with the bitter seed is a large tree, native to California; that with the sweet seed is smaller and imported. The Indians eat the latter and the animals the other, of the branches of which horses, sheep, and goats are very fond. Both the acacias produce long pods, and have twisted trunks and branches; their wood is very hard and heavy; for this reason it is very suitable for the curved parts of a ship. The sprouts when bruised and applied to the eyes are believed to be a preventive against ophthalmia. The acacia is abundant on the narrow plains which are between the mountains and the coast of the Gulf. The Cochimìes call it *huahà*, the Mexicans *mizquitl*, and the Spaniards of all those countries, *mezquite*.[88]

The *palo chino*,[89] or the Chinese tree, called thus by the Spaniards (I do not know why), is a large and upright tree, which has small green leaves that border on ash color; the bark of its trunk and branches is gray, and its wood is red and easily worked; it loses its color when it is moistened, and, even though it has never been wet, it loses color with the passing of time. This tree is native to the southern part. In the northern countries another tree is found, which is also known by the name of *palo chino*; it has white wood which is often worm-eaten; it does not produce any edible seed.

---

[88] The plant (*Prosopis juliflora*) is found almost everywhere in Mexico and southward into South America. The leaves and bark of this tree, as well as those of the small acacia (*mezquitillo*), are used as medicine yet by the natives. The seeds, when variously prepared, are used for rheumatism, for dropsy, as a hair dressing, and as an ointment for the body (*United States National Herbarium*, Vol. XXIII, p. 404). It grows to a height of from twenty to forty feet, and its roots are said to go seventy-five feet to water-bearing strata (*United States Bureau of American Ethnology*, Vol. XVII, p. 32).

[89] *Pithecollobium mexicanum*. It is found also in the mainland, chiefly in Sinaloa and in Sonora. It is used considerably for making furniture.

The *gkokiò*, called *palo blanco*[90] by the Spaniards because it has white bark, is a tree of medium height, having little foliage, and very few branches. It has white wood also in the beginning, but on reaching a certain age the innermost part of the trunk turns almost black and becomes very hard and strong. The neophytes were accustomed to make beautiful pieces of it, which look like ebony, curiously engraved and inlaid with shell. These trees grow near dry stream beds.

The *uña de gato*[91] is a leguminous tree the leaves of which are very small and narrow and of a greenish color which shades off to white. It produces its seeds in pods. Its branches bristle with curved thorns, similar to a cat's claw, for which reason it has this name, by which it is known in all Mexico. The innermost part of the trunk, or rather, the pith, also turns black, with some yellow stripes, which make it beautiful. Since this wood is hard and heavy, they make pieces out of it, worked by lathe. But if the tree is permitted to grow to a certain age the pith consumes it so that it remains hollow.

The mangle,[92] although not a very large tree, extends its branches horizontally so much that some touch the ground. Its leaves are small, oblong, notched, smooth, and of a light green which is pleasing to the eyes. Its wood is hard; and they use it for making oars. These trees grow near the coast, provided the soil is not sandy.

The *corcho*[93] is a small tree which grows on those level

[90] A tree (*Lysilomax candida*) widely distributed on the peninsula and in northern Mexico. It was used to construct some of the early Mission buildings, villages, and ships. The Mexicans call it *guaribo*, and it is probably the tree that Father Ugarte used (1719) to build the ship in which he explored the coast of the peninsula (Edward W. Nelson, *Lower California and Its Resources*, p. 105). It was also used to make wine casks, but the wood gave the wine a disagreeable taste. Today it is used considerably in tanning leather.

[91] Cat's-claw. This name is applied to several species of the different genera of *Leguminosae*. The plant grows to a height of from fifteen to twenty feet, is very durable, and takes a fine polish. It is found abundantly throughout Mexico, in the southwest, and in the Caribbean region. The name "ironwood" is often applied to this tree.

[92] Found also from Sonora to Yucatan, in southern Florida, and in Cuba.

[93] *Ammona palustris*, seen in all tropical America. It grows commonly

stretches which are at the foot of the mountains. There it is seen usually without leaves; but yet it makes a very beautiful bouquet of flowers of a very vivid purple color. Its trunk, when dry, becomes as light and spongy as the bark of the cork tree, and for this reason it has been given the Spanish name *corcho*. With it the Indians make rafts on which they are accustomed to fish, as we shall mention later. It also serves as cork bark and for corking bottles and other vessels.

The *nombò*[94] is a shrub having flexible, upright, and long stems of whitish bark, and it is usually leafless. Only when it rains is it covered with leaves broader than they are long, but scarcely does a month pass after the rain before they remain leafless again. The bark is whitish. No use is made of this plant in California; but its stalks could be useful for making baskets and especially dye, because it contains a blood-colored liquid which dyes cloth so fast that, regardless of how often it is washed, the spot cannot be removed from it. What would that dye probably be if it were prepared suitably?

There is another shrub the name of which the author of the manuscripts which we are using does not remember; it is similar to the *nombò* in the flexibility of its stems and its lack of leaves. This plant is invaluable to the Indians because they make of it two kinds of utensils which are very useful to them, that is, certain basins and bowls, of which we shall speak later.

The *batamote*[95] is another shrub, which grows on the banks of some dry stream beds, and which has upright stalks of three or four feet in length, and long, sharp-pointed leaves, but very delicate and of a very fine green. These stalks are useful for restoring the movement to injured limbs by bathing them often

---

near salt water or where the soil receives much moisture. In some places it is known as "monkey-apple," or as "alligator-apple," because it is said that alligators eat its fruit (*United States National Herbarium*, Vol. XXIII, pp. 281–82).

[94] It may be *Jatropha cineres*, although this plant might be *Elaphrium microphyllum*.

[95] Very likely *Bacchais glutinosa*, whose range seems to extend throughout northern Mexico (*Estudios Biológicos. Catálogo Alfabético de Plantas en México*).

George E. Lindsay

Fig. 11 — *Agave deserti* or *mescal* with many clumps in bloom. This small species of the interior of the peninsula seems to have been the preferred food source. Clumps of *viznaga* and platyopuntias are scattered on the hillside.

George E. Lindsay

Fig. 12 — *Palo blanco* (*Lysiloma candida*) or *gkokio*. The bark, purplish-brown beneath the white skin, has excellent tanning properties.

with a decoction made of its shoots or by giving rubbings to the joints with the roasted stalks themselves and afterward by applying a plaster of them.

In some places near the dry stream beds, there grows a small, common reed grass, the thickness of the little finger or, when larger, the index finger. The Indian women choose the most slender reeds of it for their clothing, as we shall explain later on. This little reed is the only plant in California on which manna is seen. This is a very sweet and whitish substance called by the Cochimìes *cadesè*, which means "cane juice." And they gave this very name to sugar when they became acquainted with it and tasted it. From this it is seen that, although barbarians, they thought about the origin of manna better than did our ancient philosophers, who considered it dew. At the present time there are thick, reed grasses in the peninsula which were brought from other countries.

California has no plant more esteemed by the Indians because of its shoot than the mescal.[96] This is a plant of the aloes family, similar to the maguey[97] in the manner of issuing sprout and flowers; but the mescal is smaller, more thorny, and a deeper green. When this plant is permitted to grow, it throws out, as does the maguey, an upright stalk of the thickness of a man's arm and from ten to fifteen feet in length; and at its top it has some bunches of yellow flowers and then the fruit. These flowers are full of a sweet liquid, and they have so much of it that the Indians collect an excessive amount of it to sustain themselves. It has, however, a very sweet and pleasing taste. The mescal thus grown is useful only for multiplying the

[96] Should not be confused with *mezcal*, which is a distilled brandy much used by the Mexicans.

[97] Commonly known as the century plant or the American agave. It is perhaps put to more different uses than any plant of the peninsula. It is used for building, in medicine, in making cloth, and as food, especially for the poorer people. From it is obtained a very strong intoxicant which has a use throughout all Mexico. Professor Priestley notes that its use "is responsible for a large part of the crime which prevails among the lower classes" in Mexico. In recent years the government of Mexico has tried, rather unsuccessfully, to regulate its consumption (Herbert Ingram Priestley, *The Mexican Nation*, pp. 11–12).

plants of its own species, by producing them either by its roots or from its seeds scattered about.

The Indians, nevertheless, do not let it grow, but as soon as the inner leaves begin to separate from the stalk, when it is scarcely two feet high, they cut it and then the others which are found equally ripened.

When they have provided themselves sufficiently with them, they take them to their homes; and, having made a hole in the earth, in which they light a fire, they then put in some stones. When the firewood has been consumed and the stones are red hot, they place the pieces of mescal among them; they cover them well with earth and leave them there almost twenty-four, or thirty, or thirty-six hours. This method of cooking mescal and other foods, called *tlatema*[98] by the Mexicans, was in use among the barbarous Chichimecas[99] before they were subjugated by the Spaniards. Mescal thus cooked is sweet and savory. It was the principal food of the Californians from October to April, a time in which the wild fruits on which they were accustomed to live are very scarce.

This is not the only use which they derive from that plant, since they extract fibers from their leaves for making those nets which they use instead of sacks, and for making two-handed frails and baskets for carrying on their backs all that they wish. Mescal as a rule grows only on the mountains and hills. There are different kinds of it: some have a bitter juice, and others cause stomach-ache. A missionary had some mescal transplanted there from Nueva Galicia which are larger and better than all the California varieties. In some places in Mexico, where mescal is abundant, they extract a spirituous liquor[100]

[98] In Mexico called *"barbacoa"* (barbecue).

[99] A name given to the various Indian tribes that inhabited the mountains north of the Valley of Mexico. They are believed to have been descendants of the Toltecs, a people who came into Mexico at an early date. Little is known of their true origin. Those who have studied the early ruins of Mexico have produced rather convincing evidence that the first people in Mexico closely resembled the early Egyptians. The Chichimecas were ruled, about 1500, by a man named Nezahnae Coyatle (Hungry Coyote). These people dwelt chiefly in caves.

[100] Called "mezcal," the same word often used to describe the distilled

from it; although it appears natural water at first sight, it is too strong to drink. Some take it to become intoxicated, and others for medicine, since it is considered a diuretic and good for the stomach.

Chapter Nine
━━
PLANTS USEFUL FOR THEIR ROOTS

PLANTS with useful roots are few in California. Those which were there before the entrance of the Spaniards are the *guacamote,* the *xìcama,* and the *mezquitillo.*

The *guacamote,* or sweet yucca, called *ujuì* by the Cochimìes, is a plant full of shoots with a long root, not very thick, gray outside, and white inside and fibrous. It is eaten cooked and has a good flavor.

The *xìcama*[101] is a leguminous plant full of shoots which has long and slender branches, leaves arranged by threes in the form of a cross, purple flowers, seed like lentils enclosed in black pods, and roots the shape and size of an onion, although in other respects very similar to the turnip. It is white, succulent, savory, and cooling; and it is always eaten raw. The *xìcama* of Mexico is ordinary; but that of California, although smaller, is better in the opinion of many.

The *mezquitillo,* or small acacia, is a little tree which has that name because it is similar in the shape of its branches and leaves to the acacia. In California they make use of its roots for dyeing deer skins cinnamon color.

The missionaries have taken *camotes,* onions, garlic, turnips, radish, and fennel to the peninsula, and all have grown well

---

spirits made from the maguey plant. Sinaloa produces annually about 3,500 tons of mezcal (Schnitzler, *op. cit.,* p. 144). In the vicinity of La Paz about 20,000 liters are produced each year (*Twenty-second Report of the Missouri Botanical Gardens,* p. 43).

[101] It undoubtedly belongs to the genus *Pachyrhizus.* The species might be *angulatus,* or it may be *erosus.*

there. The *camote*[102] is a tuber esteemed in New Spain, and we have made mention of it in the *Ancient History of Mexico.*

Chapter Ten

PLANTS USEFUL FOR THEIR JUICE OR GUM

THE PLANTS valuable for their resin or gum or for their oil or juice are the copal, the brazilwood, the pitchtree, the castor-oil plant, the indigo plant, and sugar cane.

The copal is a tree which produces copal gum, so well known in Europe. This tree grows in all California except in the very gravelly or sandy places. Brazilwood, which is usually a large tree in other countries, is small in California and grows only in the southern part. The pitchtree, or *pegola,* is also small. Its trunk is greenish and its bark is filled with excrescences through which the pitch exudes, which is stuck here and there to the bark in the shape of small balls. The Indians make use of this resin for gluing their arrows, as we shall mention later; and they use it prepared with tallow to mend any broken clay vessel.[103] The sailors use it to calk their ships, but it is so scarce that it is not sufficient for all these needs. It is gathered by scratching the bark, which should be done before it rains, because if the rain is heavy it carries the gum away with it. The castor-oil plant, or infernal fig, contains in its bean oil good for making a light. And it is also useful in medicine, but it is a very severe and dangerous purgative. In some places in the southern part the indigo plant is found; but it is not used, perhaps because there is little of it. In the same section sugar cane, which was transplanted to those places by the missionaries, is cultivated to the advantage of the Indians.

---

[102] The sweet potato (*Ipomoea batatas*) is still grown widely in Lower California.

[103] A tree commonly used for this purpose and to mend broken glass was called *"cuajiote"* (*Bursera optera*) (Schnitzler, *op. cit.,* p. 475).

Chapter Eleven

NOXIOUS AND GROTESQUE PLANTS

AMONG the few plants of California there are some harmful ones. One of these is a certain little tree, called arrow tree[104] by the Spaniards of that country, because the Indians of the Sonora coast derive from it that terrible poison with which they poison their arrows in order to make the wounds fatal. The Californians, although they were aware of the bad quality of this plant, have never misused it.

In the southern part there is a plant full of shoots the name of which we do not know, and its tender and fibrous shoots have a tart, strong flavor. The Indians cut them in pieces two or three spans long; they put them to roast within the hot ashes, covering them with earth to take out the sourness; and afterward they eat them. But it seems that when this roasting is done it is not enough to purge the branches of their biting quality, because they still cause a severe stomach-ache to the one who eats them and certain ulcers in the mouth and throat which sometimes cause death.

Poison ivy is a plant which grows in the mountains, and its runners are extended and interlaced with the branches of the

---

[104] This tree (*Sebastiania bilocularis*) has a light-gray bark and attains a height of from twelve to twenty feet. It is known in various places as "*hierba mala*," "*magot*," and "*hierba de la flecha*." The bark contains a poison which was used to poison arrows, and an enemy using such arrows was never forgiven. The juice of the tree acts as a violent cathartic; the leaves and fresh bark were put into the water to stupefy the fish that they might be caught more easily. But it is believed that the properties of this tree were much exaggerated. The Indians also believed that the smoke from the burned green wood, or simply sleeping in the shade of the tree, would cause sore eyes and at certain seasons of the year partial blindness. Indian doctors wore about their necks poison arrows to ward off danger and disease (*United States Bureau of American Ethnology*, Vol. XVII, p. 259). The leaves and bark of a similar tree, called "*We un kali*" by the Pomas Indians, was used by the Indians of Mendocino County, California, to make fish sleepy. The amole plant (*Chlorogalum promeridianum*) and the Turkey-mullein (*Eremocarpus setigerus*) were thought to have the same properties (*Zoe*, Vol. V, p. 136).

trees near by. This ivy is quite deserving of the name of poison ivy, because touching it causes one to become swollen and covered with sores. It is true that this illness has a quick remedy, but perhaps it would be mortal if the contact with the ivy were of longer duration.

The *guigil*[105] is a fruit produced by a shrub similar in size and color to the sour cherry, but smaller. The Indians eat it in spite of its bad flavor, because it is produced in the months of March and April when they have no other food than the mescal. It has been observed that if the Indian women eat much when they are nursing their babies the infants become so ill that some die.

In various places in the peninsula there is another shrub the fruit of which is the size of a chick-pea and round and black when it is ripe. The Cochimì Indians are very careful not to eat it, because they well know that it is very harmful; but as their little ones do not know it and do not fear anything they eat it sometimes, instigated by hunger or greediness. The effect which it has on them within a few days causes them to become helpless; and from then on other privations of sensation follow which, at last, deprive them of life. For this reason the missionaries tried to exterminate that plant everywhere. The Pericùes, nevertheless, eat the fruit without ill effects because they first take out the seed, which, they say, contains the poison. There are also various other grotesque and curious plants besides the *pitaji, cardoni,* and *viznagas,* which we have already described.

The *tasajo*[106] is a plant similar to the *pitajo* in the inner configuration of its branches, which are leafless also and thorny.

---

[105] This name is sometimes applied to the cherries found among the Indians in Mexico. The description is so brief that it is difficult to be sure of its classification. It may be the *Castella tortuosa,* or one of the *Prunus,* a form of the wild cherry (*ibid.,* Vol. XI, p. 147).

[106] The fruit of this tree (*Opuntia imbricata*) is used for making dye, and is cooked as a food with pinole. The Indians of some of the tribes bound on their bare backs bundles of the thorny branches of the *tasajo* when they participated in certain religious rites. The fruit is often called "*Vella de coyote*," "*Cardenche*," "*joconytle,*" and "*tuna juconxtla*" in some sections of Mexico (*United States National Herbarium,* Vol. XXIII, p. 874).

Fig. 13 – A stand of *cirio* (*Idria columnaris*) or *milapa*. The bizarre plants are present only in the northern part of the Jesuit area of Baja California.

George E. Lindsay

Fig. 14 — A plant association near the northern limits of Jesuit missionization. The thick trunked trees are *Pachycormus discolor* (elephant tree). *Cirio, cardón,* and some cylindropuntias are also present.

George E. Lindsay

The branches of the *tasajo* are not grooved, nor so large and thick, nor all of one piece, as are those of the *pitajo;* each branch is composed of various pieces of three to four fingers' width in length and attached by means of certain stems; a strong wind or the touch of a traveler or any quadruped is enough to separate them. The branch, broken and lying on the earth, keeps green for many months, even if there be no dampness; and if any rain comes before it dries up, it throws out a few roots and forms a new plant. It bears a fruit similar to that of the *opuntia;* but it never ripens. This plant is not useful to the Californians; on the contrary, it is harmful, because it obstructs the roads; and in some places where firewood is scarce they use the dry branches of the *tasajo* for fuel, because they burn well, although they are consumed quickly.

There is another plant called *cholla*[107] (which should be pronounced *cioglia* in Italian) similar to the *tasajo* in the structure of the branches, and likewise leafless, but so low that it rises scarcely a span from the soil. Its branches are intertwined in such a manner that they do not permit the trunk to be seen; and they are so thickly covered with thorns that one cannot see the color of their branches. The parts of which they are composed, like those of the *tasajo*, are neither so long nor so thick as the index finger. Woe to the one who steps on these branches when he is walking, because not even the soles of shoes or boots can be of value for protection against the pricking of the thorns, which are difficult to extract.

Much more curious is another tree called *milapà* by the Cochimìes, which is found frequently from 29° to 31°. It had not been seen by the missionaries before the year 1751, because they had not gone into the interior of that country. Nor do I believe that it has been known until now by naturalists. It is so large that it grows perpendicularly to a height of seventy feet. Its trunk, thick in proportion, is not woody but soft and succulent like the branches of the *pitajo* and the *cardón*. Its branches are certain little twigs about a foot and a half long,

---

[107] An arborescent opuntia, regarded by the natives as the most detested plant on the peninsula, and referred to as the criminal plant.

covered with small leaves and protected by a thorn on the end; they do not extend upward or horizontally, as the branches of other trees do, but they hang downward like a beard, from the top to the bottom of the trunk, and the top produces some little bunches of flowers, where no fruit is ever seen. No use is made of this great tree; it is neither dry nor good for firewood, but at the Mission of San Francisco de Borja[108] they burn it because of the lack of fuel.

There is also another small tree, bristling with long thorns and almost always leafless and nude. On this account the Spaniards named it "Adam's tree."[109] When it rains, it often puts forth some small leaves, but at the end of a month it is devoid of them again and remains leafless all year.

Likewise, those Spaniards call another shrub "ironwood," because it resembles iron rather than wood on account of its great hardness. Moreover, it is tortuous in its trunk as well as in its branches, which are full of thorns, and by growing horizontally they succeed in touching the ground. The hardness and the sinuosity of this wood make it absolutely useless.

Chapter Twelve

INSECTS

SUCH is the vegetation worthy of some mention which the dry soil of California produces. Passing from plants to the animal kingdom and beginning with the smallest living things, there are ants, spiders, centipedes, scorpions, crickets, mosquitoes, different kinds of moths, gnats, locusts, cicadas, fireflies, wasps, cockroaches, and various kinds

---

[108] See *infra*, pp. 333–34.

[109] A tree (*Fouquieria spinosa*) having long thorns, and being leafless almost the year round. The leaves fall in April when the tree is in full bloom. It is found also on the Magdalena and Santa Margarita Islands, and northward to 28° (*Proceedings of the California Academy of Sciences*, Vol. II, p. 132).

of worms. There are no bees,[110] nor fleas, nor bedbugs, nor jiggers.

The spiders are larger than those found in Mexico, and in other places they are improperly called tarantulas. It has never been reported in California that spiders have done any harm to anyone; consequently it is probable that they have been considered poisonous only because of their horrible shapes.

Among the mosquitoes there are those on the beach at Loreto which are called *gegen* in many countries of America, and which are so small that they are scarcely perceived, but their stings cause an intolerable burning.

There are three kinds of moths: one that eats linen cloth, one that eats wool, and one that gnaws books. The first is a small, white insect the size of a louse but with a head very large in proportion to the body; it is very agile. [Moths of] this kind live together in certain little mud cells which they build on the walls, and when they eat clothes they make tiny veins in them as other moths do. This kind of moth, called *comegen*,* does not eat wool, but only linen. The second is the type which is so common in Europe, and the same may be said of the third. Moths have not multiplied greatly in California, and it seems that none of the said species is native to that country. All three are foreign, having been brought there from Mexico.

There are two kinds of cockroaches, different in size and color but similar in shape and in habits. Both have double wings, though they rarely fly; they are very quick, loathsome, and very destructive in pantries, where they eat or soil all the

---

* *Comixèn* is the name which the Indians of the Island Española gave to certain moths described by Oviedo, which gnaw not only wood but also the walls of buildings; but this altered name was afterward applied to designate that other kind of insect.

---

[110] There were wild bees then in the peninsula, but not honey bees. The honey bee was introduced into the state of California in 1852 from Europe and from the Orient. Professor Brandegee reported in 1891, after a scientific expedition which he made in Lower California, "that the honey bee is slowly traveling southward in Lower California, and is now more than half way down toward Cape San Lucas" (*Zoe*, Vol. II, p. 146).

food, provided it is not hard; they eat sweet things in particular, and they easily pass through the narrowest crevices, because they have a very flat body. Those of the largest species have a length of two fingers' width and a width of one finger. These were taken there from Matanchel in Nueva Galicia, where they were numerous, in boats which went from that port to Loreto. The other species is native to the peninsula, and is half the size of the first but more active. Both species have multiplied greatly.

The wasps of California are of at least three kinds. The first, and the largest, is that which the Mexicans call *xicotli*, described by us in Book I of our *History of Mexico*. These make a very sweet honey, but the pricks of their sting are very painful. Those of the second kind are the ones which the zoölogists call *Vespae icneumoni*, and which build their little cells on the walls of buildings, although they do not live in partnership.

In order to build the cells, the wasp takes a little mud, molds it, and fixes it on the wall by means of a sticky liquid, which she emits through the mouth; then she takes a little more and continues working in this manner until finishing a little cell. When it is completed, she lays an egg in it, fills all the rest with small spiders, which she hunts for this purpose, and closes the entrance of the little cell with mud. Next to this she continues building another four or five, laying an egg in each, and filling the rest with tiny spiders, as in the first. This mud hardens and adheres to the wall so tenaciously that a man cannot remove it with his fingers.

From each one of these enclosed eggs, fertilized by the heat of the season, a worm is soon hatched, which is changed to a pupa in a few days, and finally into a wasp, living during the time of its transformation on the little spiders which its wasp mother placed there. As soon as these new insects have strengthened their wings sufficiently, they open the little cells and, being liberated, begin to fly; and within a short time they start to build cells after the example of their mothers. In this way three or four generations in succession are raised from May to October. Those wasps do not have a sting nor do they make honey.

Those of the third class are smaller, light, and armed with a severe sting, which causes inflammation and much pain. Although they do not make honey, they make nests hanging from the rocks, but in those places which are sheltered from the rains. The Californians are very fond of these little worms, and many times they risk the danger of falling when climbing over the crags to get them from the nests.

These poor Indians find sustenance likewise from two other kinds of grayish worms, which are long and as thick as the little finger and which are found on certain plants after the rains. In order to eat them, they catch them one by one by the head with their two fingers, and with the other two they continue pressing them from the head as far as the other extremity, in order to empty their digestive system. Afterward they roast them and make a long string of those which they wish to keep for further use.

On some trees there are also certain white worms about two fingers' width in length and covered with stickers; merely touching them causes an itching which lasts for several hours.

But the most notable insects of California, for their extraordinary number as well as for the great damage which they cause, are the locusts. Since this plague is not frequent in the countries where naturalists live, the time necessary for minute and exact observations of them has not been available. Thus I shall disclose here those observations which an intelligent and sincere missionary made for thirty years, omitting the description of the internal and external parts of those insects, which had been made with much inquisitiveness and industry by Bomare.*

In California there are three kinds of locusts, similar in shape, but different in size, color, and even in manner of living. The first, known almost everywhere, is small, flies little, and jumps much. The second is larger than the first and always gray. These two kinds are not very numerous; they never exist in large swarms, and for that reason little regard is paid to them.

* *The Dictionary of the History of the Grasshopper.*

The locusts of the third class, which are feared more, have a body the size of the small finger and double wings like the others, although larger and of a more varied color according to their state, as we shall see later.

These locusts (all that we are going to say ought not be doubted) are similar to silkworms in their manner of uniting for offspring. They mate in the summer, and the females lay their eggs about the end of July or the beginning of August. The eggs are long and slender, of a yellow color bordering on red, and joined to each other by a certain gelatinous liquid, so that at first sight they seem like a silk cord. They lay these eggs in small holes which they make in the ground with certain appendices which they have on their tails. Each female lays from sixty to eighty eggs, and even more. As soon as the locusts satisfy this desire of nature, they weaken and die, without a single one being left alive; but they leave a very numerous posterity in their eggs.

The hatching of the new locusts does not have any fixed time; it depends on the rains, which are accustomed to come sooner or later; but they usually hatch in September or at the beginning of October, when the grass springs up in the country with the scarce rains of California. They are hatched without wings, but are provided with very long legs; at that time they are not larger than a small mosquito, and their color is a dark gray. Scarcely are they hatched when they begin to jump on the near-by grass; if there be none they go to another place to look for it, all those which have descended from the same mother always traveling together. After having eaten the leaves of one plant, they pass to another; and little by little their color gets lighter, and they go on uniting in different families. Then when they are half-grown, they shed their skins, as vipers do, and their color becomes perfectly green; and as their legs are stronger at this time, and as they have gathered in much greater numbers, they travel with greater jumps, forming numerous armies and laying desolate the fields over which they pass.

Then in a few days they shed their skins again and unfold their four wings, which they had had enclosed under their skin;

they then change from green to dark gray. When they have reached full size and perfection, which comes three months after their birth, they change to red with black spots, which gives them some beauty in spite of their unfortunate shape. This color lasts them until summer, at which time they change to yellow, which they retain until their death. The life of the locusts is ten months, and in this time they change their skins twice and their color five times.

Toward the beginning of January, when they have reached the end of their growth and their wings are quite strong, they fly like birds and they begin to carry desolation everywhere. Their flying armies are so numerous and form such dense clouds that they obscure the view of the sun and darken the sky. Sometimes they fly ten or twelve miles without interruption, and in flying they always follow their leader. They usually fly in a straight line either forward or toward the sides, but they never retreat; there is nothing in the world capable of making them turn back. Whenever the guides wish to halt, all the army stops. If this should occur in some woods, they occupy the same space there as in their flight, keeping the same order and the same distance between each other; but if they fall on some sown field, as all wish to eat, they narrow up and reduce themselves to a smaller space.

As they digest what they eat with great promptness, they devour much more than one might expect from their size. When they assail some woods, meadow, or sown field, they do not do anything else than devour and move on; and thus they destroy everything in a few moments, and if they ever leave something anywhere a new army follows immediately to consume it entirely. There is often more than one army, which would be sufficient by itself to bring desolation to many countries. These locusts neither eat nor fly in the night; but they rest on the trees, collecting one upon the other in such great numbers that, in spite of their smallness, they make the branches of the trees bend and sometimes break with their weight.

Now if this plague is lamentable in fertile countries, everyone can imagine how much more so it is in that miserable peninsula. The woods and the fields are laid waste; the grass is consumed; the trees are denuded, and the bark removed in parts.[111] Hence there ensues mortality among the stock through lack of food, and hunger and illness among the inhabitants, because when all that infinite multitude of voracious insects die at the same time they infest the air with their stench.

There are some plants respected by the locusts, as watermelons and muskmelons,[112] because of the acerbity of their leaves. The *pitaji* are naturally defended by their thorns, but the insects damage the flowers, if there are any, as well as the fruit of these plants if they are cracked by their ripeness. They eat only the tenderest ends of the mescal, without touching the shoot, with which the Indians nourish themselves.

If California were more populous its inhabitants could pursue those devastating insects and prevent the havoc which they make, either by destroying their eggs or by killing them when they still have no wings. This could be done, especially if some hundreds of men each year would go about with this purpose in mind and in a certain season through the southern sections, which are the true home of these terrible enemies.

As for the rest, neither great amounts of smoke, nor shouting, nor any other of the activities which are accustomed to be practiced for preventing the damage are of any service. In the winter when the locusts are benumbed by the cold and not able to fly in the mornings until they have warmed themselves somewhat in the sun, the Indians come up and, by shaking the branches of the trees where they have lighted, make them fall to the ground and then kill many thousands with their feet. A missionary of California who had offered a reward to any one of his neophytes who would bring him a certain measure of locusts used to receive from sixty to eighty sacks daily; but, although many millions were killed, it was of no use, because

---

[111] Serious plagues of this insect since that time have been noted in various sections of the Pacific Coast. In 1859 a government exploring party in the state of California found grasshoppers so numerous in one place "that vegetation was entirely destroyed throughout the valley on the west side of the Pitt and Fall rivers" (*Report of the Smithsonian Institution*, 1864, p. 429).

[112] Locusts will eat the leaves of the present variety of these plants.

an infinite multitude remained.* Nevertheless, when the field is small, it might be freed from the greater part of the danger at least if many countrymen were occupied zealously in frightening them away during the time that those flying armies are delayed in passing.

From 1697, in which year the Jesuits began the conversion of the Californians, a plague of locusts was not suffered there until 1722. But in this year they appeared, and then they ceased until 1746, during which year and the three following ones they were there without interruption. Afterward they returned to afflict the peninsula in 1753 and in 1754, and finally in the years 1756, 1766, and 1767.

Never could that luckless peninsula have recovered from its losses if the multiplication of the locusts had not been frustrated many times by various factors. Their eggs became sterile frequently; they dried up through lack of rain; and the birds ate a great quantity of them. Besides this, an incredible number of locusts died in the spring because a certain little worm developed in their stomachs and devoured them; and for this reason in the other years, outside of the ones mentioned, none have been seen there or at least they were not in such great numbers that they caused a serious evil.

Formerly the Californians were accustomed to eat roasted and pulverized locusts frequently, after they had removed the contents of the stomach. The good advice of the missionaries and the experience acquired in 1722, in which a great epidemic attacked the Indians because they ate so many locusts, diverted them, for the most part, from such food. Neverthe-

---

* In order to form some idea of the prodigious multiplication of locusts, one should see what M. de Bomare refers to from the historian Mezeray about those which were in the district of Arles, Beaucaire, and Tarascon in 1613, of which the major part having been devoured by starlings, those which survived laid so many eggs that the villagers, stimulated by the government, gathered more than three hundred thousand pounds, part of which was buried and part thrown into the Rhone, and when the number of locusts which should have been hatched from those eggs the following year was calculated it amounted to five hundred and fifty billions.

less, some continued to eat them, since they were not averse to taking advantage of what was so abundant when other foods are so scarce.

Chapter Thirteen

REPTILES

IN CALIFORNIA there are few kinds of reptiles, to wit, large and small lizards, frogs, toads, turtles, and snakes. Among the species of large and small lizards, we do not know that there are any poisonous ones. Frogs are very scarce. Toads are abundant when it rains, but they disappear entirely when the land is dry again. Among the turtles, besides the common land variety and the fresh-water ones, there are two other species of large sea turtles. One of these is that from whose shell tortoise shell is obtained to use in prized and curious work. The French call this tortoise *carret*, and the Spaniards in Mexico call it *carey*. The Californians catch them easily, because when they spy one from their little boats or rafts they plunge into the sea and overtake it by swimming and overturn it. When it is unable to move itself, they continue pushing it toward the little boat, in which they put it; but much precaution is needed in catching them, because they bite severely.

There are two kinds of snakes, the rattlesnakes or *crotali*, as Linnaeus[113] calls them, and those which are not. The latter are smaller than the former; but their poison is more active. At the end of this volume we shall give a curious account of the dangerous experiments and observations made on the snakes of California by an able missionary.

---

[113] This great Swedish scientist, born in 1707, became professor of medicine in the University of Upsala and later a noted botanist. He is said to have classified nearly all the animals, minerals, and plants known to people of his time.

Chapter Fourteen

FISH

WHEN we pass to aquatic animals whose characteristics approach those of reptiles, we find in the seas of California whales,[114] dolphins, sharks, swordfish,[115] cetaceous fish,[116] and fur-bearing seals. Among the real fish, we know of two kinds of shaddock[117] and also two kinds of porgy;[118] also colombelle,[119] haddock,[120] skate,[121] sea-bass,[122] dorados,[123] flying fish,[124] bagres,[125] sawfish,[126] rays,[127] mantas,[128]

---

[114] Of the great variety of whales in this region, the most common was probably the Humpback (*Megaptera versabilis*). At one time it was the most abundant species off the coast.

[115] Known also in Spanish as *Espadón emperador*. The swordfish referred to in the footnote, as described by M. Bomare, suggests a very confused notion of the surgeon fish, which is a small tropical species having a sharp lance sheathed on each side of the caudal peduncle.

[116] Apparently even to the time of Artedi (1705–1735), who is recognized as the father of ichthyology and who was contemporary with Linnaeus, whales were not yet distinguished clearly from fish.

[117] Probably a compound of "shad" and "haddock."

[118] A common name for sparoid fishes. Known in Spanish as *Pargos*. One common to the Gulf of California is *Calamus brachysomus*.

[119] There is no way to identify clearly this fish. One of the *palometas*. They are an excellent food fish. Reference later to the blue stripes across the back suggests the skipjack or bonito.

[120] Perhaps another species is here intended. The nearest relative to this fish which is found in the region under discussion is *Microlepedium grandiceps*.

[121] The only fish of this kind recorded for Lower California is *Raja microtrachys*.

[122] A name applied to many members of *Serranidae* or *Epinephelidae*, of which many are found off the coast of Lower California.

[123] *Coryphaena equisetis*.

[124] Two species present in the Gulf of California. One is the sharp-nosed flying fish (*Fodiator acutus*) and the other *Cypselurus californicus*, called "*Volador*" or the great flying fish.   [125] The common name for catfishes.

[126] *Pristis zephyreus*. It is found commonly entering rivers as far north as Mazatlán.   [127] Same as "skates."

[128] Called "sea devil" fish (*Manta birostris*), having immense rays with horn-like cephalic fins.

cabrillas,[129] graylings,[130] herring,[131] sardines, dory,[132] needlefish, soles, sturgeon,[133] dogfish,[134] flounders,[135] seals,[136] morays,[137] porci,[138] horned fish,[139] horse mackerel, *botetti*,[140] shad,[141] Sparus fish,[142] ciuppe,[143] bonitos,[144] sea pike,[145] roncadores,[146] and many others. Of the crustaceous there are spiny lobsters, crayfish, and various kinds of crabs. Of the testaceous there are mussels, murex shellfish, mother-of-pearl, and many other kinds of periwinkles, mollusks, and oysters.

[129] A sea-bass (*Paralobrox maculalofasciatus*).

[130] In the absence of any description these cannot be identified. Graylings of North America are salmonoid fishes of northern distribution.

[131] Three fishes of this family (*Harengula thrissina, Lile stolifera*, and *Opisthonenea libertate*) are found in this region.

[132] A name applied to the *Argyrieoses vomer*.

[133] No sturgeons are found so far south. Probably refers to the mailed catfishes, which have a considerable external resemblance to the sturgeons.

[134] Probably the small shark that abound off the coast of this region. It is believed that the Pacific dogfish extends south only as far as Santa Barbara.

[135] Most numerous along the Pacific Coast, and especially along the Gulf of California.

[136] Perhaps the sea lion. The Guadalupe fur seal may have extended its range at that time to Lower California.

[137] This fish is still abundant there.

[138] This is doubtless the *Anisotremus interruptus*; some species are known as "pork fishes."

[139] This may be the Moorish Idol (*Zanolus cornutus*), having a pronounced horn-like projection over each eye, which gives it such a name.

[140] A species of swellfish, so called because they swell up when disturbed or irritated. They are very numerous on the Gulf coast.

[141] Possibly the thread herring (*Opisthonema libertate*), common there and belonging to the same family.

[142] The *Sparidae*, known also as the porgies.

[143] No way to identify.

[144] A word still used to describe the tunas, albacores, an skipjacks. Probably the "leaping tuna" which ranges from Lower California to the mouth of the Columbia River.

[145] Very likely one of the Belonidae, pike-like fishes such as *Tylosurus fodiator*. They are also known as "gars."

[146] Fishes belonging to the *Haemulidae*; they are known as "grunts." Several types are found in the Gulf of California. They are also known as "burro," because, when caught, they make a snore-like noise like the noise of a "burro" or donkey.

Finally, there are also different kinds of zoöphytes, white coral, millepore, and cuttlefish. Some of the aquatic creatures mentioned are very well known among Europeans; others have been described in our *History of Mexico* or in the other histories of America. Consequently, we shall mention here only what may increase the information in some way about this part of natural history.

The multitude of whales seen by sailors in that narrow space of sea which is between the peninsula and the island of Ángel de la Guardia[147] caused this sea to be named Canal de las Ballenas [whales]. But as none have ever been fished for we do not know to what species of whales they belong. Nevertheless in consideration of what is said about them they may belong to that species to which Linnaeus gave the name *physalus*.

The swordfish of California seems to be the same which Pliny named *xiphias* or *gladius*. At least what that naturalist of the ancients tells about it can be verified in no other. A few years ago one of these monsters fixed its sword in such a way in the side of a sloop anchored in the port of Loreto that, not being able to pull it out, it shook the boat violently until it broke its own weapon with similar efforts and retired defeated.*

The *colombella*, in Spanish *palometa*, which is, as we have said in the *History of Mexico*, one of the most tasty and delicate fish, is easily recognized by the four or five stripes of a deep blue color which it has across its back. It is common in the two seas of the peninsula, and the Mexicans give it the name

---

* The swordfish has a pointed head; boats pierced through by this fish are sunk in the ocean. Pliny's *Natural History*, Book 32, chap. 2.

M. Bomare gives this name to the emperor fish of the Sea of Greenland; but this type does not have its sword on the upper jaw, like the swordfish, but on the posterior part of the body; nor does it have it unsheathed, as the former does, but sheathed, and consequently less fit for wounding. The same author adds that it seems that the emperor fish makes use of its sword rather for holding fast to its course or for restraining its too great agility than for defending itself.

---

[147] The island of Ángel de la Guardia (Custodio); see *supra*, p. 20.

cozamalomichin, or rainbow fish. Dr. Hernandez[148] says that the *colombella* is the *glaucus* of the ancients.

The dorado, or gilthead fish (thus named because it seems entirely of gold in the water) is very different from the gilthead of the Mediterranean. The former is larger, much more delicate, and has more savory flesh. It is very common in the seas of Mexico and is easily recognized by the persistence and fury with which it pursues flying fish.*

The bagre of California and Mexico, very different from that to which Linnaeus gave the same name and placed among the catfish species, is a scaleless fish, with two large, thick feelers hanging from the lower lip. It has a cleft tail and six fins, among which one is a large dorsal fin, two are pectoral, and two are under the stomach, while a small one is near the tail. It has a black back and a white stomach, with two straight and lateral lines which separate both colors. Its flesh is white and delicate, and the length of its body is from one to three feet.

The *porco marino*[149] of California, and of both the seas of Mexico, is also different from the *porci* described by Linnaeus, Bomare, and others. The Californian kind is scaly, and almost cylindrical in shape; it has a round and compressed head and a lunated tail. It is provided with two long fins, which extend from the middle of the back and from the stomach to the tail. Its flesh is tasty and healthful.

In the sea of California, as well as in the seas and rivers of Mexico, there are two kinds of *sparus,* called *"mojarras"* by the Spaniards, because their shape is somewhat similar to some

* In the enumeration of the fish of Mexico which I made in Book I of the *Ancient History* of that country, I gave the name of gilthead to the giltfish, because, deceived by the name, I thought them identical; but after having seen the *dorado* in Italy I was undeceived.

---

[148] A noted Spanish naturalist and physician. He visited North America to study the minerals, plants, and animals, following which he published (1615) a natural history of New Spain. He was the first European naturalist to make a scientific study of the fauna and flora of Mexico.

[149] Difficult to identify. Probably the "*Blanquillo,*" *Cauliolatilis princeps,* common along the Pacific Coast from Monterey south to tropical America. It is a food fish of considerable importance.

daggers which bear this name. The white dagger-head, which is called *papalomichin,* or butterfly-fish by the ancient Mexicans, is broad, about eleven inches long, scaly, and very good for eating. It has a lunated tail and seven fins, two near the gills, two near the stomach, one near the tail, another small one on the back, and another large one which extends from the head to the tail. The black dagger-head, which the Mexicans called *cacalomichin,*[150] or crow-fish, is entirely black, twice as large as the other, and it has a circular tail and six fins, two near the gills, two under the stomach, one large one on the back, and a small one near the tail. Its back is covered with thick scales and armed with spines; but its flesh is as good and healthful as that of the white dagger-head.

The *ronfatore,* in Spanish *roncador,* is thus named because when it is out of the water it snores as if it were sleeping. Dr. Hernandez believes that this fish is the *exocaetus*[151] described by the ancients; at least, what Pliny says about it is more fitting the roncador than that flying fish to which Linnaeus and Bomare give the name *exocaetus.*

The manta, or giant cuttlefish, that formidable creature of which mention has been made in the *Ancient History of Mexico,* may be considered as a species of ray. And I suspect that the one which Father Labat[152] measured on the island of Guadaloupe,[153] one of the Antilles, and named *raya prodigioso,*[154] was a real manta. Its width was twelve feet, its length from the nose to

---

[150] Seems to be the *"Mojarra verde,"* a dark, spiny-rayed fish with a rounded caudal fin; it is an excellent food fish.

[151] The confusion of *"ronfatore"* with *exocaetus* is due to the etymology of the word. The ancients applied this word to a fish which was supposed to come out on the land at night to sleep, *exocaetus* meaning "sleeping outside." However, no reference seems to be made to its snoring.

[152] A French Jesuit, who was born in 1663 and died in 1738. He went to the West Indies as a missionary in 1694, returning to Paris in 1706. He published (1722) a work of six volumes entitled *Description of the West Indies.*

[153] Discovered by Columbus on November 4, 1493, and so named in honor of Madonna of Guadalupe of Spain. France has owned this island since 1653. It has an area of about 687 square miles.

[154] No doubt the manta; it is not a cuttlefish but rather a giant ray.

the beginning of its tail was nine and one-half feet, and the thickness in the middle of its body two feet. Its tail was fifteen feet in length, and its skin, thicker than that of an ox, was covered with strong spines like thorns.

In the Gulf of California the *occhione*, that singular flat fish which we described in Book I of the *History of Mexico*, and which has an eye[155] the size of that of an ox in the middle and most elevated part of its body, has been fished for many times. The name *boops* (ox eye) would doubtless suit this fish better than that one which Linnaeus places in the genus *Sparus* with this name.

The fish called *mulier*,[156] seen at various times on the coast of the Pacific Sea, deserves particular mention. This fish is so named because it resembles the upper part of the body of a woman. It has very white breasts, neck, and eyes. The rest of its body is covered with scales, like other fish, except that the tail is lunated. The missionary, Father Arnés,[157] at the time of establishing the last Mission of Santa María, saw one of them dead on the sea beach; but as it was dry and mangled, he could not observe it as he would have wished. The length of those which we know have been seen does not exceed two palms and a half, the length [*sic*] in proportion.*

* M. dell Harpe, in *A Brief of the History of Travels*, mentions a fish by this name and that of *douyon*, which is found in the islands of the Philippine Sea. He says it is similar to a woman in the breasts and sex, and that its flesh is like that of the *porco*. There is also another fish thus named at the mouth of the Loire.—M. de Bomare. V. Mulier [*sic*].

---

[155] All fish, except some blind cave-dwellers, have two eyes. But a species of ray have a striking eye-like mark in the middle of the back. They are very rare.

[156] The fabled mermaid. There were many such beliefs among the ancients. On one occasion the great Linnaeus was forced to leave Holland for questioning the genuineness of a mermaid on exhibition which belonged to a high official of that country (David Starr Jordan, *The Study of Fishes*, chap. xx).

[157] Little is known of him. He was born in 1736, and arrived in Lower California in 1764. Two years later he and Father Juan José Diez were appointed to found a Mission, which they did at the Indian village of Calag-

On the beach of the Pacific Sea from 27° to 31° there is an unbelievable multitude of univalve shellfish[158] which are considered the most beautiful of all that are known. They are shaded a very lovely lapis-lazuli color on a silver white background, with five small holes in one side.

There are also peculiar species of testaceans, which we may call *polpari,* because they share the nature of shellfish and that of cuttlefish, if they are not of that kind of cuttlefish which the modern naturalists call *ceratophytes.* The latter, which the Spaniards call *hachas* because they have a shape somewhat similar to the ax of a woodcutter, are bivalve shellfish, provided with many feelers or arms, with which they adhere so firmly to the ground that the strength of a man is not sufficient to loosen them if the soil is not excavated first. They are found underneath the sand on the coast of the Gulf, but always at sea level.

Those which they call burros, that is, asses, are also bivalve shellfish, and are likewise provided with feelers, but thinner and much more numerous, with which they adhere to the bottom of the sea in such a manner that it is impossible to tear them out or to uproot them without the aid of some iron instrument. It is said that pearl divers when they are on the bottom of the sea run the risk of being caught by these animals, because if they step inadvertently on one of them when it has its shells open it closes on them suddenly and does not let them come out of the water to breathe. The divers, therefore, are pursued by three kinds of terrible enemies, viz., by the testaceans, the sharks, and the mantas; but all these are conquered by the hope of lucre.

Although the murex shellfish of California are very much valued, no one has devoted himself, up to the present time, to fishing for them and using their dye, because pearls have attracted all the attention of the fishermen. The abundance of pearls, which has contributed so much to making the peninsula

---

nujuet (see *infra,* pp. 363–65). The following year it was moved to a new location. This Mission (Santa María) was the last one founded on the peninsula by the Jesuits.

[158] The abalones.

famous, which is otherwise so miserable, was very great in the Gulf near the eastern coast of the peninsula itself and near the adjacent islands, but there was a great variety in the quality of the pearls. Those which were found from the cape of San Lucas as far as 27° were in general white and gleaming, or, as the merchants say, "good Oriental" pearls; those which were found from 27° toward the north were usually somewhat dark and for the same reason less valued.

At the end of the sixteenth century in which those maritime mines (we shall express it thus) were discovered, the inhabitants of Nueva Galicia, Culiacán, and Sinaloa began to seek wealth in them; and in fact, some did become wealthy during the past two centuries. But by 1736 pearls became so scarce that fishing for them was unprofitable to many. In 1740 the waves washed a very great quantity of mother-of-pearl on the beach from 28° on. The Indian inhabitants of that coast, who were then newly converted to Christianity, knowing how much the Spaniards esteemed pearls, carried many to the soldiers of the Mission of San Ignacio,[159] at that time the frontier of the gentiles, and gave them away in exchange for some little things which they valued more because they were more useful to them.

Don Manuel de Ocio, one of those soldiers and the son-in-law of the captain-governor of California, hoping to make a great fortune, asked for his discharge and went to Nueva Galicia, where he used all his capital in buying small boats, in bringing there *palombari** (divers), and in providing for all the necessities for pearl diving. With the proceeds from what he took out in 1742 he made greater preparations for the following year, in which he obtained one hundred and twenty-seven Spanish pounds of pearls. But this catch, although abundant, was not comparable to that of 1744, which amounted to two

---

* Italian lexicographers place the word *"palombaro"* among obsolete words, but I have been obliged to use it because of not having been able to find another corresponding to *"urinator"* in Latin or *"buzo"* in Spanish.

---

[159] See *supra*, footnote 64, p. 31.

hundred and seventy-five pounds. This excessive quantity of pearls, although they were of inferior quality because they were found beyond 28°, enriched Ocio quickly; but from then until now the catch has been growing smaller to such an extent that it has been almost absolutely abandoned, while the few who have devoted themselves to it have scarcely been able to make expenses, especially in these last years, in which European economy has introduced the use of imitation pearls into Mexico.

The best season for this fishing is from the first days of July to the last of September. As soon as the pearl-diving outfitter (the person at whose expense the fishing is done) has the boats ready and has provided all the necessary things, he goes to the eastern coast of California and there selects a port near the pearl beds where mother-of-pearl[160] is abundant, provided there is water for drinking there. During the three months which the diving lasts the boats with the *palombari* (divers) go there daily and return to the port.

The fishing begins two hours before noon and continues until three hours after midday, because the sun, being more perpendicular then, greatly clears up the bottom of the sea, and it makes visible the shells which are there. They do not fish during the remainder of the day, nor when the sun is clouded.

The oysters are fished for at a depth of eight, twelve, sixteen, and even twenty-four *pertiche*,[161] according to the skill of the divers. They dive, each one taking a net tied to his body to hold the oysters and a well-sharpened stick to defend himself from mantas, and for other uses. As soon as they have filled the net or cannot hold their breath any longer they come out of the water and return to the boat either to empty the nets or to take a few breaths, because the fatigue which they suffer is quite considerable on diving to the bottom as well as

---

[160] The hard, pearly part of the inside of various river and sea shells, such as the mussels, abalones, and pearl oysters. Used in making buttons, handles of toilet articles, and for inlay work.

[161] Evidently a misprint. Derived from the Latin word "*pertica*," which was a measuring-rod used to measure land. It was usually called *decempeda*, a rod ten feet long. Naked divers could scarcely go deeper than fifty or sixty feet.

coming up. When the catch of the day is ended they return to port, where the count and the division of the oysters are made.

In regard to the divers, there are some hired for a salary who have from the catch only the wages on which they have agreed with the pearl outfitter. Then there are those who are not hired but receive half of the oysters which they gather; but both are fed by the outfitter during the fishing season and must be returned by him to the place from which he took them.

Every day, as soon as they return to the port from fishing, the counting and the distribution of the oysters are made in this manner: If the diver is on a salary, four are taken from the entirety of all the oysters for the pearl outfitter and one for the king. If the diver is not on a salary, the first is taken for the outfitter, the second for the diver, the third for the outfitter, the fourth for the diver, and the fifth is set aside for the king; and so they go on counting in this manner until the heap is finished.

The Catholic king gets one-fifth of all the oysters that are caught. The exaction of this tax has been entrusted by the viceroy of Mexico to the captain-governor of California, who delegated another who collected it in his name because he could not do it personally; and when the fishing season was finished he used to send all the quantity of pearls belonging to the royal treasury, with the corresponding records, to Guadalajara,[162] the capital of Nueva Galicia. As all those governors who have held this commission have been good Christians and very honest men, they have conducted themselves in it with the greatest fidelity, without any reward or other interest than that of serving their sovereign.

After they have made the division, they open the oysters to take out the pearls. Some oysters have absolutely nothing; others have one, and frequently some have two pearls or more. The outfitters buy those which fall to the divers, or they trade them for merchandise which those who undertake the fishing usually bring with them for this purpose.

---

[162] The capital of Jalisco, and the second city in size in Mexico, having a population of 180,000. It is famed for its production of beautiful pottery.

Mother-of-pearl shells are generally five inches in length, and from three to four in width; their color outside is a dirty greenish, but they are beautiful inside. The pearls are formed in some creases in the body of the animal, although some are found adhered to the inner surface of the shell. This kind of a pearl is called *topo* by the Spaniards; and however large and beautiful they may be, they have no value, because the part in contact with the shell is flat. The most esteemed ones are those which, besides being large, white, and lustrous, are spherical or oval; and especially valuable are those which are pear-shaped.

Chapter Fifteen

BIRDS

WE HAVE, however, little to say about the birds of California, although there are many species. Almost all of them are known in Europe, either because they are already common to both continents or because the historians of America have already spoken of them at length. Among the birds of prey there are vultures, falcons, sparrow hawks, crows, and eagles. Crows are very abundant, but eagles, on the contrary, are very rare; and they are found only in the mountains of the southern part. There are also many *zopiloti* birds[163] described in our *History of Mexico;* and although they are not properly in the class of birds of prey they are similar to them in many ways.

Among the nocturnal birds there are owls, barn owls, red owls, cuckoos, and other birds the names and shapes of which we do not know.

Among the aquatic birds, which either live ordinarily in the water or which seek their food in it, there are many kinds, especially of sea birds. The best-known are ducks of various

---

[163] The common buzzard. This word is also used to describe a tree (*Dwietenia mahogani*) which is much used for cabinet making (Schnitzler, *op. cit.*, pp. 194, 478). An Indian tribe was also known by this name.

kinds, geese, pelicans, gulls, purple heron, coots, and *forsici* (in Spanish, *tixeras*). The latter are so called because on flying they take the shape of a pair of scissors with their feet and wings. What we said in Book I of the *History of Mexico* about the admirable traits of the pelicans in supporting the members of their kind that are helpless as to seeking sustenance, and the ingenuity of the Indians in taking advantage of the catch of these same birds, was observed by many Spaniards in the island of San Roque,[164] a short distance from the western coast of California.

Among the many birds which are sought for the table are turtledoves, wild pigeons, and quails in great abundance, besides many other species of aquatic birds. The missionaries brought domestic hens, turkeys,[165] and doves from New Spain.

Among the singing birds are nightingales[166] (although few), *cenzontli* or mocking birds, larks, sparrows, Mexican sparrows, cardinals, and others, which bring some alleviation with their sweet and melodious songs to those who travel through those arid and melancholy wastes.

Finally, there are various birds valued for their beauty of plumage, and among others, besides those cardinals mentioned above, are the marvelous hummingbirds.

Chapter Sixteen

QUADRUPEDS

As FAR as is known, the kinds of quadrupeds of California are only twenty-six, to wit, oxen, horses, donkeys, sheep, goats, pigs, dogs, and cats—all brought from New Spain by the industry and at the expense of the

---

[164] A mile long and nearly as wide, located two miles from the San Roque Bay. It is noted for the white-footed mouse.

[165] It is believed that the turkey went from the New World to Asia, from there to Europe, and then to the American colonies on the Atlantic Coast.

[166] Not the true European nightingale.

Jesuit missionaries—and lions, wildcats, deer, *tajès*, antelopes, coyotes, foxes, badgers, hares, rabbits, otters, skunks, agoutis,[167] Swiss and palmist squirrels, *portasacos* mice, and moles. To these twenty-five species there should be added that of a certain wild animal similar in color to the American lions, although less fleshy than they, which the Spaniards of California improperly call *onza*.

The wildcat, which the Cochimì Indians call *chimbì*, is larger, more vigorous, and fiercer than the domestic one; but it has a shorter tail. It is so bold that it will attack other larger quadrupeds and sometimes even those men who walk carelessly through the woods.[168] But this kind of wild animal is not numerous.

Not so is that of the *chimbikà*, or the California lion.[169] Because the Californians have not dared to kill these dangerous wild animals on account of a certain superstitious fear, which they had before Christianity was introduced there, they have gone on multiplying to the great detriment of the Missions which were then founded there; they made havoc on the herds and sometimes even on men, some tragic examples of which were seen in the last years that the Jesuits were there. The missionaries, after having persuaded their neophytes to lay

---

[167] The gopher.

[168] Rarely if ever attacks people. It is often called bobcat, California lynx, lynx cat, American wildcat, and spotted lynx. It ranges from sea level to altitudes of more than ten thousand feet (*North American Fauna*, September 11, 1890, pp. 79–80; also *Zoe*, Vol. III, pp. 309–11).

[169] Known also as the California cougar, panther, Pacific Coast cougar, and the Northwest puma. It is commonly found throughout the Southwest and along the coast. It became so destructive to sheep, young calves, deer, and even pigs some thirty years ago in California that the state (1907) began to pay a bounty of twenty dollars for every lion killed. For many years the state has had a professional lion hunter (Jay Bruce), and through his work the number of these animals has been greatly decreased. In 1932 about six hundred lions were killed. The bounty now is thirty dollars for female skins, and twenty dollars for male skins. Stories that these animals follow people to attack them may well be doubted. Several years ago a woman school teacher and a pupil were attacked by a large lioness near Morgan Hill, California, but the animal doubtless had rabies, because both persons died from this disease shortly after being bitten by the animal (*Report of the California Fish and Game Commission*, 1925, pp. 8–9).

aside their fear, and in order to encourage them more, as we shall relate farther on, used to give a bull as a reward to the one who killed a *chimbikà*, which practice those who governed those Missions observed all the time.

The *chimbikà* is as large as a fat mastiff, and it is protected by very strong claws; it has the very same color as the African lion but is without a mane. When the *chimbikà* captures some animal it clinches with it in such a manner that it does not let loose of it unless mortally wounded. As soon as it can it cuts the victim's throat, drinks the blood, devours the neck, and covers the rest with withered leaves so that it may come to eat when it is hungry. But seldom does it find the carcass, because the hungry Indians or the *zopiloti* feed on the dead body.

When the Indians observe that the *zopiloti* gather in large numbers and fly about above some spot, they infer that there is a dead animal near by, and they go there at once; and if the flesh is not entirely decayed and evil smelling, they take it to their homes or they light a fire right on the spot to roast it.

In spite of the *chimbikà* being so daring it runs away from dogs; and when it sees itself in danger of being overtaken it climbs some tree, and from there looks at them with threatening eyes but without ever venturing to descend until they have retired. This is the opportune occasion for shooting it. The *chimbikà* of California is the same as the *miztli* of the Mexicans, the *pagi* of the Chilenos, and the puma of the Peruvians, although it may appear different in some respects.

The coyote is the quadruped described by us in the *History of Mexico* which forms the link between the wolf and the fox, combining the astuteness of the latter with the voracity of the former, and resembling each in shape.

The deer of California are distinguished from the common deer of Europe only in having horns not set perpendicularly on their heads but inclined toward their backs.

The antelopes, called *ammogokiò* by the Indians, are larger, more agile, and fleeter than the goat. They go in flocks, and they climb over the boulders with incredible ease. There are black ones and white ones. Their hide is valuable, and their flesh good for eating.

The *tajè* of California is the ibex of Pliny[170] and the *bouquetin*[171] of C. de Buffon, and the same thing that Pliny says about the ibex* the Californians tell about the *tajè* without ever having read or heard about that naturalist, which proves the truth of Pliny's description and the specific identity of those animals. The shape, color, and size of the *tajè* is the same as that of the *bouquetin*. The flesh of these quadrupeds is very good for eating.

The American skunk, given so many names in the different countries of the New World, has the name of *iijù* among the Cochimìes. At the present time this curious quadruped is well known in Europe; but since some of the missionaries of California had the opportunity to observe it frequently in its own home we can describe it more in detail.

The skunks of California are of that species of very small animals which the Mexicans call *conèpatl*. The size of their bodies, without their tails, does not exceed eight inches, and their heads are also small; the color of their fur on the stomach and legs is white, and on their backs, sides, and tails it is alternated with black and white stripes in some members and white and tawny in others. Their tails terminate in beautiful fringes which seem showiest when they carry them raised and erect, as they are accustomed to do when they run away.

They live on black beetles, centipedes, and other insects; but they especially like the blood and eggs of hens, and are, for the same reason, the exterminators of the poultry yards. They commit their systematic thefts by night and thrust themselves

---

* Ibex have wonderful fleetness, although their heads are burdened with enormous horns. . . . . In these ways they free themselves from any missile by whirling around on the rocks, especially seeking to jump from any mountain to another, and they spring vigorously with a quick rebound where they please (Pliny's *Natural History*, Book 8, chap. 53).

---

[170] A noted Roman writer and scientist who was born A.D. 23 and lost his life in A.D. 79 during the eruption of Vesuvius. Of his various writings on law, medicine, history, and rhetoric, only his *Natural History* has been preserved.

[171] Mountain sheep.

into the hen roosts through holes narrower than their normal bodies. The hens make a great noise when they hear them but do not move from their places. The skunk then takes the head off one or two of them, sucks the blood from them, and eats a little of the flesh. Skunks live in small cavities which they make among the rocks; but they rarely permit themselves to be seen unless it is in the autumn or in the beginning of the winter.

Dr. Hernandez says in his *New History of the Plants, Animals, and Minerals of Mexico* that the excreta of the skunk emit an offensive odor, and this is commonly believed; but it is certain through repeated observations made in California that those quadrupeds have not used these as a defense against their pursuers nor have they ever left signs of having done so.[172]

The powerful protection, which they use constantly in great dangers, is that unbearable scent which they emit behind them. The air around about gathers this so perceptibly (as a serious missionary explains) that it seems that it can be touched. All the objects near by are so defiled with it that for a long time they keep the stench, which is extended to places indeed distant, although they may be exposed to the open air. The dogs which have followed a skunk are terrified by the evil scent and shake their noses forcibly, as if they wished to get away from the disagreeable odor.

That curious quadruped to which C. de Buffon gives the name *swiss* and the Mexicans that of *tlalmototli* or ground squirrel, in order to distinguish it from the true squirrel which lives in trees, has been described by us in the *History of Mexico*. This kind has its holes in the ground and damages the sown fields.

[172] Clavigero was correct in his deductions. The sickening fluid, which is the animal's chief weapon of defense, is ejected from two small glands located on either side of and just under the tail. The secretion has no relation to the urine. By a violent and rapid contraction of these two glands the skunk is able to throw the liquid from four to six feet. If the spray is thrown in the direction of a strong wind, it may go fifteen and even twenty feet. The liquid is not thrown by the tail, as is commonly supposed, but the tail is elevated to prevent obstruction of the spray. The skunk belongs to the same family as the mink and the weasel, and it ranges over the entire North American continent.

The *agoutis*, quadrupeds of the mole family, but larger, more beautiful, and different in the eyes as well as in the rest of the body from the ground squirrel, as we have stated in this history, do the same damage.

Another common quadruped in California is somewhat similar to the squirrel in shape, although smaller; its thickness is that of a common mouse, notwithstanding the fact that it is twice as long. Its tail is hairy like that of the squirrel, and its back is striped in a light and dark color. This is surely the *palmista*[173] of Buffon and the *sicurus palmarum* of Linnaeus.

The mouse of California, although similar in shape, color, size, and manner of living to the common mouse, is nevertheless of a species very different from the common one and all those known by naturalists. It has underneath each ear a membrane in the shape of a little sack which communicates with its mouth. All that it picks up with its mouth it introduces into the little sacks to take away and place in its cache. Consequently, the damage which these little creatures cause in the granaries is greater than that which they should inflict, bearing in mind their smallness. When the membranes are empty and slack they are scarcely perceived, and when boys kill one and blow it up through its mouth, the membranes become inflated with their breaths and appear as large as a pigeon's egg, the sight of this very ridiculous figure causing them great amusement.*

The climate of California is suitable to all the animals brought there from New Spain, but their increase is retarded both by the scarcity of pastures and by the abundance of lions. Since the pastures are few, it is necessary that the horses, cows, sheep, and goats be scattered in different places where grass or sprouts of shrubs exist on which to graze. Since they cannot be in sight of their herdsmen, they are attacked by lions, which

---

* The two species of the *palmista* squirrel and the pocket mouse can be added to those fifty-two American quadrupeds which we have enumerated in the Catalogue placed in Volume IV of the *History of Mexico*.

---

[173] The common ground squirrel.

kill the colts and calves and sometimes the mares and cows; and they create great havoc with the sheep and goats. For this reason it becomes necessary to bring new horses for the needs of the presidio yearly from Sinaloa. It is believed that only the dogs have degenerated in California, because the affection which they have in other countries for their masters is not observed in them, and they desert their master easily for another. Who knows but that the poverty of the masters is what obliges those hungry animals to seek their sustenance in other places?

Chapter Seventeen

THE INHABITANTS, THEIR LANGUAGE, ARITHMETIC, AND YEAR

THE SAVAGE inhabitants of California were slightly different in their manner of living from the animals we have described. But if we study those few vestiges of antiquity which remain there, we shall be persuaded, perhaps, that this vast peninsula was inhabited previously by less barbaric peoples[174] than the ones whom the Spaniards found in it, because the Jesuits, in the last years that they were there, discovered in the mountains situated between latitude 27° and 28°, various large caves made in enduring rock and figures of decently dressed men and women and different kinds of animals painted on the walls. These pictures, although crude,

---

[174] Little scientific investigation has been made of these prehistoric people. In 1893 Mallery found in the caves and on smooth rocks pictures in four colors, yellow, red, green, and black, cut high up, indicating at least that some of the people were giants. These pictures showed men clothed in garments which suggest a different race, since the Californians wore little or no clothing (*Annual Report of the Bureau of Ethnology*, 1888–89, pp. 132–36). Arthur North calls these ancient people "Petroglyph Makers." He thinks there were at least "five distinct groups of cliff writings" of these early inhabitants of the peninsula (*American Anthropologist*, N.S. 1908, Vol. X, p. 244). For the petroglyphic and pictographic work of Lower California, see *University of California Publications in American Archaeology and Ethnology*, Vol. XXIV, No. 2, pp. 47–238.

represent the objects distinctly. The colors which they used for them, as is plainly evident, were taken from the mineral earth that exists in the vicinity of the volcano of Vírgenes. What surprised the missionaries most was that those colors had remained on the rock for so many centuries without ever receiving any damage from either air or water.

Now these pictures and clothing are not characteristic of those brutish and savage nations which inhabited California when the Spaniards reached it. They belong, without doubt, to another ancient nation, but we are unable to say what it was. The Californians affirm unanimously that these pictures were the work of a giant-like nation which had come there from the North.[175] I do not pretend that belief should be given to this tradition, but surely it cannot be doubted that some men of disproportionate stature were there in former times, as may be inferred from different human bones exhumed by the missionaries. Among others, Father José Rotea,[176] the missionary of Kadakaamang, was an inquiring and sincere man, and, having learned that there was a gigantic skeleton at a place in his Mission (now called San Joaquín), he ordered it dug up, and, in fact, found all the backbone (although with the vertebrae then loosened), a long bone, a rib, several teeth, and especially a large fragment of the skull. All the skeleton might have been found if a dry stream-bed near by had not eaten away the soil by degrees and forced out some bones there. The rib, although not entire, was still about two feet in length.[177] The long bone could not be measured, because it crumbled when it was taken out. Therefore, after having considered the magnitude of the skull and having measured the place which the skeleton occupied, and after having compared its vertebrae with those of

---

[175] The origin of the Indian is wrapped in mystery. Father Baegert and others believe that the Indians of the peninsula must have been driven, at some remote time, from the North because, they argue, nothing would induce a people to migrate to such a sterile, worthless land as was Lower California.

[176] A Mexican Jesuit, born in 1732, who went to Lower California in 1759. He found this skeleton in 1765 near the Mission of San Ignacio.

[177] No race of people has been found whose height averaged more than six feet. This skeleton could scarcely have been that of a man.

other usual skeletons, it is believed that the man to whom those bones belonged was almost eleven feet in height.*

The same missionary went to inspect some of the caves mentioned, one of which he describes. It was made after the fashion of an arch, divided into half and resting on a floor; it was about fifty feet in length, fifteen in width, and the same in height. As it was entirely open at the place of its entrance, there was sufficient light so that the pictures of its innermost and highest part could be observed. Men and women with clothes similar to those of the Mexicans were represented there, but they were absolutely barefooted. The men had their arms open and raised somewhat; and among the women there was one who had her hair loose over her back, and a crest on her head. Different kinds of animals, native to the country, as well as imported ones, were also seen there.

But leaving aside the vestiges of that ancient nation, of which we know nothing, and coming to speak of those found there by the Spaniards, which exist even today, we find there are three in Christian California,[178] to wit: the Pericùes,[179] the Guaicuras,[180] and the Cochimìes.[181] The Pericùes occupy the

---

* Whenever we make mention of *pertiche,* feet, or inches, the measures of Paris, which are the most generally known, should be understood.

---

[178] As far north as the Mission of Santa María, the most northerly Mission founded by the Jesuits.

[179] Also spelled Pèricos, Peruiches, and Pericùis. They probably numbered less than four thousand when the Jesuits first entered the peninsula. When the white man, especially the pearl fishermen, introduced to them whisky and many diseases, like other tribes they rapidly decreased in numbers. When the Franciscans left the peninsula to work in Upper California, the Pericùes numbered about four hundred (*The Catholic Encyclopaedia,* Vol. XI, p. 668; see also Bancroft, *Native Races*).

[180] Pronounced "Waik-u-rí," and often spelled Waikuros, Guarienris, Guayricor. They probably never numbered more than ten thousand. The Spaniards gave them this name on first landing on the peninsula, because the Indians called out "Guaxora," which means "friend" in their language, when they first saw the white men (Charles Anthony Engelhardt, *The Missions and Missionaries of California,* Vol. I, p. 171).

[181] Probably the most superior Indians on the peninsula, but they were last to be provided with Missions. They are believed to be akin to the Yuma

most southern part from the cape of San Lucas as far as 24° and the adjacent islands of Cerralvo, Espíritu Santo, and San José. The Guaicuras were established between the parallel of 23½° and 26°, and the Cochimìes took the northern part from 25° to 33° and some near-by islands of the Pacific Sea. Each one of these three nations[182] had its own language.

At 33° another nation begins which speaks a tongue entirely different from the ones mentioned. There are others on the banks of the Red River, but as these are little known and foreign to our purpose we shall say nothing about them.

The Pericù language is extinct today, and the few individuals of that unfortunate nation who remained there speak Spanish. The Guaicura language had as many dialects as there were branches of that nation, viz., those properly called Guaicuras, and Aripas,[183] Uchitas,[184] Coras,[185] and Conchò Indians,[186] afterward called Lauretanos, because of the pueblo of Loreto which was founded near them. The branch of the Uchitas is extinct and that of the Coras nearly so. The Lauretanos abandoned their language for Spanish, but in the other remaining tribes of that nation, even now, their former language is maintained. The Cochimì language has likewise been kept by all, although very many of this nation have learned Spanish.

Indians. In 1908 it was reported that not more than a hundred Cochimìes still lived near the Missions of San Borja, Santa Gertrudis, and San Xavier (*American Anthropologist*, N.S., 1908, Vol. X, p. 241).

[182] There are various estimates of the number of Indians in the peninsula when the Jesuits arrived there. Father Baegert thought that the total did not exceed fifty thousand. The Mission area of the Jesuits probably never contained more than half this number. By 1840 less than four thousand Indians lived in the peninsula, and today only a few hundred remain (*Catholic Encyclopaedia*, Vol. VII, p. 45). Those in the upper part of the peninsula were very similar in their living, religious, and tribal relations to those in the southern part of the state of California (*University of California Publications in American Archaeology and Ethnology*, Vol. VIII, Part III, p. 75).

[183] They lived mostly south of Dolores.

[184] They dwelt principally south of Loreto.

[185] They dwelt chiefly between La Paz and the Mission of Loreto. They were noted for their opposition to Christianity.

[186] Those surrounding the Mission of Loreto. Early letters from this Mission were frequently dated at Loreto Conchò.

There are four dialects, so different from each other that any one little versed in them will probably believe that they are four different languages.

The Cochimì language, which is the most widely used, is very difficult, is full of aspirates, and has some ways of pronunciation that cannot be explained. These people have only the following numeral numbers: *tejueg*, one; *goguò*, two; *kombiò*, three; and *magacubuguà*, four. In order to say five, they express themselves as follows: *nagannà tejueg ignimel*, that is, one entire hand. When they exceed this number the most uncivilized are confused and can only say "many and very many." But those who are more ingenious continue their enumeration by saying: One hand and one, one hand and two, etc. In order to express ten, they say: *Nagannà ignimbal demuejueg*, that is, all the hands. For fifteen they say, all the hands and one foot; and for twenty, all the hands and feet. And this is the end of the Cochimì arithmetic, but those who have learned the Spanish also know our method of counting.[187]

After the custom of other nations, they give the same name to the day as to the sun, called *Ibò*.[188] They call the year *mejibò*, which name means, chiefly, the most abundant and cheerful season. They divide the year not into months but into six seasons. The first, which is called *Mejibò*, comprises part of June, all of July, and part of August. This season is the most cheerful one for them (as has been said), because the *pitaje* is gathered then. The second, called *Amadà-appì*, begins in August and comprises all of September and part of October, at which time the plants grow green again with the rains which, though scarce, are accustomed to fall at that time.

Amadà-appigalà is the name of the third season, which comprises part of October, all of November, and part of December,

---

[187] Father Baegert gives a different story of the Indians' ability to count. He states that their arithmetic "extends as far as three, at most six, because they have nothing to count. They care little how many fingers they have, whether the year consists of six or twelve months, or whether the month counts three or thirty days, because with them there is perpetual holiday, or blue Monday" (Engelhardt, *op. cit.*, p. 159).

[188] Means "sun."

a time in which the grass sprung up in the previous season begins to turn yellow and dry up. This season is also as pleasing to the Californians as the first, because the *tajuà*, or bitter-sweet *pitaja*, *opuntia*, and other fruit and seeds prized by them ripen then. The fourth season, which is called *Majibèl*, and which is the coldest, begins in December and comprises all of January and part of February. The fifth, which is called *Majibèn*, commences in February and includes all of March and part of April. Finally, the sixth begins in April and comprises all of May and part of June and is called *Majüben-maajì*, that is, the bad season; it is to them what the winter season is to other peoples, since provisions are scarcer then than ever, and these poor people have for food only mescal and those toasted seeds which they have gathered in the other seasons. Thus the following season is as much more pleasing to them as their poverty is greater in this one.

Chapter Eighteen

THE ORIGIN AND CHARACTER OF THE CALIFORNIANS

WE CANNOT say anything about the origin of these uncivilized people, nor could they themselves when questioned by the missionaries say anything else but that their ancestors had come to that country from the northern regions. The Mexicans and all those nations which populated the vast country of Anàhuac[189] asserted this same thing about their origin; but in regard to the Californians it seems that it should be believed even though they had not said so, because the peninsula, surrounded by sea on every side, communicates with the continent only on the north. When they were asked the occasion of this coming, they answered that there had been a war stirred up between their ancestors and another people of the north in which the former were conquered

---

[189] A large and very fertile plateau lying northwest of Mexico City, the average elevation of which is nearly eight thousand feet.

and fled toward the south, and there they took refuge in the mountains of the peninsula.

Thus they declared their tradition sincerely without being ashamed to confess that they were descendants of those fugitives. Examples of similar ingenuity are not lacking in the old continent, says a learned author, because those two most famous peoples of antiquity, the Carthaginians and the Romans, boasted of their origin—the former in the fugitive Tyrians and the latter in the conquered Trojans.

The Californians are of good stature, healthy, and strong. The illnesses which they are accustomed to suffer do not come from their bad constitutions, but they contract them either through contagion, as smallpox, or because of the bad foods which they ordinarily use and which cause certain ulcers and tumors. *Morbus gallicus*,[190] believed to be an endemic disease of America, has not been seen in California up to the present[191] time, because it has not been brought there by any foreigner.

The Californians are similar to the peoples of Mexico in their faces, hair, beard, and color. Like them, they have thick, straight, black hair, scanty beards, and no down on their arms, thighs, and legs; their foreheads are narrow; their noses are a little thick; their teeth are white, even, and strong; and their mouths, eyes, and ears are regular, except those who are brought up in savagery and who disfigure their noses and ears with earrings which they place in them for ornaments. The color of those who live in the inland places is a light chestnut; but those who live continually on the beaches are darker. Deformed persons[192] are as rare among the Californians as among the Mexicans.

[190] Syphilis.

[191] This may have been true for some of the Missions, but Palóu states that when the inspector visited the Mission of Santiago he found there only a few Indians, most of whom were suffering from *galico*. Those who were thus afflicted and living at the Mission of Todos Santos were removed to the Santiago Mission in October, 1768, and placed under the care of a physician (Engelhardt, *op. cit.*, p. 423). It would appear that this disease did not become common there until near the close of the Jesuit period.

[192] This may be accounted for from the custom found among so many primitive people of putting deformed children to death at birth.

In regard to their souls they are not different from the rest of the sons of Adam. Those who have been brought up in the wilds have those vices and imperfections which are consistent with savage life in all countries. They are uncultured, very limited in their knowledge through lack of ideas, lazy through lack of stimuli, inconstant, hasty in their resolutions, and very inclined to gambling and to childish diversions through lack of restraint. On the other hand, they lack certain vices very common among other barbarians and even among educated peoples. Drunkenness, that dominant vice of Americans,[193] has never been in vogue among the Californians. They do not steal from each other the little that they possess; relatives do not quarrel or fight among themselves, nor do those who are of the same tribe. All their hatred and fury are directed against other nations or other tribes with whom they have enmity. Finally, they are not obstinate and stubborn but docile, and easy to guide to what is desired.

We have several strange examples of their childish simplicity. When some Indians found among the sands of the Pacific Sea some large earthen jars, left there without doubt by the sailors of some ship from the Philippine Islands, they marveled at them because they had never seen similar vessels. They carried them to a cave a short distance from their usual habitation and placed them there with the mouths turned toward the entrance, so that all might observe them well. Afterward they went frequently to look at them without ever failing to wonder at those great mouths always open; and in their dances, where they imitate the movements and cries of animals, they imitated the mouths of the jars with theirs.

Meanwhile sickness came upon them, and because they did not know what to do to free themselves from it, they met in council; after long deliberation the most exalted one of them all said that those jars had transmitted the epidemic without doubt by their mouths and that the remedy would be to stop

---

[193] The Indian seemed to have an ever increasing desire for liquor. Many of the early trappers in North America used whisky to secure from them valuable furs. When intoxicated the Indian frequently traded his pack of valuable beaver skins for a glass of whisky.

them up well. The suggestion seemed good to all. But as it was necessary to approach the jars to do this, and as they believed that this could not be done without danger of death, it was determined that some young, strong men should approach them from the back and stop up those fatal mouths with handfuls of grass, as actually was done.

Shortly after the Jesuits began to establish their missions in California one missionary sent two loaves of bread (a gift much esteemed then because of the scarcity of wheat) by an Indian neophyte to another missionary with a letter, in which he told him about this gift. The neophyte tasted the bread on the way; and, finding it good, he ate it all. When he reached the missionary to whom he was sent he handed him the letter; and when the bread was demanded from him he denied having received it, as he could not guess who could have told that to the missionary. He was advised that the letter had told it to him. Notwithstanding this, he insisted in the negative, and so was dismissed.

In a short time he was sent again to the same missionary with another gift, also accompanied by a letter. On the way he yielded to the very same temptation. But just as he had been betrayed the first time by the letter, so now, in order, as he imagined, to avoid being seen by the letter, he hid it under a stone while he devoured all that he was taking to the missionary. After he had handed him the letter, and had been newly convicted of theft, he replied with this strange simplicity: "I confess to you, Father, that the first letter told you the truth, because it really saw me eat the bread; but this other one is a liar in affirming what it certainly has not seen."

Chapter Nineteen

ARTS, MEALS, AND DRINKS

THE CALIFORNIANS were entirely barbarous and savage. Neither achitecture, agriculture, nor the many arts useful to human life were known to them. In all that peninsula there was not a house, nor the vestige of one; not even a hut, nor an earthen jar,* nor an instrument of metal, nor a piece of cloth. They maintained themselves with those fruits which grow wild or with the animals which they hunted, or fished for, without taking the trouble to cultivate the land, sow crops, or raise some animals.

Because of their poverty they used to eat and still do eat at the present time many things which are never considered edible by us, as roots, very bitter and insipid fruits, worms, spiders, locusts, lizards, snakes, cats, and lions, and even dry hides.[194] A dog is as valued by them as is a calf[195] by us. But never did

* On that trip which he made in 1746 to explore all the eastern coast of the peninsula, Father Consag found some earthen jars among some gentiles who lived on the coast toward 31°. This fact is an exception to what we have stated above; but I suspect that those gentiles had those vessels from another more northern people or from some pearl fishermen.

---

[194] There seem to have been few animals which the Indian did not eat. Father Baegert states that they lived chiefly on dogs and cats, horses and mules, mice and rats, lizards and snakes, grasshoppers and crickets, owls and bats, green caterpillars, "an abominable white worm of length and thickness of the thumb," and other insects and small animals (*Report of the Smithsonian Institution*, 1864, pp. 364–67).

[195] Under the instruction of the missionary the Indian was induced to give up the eating of many kinds of insects and worms, and to eat beef. From an economic point of view this was a mistake of the missionaries. The Mission Indians required an enormous amount of beef. It was not uncommon to have an Indian consume in a day from fifteen to twenty pounds of beef. Cattle stealing became a favorite pastime of the Indians, and at first it was difficult to increase the number of cattle at a Mission. Father Baegert wrote that "for eight years I kept, ranging at large, from four to five hundred head of cattle, and sometimes as many goats and sheep, until the constant robberies of my own and the neighboring missions compelled me to give up cattle breeding. In the bodies of nineteen cows and oxen that had been killed in one day at the mission, there were found more than eight flint-points of arrows, the shafts of which had been broken off by the wounded animals while passing through the rocks and bushes. I believe that more of these animals were killed and eaten by the natives than were brought to the missions for consumption; horses and mules suffered in like manner" (*ibid.*, p. 380). As for the number of cattle kept by the Missions on the peninsula during the period of the Jesuits, it is probable that there were never more than twenty thousand at any one time. The Indian never learned to eat pork nor to drink milk, and so he always demanded a generous supply of beef. The Indians of the northwestern

their hunger drive them to nourish themselves on human flesh, and they even always abstained from eating badgers because they somewhat resemble men.

They do truly strange things at their meals. At the time of the gathering of the *pitaje* they eat until they are satiated; but in order to make use of them again after having eaten and digested them, they do not put aside their deposits. With inexpressible patience, from what was previously *pitaja*, they separate the very tiny seeds of the fruit which remain without being digested; they toast them, grind them, and keep them, thus reduced to flour, to eat afterward during the winter. Some Spaniards jokingly call this the second *pitaja* gathering.

Those barbarians who live in the northern part of the peninsula have found the secret, unknown to most mortals, of eating and eating repeatedly the same tidbit. They tie a mouthful of meat which is dried and hardened in the sun securely with a string; they put it in their mouths, and after having chewed it a little, they swallow it, allowing the string to hang from the mouth; they keep it in their stomachs two or three minutes, and then they bring it back to the mouth by pulling it up by means of the string, and they repeat this act as many times as are necessary for consuming that mouthful, or until it becomes soft so that it is no longer useful for such a purpose. When they extract it from their stomachs, they make such a noise that it seems to one who has never heard them that they are going to choke.

When many individuals eat together in this manner, they practice it with the greatest show. Eight or ten Indians sit down on the ground, forming a circle. One of them takes the morsel and swallows it, and, after pulling it out, he gives it to another, and the latter to still another; and thus they proceed through all the circle with the greatest pleasure until the morsel is consumed.

They learn this game as children, to the astonishment of the Spaniards who have observed it. In fact, it would not be cred-

---

part of the state of California "regarded dog meat as virulent poison" (*University of California Publications in American Archaeology and Ethnology*, Vol. VIII, Part I, p. 13).

ible if it were not attested unanimously by all those who have been in the country. Some Jesuits, who did not want to believe it, in spite of so many serious and sincere persons who had affirmed it, saw it with their own eyes when they went to California later. Because of the continuous reprehensions of the missionaries, this very filthy and dangerous manner of eating has gone into disuse among those Indians who have adopted Christianity.

They do not use any seasoning in their food. They eat fresh meat almost raw, dried in the sun, half roasted or rather burnt. They eat those insects and toasted and ground seeds which are common among them. They use only natural water as drink.

Chapter Twenty

HABITATIONS, CLOTHING, DECORATIONS, AND HOUSEHOLD GOODS

EACH tribe, composed of several consanguineous families, usually lives near some spring, but with only the sky for a roof and the bare ground for a bed. When the sun is too hot, they take shelter under the trees; and on cold nights they retire to caves in the mountains. Some few build bowers in the shape of hovels for sleeping; others make holes or pits about two feet in depth. But the most usual little abodes are certain circular fences of loose stone piled up, which are five feet in diameter and less than two in height. Within each one of them a family sleeps under the open sky, and they are so accustomed to it that the missionaries have used much effort to make them sleep in those little houses or huts that they have had built for their homes, since they suffer anxieties when they begin to sleep under roofs and it seems to them that they are to smother; but afterward they become very willing. In their homes they are always near the fire except in the great heat of the summer, and each time they awaken in the night they are careful to stir it up.

Their clothing corresponds to their dwellings. That of the

men is only their own skin, and far from being ashamed of their nakedness they wondered that they were censured for it by the Spaniards, regarding which point it cannot be exaggerated how much the missionaries have had to endure. The first Californians to be clothed by them appeared so ridiculous to their fellow countrymen and were made fun of so much that they seemed compelled to lay aside their clothing. A missionary dressed two boys, servants of his, cutting and sewing the garments himself. But as soon as they appeared dressed they were ridiculed by the others with so much mockery and laughter that, not being able to endure it and, on the other hand, not wishing to annoy their benefactor, they went naked by day in the woods with their relatives and at night presented themselves dressed to the missionary. But the missionaries by means of frequent admonitions and kindness and generous expenditures succeeded at last in covering the indecent nakedness of all their neophytes.

The women of California conduct themselves in this regard in a very different way from the men, since in all the peninsula not one has been seen who failed to cover herself with something. The most clothed women are those of the Pericù nation, who wear two different kinds of garments. The first is a cape which covers them from the shoulders to the waist; and the other is a kind of petticoat composed of two square pieces, of which one extends from the waist to the middle of the leg and covers the posterior part and the hips and the other covers the anterior and extends from the waist to the knees. These clothes are not of cloth, but are composed simply of loose little cords hanging in great number partly from a cord which they tie to their necks and partly from two others tied at the waist. They get these little cords by pounding, as is done with hemp stalks, the leaves of a certain palm which grows in those countries and which gives a whiter thread than that of hemp itself.

The Guaicuras do not wear a cape. Their entire clothing consists of little skirts, which extend from the waist to the knees, or a little farther and which in the back are composed of small cords similar to those of the Pericùes, and in the front of a great quantity of slender reed-grass joints that are pierced.

Perhaps they wear the joints and not the reed, because the former are more difficult to break.

The Cochimì women, who live between 26° and 30°, have the same apron of nodes of common reed grass as the Guaicuras, and they cover the back part with a deer skin or that of any other animal. Those women who live from 30° on toward the north wear, in addition, a cape of beaver skin, or of hare, rabbit, or other animal. All are very careful about their modesty and that of their daughters. Scarcely is a daughter born when they cover her with little skirts prepared from the time of their pregnancy, and they were greatly embarrassed when they saw this duty omitted with the little daughters of the Spanish soldiers.

When the Californians do not travel they go absolutely barefooted. But when making a journey they use the same kind of footwear as the Indians of Mexico and other American countries; that is, some wear leather soles fastened on with straps, so that only the sole of the foot is covered by them. Previously they used to make these soles of deerskin; but now they usually make them of ox-hide, because it is thicker and stronger.

Although all the men in California were alike in their nakedness, those of each nation distinguished themselves by their finery. The Pericùes wore long hair, adorned with pearls and interwoven with white feathers, so that from a distance it appeared like a peruke. The Guaicuras, at least those of Conchò (afterward called Lauretanos), girded their waists with a beautiful belt, and wore a curious net like a fillet on their heads; and some added to this a collar of little pieces of mother-of-pearl and certain berries strung together, and little bracelets and armlets of the same material. The Pericùes also used fillets of certain white, round snail shells, which at first sight seemed to be pearls. The women of this nation wore their hair long, loose, and spread over their backs; and they wore, hanging from their necks to their waists, many strings of small snail shells, pearls, pieces of mother-of-pearl, berries, and little internodes gaudily arranged. The Cochimìes did not wear their hair long, but only as some short locks; nor did they adorn themselves with pearls either, but with a kind of crown composed of many little pieces of small mother-of-pearl, which were of even size and strung on a string.

The household goods of the Californians were so scanty that the entire outfit of a family could be carried easily by a boy. It consisted of a tray, a bowl, a small stick for lighting fire (according to the custom of the rest of the Americans and the ancient shepherds of Europe), a sharp bone that was used for an awl, and two nets, in one of which the women carried their children on their backs, as we shall explain later, and in the other, maguey sprouts, *pitaje,* and other fruits which the men gathered in the woods.

The tray, called *batea* by the Spaniards, is round, somewhat deep, and varies in its size; it is usually a foot and a half in diameter. It is made from the twigs of a certain plant, flexible as the willow after they have flattened it and cut it lengthwise. They make it in a spiral form, beginning in the center, and fasten it strongly with strips of the same material. The spirals are held together so closely and the tray is so solid that it holds water without even a drop being able to get out. The Pericùes make their trays oval; they are composed of staves which are eighteen inches in length and from four to five fingers' width wide, similar to those of barrels, made from the bark of a certain small palm and fastened together with flexible little twigs, like those trays of the Cochimìes. These trays are of use to the women principally for cleaning, and also for toasting the seeds which they use for food. For this purpose they put coals among the seeds and they shake the tray continually.

Those Indians who live on the banks of the Red River make their trays like those of the Cochimìes, but much larger. They use them, as they wish, for moving their things on the river from one bank to another by swimming and pushing the trays with their hands. Such trays are called *coritas* in that country.

The bowl of the Californians, called *addà* by the Cochimìes, is made of the same material as the trays, and as firmly and closely woven as they; but it is smaller and has the shape of the crown of a hat. Those Indians use them as plates for eating, as glasses for drinking, and even as hats for the women. And for that reason, when they saw the hats of the Spaniards, they gave them the name of their bowls, that is, *addà*.

Chapter Twenty-One
╬╬╬

OCCUPATIONS

THEIR fishing nets, as well as those for transportation, are made of fiber from the leaves of the mescal. The women are the ones who make the nets, repair the trays made by the men, assist them in gathering the fruits and seeds upon which they live, and prepare the food. Occupations followed by the men are hunting, fishing, and war.

For the hunt they use chiefly the bow and arrow. The bow is simple: it is made of pliable wood hardened by fire and thicker in the middle than at the ends; and the bowstring is made of twisted deer tendons. The length of the arch varies from four to five feet, according to the size of the bow. The arrows are about two and a half feet long and are made of two pieces joined with the pitch of that tree which we have mentioned in another part and bound with slender deer tendons. The piece of the point, which makes the third part of the arrow, is a hard and slightly sharpened little rod, and the other is a reed with three hawk feathers near the indentation. These are the arrows which they use ordinarily for hunting birds and small quadrupeds; but for deer, lions, and other similar animals, as well as for war, they arm the point with flint so that the wounds may be larger and that the arrows may not be loosened easily from the body.

In order to hunt deer they use a curious strategem. An Indian takes the head of a deer kept for this purpose and, placing it on his head, he hides behind the thickets which permit only his false head to be seen, which he moves so that it will appear as one of those animals. The deer, deceived on seeing it, approach and are easily killed by other hunters who lie in ambush for them.

In order to hunt hares, besides the nets and snares which

they use ordinarily, the Cochimìes avail themselves of an easier and more direct method, without any other appliance than a small curved stick about a foot and a half in length. When they see a hare, as they travel along, they throw that little stick, which they dragged along the ground, so skillfully that it breaks their legs; and in this manner they are accustomed to catch many without interrupting their travel for a moment.

The perspicacity of the Californians is truly admirable in scanning the tracks of quadrupeds in order to follow them and in distinguishing men by theirs. If the man who has passed over the road belongs to their tribe and went barefooted, they know infallibly who he was by the tracks which he made. The same thing happens in distinguishing the arrows of the members of their tribe. However similar and uniform they appear to the Spaniards, the Indians by some almost imperceptible signs recognize who the owner of each one is, just as we are accustomed to recognize a writer by the shape of his handwriting.

They fish in two ways, either with nets on the beaches in the backwaters of the tide or with small forks on the high sea. In order to fish on the high sea in this second way they use a simple raft composed of three, five, or seven logs fastened together with sticks and well tied; the log in the middle, which extends farther because of being longer, serves as a prow. The wood from which these rafts are made is cork (a tree already described by us), because it is the lightest. On each one of them, according to their size, two or three men take their places and depart four or five miles from the coast, without fear of the very high waves of the Pacific Sea, which, at times, seem to lift them as far as the clouds and at times to bury them in the bottom of the sea. The most productive fishing is done in the port of Magdalena.

Besides the bow and arrow they use for war small darts or lances, which are sharpened sticks hardened by fire. Among the Indians who live from 31° toward the north, weapons of another kind are found for wounding from close by; but all are of wood. The first is a mallet with its handle, made of one piece, and similar in shape to a weather vane. The second is like the ax of a wood-chopper, also in one piece. The third has the shape of a small scimitar. In this respect it seems that men are accustomed to be more ingenious in seeking the harm of another than in procuring suitable comforts for themselves.

When the Californians were still gentiles there were frequent wars, now among two different nations, then among two or more tribes of the same nation. The motive for starting it was usually some injury done to an individual, or some damage caused one tribe because of going to fish, hunt, or gather fruit in those places in which the first were accustomed to go. Before beginning the conflict they mutually directed great threats at each other in order to intimidate each other. Their manner of fighting was more or less the same as is used commonly among other savage nations of the world; that is, they began with fearful howls, with more fury than bravery, and without any order, except what they had for getting in the front of the army in succession when the vanguard could not maintain themselves through weariness or through lack of arrows. Among other benefits for which they are debtors to Christianity are those of peace and charity, which have gathered them to Jesus Christ, making their old discords and dissensions disappear entirely.

Chapter Twenty-Two

HOLIDAYS AND SOCIAL RANK

IN TIME of peace, besides exercising in the hunt and in fishing, the Indians amused themselves in dancing, in contests, and in races. Father Salvatierra,[196] the

---

[196] Born in Milan, Italy. He became a Jesuit at twenty-seven years of age and arrived in Mexico in 1675 to work among the Indians. He was assigned to the Missions in the Sierra Madre Mountains, located northwest of Mexico City. Here he labored for ten years, when he was made inspector of the Missions in Sinaloa and in Sonora. On one of his trips he met Kino. The two traveled about the country exploring the land for Mission sites and studying the Indians. Venegas says that as they went about the country the

famous founder of those Missions, makes the following explanation when speaking of their dances: "We had spent the holiday of the Blessed Nativity of the Master with much consolation and devotion on our part as well as on that of the Indians among whom were present some hundreds of our catechumen. The Indian children executed their dances, of which they have more than thirty kinds, all figurative and representing the hunt, war, fishing, their trips, their burials, and other similar things. It gave one great pleasure to see a tiny child of three or four years who gloried in doing his duty in the dance."

They held these dances for celebrating their weddings, the birth of their children, success in the hunt and in fishing and the gathering of fruits, or for victory attained over their enemies. These dances were neither very frequent nor very solemn, as in the joyous season of the *pitaje*. As Father Salvatierra states, this was their carnival in which they found so much happiness that they went out of their senses. They were accustomed to invite other tribes to these festivals and to challenge them to wrestling and races.

One of the most celebrated California holidays which the Cochimìes used to hold annually was the time of distributing the deerskins. On the predetermined day the different border tribes gathered at a definite place, each one taking the skins of all the deer which they had killed that year. There they made a great circular bower; they opened a street which ended in it; and they hung it with all those skins. Within the bower the principal hunters were given the game and the fruits which were prepared, and, after having eaten, they smoked wild tobacco in reed pipes, according to their custom.

---

conversion of California "was the subject of both their public and private conversation" (Miguel Venegas, *Juan María de Salvatierra* (translated and edited by Marguerite Eyer Wilbur), p. 35. In 1697 the Jesuits were given permission by the king to go to California; and Salvatierra and Kino were appointed to establish Missions in the peninsula. Before he went to California, Salvatierra had founded two Missions (Santa Teresa and San Francisco de los Guazaparis) in Sinaloa. In Book II Clavigero gives a most graphic story of the work of Salvatierra in the peninsula.

A *guama*,[197] that is, one of their charlatans, sitting near the entrance of the bower, proclaimed the panegyrics of the hunters with fearful shouts. Meantime, the other Indian men kept running through that street hung with skins, and the Indian women danced and sang in it from one end to the other. As soon as the charlatan ceased shouting, because of weariness, the running ceased also. Then the principal men, after coming out of the bower, distributed the skins among the women, to the great happiness of all, especially to that of the women themselves, who appreciated those skins like a gift come from heaven, since they had nothing else with which to cover their backs.

On hearing the principal men mentioned one would conclude that there was no superiority of authority or any pre-eminence of nobility among the Californians. Neither the nations nor the tribes were subjected to any chief or superior; nor did they distinguish those different gradations which result from birth, occupations, or wealth. Uniformity of language was the only thing which united the different tribes of each nation; and consanguinity and relationship caused the different families of each tribe to live together. Among the Californians the chief men were those who made themselves feared and respected

[197] It would seem from Clavigero's account that only men acted as "doctors." Father Baegert says that women also practiced sorcery, and that they were just as accomplished in their deceit as were the men (*Report of the Smithsonian Institution*, 1864, p. 389). Bancroft says that in general there were two kinds of quacks or *guamas*. One type was known as "root doctors" and the other as "barking doctors." He says that women occasionally practiced medicine (*Native Races*, Vol. I, chap. iv). It was believed by the Indians that the *guama* could cause as well as cure disease. Sometimes one *guama* diagnosed the disease, and the other one applied the remedy. Little medicine and few drugs were used. Customs differed widely as to the pay of the *guama*. If he failed to cure the patient, he was often compelled to return his fee, or he was killed by relatives of the deceased. And if he were called to see a sick person and refused to go he had to return to the relatives of the deceased the fee which he had accepted or been offered. Professor Kroeber says: "The causing and prevention of disease and death were therefore even more largely the predominant functions of the person who had acquired personal supernatural power in California than elsewhere in America" (*University of California Publications in American Archaeology and Ethnology*, Vol. IV, No. 6, p. 332).

by others through their bravery or skill. These were the ones who acted as generals in war or as guides in fishing or hunting; and to them the others left the care of indicating a day and a place for such expeditions. As for the rest, they recognized no other superiority than that which each father has by nature in his own family.

The authority of the husbands was unlimited, especially among the Pericùes, among whom polygamy was generally practiced. They had as many wives as they wanted; and the greater their number was, instead of being expensive, the more useful they were in looking for fruit and edible seeds for their husbands and in preparing the meal; and all the other domestic occupations weighed on the poor women, while the men amused themselves in dances or other similar exercises suited to their taste.

The fortune of the women depended on the caprice of the husbands, who repudiated them when they liked; and the one who was once cast off did not easily find someone who would want to take her for a wife. Consequently, through fear of seeing themselves subjected to this misfortune, they were very solicitous about pleasing their husbands and were always competing with each other in bringing them the tastiest fruit in the greatest quantity. Who would believe now that, in a country where at that time the number of the women greatly exceeded that of the men the women should have diminished in such a way that today many men are obliged to remain single, or to go elsewhere to seek a wife, as we shall state later. The Pericùes in this regard as well as in others were the most demoralized and are still today the least docile and peaceful.

Among the other nations of that peninsula polygamy was rare, and almost all were contented with only one wife. Their habits were more honest; this should be attributed largely to their more laborious lives.

Chapter Twenty-Three

WEDDINGS

THE MANNER of celebrating weddings was not the same everywhere. Among the Guaicuras the one who wished to marry sent the young woman a tray of the kind used for cleaning and toasting edible seeds. If she accepted she answered the gift with a net, and the matrimonial contract consisted of the mutual sending and accepting of these gifts. Among other nations the contract was made after a great dance to which all the tribe of the man who wished to get married were invited. The widow among the Californians, according to the custom of the Hebrews, married the brother or nearest relative of the deceased husband. Adultery committed without the consent of the husband was considered a grave crime by all the Californians and an injury which never remained unavenged, even to causing bloody wars. Sometimes in the case of a challenge to a wrestling match or a race the wife of the vanquished was accustomed to become the prize of the victor.

The love which they professed for their little children was not so tender but that at times they destroyed those whom they could not support.* But as soon as the early missionaries learned the reason for such inhumanity they arranged, in the daily distribution of food which was made among the neophytes and catechumen, for a double ration to be given to the women who needed it on account of their children. Abortions, secured intentionally, were also very frequent, especially among women newly married, because they believed that the first child would usually be weak and sickly. They did this without any concealment, because custom or example succeeds many times in suffocating the sentiments of people, especially among barbarian nations.

* More barbarous still was the inhumanity which was practiced in Poland in the thirteenth century. Albert the Great was sent as a Nuncio to that kingdom to abolish the barbarous custom of killing children who were born imperfect, and helpless old people (Fleury's *Ecclesiastical History* [1260], Book 84).

In that peninsula the unreasonable practice which is common to many barbarous peoples of both continents, namely, putting the husband to bed instead of his wife when the latter gives birth, was never practiced.* What frequently happened was that the women, not keeping account of their time, gave birth to their children while they were in the woods gathering fruit; and then they returned immediately to their usual abode to rest.

As they had no cloth with which to cover their newly born children, they varnished the tender little bodies with ground charcoal and fresh urine to protect them somewhat from the inclemency of the air. And this was not the only use which they made of urine; the women used to wash their faces with it and do so even today, imitating in part the example of the ancient Celtiberians.†

A few years ago near 31° another still more outlandish manner of protecting children from the air was found. They make a hole in proportion in the sand and they heat it with a fire; afterward they take out the fire and, when the heat abates, they bury the child there up to the neck. But the missionaries have insisted on eradicating this custom, which is dangerous for many reasons.

The ways are many in which the women carry their children. The Pericùes carry them on their backs on an oval tray similar to that which they use for cleaning edible seeds but deeper, so that the baby can be in it with greater comfort. In the rest of California they are carried on the backs of the mothers in nets hanging from their foreheads, and in order that the delicate limbs of the babies may not be hurt with the fibers of the nets they place grass in them or some soft hare or rabbit skin. In some places they are accustomed to carry the net perpendicularly from a short javelin, which they support with one hand over the

---

* No care is administered to any woman struggling in childbirth; but her husband, instead, just as though having the badly weakened body of a confined woman, lies in bed for certain days. In the Spanish history of California it is asserted that such a custom is common in that peninsula; but this is a mistake.

† They bathe all the body with urine and furthermore even brush their teeth with it (Diodorus Siculus, Book 5).

shoulder;* and when they wish to nurse the child they drive the javelin in the ground, leaving the net and the baby hanging from it. When the infant is a little larger, the mother carries it in her arms; but when the child is two or three years old, she carries it on her back, holding it by the feet, the child grasping her hair. It is not unusual to see a mother take her child on her back with her household goods, having another one hanging in a net, and leading a third larger one by the hand.

When the children reached a certain age they pierced their ears and the cartilage of their noses in order to put rings in them. This was done at a great dance which all the kinsfolk attended, so that the weeping of the children might not be heard above the noise.

Chapter Twenty-Four

RELIGION AND DOGMA

IN REGARD to religion,[198] which is one of the essential elements in the history of nations, we can say little, because there was scarcely any among the Californians. As they had neither churches, altars, images, priests, nor sacrifices there is found among them, consequently, no trace of idolatry and no external worship of Divinity. They had, nevertheless, some idea of a Supreme Being, the Creator of the world; but it was as unintelligible and confused as among other barbaric peoples, and senseless, foolish, and childish. In regard to their dogmas and superstitions, we shall state here what some

---

* In the Spanish history of California, the custom of carrying their babies in a net hanging from a javelin is attributed to all the women of that peninsula; but it was not so, since this was used only in some places.

---

[198] For a scholarly treatise of the religion of the Indians of the state of California, see Professor Kroeber's study, *The Religion of the Indians of California* (*University of California Publications in American Archaeology and Ethnology*, Vol. IV, No. 6).

grave and learned missionaries have related after diligent investigations.

The Pericùes said that in Heaven there lived a great lord, called Niparaja in their language; that he had made heaven, earth, and sea, and could make all that he might desire. This Lord, they added, had a wife called Anajicojondi, and although she lacked a body he had nevertheless three children by her. One of these, called Quajaip, was born to Anajicojondi in the mountains of Acaragui. He was a real man, and he lived a long time among our ancestors to teach them. He was powerful, and he had many people under his command; whenever he wished, he entered under the earth and got men out of there; but these ingrates, scorning the many benefits which they had received from him, conspired against him and killed him, and, after killing him, they pierced his head with a wreath of thorns. Thus those barbarians explained their belief.

They added that there was a fearful war at another time in Heaven, which was more populated than the earth, because a great personage of the former country, called Tuparàn by some and Bac by others, conspired with all his men against the Supreme Lord, Niparaja; but the latter, being victor in the war, after having deprived Tuparàn of the *pitaje* and all the other delicious fruits which he had, threw him out of Heaven with all his followers and imprisoned him in a cave next to the sea; and that then Niparaja created the whales to guard him and to prevent Tuparàn from getting out of the cave. They said also that Niparaja did not want the war, and that, on the contrary, Tuparàn craved it; and for this reason, those who were shot by arrows and died did not go to Heaven but were confined in the cave of Tuparàn.*

From such a doctrine there grew up in the country of the Pericùes two factions, or sects, as opposed in their customs as in their opinions. The followers of Niparaja were generally

---

* This dogma of the Pericùes was diametrically opposed to that of the Mexicans, of which we have made some mention in Book VI of the *History of Mexico;* the latter said that all those who died in war went to the house of the sun.

grave, circumspect, and amenable to reason; and so it was not difficult for the missionaries to convince them of the evangelical truths which predominated over their very dogmas. Those who followed Tuparàn were liars, treacherous, restless, and obstinate in their mistakes. The latter said that the stars, which in their opinion were of metal, had been created by a deity called Purutabui, and the moon by another called Cucunumic.

The Guaicuras, who are divided into several branches of different dialects (as we have stated), said that toward the north there was a principal Spirit called Guamongo, who sent sickness to the earth and who, in ancient times, had sent another Spirit called Gujiaqui to visit the earth in his name; that in his trip over that peninsula he went sowing *pitaje* and preparing fishing places as far as a great stone, which is on the eastern coast near a port afterward called the port of Escondido, or Hidden Port, where he shut himself up for some time; that he was served by other inferior spirits, who took him good *pitaje* and fish daily to eat while he was occupied making from hair, which his devoted followers presented to him, the capes (which we shall mention later) for the medicine men or charlatans of California; that from there Gujiaqui left to continue his visit to the peninsula; and when this was concluded he returned to the northern country from which he had come. The Guaicura medicine men also affirmed that the sun, moon, and other heavenly bodies, apparently larger, were men and women, who fell into the sea every day at sunset and came swimming out of it the following day; also that the stars were firesides lighted in the sky by the Spiritual Visitor and kindled again after being put out in the water of the sea.*

The Cochimìes said that in the sky there lived a great Lord whose name in their tongue means "he who lives"; that the latter, without concourse with any woman, had a son who had two names, one of which means the "Swift One" and the other "Perfection" or the "End of Clay"; and besides these, there

* Because the Guaicuras lacked a suitable word in their language to signify Heaven, they made use of the word "Notù," which means above or in the high part.

was another personage called "He who makes Lords." To all these three they gave the title of Lord;[199] but when asked how many lords there were, they answered only one—he who created heaven, earth, the plants, animals, man, and woman. They say also that when "He who lives" had created certain invisible beings, these conspired against him and declared themselves the enemies of men also; and these spirits, whom they call "Liars" or "Deceivers," caught men when they died and put them under the ground so that they might not see the "Lord who lives."

Those Cochimíes, who live beyond 30°, made mention of a man who came from Heaven in ancient times to benefit men. And for this reason, they call him *Tamà ambei ucambi tevivichi*, that is, "the Man come from Heaven." But they were unable to say in what manner he had benefited men or that they worshiped him in any way. It is true that they celebrate a holiday named after "the Man come from Heaven"; but this day, instead of witnessing any religious act, is confined entirely to enjoying the pleasures of eating and dancing.

Some days before the holiday the women are charged strictly to seek everywhere for things that serve as tidbits, in order to regale, as they said, that Deity who was to come to visit them; all these provisions were kept in a bower constructed for this purpose. When the day designated for the feast arrived, they selected a youth to represent the person of that deity and they dressed him secretly with skins, after having painted him with several colors so that he would not be recognized. The youth hid himself on some hill near the bower, which the men entered

---

[199] This implies that the Indian had the conception of the Trinity. Father Baegert differs from Clavigero on the religion of these Indians. He says: "I made diligent inquiries, among those with whom I lived, to ascertain whether they had any conception of God, a future life, and their own souls, but I could never discover the slightest trace of such a knowledge." He states further, evidently to refute Clavigero's view: "I am not unacquainted with the statement of a certain author, according to which one California tribe at least was found to possess some knowledge of the incarnation of the Son of God and the Holy Trinity; but this is certainly an error, considering that such knowledge could have only been imparted by preachers of the Gospel" (*Report of the Smithsonian Institution*, 1864, pp. 390–91).

to wait for him; the women and children remained at a distance, although in sight of the bower and the hill. The disguised youth, when it was at length time to let himself be seen, appeared on the summit of the hill, and from there descended, running very swiftly to the bower, in which he was received by all with much rejoicing. There they ate gleefully at the expense of the poor women, who, because they did not know the secret, remained firmly persuaded that what their lying husbands pretended was true. When the meal was finished, the false deity returned by the same road and disappeared.

The Cochimìes on the anniversary of their dead practiced a similar deceit with the same purpose. They pretended that their dead who resided in the northern countries came yearly to make them a visit. When the men had agreed on the day of this visit, they compelled the women, even with threats of punishment, to look for a great quantity of food in the woods and in the country, with which to regale their dead. On the day designated for the anniversary, the men, having gathered in a bower, ate all those provisions, while the women and children who were distant from that place wept abundantly over the deaths of their relatives for whose dinner they had so wearied themselves. The men were so careful to keep that mystery hidden from the women that a youth was killed immediately by his father himself for having revealed it to his mother.

The finding of so many signs (although distorted) of Christian truths among the dogmas of the barbarian Californians cannot fail to cause wonderment to those who read these stories. It could be suspected that they had been taught previously by some Christians who had arrived there, because in the fifty years which preceded the entry of the Jesuits in California[200] many ships from Mexico and some from other countries landed there; but no one ever remained there long enough to learn any of those very difficult languages. And the Californians themselves, when questioned about the origin of their doctrine, steadily as-

---

[200] Clavigero fails to note that more than a century before this Indians had accepted Christianity in parts of Mexico and that during this period it was possible for such Indians to make their way into the peninsula.

serted that they had received it from their ancestors. Besides, if some Christian had taught them the mysteries of the Trinity and the Incarnation, surely he would not have failed to instruct them in the necessity of baptism; but not a trace or any information about this was found in all the peninsula. As a historian, I limit myself to relating facts that are sure, leaving to others the liberty of making conjectures.

Chapter Twenty-Five

GUAMAS, OR CHARLATANS, AND THEIR POWER

THE PRINCIPAL propagators of those false doctrines were certain charlatans who, according to their sects, had the name of Niparaja or Tuparàn among the Pericùes, among the Guaicuras that of Dicuinocho; and among the Cochimìes that of Guama, which we shall call them all. These acted as instructors, teaching their dogmas to the children; as physicians, applying remedies to the sick; and as soothsayers, pretending that they were inspired by Heaven and that they were confidants of the spirits. Some have honored them with the name of priests, others have defamed them by calling them witches; but certainly they were neither the one nor the other. They were not priests because there is no priesthood where there is no worship of divinity nor any practice of religion; they were not witches because by virtue of the information given by the ablest missionaries it is known that they had no communication with the Devil, although they pretended to have it for the sake of their interest. They were nevertheless great impostors and very wicked men, and they presented a very extensive resistance to the introduction of the Gospel.

These *guamas*, or charlatans, were selected from those children who seemed to them most astute and fit for this office. After taking them to the most secret places in the woods they trained them in their mysteries, and especially to make on certain little boards some strange figures which they pretended were copies of those which (as they said) the visiting Spirit had left them on departing. These little boards were their books, in which they professed to read the nature of illnesses, the remedies suitable for them, the future changes of the atmosphere, and even the destiny of men. They were so careful about the secret of such instructions, and they commended it so earnestly to their pupils that the missionaries could not find out about it until some years had passed.

Every time that any Californian fell sick, the *guama* was called immediately. In order to cure him, he made use of plasters of herbs or unctions of some juice; and if the patient had a daughter or a sister he made an incision in the little finger of either and obliged her to let the drops of her blood fall on the body of the patient. But the remedy which they considered most efficient was the fumes of tobacco made with a bellows, or reed pipe, and applied to the sick member.

They also used the reed pipe for extracting the evil from the body with their breath (as they pretended); and if they did not succeed in this manner they tried to extract it by the force of the hands, by placing their fingers in the mouth of the sick person. This remedy of the reed was applied also at the request of the patient himself and by all his relatives who were called there by the *guama*. When the relatives saw that the patient was beyond hope, they placed themselves, drawn up in a line, near him and broke out in great weeping and outcries; and if they saw him fall asleep they struck him on the head to awaken him and restore him to life.

If the patient, after being aided in this way by the *guama* and his relatives, finally ended by dying, then the weeping was greater and the cries louder, especially among the Guaicura women, who were accustomed to strike their heads furiously. It was necessary for the missionaries to exercise particular vigilance in order to prevent these barbarous demonstrations of grief, which the Indian women did not give up even after they were baptized.

As soon as the sick person died they proceeded quickly without any preparation or ceremony for the funeral, which was held indifferently, accordingly as it was most convenient for them, either by burying[201] the corpse or by burning it. But to do either they did not always wait to be assured of his death.

A barbarian to whom such a misfortune came was liberated from death by the famous Father Salvatierra. On hearing the noise that those gentiles were making at a funeral and on approaching it, he observed some signs of life in the supposed corpse; he took him out of the fire in which he was already beginning to burn and succeeded in restoring him and curing him;[202] and Father Salvatierra reproached those barbarians for their inhumanity. They were accustomed to honor the memory of some of the deceased by placing their figures, crudely made of branches, on the end of long javelins near which a *guama* took his place to preach their praises.

The *guamas* made use of promises and threats to make themselves respected and feared by those savage tribes. They promised many riches and great happiness to those who brought them contributions of the best fruit and the choicest of the game and fish; on the other hand, they threatened with sickness and other misfortunes those who omitted that homage or who did not know how to please them.

At those public gatherings which most of the tribes of a nation attended, the *guamas* appeared in ceremonial dress. This consisted of long capes which covered them from head to foot and which were made entirely of hair that was contributed by the boys (their disciples) and by their patients; the "doctors" had to be paid with hair, whether the sick recovered or died. Besides the capes they wore on their heads crests of sparrowhawk feathers, and in their hands they carried fans of the same. The *guamas* of the Pericùes were accustomed to wear crowns made of deer tails instead of crests, and the Cochimìes wore, besides, two strings of deer hoofs at their waists.

---

[201] It seems to have been a universal custom, not only among these Indians but among many tribes of other parts of North America, never to mention the name of a dead relative after the funeral.

[202] Father Baegert records that a person whom he knew "restored a girl to life who was already bound up in a deer skin, according to their custom, and ready for burial, by administering to her a good dose of chocolate. She lived many years afterward" (*Report of the Smithsonian Institution*, 1864, p. 387).

It fell to their lot to start the celebration by smoking tobacco in a stone pipe, which was called *chacuaco* by the Spaniards of those countries. As soon as the *guama* had his head somewhat disturbed with the smoke, he began, after the manner of a man inspired by Heaven, to preach their dogmas, with grimaces, extravagant gestures, and audacious actions. He passed from the exposition of their doctrine to a panegyric of his partisans (those who were more liberal toward him), and directed the invectives against those who had not been diligent in bringing him the best fruit. And not content with censuring these for their defects, he imposed penances on them, the most common of which was that of fasting, and threatened them with great misfortunes if they did not do them.

Not only private individuals but even entire tribes were often subjected to these penalties. Likewise in the punishment of similar sins they were obliged frequently to open some new road in the mountains so that the spiritual visitor could descend with more ease and to erect on it at certain distances some heaps of stones on which he might rest. Perhaps the *guama* commanded someone to hurl himself from the cliff of a mountain; and he was obeyed without fail, either willingly or by force. Such was the authority of these impostors over those barbarians.

Among their superstitious instructions they taught that lions should not be killed, because the dead lion would bring death to the one who killed it; that he who killed a deer ought not to taste its flesh, because if he tasted it, he would not be able to kill another from then on; that young people who did not yet have children should eat hare meat if they wished to have them; that the mother-in-law should not look at the daughter-in-law, because the former would have trouble with her eyes for no other reason. Such were the instructions of those impostors, and such was the condition, as we have explained it, of that miserable peninsula before the sublime doctrine and the holy religion of Jesus Christ were preached in it.

BOOK II

ATTEMPTS OF THE CONQUEROR CORTÉS AND MANY OTHERS TO DISCOVER CALIFORNIA. THE INSISTENCE OF THE CATHOLIC MONARCHS ON THE ESTABLISHMENT OF SOME COLONIES THERE. THE ENTRY OF THE JESUITS TO THAT PENINSULA. THE DIFFICULTIES, NEEDS, AND OPPOSITION ENDURED BY THE MISSIONARIES. THE ESTABLISHMENT OF SIX MISSIONS UP TO 1711. THE STRICT ORDERS OF KING PHILIP THE FIFTH IN FAVOR OF THE MISSIONS. EXPEDITIONS, UNDERTAKINGS, AND THE DEATH OF FATHER KINO

As THE Californians had remained for so many centuries shut up in their wretched peninsula, deprived of all outside communication and buried in the most fearful barbarism, so they had no information of the other peoples of the earth. Nor did the latter know about them until the sixteenth century, during which that execrable thirst of gold which carried Europeans to other countries of the New World urged them to California also.

Chapter One

THE ATTEMPTS OF THE CONQUEROR CORTÉS TO DISCOVER CALIFORNIA

FERNANDO CORTÉS, that very enterprising and intrepid conqueror, who became neither weary with fatigue nor disheartened by difficulties, dangers, or misfortunes and who was not content with the conquests which he had made (although great and beyond his hopes), after having subjugated the vast empire of Mexico and after having taken possession of the pleasant and prosperous kingdom of Michoacán,[1] gave his attention to the discovery of other countries, hoping to find and conquer another Mexico in order to extend the dominions of his sovereign still farther and to augment his own glory and grandeur.*

With this purpose, after other useless and expensive attempts made on the Pacific Sea, in 1534[2] he built and equipped two ships in Tehuantepec[3] (a port of that sea), and sent them

---

*Cortés, in a letter of October 15, 1542, to the Emperor Charles V, informs him that he hopes to discover very rich and large countries, greater yet than all the numerous ones known to the Spaniards up to that time.

---

[1] One of the present states on the western coast of Mexico, having an area of 26,261 square miles.

[2] Two years before, Cortés had sent out two vessels from Acapulco to explore the northern coast of Mexico. The ships were commanded by Diego Hurtado de Mendoza. One was wrecked in the Bay of Banderas, and most of the sailors were murdered by the Indians. The other vessel was lost, probably on the coast of Sinaloa (Hubert Howe Bancroft, *History of the North Mexican States and Texas*, Vol. I, pp. 40–45).

[3] An Indian word meaning "mountain of the man eaters," so named because in the early days the natives claimed that the surrounding mountains contained so many man-eating animals. It is located on a river by this name,

out under the command of Diego Becerra de Mendoza,[4] a relative of his, and Hernando de Grijalva.[5] Both weighed anchor together; but after the first night they were separated, never to see each other again.

After Grijalva had sailed for some months, he returned to the port of Acapulco, without other success than the discovery of a deserted island.[6] Becerra was more unfortunate, because the pilot of the ship, who was a Biscayan named Ordoño Jiménez, and could not tolerate his harshness and excessive haughtiness, killed him while he was asleep, wounded the others who might have avenged him, and, aided by his partisans, took possession of the ship. After he had put ashore on the coast of New Spain the two Franciscans[7] along with the wounded men, whom he permitted to live because of the influence of these same Franciscans, he fled in order to escape the punishment due him; and after going toward the northwest he landed at a port of California which was called the bay of La Cruz.

He was the first European who set foot on that peninsula.[8] But he paid for his evil deeds there; he was attacked by the barbarians and lost his life, together with some twenty other Spaniards. Those who escaped in the ship weighed anchor and after crossing the Gulf reached Chiametla,[9] a port of Nueva Vizcaya, bringing information, though false, that the country

---

some twenty miles from Salina Cruz, and has a population of ten thousand, largely composed of Indians who are descendants of the Aztecs.

[4] One of the members of the Becerras of Badajoz or Mérida family. He was murdered shortly after starting, while asleep (Bancroft, *History of the North Mexican States and Texas*, Vol. I, p. 46).

[5] He returned safely to Acapulco, and the next year was in command of another expedition (*ibid.*, p. 49).

[6] Revilla Gigedo Islands, situated some three hundred miles south of the peninsula of Lower California.

[7] One was P. Martín de Jesús (Bancroft, *History of the North Mexican States and Texas*, Vol. I, p. 46).

[8] Some doubt exists whether Jiménez discovered the peninsula in 1734 or in 1735. His survivors carried to Mexico City reports of pearl beds, and new expeditions were soon sent out to find them.

[9] A province just south of the present city of Mazatlán. A small river as well as a town near there is still known by that name.

which they had discovered was good and well populated. The ship was seized by the wicked Nuño de Guzmán,[10] who then ruled as conqueror of those countries and who was the declared enemy of the conquerors of Mexico and especially of Cortés himself.

Cortés, in spite of the unfortunate outcome of that and other expeditions, made ready three other ships in Tehuantepec and from there he sent them to Chiametla, for which place he himself left, as he did not wish to entrust that enterprise to another. And he took with him many soldiers for the conquest of the new countries, some families for settling them, and several priests and friars to establish Christianity there. After he had ordered there the ship, which had been pillaged previously by his rival Guzmán, he embarked with the greater part of his people; and after crossing the Gulf of California, which was then beginning to be called the Sea of Cortés, he reached on May 1, 1536,[11] that same port of California in which Jiménez was killed with the other Spaniards.

As soon as he landed there he sent three[12] ships to bring that part of his people and the provisions which he had left in Chiametla. But when they were returning loaded they were scattered by two furious storms; and only one could reach the port of La Cruz, though without provisions. For this reason Cortés embarked anew to go in search of the other ships; and after a course of one hundred and fifty miles he found them standing high and dry. He had them taken out of there; and after he had them repaired he returned with them to the port of La Cruz. Meanwhile, some people had already died of

---

[10] As a conqueror of the Indians, Guzmán ranks next to Cortés. Following the marked success of Cortés in subduing the natives, Guzmán left Mexico City in 1529 with an army of several hundred Spaniards and ten thousand Indians to conquer the northwestern part of Mexico. Within three years he had crossed Mexico and brought under his complete control the provinces of Jalisco and Sinaloa. He founded Culiacán (1531), and became the ruler of Nueva Galicia. He ruthlessly opposed all those who dared to cross his path, devastating many of the Indian villages that he came upon. It is said of him that in order to promote his plan he would kill a Spaniard as soon as an Indian. [11] Cortés landed May 3, 1535.

[12] It seems that Cortés sent back only two ships for supplies and for more settlers.

hunger, and after the provisions arrived others died from gorging themselves, in spite of the precautions taken by that prudent general.

Saddened by such great misfortunes, Cortés set sail again to explore other countries of the peninsula, leaving the greater part of his people in that ominous port under the command of Captain Francisco de Ulloa.[13] At that time he discovered near the cape of San Lucas a port which he called California, a name[14] which was extended afterward to all the peninsula.

At this time rumors had been spread in Mexico of the death of Cortés. On account of this a great rebellion of the Mexicans was feared. Moreover, Pizarro,[15] the conqueror of Perú, in need of soldiers and weapons, asked him for help. Cortés was recalled by the viceroy,[16] by the *audiencia*[17] of Mexico, and by

---

[13] Later Ulloa made a voyage up the Gulf of California. He was the first white man to describe the coastline of both sides of the gulf. His idea that California was not an island was still not accepted by all navigators a century later.

[14] It is now maintained by the best authorities that Cortés never applied the name "California" to the peninsula (Charles Edward Chapman, *A History of California: The Spanish Period*, chapter vi).

[15] He sailed from Panama in 1531 to conquer the Indians who lived along the northwestern coast of South America. He quickly overran their country and ruthlessly subdued them as far south as Lake Titicaca. Returning to Spain he was held in prison for twenty years because of his cruelty and because he had murdered Diego de Almagro, his old friend and close partner in the conquest of the Incas. For a brief but excellent account of Pizarro, see Irving Berdine Richman, *The Spanish Conquerors*, chapter vi.

[16] Antonio de Mendoza, the first viceroy of Mexico (1535–1550). The viceroy was the king's representative in the government of the Spanish colonies, being governor, military commander, and judge over all matters relating to the general welfare of the colony. He took special care of the Missions. A complete list of the viceroys in Mexico from 1535 to 1821, when Mexico became an independent state, is given in Herbert Ingram Priestley, *The Mexican Nation*, pp. 505–6.

[17] Meaning "hearing" or "audience." In the early days the king of Spain invited persons having complaints to present their cases personally before him. He gave them an audience to listen to their pleas, and when he was unable to do this he appointed certain officials to hear them. Later these men constituted a court and took the name of *audiencia*. It exercised wide jurisdiction over the general affairs of the people, and with the approval of the king it was sovereign in matters relating to the progress and development of the colonial possessions. It administered justice, enforced royal decrees, looked after finan-

his wife (the Marquesa del Valle) with very urgent letters. Cortés was not annoyed by having this decorous pretext for abandoning, without lack of honor, an enterprise in which he had spent fruitlessly two hundred thousand ducats.[18] He returned, therefore, to Acapulco at the beginning of 1537[19] to go to Mexico; and in a short time he was followed by Captain Ulloa together with all the people who had remained in California, because he could absolutely not have lived there for lack of provisions.

Cortés, not disheartened by so many misfortunes nor embarrassed by those many grave responsibilities which he then had in Mexico, again sent three[20] ships in May[21] of that same year under the command of Ulloa. Captain Ulloa spent an entire year on that voyage; he observed all the coast of the Gulf of California, and he coasted along both sides of that peninsula until he was compelled through lack of provisions to return to New Spain.[22] This voyage made known clearly that California was a true peninsula, and it was thus represented on the geographical maps of that century,* although the geogra-

---

* Among other maps which I have seen, there is one drawn in 1541 by the pilot, Domingo del Castillo, in which California is represented as joined to the continent of America and the mouths of the Red River are shown well located, although under a different name. I have a copy of this map, which was printed in Mexico in 1770.

---

cial affairs, and kept the home government informed about conditions in the colonies.

[18] An old Spanish coin of varying value. It was first coined in Venice in 1284.

[19] Cortés probably left the peninsula in 1536. Bancroft says (*History of the North Mexican States and Texas*, Vol. I, p. 52) Ulloa was left there with thirty Spaniards, twelve mules, and provisions for ten months. It is thought that Cortés sent a ship there in 1536 to get these people and return them to Mexico.

[20] The "Agueda," the "Trinidad," and the "Santo Tomás"; the largest was of only 135 tons burden.

[21] Most accounts give July 1539 as the date of his sailing.

[22] Coming south along the peninsula, Ulloa rounded Cape San Lucas and followed up the Pacific side of the peninsula somewhere beyond Magdalena Bay. He seems never to have returned to Mexico. He was probably shipwrecked or killed by the Indians, although some think he returned to Acapulco in May 1540.

phers were led in later times (I do not know why) into the mistake of making it an island.

Cortés no longer made new attempts to colonize, because serious trouble arose between him and the viceroy, who wished to restrain his use of authority and the favors granted him by the sovereign as a reward for his very eminent services; and he had to return to Spain, where, after several years of annoyances, fruitless claims, and undeserved neglect, he left this life in 1547.

Chapter Two

THE ATTEMPTS OF THE VICEROY, INCITED BY CERTAIN ACCOUNTS

WHILE Ulloa was carrying on those discoveries of California by the order of Cortés, there appeared in Mexico the famous Alvaro Núñez Cabeza de Vaca,[23] with his three companions,[24] who, after having been shipwrecked in 1527[25] off the coast of Florida and after an exceptionally strange pilgrimage of ten years[26] among barbarous and unknown nations, reached Culiacán and from there Mexico [City] in 1537.[27] Among the many curious things which they related about those countries through which they had passed, Vaca asserted that there was a great abundance of pearls in the Gulf of California.[28]

[23] He was a member of the Narváez expedition that was shipwrecked on the shores of Florida in 1528.

[24] Andrez Sorantes, Alonso del Castillo Maldonado, and a Negro named Estevanico who "played a conspicuous part in later history in America" (Herbert Eugene Bolton, *The Spanish Borderlands*, p. 45).

[25] In 1528.   [26] About eight years.

[27] Vaca reached Mexico City in July 1536.

[28] In Texas Vaca and his companions were captured by the Indians, but they managed to escape, passing through New Mexico and Arizona and entering Mexico, probably near the present city of Douglas, Arizona. They passed south near the Gulf of California, and, on reaching Culiacán, turned eastward and arrived in Mexico City. They were the first white men to cross

At the same time a trustworthy friar[29] (or religious) who had made a long trip through the northern countries related (rather because of what had been told him than because of what he had seen), when he returned to Mexico, that there were very rich kingdoms and very large cities in those countries.

The viceroy, induced by both stories and desirous of surpassing Cortés in the glory of his conquests, to whom the supervision of the Pacific Sea belonged according to the agreement made with the Catholic Monarch, sent two armies in 1538. One went by land under the command of Francisco Velázquez Coronado,[30] the governor of Nueva Galicia, and another by sea, entrusted to Francisco de Alarcón,[31] a close friend of his, with the order to meet at some port of the Pacific Sea at 36°. But neither did the armies ever meet, nor did they do anything worthy of note. Alarcón had a strange conference with the barbarians, as can be seen from the story that he himself wrote

the southwestern part of the United States. Vaca brought to the viceroy the first direct word about the "northern mystery," as the country north of Mexico was then called.

[29] Marcos de Niza, who had been with Pizarro in Peru. Crossing Mexico westward almost to the coast, Fray Marcos went north not far from the coast, accompanied by a few Indians and by the Negro who had been with Vaca. Fray Marcos probably went no farther north than just beyond the boundary of Arizona; and on returning to Mexico City he told more marvelous stories about the strange country than had Vaca. Either the vivid imagination of the good friar, a mirage, or his full faith in the legends of the Indians caused him to express his belief in the existence of the wealthy seven cities of Cíbola. Accepting the credence of Fray Marcos, the viceroy soon sent out other expeditions to explore the distant north.

[30] He was not made governor until 1539. The next year he collected his army in February at Compostela, a settlement near the Pacific Coast and then the capital of Nueva Galicia. From here he marched north to conquer the country. He went nearly to the Colorado River, and then turned eastward, passing into Texas and into southwestern Kansas, where his men saw some "humped-backed cows" (buffaloes). While going north, one of his lieutenants, López de Cárdenas, came upon a great canyon, his descriptions of which have led historians to believe that he was the first white man to see the Grand Canyon of the Colorado River. For an interesting account of this expedition see Bolton, *The Spanish Borderlands*, chapter iv.

[31] He went up the Colorado River probably as far as the mouth of the Gila River. At the same time Melchor Díaz crossed the Colorado and continued southwest to the peninsula of Lower California. It is probable that he was the first white man to enter overland what is now the state of California.

and which Ramusio[32] published afterwards. With more than a thousand picked men Coronado went through Culiacán, Sinaloa, and Sonora to the countries of Cíbola and Tiguex, and some of the division penetrated into the interior as far as Quivira, a town situated, as they said, at 40°. But having seen neither those great cities nor the wealth that they had heard of, they were compelled by the intolerable hardships and troubles of that very long trip to return to Mexico without having derived any benefit.[33]

In the meantime, Pedro de Alvarado,[34] the very wealthy governor of Guatemala, who was first the friend and companion of Cortés in the conquest of Mexico and afterward the rival of his glory, also wishing to make discoveries in that sea, had equipped a fleet composed of twelve vessels and other smaller boats at great expense; and he had come with it to the Port of Purificación[35] in Nueva Galicia. Then it occurred to the viceroy to attract him to his party (as he wished), the two promising to defend each other mutually. But with the unfortunate death of that governor, which happened in 1541, the fleet was dispersed, and all that great enterprise was reduced to nothing.

The viceroy was not discouraged by this; and he sent out two of those ships in 1542 under the command of Juan Rodrí-

---

[32] A noted Italian scholar and translator, born in Italy in 1485. He published three volumes (1550–1559), entitled *Raccolta di Navigazioni*, which were widely read by all navigators seeking information about the New World.

[33] Coronado marked out a new path to this "land of mystery," and brought back much additional information about the country and its people.

[34] One of the officers in the army of Cortés. Alvarado went with Grijalva (1518) to explore and conquer Yucatán, and his success there brought him his appointment as governor of Guatemala in 1524. Ten years later he was on the coast of Ecuador, South America, with several ships. He marched inland, but came in conflict with Pizarro's interests. On returning to Mexico Alvarado made an agreement with Cortés in 1540 to work jointly in the further conquest of Mexico. The viceroy (Mendoza) was given one-half interest in a fleet, and Alvarado was to receive one-fifth of all the profits made in the expeditions. He was killed in Guadalajara in the Mixton War in an Indian encounter in 1541 (*Catholic Encyclopaedia*, Vol. I, p. 372).

[35] On the coast of Jalisco, just north of the city of Manzanillo. The Purificación River flows into this port.

guez Cabrillo,[36] an honorable Portuguese, brave and very skillful in the art of navigation, and ordered him to explore the western coast of California and then to continue his voyage until he found the end of the continent of America in that direction. Cabrillo, having sailed from the port of Navidad[37] in Nueva Galicia, went to that of Magdalena in California. Then, after having explored various ports and capes, he saw at 40° some mountains covered with snow; and farther on he discovered a cape which he named Mendocino in honor of the viceroy, Antonio de Mendoza. In January of 1543 he found Cape Fortuna, and, finally, in March he went up as far as 44° latitude, where all experienced great cold. This was the end of that voyage; since the ships were not in a condition to continue it and provisions were beginning to fail them, they were compelled to return to the port of Navidad from where they had set out ten months before.

Chapter Three

EXPEDITIONS ORDERED BY THE KINGS, PHILIP THE SECOND AND PHILIP THE THIRD

No ATTEMPTS were made to explore California in the fifty years following. During this interval, Francis Drake,[38] the celebrated English privateer, landed

---

[36] He is the discoverer of what is now the state of California. On September 28, 1542, he sailed into a spacious bay which he named San Miguel (now San Diego Bay). Cabrillo went north perhaps no farther than Drake's Bay; and on account of the severe storms he returned south and stopped on the Santa Barbara Islands for the winter. Here he died in January 1543. His chief pilot, Bartholomé Ferrelo, then sailed north to the Oregon coast. His crew faced starvation, and he returned to Mexico, arriving at Navidad in April of the same year. Cabrillo rests in an unknown grave. Point Loma, California, was set aside a few years ago by the federal government as a national monument to his memory.

[37] About twenty miles from the harbor of Manzanillo, and one of the most important seaports today of the west coast of Mexico. Into it came many of the Manila galleons loaded with their treasures from the Philippine Islands.

[38] He made no landing on the peninsula. Drake was one of the many famous "sea dogs" that preyed upon the Spanish trade. When only twenty-

on the northern part of the peninsula and gave it the name of New Albion, which it retained for some time on the geographical maps. The hostile acts committed by this bold privateer on the slightly populated and entirely defenseless coasts of the Pacific Sea caused King Philip II[39] to give an order to the count of Monterey, the viceroy[40] of Mexico, to have the ports of California fortified and settled.

Sebastián Vizcaíno,[41] a man of great merit, who united naval skill, bravery, and prudence to affability of disposition, was named by the king for this expedition. Accompanied by four Franciscan friars[42] and a great number of soldiers, Vizcaíno left Acapulco in 1596, taking three ships well provided with everything necessary.[43] After having gone up to some places

---

seven years old, he achieved honors following a plundering expedition which he made in 1572 upon the Spanish colonies in the New World. In 1577 he left England with five small ships to go to the "South Sea" and "about the whole Globe of the Earth." He crossed the Atlantic Ocean, and after rounding Cape Horn he had one ship left. With the "Pelican," which he renamed "Golden Hind," as a good omen, he sailed up the coast of South America and Mexico, capturing ships and plundering towns until his small ship of a hundred tons burden was loaded with gold, silver, and jewels, valued at several million dollars. Authorities differ as to how far north he sailed. He probably went no farther than the coast of northern Oregon. On his return he landed on the coast of California at a place which was later called Drake's Bay. Here he remained a month, repairing his ship and exploring the land. He erected a cross, preached a sermon (the first Protestant one on the Pacific Coast), and took possession of the country in the name of England (William Wood, *Elizabethan Sea-Dogs*, chapters vi-xi.

[39] Born in 1527, the son of Charles V. Philip became ruler of Spain in 1556, and died in 1598. He left Spain almost bankrupt and her people facing misery and poverty.

[40] Gaspar de Zúñiga y Acevedo acted as (the ninth) viceroy from 1595 to 1603. He sent out Vizcaíno.

[41] Vizcaíno was a man well fitted to undertake such a task, having served the king upon the seas for most of his life. He had made voyages to the Philippine Islands, one of which brought him a profit of more than two thousand ducats (Chapman, *A History of California: The Spanish Period*, p. 124).

[42] Fathers Francisco de Balda, Diego Perdomo, Bernardino Zamudio, and Nicolás de Saravia (Bancroft, *History of the North Mexican States and Texas*, Vol. I, p. 148). Brother Nicolás López accompanied them.

[43] He arrived at Acapulco from Mexico City with 126 men. Father Ascención, who kept a diary of the expedition, states that Vizcaíno set sail with some 200 men, of whom 150 were "select and experienced soldiers"

on the inner coast of California and after having abandoned them because of the sterility of the soil, they finally anchored in a port at 23° 30½', or a little more,[44] to which they gave the name of La Paz,[45] because they were received so peaceably there by the Indians. After they had landed there,[46] they built some cabins for their dwellings, and among them a larger one to be used as a church, in which they began at once to celebrate holy mass, which the barbarians, filled with astonishment, attended sometimes.

The Indians approached the Spaniards fearlessly and brought them fish, fruit, and even some pearls. The friars kept trying to interest them in Christianity with good examples, with demonstrations of kindness, and by caressing their little ones and presenting them with glass beads and other similar things which the barbarians greatly esteemed. But they could not learn the language of the country in the mere two months that they were there. So they did not derive the benefit that might be expected from those barbarians who were so well disposed to them and so docile.

Meanwhile, the general of that Armada, wishing to become acquainted with all that coast which extends from the port of La Paz toward the northwest, had sent one of his ships to explore it, ordering those who went in it not to land except in those places where they saw the Indians inclined to receive them in a friendly fashion. So they did, sailing in view of the coast for about three hundred miles. When fifty of the best men of the fleet landed in the last place that they examined, nineteen of them perished; part of them were killed by the Indians, and part of them were drowned when they wanted to take the rowboat to return to the ship, which was more than a mile distant from the shore. Then they returned to the port of La Paz, where they informed the general how barren all that coast was which they had explored. The general, seeing

(Herbert Eugene Bolton, *Spanish Explorations of the Southwest, 1542–1706*, pp. 53, 106).

[44] Just north of 24°, the same place where Jiménez landed, and where Cortés had stopped and had named Santa Cruz.

[45] Meaning peace.   [46] In 1597.

that they could no longer exist there for lack[47] of provisions, decided, with the advice of his officers, to abandon the enterprise of the settlement and to return to Mexico with all his people in order to give an account to the viceroy of the outcome of the voyage. This was done, in fact, at the end of that same year.

In 1599 the same viceroy[48] received an urgent order from King Philip III[49] to equip a new fleet at the expense of the royal treasury, regardless of cost, and to send it, under the command of the same person, not now to the eastern coast of California (as had been done before) but to the western coast. When the viceroy had carried out diligently all the commands of the court, Vizcaíno set sail from Acapulco on May 5, 1602, with two large ships, a frigate, and a long boat in order to be able to approach land more easily and explore it better. He took with him three Barefoot Carmelites,[50] one[51] of whom wrote a very long and minute log of all that voyage. They went as far as Cape Blanco (San Sebastián), situated at 43° latitude.[52] As they navigated against the northwestern wind which rules those seas, they kept stopping to sound the ports and to explore the coast; they spent nine months on that voyage, which they probably would have concluded in a single month with a favorable wind and without stopping to make observations. The general would have liked to continue his voyage until he discovered the end of that land in the Strait of Anián;[53] but it was not possible for him to do so because he

---

[47] Some say that he left because of Indian troubles (Herbert Eugene Bolton, *The Spanish Borderlands*, p. 114).

[48] See note 40, above.

[49] Philip III ruled from 1598 to 1621.

[50] Fathers Andrés Asumpción, Antonio Ascención, and Tomas Aquino. Father Ascención had formerly been a pilot. Vizcaíno had his son with him. See Bolton, *Spanish Explorations in the Southwest, 1542–1706*, p. 52.

[51] Father Antonio Ascención. For his diary, see Bolton, *ibid*, pp. 104–34.

[52] Vizcaíno was ordered by the king to stop at 41°, but he was caught in a severe storm which drove him farther north (George Davidson's *Early Voyages*, pp. 231–33). He reached Cape Mendocino on January 12, 1603.

[53] A mythical body of water that was supposed to connect the Atlantic and Pacific Oceans. The Indians in every section of western North America said

had scarcely anyone to man the rudder and the sails;[54] almost all were seriously ill with scurvy, and some had already died. And on the ships only laments and groans, caused by the severe pain which they suffered, and prayers to Heaven were heard.

Compelled therefore by necessity to turn back, they passed by the western coast of the peninsula in a few days; and after crossing the entrance of the Gulf of California they entered a port of the islands of Mazatlán,[55] situated at 22½°, near the province of Chiametla,[56] from where the general sent a courier to Mexico [City] to give the viceroy an account of the expedition and to ask for orders about what he should do. After several sick men from the fleet had landed on those two islands, they found health accidentally in a fruit called *xocohuiztli** by the Mexicans. Of all those who ate it none died. As soon as they had eaten it once or twice, it took away the inflammation of their gums by purifying the bad blood and within a very few days they were perfectly well; so that when they had left there by the command of the viceroy to return to the port of

---

* In Michoacán they call this fruit *tumbirichi*. The Spaniards of Mexico, accommodating the Mexican name to the Spanish language, call it *xocuistle*; in Guatemala, and in other countries they call it *piñuela*, or little pineapple, because the plant which produces it has leaves similar to those of the pineapple. Its stalk is about three feet tall; on it the fruit is borne, forming a raceme like small bananas. It also greatly resembles the smallest species of the banana in size and shape, though not in color. It is one and one-half to two inches in size, and has white pulp and a white rind with a tint of red. The taste is bittersweet but not disagreeable.

---

that such a "river" existed. Early navigators located it on their maps. Cabrillo, Vizcaíno, Drake, Hudson, Baffin, Davis, and others searched in vain for it. Even as late as 1742 the noted French explorer La Verendrye spent months going about the country west of the Lake of the Woods and south into the Dakotas looking for this river.

[54] Father Ascención said that when Vizcaíno landed on the northwest coast they would have sailed through the continent to the Atlantic Ocean if there had been fourteen able sailors.

[55] Discovered by Vizcaíno in 1596, and named by him San Juan de Mazatlán (*California Historical Society Quarterly*, Vol. VII, p. 380).

[56] Extending from Compostela to Culiacán.

Acapulco they arrived in good health. On the other hand, forty-eight who did not have the good fortune to eat that fruit died. No other advantage was derived from that uncomfortable and very expensive voyage of eleven months than having discovered a very efficient antiscorbutic and having acquired clearer knowledge of the western coast of California.[57]

General Vizcaíno, being persuaded how useful the acquisition of that peninsula would be to the crown, proposed to the viceroy that he should make a new attempt at his expense. The advantages which were expected consisted not only of pearl fishing (the abundance of which there was no doubt) and of precious metals, which they imagined would be discovered in those mountains, but it would also prevent pirates[58] of other nations of Europe from taking refuge in the ports of the peninsula, as they were accustomed to do in order to leave from there and commit hostilities on the coasts and on the ships of the Spaniards; and also there would be an advantage of finding a

---

[57] Clavigero fails to mention that Vizcaíno discovered a great harbor while sailing north. After leaving San Miguel Bay, which he renamed San Diego in honor of his flagship, he sailed into another spacious, beautiful harbor, the Bay of Monterey, on the evening of December 16, 1602. A landing was made, and mass was said under a large oak tree. Vizcaíno commented at length on the harbor, the trees covering the hills, the whales playing in the bay, and the great variety of wild game. He named the bay in honor of the viceroy, Monte Rey, who had sent out the expedition. Some say that Rodríguez Cermenho, a commander of a Manila galleon, had sighted this bay some years before. More than one hundred and sixty years after Vizcaíno's visit Father Junípero Serra founded there the second Mission in the state of California. A presidio was also built. It is believed that Serra said mass under the same tree that Vizcaíno had used. This tree was still standing until about thirty-five years ago. Years after the tree was dead it was cut down and cast into the bay by the city officials of Monterey. A local priest of San Carlos, Father Mestrer, was able to rescue the trunk of the tree and it is today kept as a most valuable relic (*California Historical Society Quarterly*, Vol. VIII, p. 390).

[58] A hundred years later English and Dutch pirates still infested the Pacific Ocean. Among the more noted English ones (1700) were Woodes Rogers, William Dampier, and Captain Clipperton. One Spanish galleon, the "Santa Ana," bound for Acapulco and having on board a rich cargo of silk from Asia and 122,000 pesos in gold, was captured by the English sea dog, Cavendish, off the coast of Mexico, after six hours of fighting, and towed to Magdalena Bay, where the booty was divided (Hubert Howe Bancroft, *History of Mexico*, Vol. II, pp. 744–50).

suitable port in which the ships that came from the Philippines[59] to Mexico would find aid on such a long and painful voyage. The viceroy, nevertheless, did not accept the proposal of Vizcaíno because he feared that the court would disapprove, since it seemed determined to take charge of that enterprise.

Vizcaíno therefore proceeded to court for the purpose of asking the king himself the permission which he desired, but, not receiving assistance there, he returned quickly to Mexico [City] with the plan of passing the rest of his life peacefully in his home. Nevertheless, scarcely had he returned when another new order from the king arrived in 1606 commanding that a suitable port be looked for and settled in California which would serve as a stopping place for the ships from the Philippine Islands; that the expedition be entrusted to Vizcaíno himself and, in case the latter had died, then to the one who had been his lieutenant on the previous voyage. Vizcaíno accepted the commission willingly. But while he was making the preparations for the voyage he died,[60] and the enterprise was abandoned for some years in spite of the urgent orders of the court.

[59] Magellan discovered these islands in 1519 when he circumnavigated the globe. A Spanish expedition under the command of Villalobos crossed the Pacific Ocean in 1542 and opened up trade with the Philippine Islands. Villalobos named them in honor of Philip II of Spain. A lucrative trade was soon developed between Spain and these distant islands. The ships used in this trade were known as Manila galleons. Some of them went around the Horn; others landed on the east coast of Mexico and were loaded with goods brought overland from some seaport on the Pacific where the galleons stopped. The trip from the ports on the west coast of Mexico to the Philippines, not a dangerous one, was usually made in three or four months. The return voyage often took twice as long. Sometimes heavy typhoons would be encountered, and ships would be carried several hundred miles northward out of their course. Then they would be obliged to follow down the coast of California to Mexico. Ships often reached this coast greatly damaged and the crews entirely disabled.

[60] During 1611–1613 Vizcaíno made a voyage to Japan.

Chapter Four

THE ATTEMPTS WHICH SOME MADE AT THEIR OWN EXPENSE.
THE FABULOUS VOYAGE OF ADMIRAL FONTE

Captain Juan Iturbi[61] in 1615 obtained permission from the viceroy to go to California at his own expense. One of the two[62] ships which he equipped was stolen by a European pirate; and with the other he sailed up the Gulf of California[63] as far as 30°, where he observed that the farther he advanced toward the northwest, the nearer the two coasts approached each other, from which the union of California with the continent of New Spain could be inferred. When he returned to Mexico he brought very many pearls, partly fished for on his own account and partly acquired from the Californians in exchange for some things of small value. This revived a desire among individuals as well as within the government that the peninsula be conquered and settled.

Among the pearls was one which was valued at 4,500 *scudi*.[64] From then on, several residents of the provinces of Culiacán and Chiametla began to frequent the Gulf of California in small boats; and from the traffic in pearls which they had the Californians fish for or which they bought from them some people became rich, one of whom, Don Antonio de Castillo, a merchant of Chiametla, deserves particular mention. The Indians of California, on account of this trade, had to suffer a thousand vexations from those greedy fishermen;[65] but sometimes they knew how to avenge themselves.

---

[61] He could afford to do this because under a contract made with Tomás Cardona, who had been given a monopoly in pearl fishing in the New World, Iturbi expected to become rich.

[62] He had three ships, one of which was captured by a Dutch pirate.

[63] This was in 1616, on which voyage he had two ships.

[64] A silver or gold coin used in Italy, the value of which was about ninety-seven cents. Some writers put a value of 4,500 pesos on this particular pearl.

[65] Father Francisco Palóu, who worked in Lower California, denies that the Indians were forced to dive for pearls "in any part of the peninsula" in his time, and he was convinced that any trouble or mutiny that arose among them came from the low pay they received and not from being forced to dive

There were some who solicited permission from the government to undertake the conquest of California at their own expense. But none attained it then, with the exception of Captain Francisco de Ortega, a man more fortunate or more industrious than the rest. He embarked in a small frigate in March 1632. He landed on that peninsula on May 2,[66] and after he had explored that country, while trading in pearls from the port of San Bernabé to that of La Paz, he returned the following month to a port of Sinaloa and from there gave an account of his voyage to the viceroy.[67] It seems that he was not unsuccessful in this business, since he repeated the voyage during the two following years with the idea of establishing a settlement in the peninsula; and for this purpose he took with him two[68] priests who were to be engaged in the conversion of the Indians, which seemed very easy to him on account of their docility. But at the same time, he found such barrenness everywhere and such lack of food that he was compelled to abandon the enterprise. In order to overcome that obstacle and make the settlement secure against the attempts of that tribe of Indians which had become enemies of the Spaniards because of the extortions suffered from the pearl fishermen, he proposed two projects to the viceroy—so suitable that, if they had been carried out, perhaps the undertaking of the settlement would have been attained. The first was that the presidio established at Acaponeta[69] be transferred to California, since it was no longer needed there because of the great peaceableness of those people; the second was that a sum of money be raised in Mexico to furnish what was necessary to the new settlers until they could support themselves with agriculture and the trades of social life.

(*Historical Memoirs of New California*, by Fray Francisco Palóu, translated and edited by Herbert Eugene Bolton, Vol. I, p. 220).

[66] May 4, according to Chapman, *op. cit.*, p. 164).

[67] The Marquis of Cerralvo, Rodrigo Pacheco Osoris.

[68] Bancroft mentions one, Father Roque de Vega, who was probably the first Jesuit to enter the peninsula (Bancroft, *History of the North Mexican States and Texas*, Vol. I, pp. 174-75).

[69] A small seacoast town on the coast of Nueva Galicia, now a city of 7,449 population in the state of Nayarit.

While Ortega was trying to influence the government to execute his projects, Estevan Carbonel,[70] who had been his pilot on the previous voyages, obtained permission from the viceroy to take colonists to California. In fact, he left for that country, hoping to find the soil fertile in the northern part of the peninsula; but not having found it he returned to Mexico, covered with humiliation, although consoled, on the other hand, by the acquisition of some pearls.

Various English authors place at this time the famous voyage of Admiral Fonte[71] which he made (as they say) at the orders of the king of Spain and the viceroys of Mexico and Perú from Lima to the coast of California and from there to the western extremity of America. But this voyage is a chimera; and the story which was published about it in London is a tissue of falsehoods, badly warped and entirely groundless, which, adopted thoughtlessly by M. L'Isle, M. Bauche, and other geographers of note, has occasioned many errors in the geographical maps of America.

Chapter Five

NEW ORDERS AND ATTEMPTS

THE MARQUÉS DE VILLENA,[72] the viceroy of Mexico, in 1640, directed Don Luis Cestin de Cañas,[73] the governor of Sinaloa, to go and explore all the coasts

---

[70] A Frenchman, who built a ship secretly near San Blas, intending, it was believed, to sail north to find the straits of Anián. Bancroft says that he obtained fraudulently his license to fish for pearls. Chapman thinks this may be doubted (*A History of California: The Spanish Period*, pp. 164–65).

[71] He claimed to have made this voyage in 1640, and that he went north to the waters of Alaska. He met boats there which he said had come across the continent from New England! He, too, must have believed in the existence of the inland waterway across the continent. His imagination also led him to record that Jesuit Missions had been established as far north as 66°.

[72] He was viceroy from 1635 to 1640. The duke of Escalona, Diego López Pacheco, who succeeded Villena, served only two years. It may be doubted which viceroy sent out Cañas.

[73] He was the captain of a presidio in Sinaloa rather than the governor of that province. Some place his voyage at 1642. He explored the coast of the

of California and the neighboring islands. And he got the *provincial*[74] of the Jesuits to send an able missionary[75] with him. The reason for repeating so many trips at such expense was that, instead of publishing the logs and the geographical maps of the early discoverers, they sent them to Spain where they were buried in some archive;[76] and so those who were entrusted anew with similar discoveries could not profit by that information. This trip of the governor of Sinaloa was useful only for confirming what was known already about the abundance of pearls in that sea, the sterility of the soil of that peninsula, and the docility of those barbarians.

In spite of this the viceroy himself, having been called to Spain, inflamed the spirit of the court in such a way with his accounts that it undertook the conquest of California; for King Philip IV[77] sent Admiral Pedro Portel de Casanate[78] to Mexico in 1643, giving him ample powers to build fleets, conquer and settle the peninsula, and do all that seemed advantageous for reducing those barbarians to Christianity. The count of Salvatierra,[79] the viceroy of Mexico, paid attention to the orders of the court in every respect and entreated the provincial of the Jesuits to have the admiral accompanied by two missionaries,[80] as in fact was done. But when the fleet was on

peninsula for some leagues south of La Paz (Miguel Venegas, *Noticia de la California*, Vol. I, pp. 209–11).

[74] An officer who acts under the orders of a superior general and presides over a certain section of the country. He is elected for a period usually from three to six years. He is required to make regular visits to the churches and institutions in his territory and to report upon the religious, educational, and financial conditions of the district under his jurisdiction.

[75] Father Jacinto Cortés, one of the first Jesuits to arrive in the peninsula.

[76] The object being, no doubt, to keep the king in ignorance.

[77] He became king when he was sixteen years old.

[78] He was granted permission in 1636 to make a voyage to California, but for some reason the license was later revoked. The king of Spain in 1640 gave him a license to make such a voyage, but he did not start until 1643. He made another voyage to California in 1648.

[79] Barcia Sarmiento de Sotamayor. He served as viceroy from 1642 to 1648, when he was sent to Peru.

[80] Probably Andrés Baez and Jacinto Cortés, who went with Casanate to California in 1648.

the point of setting sail for California, some wicked enemies of his burned the two ships. For this reason he was compelled to delay the trip until the ships were built again. Finally he went there in 1648 with two missionaries and a sufficient number of soldiers; and he explored all the eastern coast accurately, seeking some place suitable for establishing a presidio; but having found that the land was sterile everywhere, he returned to Mexico to state the difficulty of that enterprise to the viceroy.

The experience of so many unsuccessful expeditions was not enough to keep the court from thinking of California, for the same king, Philip IV, repeated the order to make another attempt there, commissioning Admiral Bernardo Bernal de Piñadero[81] for it, under certain conditions. He went there in 1664 with two small ships; but those who accompanied him, instead of doing what they should have done, devoted themselves to fishing for pearls, doing the Californians a thousand wrongs and exciting such discord among them that they fought each other; and some were killed.[82] Therefore the admiral, in order to remove the source of those abuses, soon set sail and returned to New Spain, where he was poorly received by the viceroy.[83] The latter informed the court about it; and the queen, who was then ruling the kingdom in the name of her son, Charles II,[84] commanded that Piñadero be compelled to fulfill all his promises according to the contract made with the deceased king. Piñadero, not being able to help himself,

[81] He was too much interested in fishing for pearls and in other commercial pursuits to advance the interests of the king (Venegas, *Noticia de la California*, Vol. I, pp. 216–17). He made no serious efforts to found a settlement, and his voyages have little significance.

[82] It is believed that the quantity of pearls obtained was very large and that the quarreling occurred over the proper division of the pearls.

[83] The marquis of Mancera, Antonio Sebastián de Toledo, who held the office from 1664 to 1673. During his administration the beautiful cathedrals in Mexico City that had been started a century before were completed.

[84] He became heir to the throne in 1665 when he was four years old. He was so weak in mind and body that he was barely able to learn to read and write. He was deformed, and his epileptic fits caused many people to think that he was bewitched by the Devil. Although he ruled Spain for thirty-five years, he was always so mentally incompetent that agents managed the state for him.

equipped two smaller boats[85] in the port of Chacala, from where he left for California in 1667; but this trip was as unsuccessful as all the others.

Not more fortunate, in truth, was Captain Francisco Lucenilla, who obtained permission (1668) from the government to undertake a new voyage. The two Franciscan fathers[86] whom he took with him devoted themselves with great zeal and industry to the conversion of the Californians; but provisions having failed them, they were compelled to abandon that very miserable country.*

Chapter Six

THE FAMOUS EXPEDITION OF ADMIRAL OTONDO

THE VICEROY[87] of Mexico in 1677 received an order from King Charles II to send a new expedition to California. Admiral Don Isidoro de Otondo y

---

* In the edition of the letters of the conqueror, Cortés, published in Mexico in 1770, it is said that *"these two Franciscans penetrated successfully through the interior of California; but because they were hindered by the Jesuits, they returned."* This, however, is a gross calumny, since everyone knows that there were not even Jesuits in California then and that the latter did not become established there until thirty years afterward. Betancur, a Franciscan and the chronicler of the Franciscans, who was living in Mexico then, states clearly that those friars were compelled to leave California because of the scarcity of provisions, and no one has ever fancied what that editor asserts. So then the success which the friars had there was not very considerable; in the short time that they were there they could not have learned the very difficult language of those Indians. Even the most that could probably be believed was that they baptized some children.

---

[85] These two ships were built from money that he was able to borrow. See Herbert Eugene Bolton, *Kino's Historical Memoir of Pimería Alta*, Vol. I, p. 220 (hereafter cited as Bolton, *Kino*).

[86] Juan Caballero y Carranco and Juan Bautista Ramírez. It is not known how successful they were for the short time they lived among these Indians.

[87] Archbishop Payo Enríquez, a relative of the noted Cortés, who held this office from 1673 to 1680.

Antillon was entrusted with it, who, after he had made the agreement with the king and had built two ships in the port of Chacala,[88] weighed anchor from there on March 18,[89] 1683, with more than a hundred men. Among them were three Jesuits[90] appointed by the court for the conversion of the Indians, one of whom was Father Eusebio Francisco Kino[91] of Triente, a learned mathematician and a very industrious missionary, who obtained the employment of cosmographer from the king.

A sloop laden with provisions was to have followed these two ships, but it was never able to join them. After they had reached the port of La Paz in California after fourteen[92] days of sailing they did not see an Indian in the first five days. But, as soon as they landed and began to make their camp there appeared in the distance some armed savages who were painted several colors (as they were accustomed to do when they go to war) and who gave the Spaniards to understand, with outcries and signs, that they did not want them in their country.[93] This demonstration occurred solely because their natural mildness was wearied from suffering so many vexations from the pearl fishermen.

The Spaniards did not wish to move their camp. The three missionaries went toward them, carrying some food in their hands and trying to make them see that they sought their

[88] At the mouth of the Sinaloa River.
[89] Kino gives the date as March 25 (Bolton, *Kino*, Vol. I, p. 221). Several authorities agree with Clavigero, but Bancroft gives January 18 (*History of the North Mexican States and Texas*, Vol. I, p. 187).
[90] Fathers Kino, Matías Goñi, and Antonio Suárez. For some reason Goñi did not go on the expedition. Father Copart went in place of Goñi (Bolton, *Kino*, Vol. I, p. 39).
[91] Kino was made mapmaker, surveyor, and astronomer. At first he thought the peninsula to be an island, and he sketched it thus on some of his maps. But further examination of the country convinced him that the land could not be a peninsula (*ibid.*, p. 334).
[92] Kino says they landed on April 1, being then only seven days in crossing the Gulf (*ibid.*, p. 39).
[93] Accounts differ as to the reception that the natives gave the white men when they entered the land of the savage. On this occasion it would be natural for Otondo and his soldiers to exaggerate the hostile demonstrations of the heathen, and for Kino to excuse many acts.

friendship and that they were not coming to do them harm. After they had approached the Indians a little they put what hey carried on the ground and retreated. Those barbarians devoured that food in a moment and ran after the missionaries asking for more, until they entered the Spaniards' camp fearlessly with them. Very great was their hunger and their simplicity!

The same thing happened with another group of barbarians who appeared after two days. The Spaniards constructed some cabins there for divine worship as well as for their own dwellings.[94]

Wishing to become acquainted with the interior of the country, the admiral started in one direction with Father Kino and twenty-five soldiers and sent a captain with another missionary in another direction. But they returned to the camp after having gone about twenty miles with great fatigue because only very narrow footpaths existed there for the use of those unclothed barbarians and it was necessary for them to open a road with much labor by cutting down branches and uprooting trees. Those who went with the captain met some tribes of Coras[95] who were so friendly and peaceable toward them that from that day on they came to the Spaniards' camp frequently, and sometimes they stayed to sleep in it, lying down among the soldiers.

In the opposite direction the admiral met the tribe of Guaicuras who, always armed and little content with their arrival in that country, threatened several times to come upon him with all the force of the tribe if they did not leave that country. The Spaniards suffered such insults patiently, hoping to soften the ferocity of the barbarians in this manner. But on June 6 two crowds of Guaicuras appeared near the camp, and, not content with making shouts and threats, they assaulted the intrenchment armed. The Spaniards would have availed themselves of the artillery fire if the intrepid admiral, going out of

---

[94] They built a log church, a small fort, and some huts for their homes.

[95] Afterward noted for their obstinate resistance to the work of the missionaries, they were regarded as about the most warlike and indolent tribe with which the missionaries had to deal.

the line, had not rushed upon them with terrible shouts and great demonstrations of indignation and had not frightened them until they turned their backs and hastily took to flight. In spite of this, they kept approaching the Spaniards frequently, although not without some distrust.

At that time a sailor had deserted from the Spaniards' camp. In the beginning it was believed that he had gone away with the Guaicuras to live among them of his own free will. But later the rumor was spread that he had been killed by the Guaicuras, and in order to confirm it the deposition of certain Coras was obtained; but the truth was that they did not understand the Indians. The admiral, believing that report to be true and considering it dangerous to overlook a similar offense, ordered the leader of the Guaicuras seized one day when they came to the camp, as they were accustomed to do. This caused them great annoyance; and in a few days they returned in crowds to request the liberty of the prisoner; but, not having succeeded, they determined to gather all their forces to exterminate the Spaniards.

With this purpose they implored the aid of the Coras, who belonged to their same nation, although they were enemies of theirs. But the Coras, being promised greater advantages from their union with the Spaniards against the Guaicuras, disclosed the design of their countrymen to the Spaniards. The admiral doubled the guards and ordered a cannon trained in the direction whence the Guaicuras were accustomed to come. On the day set by the Guaicuras for the attack they began to leave the mountain one by one until there were fourteen or fifteen; and as soon as they were in reach of the cannon, ten or twelve were killed and the others were wounded. On account of this their forces, which were in ambush to attack the camp at an opportune time, were so terrified that they went away to their lurking-places never to return. These hostilities, thoughtlessly begun by that admiral,[96] greatly alienated the affection of the

---

[96] Some years later (1705) in a report made to the viceroy, Father Salvatierra accused Otondo of killing several Guaicuras while they were dining as his guests(Venegas, *Noticia de la California*, Vol. II, p. 155; also Bancroft, *History of the North Mexican States and Texas*, Vol. I, p. 189).

Guaicuras for the Spaniards and retarded their conversion afterward, as we shall see further on.

Those Spanish soldiers, very different from those who conquered Mexico, became so afraid of the Guaicuras (fearing that they might make all the nations of California fall upon them) that neither the reproofs of the admiral nor the exhortations of the missionaries were sufficient to make them more courageous. Many of them, like men in despair, asked the admiral to be taken out of that country, even though it might be to leave them on some island near by. The admiral, considering that their anxiety might be turned into general sedition and that the greater part of the provisions, which were then very scarce, had spoiled for the most part, finally decided to yield to the pressing arguments of those cowards. But in order not to go too far from the peninsula, to which he intended to return, he amused himself among the adjacent islands, hoping to be joined soon by one of his ships which he had sent to Sinaloa to bring provisions, as in fact happened.

He arranged, nevertheless, to go in person to a port of Sinaloa to provide himself more abundantly with all the necessities; and having sold there a great part of the salable goods which he had brought with him and having pawned even his silver and jewelry, he returned to California, not to the port of La Paz but to another situated at about 26° latitude. To this place he gave the name of San Bruno, because he landed there on October 6.

After the admiral had made his trenches and built his cabins there (as in the other port), he left in December, well accompanied, and went more than seventy miles into the interior of the country, everywhere treating well the Indians whom he met, caressing them, and giving them presents to draw them to his friendship and to the Christian faith.[97]

[97] The history of this settlement and the activities of the missionaries from December 1683 to May 1684 are narrated by Kino. His manuscript is in the archives of Mexico. See Bolton, *Kino*, Vol. I, p. 43. This manuscript history is known as *Favores Celestiales*. It deals with the work of the missionaries in Pimería Alta (see below, note 103) between 1687 and 1710, and was written by Father Kino at the request of the Father-General of the Society of Jesus. Kino wrote it at the Mission of Nuestra Señora de los Dolores. This manuscript

While the admiral was occupied in this and other trips, the missionaries devoted themselves with the greatest diligence to learning the two languages which were spoken there. After having acquired sufficient knowledge they undertook to translate the Christian doctrine for them; but they did not know how to express the section about the resurrection of the dead because they did not find any word with this meaning.

They made use of a curious measure for the purpose of finding it out. After they had caught some flies and submerged them in cold water until they seemed quite dead, they first put them on ashes and then exposed them to the sun to resuscitate them with the heat; they were very attentive, meanwhile, in observing and writing the first words that the Indians uttered when they saw the flies revive, being persuaded that the words would mean resurrection. But they were disappointed, because the words then used by the Indians and put on the symbol, after some investigations, were these: *ibì-muhuet-ete*, which does not express resurrection but means only "It died a little while ago," or "Just now it was dead."*

* Father Kino gives an account of this fact to his teacher, Father Henry Scherer, a learned German Jesuit, who published the letter of his pupil in the second part of his work entitled *Atlas Novus*. In the Cochimì language *ibì* is a verb, which means to die; *te* is a particle which is added to the verbs to form the preterit; *muhuet* is the adverb corresponding to *nuper*, or to *modo* of the Latins, which, in adjustment with the verb, means that it is not long ago that there happened that which the verb signifies. Don Miguel del Barco, very learned in that language, as one who spoke it for thirty continuous years, surmises that the words pronounced by the Indians would be this: *Ibì-muhuet-e-te-dommò, gaijenji juajib omui*, that is, "although it has been dead a little while, it arose suddenly," and that the missionaries, attentive to the first words, did not pay attention to the rest. *Dommò* is a conjunction equivalent to *etsi* or *quamvis* of the Latins; but among the Cochimìes, it is placed not before but after the verb. *Huajib* means the one who was lying down arose; but it is used in the sense of resuscitate, as with the Latins, who used the verb *surgere* as the symbol to express the resurrection of Jesus Christ.

---

was lost until it was discovered by Dr. Herbert Eugene Bolton about thirty years ago in the Archivo General y Público in Mexico City.

As soon as they compiled the catechism in the Cochimí language, although imperfectly, they began to teach it, especially to the children. The latter learned it quickly, and every day on their knees and with their hands in front on their chests they recited it together with the missionaries. Afterward they became the teachers of their parents and relatives until by this means and with frequent short sermons the missionaries had about four hundred catechumen ready for baptism; but not being sure of remaining in that country they did not wish to baptize anyone unless in danger of death. Only thirteen were thus baptized, ten of whom died in a little while, and the three who survived were taken by the admiral with the permission of their parents to Nueva Galicia and entrusted to the bishop of Guadalajara.

The missionaries were very happy over the docility of those Indians and their favorable disposition toward Christianity. But the admiral was not happy in that country, in which it was not so easy for him to maintain the settlement. Then, the soldiers complained to him of the hardships caused by the barrenness of the land and the inclemency of that climate. With these things in mind, he called the officers and the missionaries to a meeting to learn their opinions. The officers thought that the settlement of San Bruno should be abandoned, because it was situated in a sterile and unhealthy place. The missionaries said that it was necessary to wait some time in order to form an exact idea of the country, since the drought of that year had been general, even in New Spain; and in California it had not rained for eighteen months. The admiral sent one of his ships to explore the coast toward the north and to search for a more suitable place for the settlement; and in the other he took all the sick people to the coast of Sinaloa, from where he wrote to the viceroy,[98] giving him an account of all that he had done and sending him, with his own information, the opinions of the missionaries and the officers, signed by their respective authors. And setting sail again, he went to observe some places on the Gulf where pearls were abundant.

[98] Tomás Antonio de la Cerda y Aragón, the marquis of Laguna.

The ship sent to reconnoiter the coast did not find what it sought. And the viceroy, after he had heard the judgment of several ministers of the king, answered the admiral that since such great expenditures had been made up to that time in the conquest and settlement of California he should be content to keep what had been acquired, if it were possible, without insisting on new undertakings. The admiral, because he did not find a way to live in the port of San Bruno, embarked with the missionaries and all his people and returned to New Spain. Thus terminated that famous expedition in which were consumed three years and two hundred and twenty-five thousand *scudi*[99] from the royal treasury.

Chapter Seven

OTHER UNSUCCESSFUL PLANS

THE VICEROY had this business considered in the assembly of all the royal ministers, and after various sessions it was decided that the Californias were unconquerable by the means which had been used up to that time and that, in spite of this, the conversion of the peninsula should be commended to the Jesuits, all that they might need for the expenses being furnished them from the royal treasury. The royal *fiscal*,* who was entrusted with making that proposal[100] to the superior of the Jesuits, presented it to him at various times; but the superior answered unanimously with his advisers

---

* The duty of the royal *fiscal* in the Spanish *audiencia* is partly equivalent to that of royal procurator in the French Parliament.

[99] Bancroft states that the venture cost 225,400 pesos (*History of the North Mexican States and Texas*, Vol. I, p. 193). The Spanish government made no further attempts to colonize the peninsula or to subdue the Indians until the Jesuits were given permission (1697) to work there. Every effort of the government since the days of Cortés had been a dismal failure.

[100] The *fiscal* was trained in law and was one of the most influential officials of the king, being entrusted with the most confidential proposals. He reported directly to the viceroy, and his opinions and recommendations were nearly always accepted by the king.

that the Order was very grateful to that respected tribunal for the honor which they showed it in entrusting it with an affair of such importance and was ready to appoint all the missionaries who might be considered necessary for the conversion of the Indians. But it did not find it convenient to take charge of the temporal matters of the peninsula in the manner proposed to it.

When this hope had vanished the gentlemen were so persuaded of the uselessness of any other attempt to reduce California that the viceroy absolutely denied permission to Captain Francisco Lucenilla, who wished to try it. But as difficulty itself is accustomed to inflame the desire of an undertaking, and there were (besides the interests of politics and religion) new orders from the court for undertaking the reduction of California, this business was dealt with again with much ardor.

When the computation had been made of the money which was necessary to spend there and it was found that the annual expenditure of thirty thousand *scudi* was absolutely necessary, it was determined to give that sum in advance to Admiral Otondo to undertake a new voyage to that peninsula. But the same week in which the money was to be delivered to the admiral the viceroy received a royal command to send fifty thousand *scudi* promptly to the court and to suspend the enterprise of California as long as the disorders in Tarahumara[101] lasted. Although these troubles quieted down in a short time, no expedition to California at the expense of the king was considered again at that time. But Captain Francisco de Itamarra[102] obtained permission to go there in 1694 at his own expense; this trip was as unsuccessful as all the others made up to that time. It was learned then that the Indians of the port of San Bruno and of the surrounding country had asked urgently for the fulfillment of the promise which the missionaries had made them of returning to the peninsula to instruct them in religion and to teach them the way to Paradise.

[101] A section of Mexico east of the Sierra Madre Mountains. Most of the Tarahumara Indians lived in the province of Chihuahua.

[102] Little has been written about his voyage. Bancroft says he did nothing but find out that the Indians there "had not forgotten the taste of pozole, and were clamorous for conversion."

Chapter Eight

THE ZEAL OF SOME JESUITS FOR THE CONVERSION OF CALIFORNIA AND ITS SUCCESS

THE MISSIONARIES were appointed by their superiors to other Missions. Father Kino went to Sonora,[103] the theater of his fervid zeal, whence he hoped to go to California. With this thought he left Mexico [City] on October 20, 1686, and on passing through the provinces of Tepehuana[104] and Sinaloa he inflamed the spirits of the Jesuit missionaries there in favor of the conversion of the poor and forsaken Californians.

One of the many who felt inspired for such an enterprise by the ardent words of Father Kino was Father Juan María de Salvatierra, who was then visitor-general[105] of the Missions.

---

[103] This province included what is now southern Arizona and northern Sonora, and it was known as Pimería Alta. Kino arrived in Sonora in March 1687 to take up his missionary work, which he continued with unusual zeal and success for twenty-four years. The first Mission which he founded, a few months after arriving in Sonora, was called Nuestra Señora de los Dolores. It was located on the San Miguel River. The new church was not dedicated until April 26, 1693. Within ten years Kino had founded many Missions, one, San Javier, being established in 1700 north of the present boundary of Arizona. For many years he explored the country of northern Sonora, reaching the junction of the Colorado and Gila rivers. Besides preaching to the Indians, baptizing them, and building churches, Kino was a most successful business man. He managed vast stock ranchos which supplied food for his many Missions and also those in adjacent districts. At one time he sent to Salvatierra in Lower California seven hundred cattle. When he was sixty-seven years old, Kino died at one of the Missions he had founded (Magdalena) "as he had lived, with extreme humility and poverty," and having a bed consisting "of two calfskins for a mattress, two blankets such as the Indians use for covers, and a packsaddle for a pillow." Said a co-worker of his, "These, then, are the virtues of Father Kino: he prayed much, and was considered as without vice. He neither smoked nor took snuff, nor wine, nor slept in a bed. He was so austere that he never took wine except to celebrate mass, nor had any other bed than the sweat blankets of his horse for a mattress, and two Indian blankets." See Bolton, *Kino*, Vol. I, p. 89. For the career of this great Jesuit see Bolton's life of Kino, entitled *Rim of Christendom*.

[104] A province adjacent to Sinaloa including what is now Durango.

[105] An important official of the government who was sent into any part of

This famous man was born of noble parents* in Milan in 1644.[106] After having finished his elementary studies in the Seminary of Parma,[107] he entered the Society of Jesus. Desirous of working for the conversion of the gentiles,[108] he went to Mexico in 1675 in company with his saintly compatriot, Juan Bautista Zappa.[109] Sent by his superiors to the Missions of Tarahumara, Salvatierra worked in them with the greatest success for some years;[110] and, having been summoned afterward to Mexico [City], he acquired there the chief burdens of that province[111] on account of his great talent and singular courage. He was strong, accustomed to labor and hardship, possessed of a good mind and a big heart, full of zeal, prudent, humble, and as gentle with others as he was austere with himself; and, finally, he was very well disciplined through the exercise of prayer, in which he had intimate union with God.

The luminous examples of integrity that he gave in the forty-two years which he lived in various places of the kingdom and the special divine favors with which Heaven adorned him made the name of Salvatierra famous everywhere. His memory is maintained there with great veneration after so many

* He was of Spanish ancestry on his father's side.

---

the Spanish possessions to investigate any department of state. He was frequently given power to punish and to institute reforms.

[106] Venegas gives 1648 as the date of his birth; Clavigero is doubtless correct.

[107] An ancient Etruscan city located in Parma, now a city of about fifty thousand population.

[108] A name applied to the Indians before they came into the Mission settlement.

[109] Born in Milan, Italy, in 1651, and a boyhood companion of Salvatierra. At the age of fifteen Zappa became a Jesuit. He taught in the College of Nice, and, as a missionary he was first assigned to the Indies. He spent most of his time working in Sinaloa; he died in 1694.

[110] During the time that Salvatierra worked among the Indians on the mainland his main Mission, Chinipas, located on the Fuerte River, became his headquarters.

[111] He was made father-visitor of the Mission work in Pimería Alta, and he was sent into that country immediately to investigate conflicting reports relative to the success of the Missions there.

years. Such was the man destined by God to establish the Christian religion in California and to put into practice what the Spanish government had not been able to do in one hundred and fifty years after repeated and excessively expensive attempts.

When Father Salvatierra was informed by Father Kino[112] of the docility of the Californians and their good disposition toward Christianity, he determined to do all that was possible to obtain permission to go and convert them. Therefore he asked his provincial, the supreme magistrates of Nueva Galicia, the viceroy[113] of Mexico, and even the king himself. Although his zeal was praised by all, his solicitations were denied him because the enterprise was considered not only useless but also rash after so many unsuccessful attempts had been made. Nevertheless, he did not cease to commend this affair warmly to God and to redouble his efforts before men, especially since he felt sure of success because of a letter written to him by his saintly friend, Father Zappa, in which he urged him not to cease in his petitions about California; and since God had destined him to carry the faith of Jesus Christ to those poor nations, he should try to practice more of those virtues necessary for that end and should not neglect to build in that Peninsula, as he had done in so many other places, a chapel in honor of the Virgin of Loreto, who would be his protectress in that great work.

Father Salvatierra and Father Kino, animated by Christian pity for those unfortunate souls and by ardent zeal in behalf of the glory of their Creator, had repeated in vain their peti-

---

[112] Salvatierra arrived where Kino was stationed in the district of Dolores the day before Christmas in 1690. He visited and examined many of the Missions in Sonora and Sinaloa, and then made his report to the viceroy. It was during this visit with Kino, as the two traveled about the country, that Salvatierra was converted to the idea of going to Lower California to found Missions. He was no doubt greatly influenced in this regard by Kino. As the two traveled among the Missions it was clear that "these lands so pleasant, so rich, so fertile and able so easily to lend aid to the scanty lands of California" furnished a sound argument that if Missions were founded in California they could be supplied by products from the mainland.

[113] The count of Galve, Gaspar de Sandoval Silva y Mendoza.

tions as to California for almost ten years. In 1696 the supreme magistrates of Nueva Galicia, who had constantly opposed that enterprise, consented to it at last;[114] and they began to aid it, influenced by the impressive statements made to them by the royal *fiscal*, Don José de Miranda,[115] a learned and pious man and the friend and admirer of Father Salvatierra. The *audiencia* wrote to the viceroy, stating to him the reasons that existed for undertaking anew that expedition and for looking forward to its success if it were entrusted to the Fathers of the Company of Jesus.

Meanwhile Father Salvatierra, having been given permission from the provost general of the Company to be relieved of all his duties in the colleges[116] of that province as soon as the Mexican government would permit them to enter California, also obtained from the provincial permission to collect alms[117] for that great enterprise which he was considering.

---

[114] Kino and Salvatierra arrived in Mexico City on the same day, January 8, 1696, although by different routes, to plead that they be allowed to go to Lower California.

[115] The legal adviser of the royal *audiencia* at Guadalajara.

[116] A number of colleges were started in Mexico by the Jesuits soon after their arrival. One was opened in 1616 in the province of Zacatecas, and two years later another, the college of San Pedro y San Pablo in Mexico City. It soon became an institution of high rank, and is still in existence. Other colleges were located at Puebla, Tepotzotlán, Querétaro, and Valladolid. When the Jesuits were expelled from the Spanish possessions in the Americas they owned twenty-three colleges and several seminaries. These institutions were turned over to the Franciscans. See Priestley, *The Mexican Nation*, p. 153.

[117] This is the beginning of the famous *"fondo piadoso"* (Pious Fund). Since the Jesuits were required to support financially the Missions that they would found, and since the peninsula was so barren, it developed upon private interests to help establish and maintain them. Ten thousand pesos, invested at five per cent, was sufficient capital to endow a Mission. Often gifts represented vast tracts of rich land and also city property. One man, the Marqués de Villapuente, gave almost a half million acres of land, and another gave 200,000 pesos to the fund, which is believed to have reached more than a million dollars. After the Jesuits were expelled the government of Mexico took over the fund, and in the course of a few years it was used for other purposes. In 1836 the fund was entrusted to the Bishop of California, but after 1846, at which time California became American territory, the Mexican government ceased paying to the Catholic church the interest on the money, which it had previously confiscated. Mexico in 1870 paid the accumulated

Father Juan de Ugarte, a remarkable Jesuit and one worthy of eternal memory, was then professor of philosophy in Tegucigalpa [City]. This man, born in Tegucigalpa, a city of the diocese of Honduras, in 1660, united in his person the most estimable gifts of nature and divine grace. From nature he received illustrious birth, a strong constitution, extraordinary physical strength, a sublime mind, a natural, penetrating talent, which was quick and facile for all the sciences and arts, rare industry and prudence in economic affairs, and a heroic magnanimity superior to all obstacles and dangers. By divine grace he was endowed with the deepest humility, excessive lowliness of spirit, great mortification of senses and passions, angelic chastity, ardent zeal for the welfare of souls, and intimate union with God. In the opinion of Father Salvatierra himself he was the Atlas and the Column of California; and the conversion at those Missions was due, after God, to him.

We should never finish, if we should wish to relate all that he did there; but we shall tell in the space of this history something of his work. This great Jesuit, animated by the same spirit that was in Salvatierra, joined him to facilitate the spiritual conquest of California, overcoming the obstacles which were adverse and seeking the necessary means for finishing it well.[118]

---

interest, amounting to nearly a million dollars from 1848 to 1869. The annual interest was $43,050, and Mexico paid this sum annually for thirteen years. The question was placed before The Hague Permanent Court in 1902, being the first international dispute to be considered by this tribunal. It was decided by this court that the Mexican government should pay all back interest, which amounted to $1,402,682, and also pay annually $43,050 forever. Payments were promptly made from 1902 to 1912; but since that time nothing more has been paid. See Charles Anthony Engelhardt, *Missions and Missionaries of California*, Vol. I, pp. 595–99; Chapman, *A History of California: The Spanish Period*, pp. 181–83; *The Catholic Historical Review*, January 1934.

[118] Ugarte spent several years studying in Guatemala, and became a Jesuit when he was twenty years old. He was a teacher in the College of San Gregorio when he decided to devote his life to missionary work. He died at the age of seventy at the Mission of San Javier, founded in 1730. Some writers believe that the Missions on the peninsula would have been abandoned had it not been for the unfailing devotion, ceaseless labors, and able leadership of Ugarte.

The first success of his endeavors came from the alms of two thousand *scudi* which the Count of Miravalles[119] and the Marqués de Buenavista[120] promised. Other benefactors, after the manner of these gentlemen, offered to give fifteen thousand *scudi* and in fact did give five thousand. The Brotherhood of Nuestra Señora de los Dolores, then existent in the College of San Pedro y San Pablo in Mexico [City] endowed one Mission; and Don Juan Caballero y Ocio,[121] a priest of Querétaro, not less rich than pious and liberal toward God, offered to endow two. Besides, Don Pedro Gil de la Sierpe,[122] the treasurer of the king in Acapulco, promised to lend them a galiot

---

[119] One of the four men who promised to give $1,000 each to start the Pious Fund. According to a memorial sent to the king of Spain in 1737 by Gaspar Rodero, Procurator-General of the Indies, the contributors to the Pious Fund and their contributions (in pesos) up to that time were as follows: Marquès de Villapuente (up to April 8, 1720), 167,540 pesos; Juan Cavallero y Ocio, 44,000; Diego Gil de la Sierpe, 25,000; Nicolàs de Ermiaga, 14,000; Nicolàs de Arteaga, 12,000; Marquesa de las Torres, 10,000; Duque de Linares, 11,000; Padre Joseph de Guevara (a Jesuit), 10,000; Padre Juan Maria Luyando (a Jesuit), 10,000; The Brotherhood of Dolores of Mexico City, 8,000; Damaso de Zaldivia, 4,000; Her Excellency Señora Duquesa de Sessa, 2,000; Luis de Velasco, 10,000; The Jesuit Fathers of Sinaloa, Sonora, and Tarahumara (up to 1720), 105,000; The cities and villages of Mexico, 115,500; Total, 548,040 pesos.

All the individual donors, except three, had died by 1737. (From the memorial of Gaspar Rodeo, entitled "Señor," in the Henry E. Huntington Library.)

[120] Another of the four men to give $1,000. The other two men to give an equal sum each were Alonso Dávalos and Matheo Fernández de la Cruz (Engelhardt, *op. cit.*, p. 74).

[121] Born in Querétaro, Mexico, in 1644. He was mayor of this city, and he gave large sums of money to erect churches, schools, hospitals, convents, and colleges. Two of the beautiful churches that he helped to build are the Santa Clara in Mexico City, and St. Dominic in Guadalajara. He gave $150,000 to found and aid the Missions on the peninsula, and at one time he told Salvatierra that he would honor any bill of expenditures that might be sent him, provided it carried his signature. At his death he left the remainder of his wealth to charity.

[122] During the visit of Salvatierra to Sierpe's home in Guadalajara he won his support so completely that Sierpe, "without speaking a word, made evident, by his many tears, his interest and joy" in the work going on in the peninsula (Miguel Venegas, *Juan María de Salvatierra*, translated and edited by Marguerite Eyer Wilbur, p. 166).

for their trip and to give them another small vessel for the transportation of supplies.

Chapter Nine

THE JESUITS ARE PERMITTED TO GO TO THE CONVERSION OF CALIFORNIA

AFTER these steps were so happily taken they thought it well to make new petitions to the viceroy[123] in order to solicit the permission which they so much desired. This was made by means of a petition which the provincial[124] of the Jesuits presented. There were some contradictions in the report about which the viceroy asked the *audiencia;* but finally, after seeing that nothing was asked from the royal treasury this time, permission[125] was granted Fathers Salvatierra and Kino to go to California to convert those peoples to Christianity, provided they took possession of the country in the name of the Catholic king and asked nothing for expenses. It was permitted the Fathers, likewise, to take soldiers at their expense for their security, to name the captain and the governor for the administration of justice and to discharge any officer or soldier whenever they thought it necessary if they gave an account to the viceroy.

These soldiers were granted all the privileges which the royal troops enjoyed, and it was arranged that their service in California should be considered as rendered in a campaign.

As soon as Father Salvatierra obtained the desired permission, he no longer wished to stay in Mexico. Leaving the care of the alms and all the affairs pertaining to California to Father Ugarte, and giving an order for the boats to go from the port

---

[123] The count of Moctezuma, José Sarmiento Valladores, who held this office from 1696 to 1701.

[124] Father Juan de Palacios.

[125] The next year Kino was given permission by the father-general in Rome, Thyrso Gonzales, to spend six months of each year in the peninsula (Bolton, *Kino,* Vol. II, p. 157).

of Acapulco to that of Yaqui, he left the capital on February 7, 1697, taking with him the Christian doctrine written in the Cochimì language and others written by Father Copart,[126] one of those Jesuit missionaries who had been with Father Kino in California.

On passing through Guadalajara he talked about his expedition with that supreme magistrate and his great friend, the *fiscal* Miranda. When he reached Sinaloa, he gave prompt notice of his arrival to Father Kino. From there he went to Lower Tarahumara, where he had been as a missionary, to visit his beloved children in Jesus Christ, and to confirm them in the faith; but on returning to Sinaloa, and being very happy with the prosperous condition of that Christianity, he received the distressing news of the rebellion of the neophytes of Upper Tarahumara and of the danger in which his missionaries were.

Impelled by his ardent charity he hurried immediately to those rugged mountains, where he remained among a thousand worries and hardships and in danger of his life until the middle of August. And then, having restored tranquillity to that country, he went to the port of Yaqui where the galiot had arrived with another vessel given by the treasurer of Acapulco, after thirty-seven days of dangerous and disagreeable sailing. He remained there for two months, providing himself with supplies and waiting for Father Kino, who, while on the way to join him and to go with him to California, was detained by the governor of Sonora and by the superiors of those Missions; they feared that the peoples of that vast province might rebel after the example of those of Tarahumara, and they thought that the presence of such a great missionary was necessary and that the love and respect which the Indians professed for him were worth more than a thousand soldiers to restrain them. Father Kino, resigned to divine dispositions, therefore remained to work as an apostle in the Missions of Sonora and Pimería; and in his place Father Francisco María Piccolo,[127] a Sicilian missionary, was appointed.

[126] See above, note 90.

[127] Born in 1650, Piccolo came to Mexico when about thirty-five years old, and worked for several years among the Tarahumara tribes in Chihuahua.

But in order not to be further delayed Father Salvatierra determined to set sail at once, as he did on October 10, 1697, imploring the protection of the Blessed Virgin and that of San Francisco de Borja,[128] whose holiday was celebrated on that day. Salvatierra's fleet for that great conquest was composed of a loaned galiot and a small vessel; and his troops numbered nine men,[129] namely, five soldiers of different nations, their commander, and three Indians. Scarcely could they have sailed two miles when a storm descended which drove the galiot on the beach and left it aground on the sand; but with the work of those few men and the aid of the tide they got the galiot out of danger and, setting sail again, saw the land of California on the third day.[130]

They landed first at the port of Concepción and afterward at that of San Bruno, where Admiral Otondo had been; but

---

In the absence of Salvatierra from the peninsula in 1701 Piccolo was made vice-rector, and in the same year he was asked by the king to make a report on the state of the Missions. This he did at Guadalajara the following year. It is perhaps the most concise and correct statement of the conditions of the peninsula Missions made up to that time. It is found in Lockman's *Travels of the Jesuits*, Vol. II, pp. 395–408; also in Bolton, *Kino*, Vol. II, pp. 46–66. Later Piccolo worked with Kino and others among the Missions of Sonora, and he was made visitor-general of the Missions there. He died in the presidio at Loreto on February 22, 1729, having been the first missionary to die in the peninsula. See Engelhardt, *op. cit.*, p. 201.

[128] The Spanish for Borgia. He was born in Spain in 1540, coming from a distinguished and wealthy Spanish family. At the age of thirty-four he was made commissary-general of the Jesuits in Spain by St. Ignatius, and two years later the Missions of the East and West Indies were placed under his care. From 1565 to 1566 he supported Missions founded in Peru, in Florida, and in Mexico. He died in 1572, and next to St. Ignatius the Society of Jesus is probably indebted most to him. See *Catholic Encyclopaedia*, Vol. VI, p. 216.

[129] Luis de Torres Tortolero (commander), Estevan Rodrígues Lorenzo, Bartholomé de Robles Figueroa (a Creole), Juan Caravana (a Maltese sailor), Nicolás Marqués (a Sicilian sailor), Juan (a Peruvian mulatto); and the Indians were Francisco de Tepahui of Sinaloa, Alonso de Guayavas of Sonora, and Sebastián of Guadalajara (Venegas, *Noticia de la California*, Vol. I, p. 228; also Bancroft, *History of the North Mexican States and Texas*, Vol. I, p. 284). Salvatierra also took with him thirty cattle, ten sheep, four pigs, and a horse.

[130] The boat in which Salvatierra was went across the Gulf in one day; but the smaller vessel did not arrive until November 15 (Chapman, *A History of California: The Spanish Period*, pp. 174–75).

having found both unsuitable, and taking the advice of the captain of the galiot, who was a man very experienced on that coast, they selected the port of San Dionisio, which is situated at $25\frac{1}{2}°$ latitude and which is in a small bay surrounded by land in the form of a semicircle whose two capes form a mouth fifteen miles long. The soil there appeared covered with verdure and shrubs, and it had the advantage, so desired in that arid peninsula, of having an abundance of fresh water.

Chapter Ten

THE PENINSULA IS TAKEN POSSESSION OF IN THE NAME OF THE KING. FATHER SALVATIERRA ESTABLISHES THE MISSION OF LORETO. A CONSPIRACY OF THE INDIANS AND THE VICTORY OF THE SPANIARDS

THEY landed there on October 19,[131] and were well received by fifty Indians who inhabited that beach and by others of San Bruno, who, on their knees, kissed the images of the crucifix and the Virgin. Father Salvatierra cherished them with great amiability, making use of those words and sentences of their language which he had learned in the writings of Father Copart. Afterward they looked for a place suitable for their dwelling, and they found it on the same beach near a spring of good water; there they landed the animals, provisions, and all that the galiot carried, Father Salvatierra giving an example to all in the hard labor of carrying packs on his back.

They made their encampment by digging a trench all around and taking advantage of all the defenses that they could for their security. In the center of that small camp they erected a great bell tent given to Father Salvatierra by a pious Mexican gentleman and designed to serve meanwhile as a chapel. In front of this they placed a cross decorated with flowers. And when all was arranged in the best manner possible

[131] October 18.

they carried the image of the Virgin of Loreto in procession from the galiot to the tent, where it was placed on October 25. The ceremony which was uselessly practiced at other times in that country for taking possession of it in the name of the Catholic king was held afterward. From that time forward that miserable camp, which afterward became the capital of all the peninsula, as well as that port was known by the name of Loreto.[132]

Father Salvatierra devoted himself at once to teaching the Indians the Christian doctrine and to learning their language. He taught them the doctrine, reading it to them in the writings of Father Copart; and afterward, with his pen in his hand to write what he observed from them, he listened to them talk upon the subject. He talked with them, and these barbarians corrected his mistakes. Patiently he endured their mockery and coarse laughter because of those errors which escaped him, now in words themselves, then in the pronunciation. Every day when the drill of the doctrine was finished, he gave all those who had attended some *pozolli,* or cooked maize, a food much prized by them. Such were the labors carried on in that dark corner of the world and among those savages by a man who, by his birth, could have been conspicuous in his native land and who, because of his talents and integrity, had acquired for himself the esteem and respect of the chief cities of New Spain.

Not content with dedicating himself to the activities befitting a missionary, he also performed those duties of a captain and soldier which were not unseemly to a priest, giving all the orders suitable for the security of that camp and even standing sentry personally during the most uncomfortable hours. Soon it was realized that such vigilance was very necessary.

These barbarians, desirous of *pozolli,* wanted a greater

---

[132] The first permanent settlement made by white men on the peninsula. When the Californias were divided in 1772 at a place about thirty miles below the present international boundary, Monterey was made the capital of Upper California, and Loreto was kept as the seat of government of Lower California. Felipe de Neve was sent from Loreto to be the governor of Upper California, and Captain Fernando Rivera was sent from Monterey to Loreto to act as lieutenant-governor. For a description of early Loreto, see Engelhardt, *op. cit.,* pp. 301–2.

quantity than that which was given to them daily. At first they asked for it persistently; afterward they began to be vexed, and later they committed some small thefts. The Spaniards tried to stop these abuses; but their efforts served only to inflame further the appetites and the anger of the Indians. Confident in their number, which was vastly greater than that of the Spaniards, they determined to kill them and take possession of all their property.

Among the barbarians there were some sensible ones of better inclinations who reproved the ingratitude and the conduct of their countrymen; but they did not succeed in dissuading them from their barbarous resolutions. Before openly declaring hostilities the conspirators had pounced upon the small flock of sheep and goats which Father Salvatierra had brought with him; and they also made it clear that they intended to attack the camp of the Spaniards; but Father Salvatierra, overlooking their wicked design, continued in his accustomed ministry of the doctrine and the daily distribution of food.

Finally they determined to make a general attack on the camp on the night of October 31. Father Salvatierra was warned in time by an Indian chief named Ibò,[133] who, being seriously ill, had persistently asked for baptism and in fact obtained it a short time afterward. Salvatierra could not help but fear the consequences; but, on the other hand, he confidently awaited help from God.

On that same night on which the attack was to be made, a harquebus shot was heard from the seashore. Those of the camp replied with another; afterward a cannon shot was heard, and another, likewise, was fired in the camp. This answered noise frightened the conspirators so much that they did not dare to attack the camp. The Spaniards surmised that their small vessel, which they thought had become lost on the trip to California, had reached the port. But the next day they found out that it was only the galiot which had been sent five days before

---

[133] One of the barbarians was a chief called "Dionisio," who was regarded by Salvatierra as "a great eater." He revealed the plot of the natives when they planned to attack the settlement (Bancroft, *History of the North Mexican States and Texas*, Vol. I, p. 287).

to Sinaloa by Father Salvatierra in order to bring Father Piccolo and some soldiers from there and, being unable to enter the port on account of contrary winds, it had returned to the island of Carmen to await favorable weather in that place.

The sight of the boat restrained the animosity of the conspirators. They were aware that it brought help to the Spaniards,[134] who had spread the report among their Indian friends. But as soon as the galiot which had set sail for Sinaloa was lost from their view they began their hostilities again. On a dark night of November some of them approached the camp without being heard, took away the only horse which Father Salvatierra had been able to bring to the peninsula, and led it away. When the theft was discovered on the following morning, two brave soldiers, the Portuguese, Estevan Rodríguez Lorenzo,[135] of whom we shall make frequent mention in this history, and a Maltese, Nicolás Caravana, decided to give chase to the thieves.

Their decision was doubtless rash, because two lone men were going against so many enemies to make their way into an unknown country. On the other hand, it seemed necessary under the circumstances to make some extraordinary effort which would place their bravery in the highest grade of repute, because these barbarians are of such a character that they become cowardly and lose courage when they see great intrepidity in their enemies but become very insolent and intolerably proud when they observe some indication of cowardice or fear in their enemy.

Some friendly Indians, who frequented the camp and who were encouraged by the bold resolution of those two soldiers, offered to accompany them. In fact, twenty men, armed after their fashion, left with them. After tracking them for more than six miles, they found them on the slope of a mountain,

---

[134] Loreto now contained eighteen men—the two padres, five sailors, seven soldiers, and four friendly Indians from Mexico (*ibid.*, p. 290).

[135] Born in Algave, Portugal. When he arrived in Mexico he became the *mayordomo* (manager) of a large rancho owned by Tepotzotlán College, a Jesuit institution. Those who served in the peninsula give great credit to Lorenzo for the success of the Missions there (Engelhardt, *op. cit.*, pp. 244-45).

flaying the horse which they had already killed to eat. As soon as they saw them approach, they fled, deserting the prey. The soldiers returned to the camp at Loreto after distributing the horse meat among their Indian friends, which they accepted as a great gift.

Meanwhile the barbarians continued their hostilities, and Father Salvatierra maintained his patience and toleration, hoping to be able to tame their ferocity with gentleness and endearing expressions, which he increased from day to day.

They finally determined to make the attack, and after having assembled almost all the tribes of the Guaicura nation for this purpose (about five hundred men), they divided them into four sections and went forward against the Spaniards on November 13. They attacked the camp on all four sides with a shower of arrows and stones. The defenders, seeing that they were too few to advance upon such a superior number of assailants, wished to fire upon them; but Father Salvatierra, being unable to suffer the loss of the souls which he had come to acquire for Jesus Christ, ordered the soldiers not to kill them except when they could defend their own lives in no other way.

Nicolás Caravana discharged the only small cannon which they had; but he fired it into the air. For this reason the Indians, imagining that because the large cannon had not done them any harm and thinking they would be less harmed by the slender barrels of the harquebuses, persisted in the attack with such fury that *Alférez* Tortolero, who acted as captain, was forced to command them to fire. Then Father Salvatierra, always impelled by his ardent charity, went forward toward the barbarians, imploring them to retreat if they wished to avoid death. The answer which he received was three arrows, which did not harm him. He withdrew to commend them to God, while the soldiers did their duty by firing on them and killing them with their harquebuses. Not many persons perished;[136] but the others, on seeing such destruction as their weapons were not accustomed to make, soon became confused and fled.

After the Spaniards had rested somewhat from the toil of

---

[136] Two Spaniards were killed by the bursting of the cannon (swivel gun).

the combat, they saw many Indian women, who were the mediators of peace, coming with their small children, according to the custom of those nations. Seated near the camp entrance, they started to weep, protesting their sorrow, promising the correction of their husbands, and offering to leave their children as hostages. Father Salvatierra heard them with kindness; and he promised to make peace and to forget the faults of their husbands, if they truly changed their ways. He gave them some little things and dismissed them, after having accepted one of their small children in order not to displease them.

When night came they all went to the tent to give thanks to the Most High for victory. They marveled that, being only ten, they had been able to defend themselves from such a large number of the enemy determined upon their destruction, and that they had saved their lives without receiving any damage from so many arrows and stones. Their wonder still grew when they saw that almost all the arrows which were shot had pierced the base of the Cross placed in front of the tent; wherefore all were then so convinced of divine protection over them that they determined to persevere in that settlement, although they might not receive the help for which they were hoping.

That night they took rest, which was so necessary for them, Father Salvatierra meanwhile standing sentry and watching. The following morning, when he was preparing to say Holy Mass, they saw a boat enter the port; they all ran and discovered, with unspeakable joy, that it was that lost ship which was so desired and which brought a reinforcement of soldiers and provisions and the news that the galiot was to arrive soon.

Chapter Eleven

RULES AND REGULATIONS AND WORK OF FATHER SALVATIERRA

WHEN greater security had been attained in this manner in that recent settlement, Father Salvatierra devoted himself to formulating rules and regulations in order to protect it better and to improve it. He assembled the people, and after reading the commands of the viceroy to them, he informed all of them of their obligations and privileges. He appointed the *alférez*, Don Luis de Torres y Tortolero, captain, and conferred other duties on those who were most fit; he made a prudent distribution of the hours for Christian training and for physical labor; and he commanded that all meet on Sundays to hear a sermon on the imitation of the virtues of the Blessed Virgin, according to the custom taught by the Jesuits in different places of New Spain.

Salvatierra returned afterward to the usual instruction of the Christian doctrine and to the distribution of *pozolli* among the Indians, who returned, a few at a time, excusing themselves as best they could for their past errors; and after administering slight reprehension that most gentle man redoubled his caresses to remove every apprehension from their minds. The tribe which had been the chief one in the past turbulences and which had incited the other tribes against the Spaniards soon found itself obliged to implore the protection of the Spaniards in order to defend themselves against the fury of the rest, who wished to avenge on them the deaths of their men killed in the attack. Later they came to the camp to hand over their weapons as a sign of friendship, and they begged that they be permitted to lodge near the camp and open up trenches to defend themselves. All was granted them; but not many remained. Father Salvatierra reconciled the hostile tribes, who, from then on, came together quietly to hear the doctrine.

Father Salvatierra took advantage of this tranquillity to consecrate the first fruits of California to God by means of baptism. The first and most solemn baptism, that of the Indian Ibò of whom we have already spoken, had been made two days before the attack; he was from the territory of San Bruno and belonged to the Cochimì nation. He had learned the rudiments of our faith and had asked for baptism when Admiral Otondo was there with Father Kino. He had been suffering for a long time from a terrible cancer, the fatal force of which seemed to have been most piously restrained by God until the arrival of Father Salvatierra.

As soon as Ibò[137] learned of the coming of Father Salvatierra, he came immediately, seeking again those other missionaries and begging them to make him a Christian. Father Salvatierra received him with the utmost graciousness and devoted himself to curing him if possible; but seeing that the illness was mortal and that, on the other hand, he was well disposed and sufficiently instructed, he solemnly baptized him on November 11, giving him the name of Manuel Bernardo.[138] He was so happy that in that very month he died with great signs of preordination.

He also wished that his two children, one of four and the other of eight, should be baptized together with him. The baptism of the former was deferred until he might be well instructed in the mysteries of the faith; the latter was baptized on November 15 with the name of Bernardo Manuel.[139] The reason for having given these names to the father and the son was that the viceroy, on taking leave of Father Salvatierra, requested him to call thus the first two Californians whom he might make Christians.

Afterward two other children were baptized, one of whom was named Juan and the other Pedro in honor of the memory of Don Juan Caballero and Don Pedro Gil de la Sierpe, benefactors of the Mission. The fifth Californian baptized was one of those who had been wounded in the attack on the camp and who was deserted by his own people and found by the soldiers; he was instructed as circumstances permitted, and he died the night following his baptism, glorifying all the merciful powers of the Master.

[137] Dionisio the "great eater." See above, note 133.

[138] Bancroft says that the father was named Bernardo Manuel (*History of the North Mexican States and Texas*, Vol. I, p. 289).

[139] Manuel Bernardo, according to Bancroft (*History of the North Mexican States and Texas*, Vol. I, p. 289.

Chapter Twelve

FATHER PÌCCOLO, MISSIONARY. A LETTER FROM FATHER SALVATIERRA. THE LABORS OF THE COLONISTS. A CONSPIRACY AGAINST THE SPANIARDS, AND THE VICTORY OF THE LATTER

On Saturday, November 23, when the first of the sermons delivered on that day by Father Salvatierra had scarcely been finished, the galiot which brought Father Francisco María Pìccolo, who had been appointed to that Mission in place of Father Kino, reached that port. He was born in Sicily, and after having become a Jesuit he went to Mexico while still a young man. And from there he was sent to the Missions of Tarahumara, where he worked for twelve years with much success, converting the heathen, building churches, and improving the habits of the Christians. He went to California in the year 1697, and in the thirty-one years which he spent there he was one of the chief pillars of that very recent Christianity, sparing no effort to extend the kingdom of God and inciting all to the practice of Christian virtues, not less by his example than by his words.

His coming was a great consolation to all. Father Salvatierra acquired a companion to help him in the ministration of the apostleship and cares of the new colony. The soldiers then had in him another priest to direct their souls, to minister to them in their illnesses, and to comfort them in their afflictions. But it was already time to give an account to the government about the success of that enterprise and to return the galiot to the treasurer[140] of Acapulco, who had loaned it. While the ship was being prepared for the voyage to Acapulco, Father Salvatierra wrote many letters to the viceroy, the benefactors, and all who had any interest in the success of the venture. Four letters were printed from these in Mexico; the first went to the viceroy; the second to the wife of the viceroy, the Condesa de

---

[140] Don Pedro Gil de la Sierpe.

Moctezuma; the third to Don Juan Caballero y Ocio; and the fourth, which contained a detailed account of all that had happened up to that date, to Father Ugarte.[141] In all there gleamed the apostolic zeal and the graciousness and gratitude of that great man.

After the galiot was sent, all devoted themselves to work to give their camp the best order that they could then. They widened the trenches; they built a palisade; they constructed a chapel of stone and mud and covered it with a thatched roof; they built three small houses, one for a dwelling for the missionaries, another for the captain, and another for the storehouse; and near them they built barracks for the soldiers. While the soldiers were engaged in these labors, the missionaries of the province sent all the provisions which they could get on two trips and, besides, five soldiers, who were useful for finishing the buildings more quickly.

The Indians who came there daily to be instructed, seeing these labors on the one hand and observing, on the other, that the foreigners did not fish for pearls nor value them, like all the rest who had been in that peninsula before, were persuaded finally that they had not come [*sic*] to return later but that they were trying to establish themselves there to introduce a new religion. Now this could not be done without decreasing the fees of the *guamas*, who, as we have said before, acting as doctors of law and as physicians and having derived advantage from the gross credulity of the barbarians, did not cease in their conventicles to embitter the minds of the Indians against the missionaries and the Spaniards. Many of the Indians, already illuminated by divine grace and very fond of the Christian doctrine, did not surrender to their suggestions; but others consented without difficulty.

On an April day of 1698 the latter went to the port and took possession of a boat which the galiot had left there, either to make use of it in fishing or only to begin a war by this deed. The two soldiers who took care of the boat and who were from

---

[141] According to Bancroft the third letter went to Ugarte and the fourth to Ocio (*History of the North Mexican States and Texas*, Vol. I, p. 289).

the vicinity could not dissuade them; but one of them ran to the camp at once to give warning. The captain went out there with ten well-armed soldiers against the thieves. A part of the thieves faced the soldiers, while the others, drawing the boat out of the water, destroyed it with large stones; and when this was done, they all fled.

The Spaniards, determined to punish them, divided into two squads and followed them. One squad, composed of the *alférez*, Figueroa,[142] three soldiers, and a friendly Californian, while traveling along a trail, fell into an ambuscade of more than fifty barbarians. They attacked the soldiers furiously with arrows and stones; but the Spaniards defended themselves with great courage, making several maneuvers in order not to be captured alive, as might have happened easily if the Indians had not been restrained by the fear of firearms. While those four men were defending themselves as well as they could from so many enemies, the Californian who accompanied them ran to give warning to the captain's squad, who had not heard a thing because of the noise of the tide and the strong wind which was then blowing. When they arrived to aid their companions the number of Indians also was increased; and both fought desperately until the Indians retired at dusk, leaving some dead and others wounded on the field. Not one of the Spaniards was killed or even seriously wounded.

So the Californians learned at their cost not to wage war on the foreigners who, although few, had better discipline and fought with very superior weapons. The conspirators, mingled with the faithful Indians, came again to the Spaniards' camp. The captain wished to punish them for their wickedness, but the missionaries interposed; and a general pardon was proclaimed. The conspirators, in order to make known their repentance and submission, brought, with barbarous simplicity, the useless fragments of the destroyed boat.

---

[142] One of the newly arrived soldiers mentioned above.

Chapter Thirteen

THE OCCUPATIONS OF THE MISSIONARIES AND THE LACK OF PROVISIONS

During that Holy Week divine services were held with much devotion by the Spaniards and with the greatest tranquillity and wonder of the Indians. The missionaries continued their work of studying the language and catechising. In order to do this to greater advantage and be on guard against the inconstancy of the barbarians, Father Piccolo instructed the children within the camp while Father Salvatierra catechised the adults outside. With their constant toil they had instructed and thoroughly prepared many for baptism; but they did not wish to baptize any, because they feared their fickleness and because the permanency of the Mission was still uncertain. Only those who were in danger of death were baptized, among whom were observed many notable indications of the divine providence of the Master.

Some strange examples also were seen of the marvelous workings of divine grace among the catechumen and among others. The one which Father Salvatierra himself relates in his letter to Father Ugarte is worthy of memory. There was a child of four years, named Juan Caballero, who, with a wand in his hand in imitation of the *fiscales* (teachers of the Christian doctrine), was guiding the others in the repetition of the prayers taught them. If he saw any talk he intimated silence to them by placing his finger on his mouth. When the doctrine was finished, he took the rosaries and relics which the soldiers carried with them and (kneeling) he kissed them and reverently put them on his eyes. Not being content with these demonstrations, he wanted others to follow his example; and he did not become calm until he succeeded in it, which affected the soldiers themselves to the degree of making them weep.

When the missionaries were most engaged in their praiseworthy duties and most satisfied with the progress of the Indians, the latter began to be absent little by little from the camp.

June had arrived and, being the time of the gathering of the *pitaje*, they went everywhere collecting the fruit they so esteemed.

This annoyance was followed quickly by another more serious one. The boat which had been sent two months before to Yaqui to bring provisions had not returned. Nor had the provisions arrived which were expected from Mexico. There was such a great scarcity of food in the camp that there were no provisions except three sacks of bad wheat flour and as many more of worm-eaten corn. The distress of all was so increased that Father Salvatierra, in an account which he wrote then, states as follows: "I am beginning to write this account without knowing whether I shall be able to finish it; because, at present, we are in such great want here for lack of food which is growing scarcer each day; and, as I am the eldest of all those of the camp of the Virgin of Loreto, I shall be the first to pay common tribute to nature."

But the most admirable thing is that the missionaries, in the midst of such calamities and dangers, knew so well how to direct the soldiers (composed of twenty-two men of different nationalities and of almost every free profession) that not any dispute or false oath or curse was heard among them. On the contrary, all punctually attended the devotional services which were held there every day, and especially a novena which was then said to the Blessed Virgin to obtain from God the help so long desired; and, having heard in a sermon which was preached to them against the vice of the false oaths that were so common among soldiers and sailors in some city in Germany (I do not know which), that any perjurer was condemned to pay a certain sum of money, they themselves spontaneously imposed a similar fine; and they were all very solicitous about applying the penalty to the one who might incur such a sin.

Chapter Fourteen

THE LOSS OF THE COLONY. THE MISSIONS OF SAN JUAN BAUTISTA DE LONDÒ AND SAN JAVIER DE VIGGÈ

They were about to finish the novena and with it the provisions also, when there arrived a new large boat, the "San José," which was built by a merchant of Nueva Compostela and sent from the port of Chacala. It brought all the provisions which Father Ugarte had sent from Mexico for the Mission, together with seven volunteer soldiers who wished to serve there. Since it was believed that the Mission boat had been lost, Father Salvatierra wanted to buy this new boat, which seemed quite good to him. The master consented willingly, because he well knew, through experience acquired on that voyage, that it was very poorly built. Then, by using a thousand rascally tricks, he sold it for twelve thousand *scudi*, which Father Ugarte was to pay in Mexico. The deception was soon discovered, and another six thousand *scudi* were spent in repairing it. In spite of this all the cargo carried on the first voyage was damaged, and on the second it floundered at Acapulco, for which reason it was necessary to sell it; and scarcely could a person be found who would pay five hundred *scudi* for it, to the great loss of the Mission.

The beneficence of the treasurer, Don Pedro Gil de la Sierpe, relieved this misfortune by giving Father Salvatierra two boats, a large one called "San Fermin," and another, a little one called "San Francisco Javier." They began immediately to make voyages, carrying all the necessities to California from different ports of Sinaloa and from Nueva Galicia, and, among other things, horses, oxen, and other animals sent by Don Augustín de Encinas,[143] a benefactor of that Mission.

Now that the missionaries knew the language of the barbarians and had horses for making trips over the arid and gravelly mountains, they decided to penetrate the country from different points. Father Salvatierra, accompanied by some sol-

---

[143] A merchant in Mexico City.

Homer Aschmann

Fig. 15a – The mission church at Loreto. This photograph was taken in 1949 early in the modern refitting of the church.

Hugh Manessier

Fig. 15b – The refitted mission church in Loreto.

Homer Aschmann

Fig. 16a — Interior of the nave of the mission church at Loreto early in its refitting period. The details of the masonry work in the massive walls indicate several reconstructions, but some of the structure dates from Jesuit times.

Homer Aschmann

Fig. 16b — Remnant of the chapel at San Juan Londó. This site was designated a mission only for a short time, and then it became a subsidiary *pueblo de vista* of Loreto.

Fig. 17 – The mission church and part of the modern village of San Javier Viggé. A carved inscription bears the date 1758 so the building is clearly of Jesuit construction and is their greatest architectural monument in Baja California.

Homer Aschmann

Hugh Manessier

Above: Fig. 18a — Looking north over the village of San Javier from the roof of the mission church.

Left: Fig. 18b — Interior of the church at San Javier.

George E. Lindsay

diers, went out first at the beginning of 1699 toward the northwest to a place called Londò, which was twenty-seven miles distant from Loreto and inhabited by many families of Indians. But he did not find any, because all had fled on seeing him arrive, in spite of the many times he had told them before that he wanted to make them a friendly visit. He waited there for two days; but because they did not even come when they had been called, he returned to Loreto with his followers. He lamented their lack of confidence; but finally he managed to dissipate their fears. Therefore when spring came he returned to the same place, to which he gave the name of San Juan Bautista, where he remained for some days with them, instructing them, treating them kindly, and giving them presents.

Some Indians had come to Loreto from Viggè-Biaundò,[144] a place situated toward the west behind a rough mountain. They showed such great gentleness and such an inclination to the Christian doctrine that the missionaries, in spite of their resolution not to baptize them except when in danger of death, gave baptism to a very quick youth better instructed than the others, naming him Francisco Javier.

Father Piccolo decided to go to that place, and he went in fact on March 10, accompanied only by some friendly Indians, because the soldiers were discouraged. There were great difficulties to overcome on the trip; the mountain was very steep and there was no open road. He was received with the greatest courtesy by the Indians of Viggè-Biaundò, where he remained four days instructing them; and he found out that the new Christian, Francisco Javier, was doing the same thing spontaneously. That place seemed suitable to him for establishing a Mission, because those Indians were very well disposed to adopt Christianity and because in the next valley there was land capable of cultivation and provided with water and with good pasture for maintaining cattle.

As regards the difficulty of the road, it was made in such a way (although with the greatest labor of the soldiers who were encouraged by Father Piccolo and aided by the Indians them-

---

[144] Biaundò was the name given the country by the Indians, and the surrounding mountains were called "Viggè" (Bolton, *Palóu*, Vol. I, p. 180).

selves) that in June a good trail was already opened on which they at once began to travel by horseback from Loreto to Viggè-Biaundò. In October the Father moved there to build, with the help of the soldiers and the Indians, a small chapel and some little houses of crude bricks for their dwellings, which they then covered with thatched roofs. And this was the origin of the Mission of San Francisco Javier,[145] the little chapel of which was dedicated by Father Salvatierra on November 1 with more devotion than dignity.

While Father Piccolo was occupied in establishing that new Mission and in exploring part of the western coast of that peninsula, Father Salvatierra made a third trip to Londò; but he attained little success from it because of the hostility which existed among the several tribes which met there. They offered some opposition, a part of which was even directed against the missionary, since some Indians had the daring to shoot an arrow at the mule on which he was riding. He managed, nevertheless, with his patience and his good reasoning to pacify and reconcile them.

Chapter Fifteen

THE MISFORTUNE OF THE COLONY, FOR THE REPARATION OF WHICH FATHER SALVATIERRA AND FATHER UGARTE VAINLY ASKED THE GOVERNMENT FOR HELP

AMONG these events, sometimes prosperous and sometimes adverse, the year 1700 arrived. In this year and the following one so many misfortunes came upon the colony[146] that it would inevitably have been ruined had it

---

[145] Endowed by Juan Caballero with ten thousand pesos. It later supplied the early Missions founded in what is now the state of California with, among other things, four good horses, sixteen mules broken to work, harness, leather bags, church vestments, a small bronze bell, and "a liquor case with six flasks" for use in mass (*ibid.*, p. 51).

[146] By 1700 Loreto had within its settlement twenty people. When this Mission was taken over by the Franciscans (1768) Loreto had only forty families, representing about 160 persons. Up to that time 1,646 Indians and

not been sustained by the especial providence of God. At that time the number of the colonists had reached seventy. All were supported by Father Salvatierra, and it was necessary, therefore, to bring a greater quantity of supplies from distant countries, since the land of that peninsula was not yet sufficiently cultivated to produce them. Besides the little boat, the "San Javier," there was the "San Fermin," because the "San José" had become disabled, as has been said.

Until that time the soldiers had appeared contented (as was right) with their subordination to the missionaries by whom they were paid. Every aid and protection in favor of the colony was rightly expected then from the government of Mexico, because after it had attempted to establish one for so many years with such considerable expense it seems that the colony should be assisted in every way. But men are so constituted that after they have exerted themselves with unspeakable efforts to get something, having obtained it, they cannot keep it.

In fact, all these hopes vanished like smoke; and all those advantages which existed there were turned into as many misfortunes. The vessel "San Fermin" was grounded on the shallows in the port of Ahome[147] and went to pieces from the force of the waves and through the neglect of the sailors, who promised to take better care of another boat when it would be constructed. There remained, therefore, only the little "San Javier," which was damaged by the heavy storms that it had suffered and which had carried Father Salvatierra at the peril of his life to Sinaloa in order to seek help to alleviate those great trials which they suffered at the Mission. But all the efforts made by him were of no avail.

Spaniards had been baptized, and 1,329 persons had been buried there; 92 people had been married (Bolton, *Palóu*, Vol. I, pp. 186–87). The Mission was completely destroyed by an earthquake in 1717, but it was immediately rebuilt. Perhaps this Mission had the most elaborate decorations inside of any Mission in the peninsula or in Upper California (*Proceedings of the California Academy of Sciences*, January 1923, p. 63). Loreto today exports fish and much tanbark, which is used in the tannery at La Paz.

[147] A seaport town on the mainland directly opposite Loreto, at the mouth of the Fuerte River. Today it is a town of about three thousand people, engaged chiefly in fishing.

In the two preceding years he had written many times to the viceroy, giving him an account of the beginning and progress of his Mission. But that gentleman had not deigned to answer him. Now, in March 1700, he drew up a long petition directed to the Royal Tribunal (composed of the viceroy, the supreme judges, and the other ministers of the king) and signed by the two missionaries and by thirty-five other persons of that colony.

In this petition he related concisely all that had happened in California. He explained the actual condition of the colony, the great sums expended on it, and the impossibility of paying the soldiers of the presidio only with alms, which, at last, had become uncertain and often late; then he implored the king's protection, asking, in order not to lose the fruit of so many labors, that the presidio be supported by the royal treasury, just as the many other presidios which the Spaniards had on the frontiers of the gentiles. He pointed out the evils which would undoubtedly have resulted if that Mission had been abandoned by the soldiers; and he concluded by testifying to his decision of staying there, together with his companion, Father Piccolo, even though they might remain alone and manifestly be exposed to the violences of the barbarians.

From Sinaloa he addressed another petition to the viceroy, pointing out to him clearly the danger which that colony ran of perishing from hunger, because it had only one vessel in poor condition for the transportation of the provisions. And he begged him to assign, for this purpose, another boat to replace the one already confiscated in Acapulco, which had belonged to a merchant of Perú.

Salvatierra could not succeed at that time in obtaining aid for the things he was attempting, in spite of his just and effective reasons and the urgent arguments of Father Ugarte, the procurator of the Mission. The latter reproved those gentlemen, although modestly and respectfully, for their total indifference to the colony, since it was already established; whereas, a few years before, after a thousand attempts no less useless than excessively expensive, they had entreated the Company of the Jesuits to take charge of that much-desired expedition, promising it thirty thousand *scudi* annually for the expenses.

The royal *fiscal* alleged that in the agreement made in 1697 Father Salvatierra had bound himself to carry out that undertaking without any expense to the royal treasury. It is certain, Father Ugarte answered, that he obtained permission to enter California on the condition of causing no expense to the treasury (as he had not done) by establishing the first colony and maintaining it for three years with great work and with only the alms of the benefactors. But there is a great difference between creating a colony and maintaining it forever; and, although he had obligated himself in this way he was now inculpably in such grave need that the interests of the Church and the state demanded that he be favored and helped.

This very great opposition of the government to the petitions of Father Salvatierra arose from the false rumors maliciously scattered against the Jesuits by their enemies. The latter could not tolerate the thought that a Jesuit should have succeeded at last in that enterprise which many brave men had attempted in vain at such expense and with such great preparation of ships, soldiers, and weapons; they could not understand how well-born men, endowed with talent and knowledge, should wish spontaneously to deprive themselves of the company of their dear brothers and those comforts and honors that they could enjoy in their colleges in order to go to remote and uncivilized countries and to lead a distressing life among the savages, unless they were encouraged by the certain hope of becoming wealthy.

As the animal man, according to Saint Paul, does not understand the things of the spirit of God, so he cannot imagine either that there is anyone capable of sacrificing all the comforts of life and all the goods of the world for divine glory alone. California had become famous for its abundance of pearls, with the fishing of which not a few have gained opulence. And it was known to all that the missionaries had little thought of engaging in this traffic; they neither fished on their own account, nor did they permit their dependents (the new colonists) to do so.

Nevertheless their enemies had been persuaded or wished to be persuaded that they were looking for nothing else in

California than to become owners of those riches. The alms of the benefactors of that Mission were, at that time, a new source of false rumors against the Jesuits, although they were certainly very insufficient for the expenses which had to be made in a country so remote and absolutely lacking in everything; they were, however, sufficient for making one individual affluent; and those who did not have the valor to endure the toil, hardships, and dangers of those missionaries envied the wealth of their Mission.

Among other calumnies the report was spread that the loss of the "San Fermin" was not genuine but was pretended by the missionaries in order to extract money from the royal treasury. This gross slander was disproved by the testimony of many respectable persons; but the rumors did not cease; they found new support in the letters of Don Antonio García de Mendoza,[148] the captain of the presidio of California. As we have already said, Don Luis de Torres Tortolero was its first captain. But after having served very well and being ill from a bad inflammation of the eyes, which that climate caused him, he was discharged in 1699, to the great regret of the missionaries, taking with him an affidavit about his services and good conduct, which was given him by Father Salvatierra and which was of use to him in obtaining some good positions in Nueva Galicia.

In his place García de Mendoza, who was a brave soldier, was appointed captain; but he was not so honorable a man. Although the latter owed his position to Father Salvatierra and was paid by him, yet he did not want to be dependent on him because he wished to be able to make use of the Indians at his free will, as some conquerors and captains of Sinaloa and other places in America are accustomed to do, with unspeakable harm to the neophytes and to the Missions. He also wanted pearl fishing to be permitted him and the soldiers with the object of becoming rich quickly, instead of doing the work that was necessary in California to put that colony in better shape; and as he could attain neither, he vented his rancor against the mission-

---

[148] The second captain of the presidio at Loreto, an old soldier who had become well seasoned by fighting the Indians in the province of San Luis Potosí.

aries in several letters addressed to the viceroy and to some of his friends. But they were so confused and filled with contradictions that it was perceived at once in them how he was blinded by passion.

In order to give some idea of this, the letter which he wrote to the viceroy on October 22, 1700, suffices. After having stated that the Fathers Salvatierra and Piccolo were saintly men, apostles, and celestial spirits, and after having praised to the stars their works, their zeal, and their detachment from worldly things, he complains bitterly of them because of the labor spent in leveling the road, in constructing some buildings, and in some other things, not very useful but absolutely necessary to the colony; and he concludes thus: "I do not find any other remedy for checking such temerity, than to inform the Most Reverend Father Provincial[149] of the Sacred Society of the Jesuits, begging him to withdraw those Fathers from California and place them where they may be punished with that penalty which they deserve; and that they put me also in a prison with a thick chain that I may serve as an example to my successors." But this good soldier endured those great hardships because he wished to. He could have freed himself from them easily by giving up his position and going where he liked it better.

The enemies of the Jesuits did not fail to scatter everywhere copies of these letters, which, although so worthy of scorn, some royal ministers and other persons believed, being persuaded that the subordination of the soldiers in California to the missionaries was the general intent of Jesuitical ambition to rule everywhere.* These and other pretexts, scattered by respectable persons among the populace, considerably discouraged the

---

* Father Salvatierra was appointed provincial of the Jesuits of Mexico in 1704; but he made so many efforts to free himself from that office and return to California that finally he succeeded in it. Now if he had been ambitious to rule he would not have left the command of such an illustrious body in such a splendid metropolis as that of Mexico [City] to go and command a few impoverished soldiers in an obscure corner of poverty-stricken and almost deserted California.

---

[149] Father Francisco de Arteaga.

liberality of the benefactors. Hence the progress of Christianity in that peninsula was greatly retarded, and the Mission was reduced to such a condition that it was necessary to send away a larger part of the people because so many could not be supported in it.

This gave the barbarians occasion to become insolent and make various attempts against the colony. In a letter to his friend, the *fiscal* of Guadalajara, Father Salvatierra, after having stated to him that he had already discharged eighteen soldiers, wrote thus: "I await only the last decision of the government of Mexico to which I have already directed my final protests for discharging the remainder of the men. When all are dismissed, we shall think about paying, as a debt, what we shall have left. However, if the Californians (my beloved children in Christ) should send us to render an account to God before we have been able to do so, then the Virgin will pay for us."

Chapter Sixteen

THE TRIP OF FATHER SALVATIERRA TO SUPPLY THE COLONY. THE ARRIVAL OF FATHER JUAN DE UGARTE IN CALIFORNIA. A BOATLOAD OF PROVISIONS

CONSIDERING that the colony could absolutely not last unless necessities were assured for the colonists, that these supplies could not be found in California, and that bringing them from Mexico [City] became each time more difficult, Salvatierra now determined to go and seek them in the Missions of Sonora. It was a country rich in mines and fertile soil, and a short distance from that of California, since the distance between the two is not greater than the width of the intervening gulf. With this object he left the port of Loreto at the end of October (1700), and, having obtained some aid in Sinaloa for his Mission, he went to Sonora to find Father Kino, his former friend and benefactor.[150]

---

[150] Salvatierra went directly to Dolores, a Mission founded by Kino early in 1687, where he met him in January 1701. Records differ somewhat about

This zealous and indefatigable missionary, not being able to work in the Mission in California as he had wished because obedience kept him in Sonora, did everything that was possible to maintain it by sending cattle, furniture, and supplies,[151] which he solicited in the mines and Missions from the port of Guaymas to Loreto. But his great zeal, like that of Father Salvatierra, was limited neither to those things nor to those times. Both, since they were eager to increase the kingdom of Christ, intended to extend their respective Missions toward the north until they met each other[152] beyond 33° and hence could aid each other mutually.

the meeting of these two noted men. Kino says that on February 20 Salvatierra arrived at Dolores and five days later Salvatierra set out westward "with twenty loads of provisions" and eighty pack animals, mostly mules. Two days later Kino started and overtook Salvatierra at Caborca. On March 31, 1701, they came in sight of the Gulf of California, where they could plainly see "the closing in of both lands of this New Spain and California." In April the two men decided to return, Kino returning to the Mission at Dolores, and Salvatierra going south to Guaymas, where he embarked on the "San Javier" for California. He arrived at Loreto in May. For account of this interesting expedition see Bolton, *Kino*, Vol. I, pp. 271–89.

[151] Kino sent across the Gulf to Salvatierra in the fall of 1700 supplies collected from various settlements in Sonora. More than 600 cattle were sent. Kino's own Mission (Dolores) gave 200 cattle. One district (Oposura) gave 100 cattle and 1,000 sheep and goats. Large quantities of lard, flour, and tallow were also sent. Ten loads of flour were sent to Salvatierra the next year. See Bolton, *Kino*, Vol. II, p. 264; also Vol. I, p. 306.

[152] It was the hope of these Jesuit leaders, and of others, that a chain of Missions could be established north through the peninsula to connect with those running north through Sonora. In the transportation of supplies from the mainland to the peninsula, this chain of settlement would then be used, thus eliminating the dangerous trip across the Gulf.

It is interesting to note that Missions were not founded on the Colorado River until 1780. The first two proved to be tragic failures. Near the juncture of the Colorado and Gila rivers was founded the Mission of Purísima Concepción, and few miles down the Colorado River a second one, San Pedro y San Pablo de Bicuñer. Immediately, serious trouble arose with the Indians, and the next year in July occurred the Yuma massacre. The preceding month, Captain Rivera, who had led one of the expeditions up the peninsula when San Diego was founded, arrived on the Colorado River with forty colonists, including women and children. While they were resting at these Missions the Indians attacked them, killing Rivera and every man, even the two padres stationed at each Mission. The women and children were made captives.

As they wished to explore all the country to which they had been assigned for their apostolic tasks, they went, when they met, toward the Red River in March 1701 accompanied by ten Spanish soldiers and some Indians. They traveled along the coast road, which was the shortest, although bad. When they had arrived beyond parallel 32°, they distinctly observed from the summit of a mountain the union of California with the continent; but they were unable to go farther forward because from that mountain as far as the Red River[153] there was sandy ground for ninety miles. The following year Father Kino repeated his trip over other practicable roads to that river, as well as to the Gila, and he had the opportunity to observe its banks attentively.

When Father Salvatierra had collected some alms in the Missions of Sonora,[154] he returned at the end of April to Loreto, where he had the great pleasure of finding Father Ugarte. The latter, after having left Mexico on December 3 of the previous year with the purpose of bringing provisions to that colony, made a trip of one thousand two hundred miles by land as far as a port of Sinaloa. And not finding anything there for crossing the Gulf but a small boat that was very old and abandoned as absolutely useless, he embarked fearlessly in it; and after three days of favorable sailing he arrived at Loreto[155] on March 19, 1701. He found the colony in the greatest want; it

---

[153] The frontier just south of the Colorado River was not a strange land to Kino. In 1691 he and Salvatierra had explored the country north from Dolores Mission to the Gila River Valley, and three years later Kino returned to the same section of the country. He made a similar trip in 1697, and during the next two years he made two more trips to the Gila River. He went down this river (1700) to its confluence with the Colorado, looking for new Mission sites and planning to found a chain of Missions to connect with those on the peninsula. From these trips Kino concluded that California could not be an island (Bolton, *Kino*, Vol. I, pp. 351-54).

[154] By 1700 several Missions had been founded in Sonora. Among those along the Altar River were Caborca, Cocospera, Dolores, Santa María, Suamca, San Ignacio, and Tubutama.

[155] It is said that when Ugarte left Mexico City to begin his important work in the peninsula he took along only a coverlet, two bed sheets, and a few reales (Bancroft, *History of the North Mexican States and Texas*, Vol. I, p. 408).

was then five months since it had received any aid. But a few days afterward they had the great joy of seeing the vessel "San Javier" reach that port loaded with provisions collected three months before by Father Ugarte himself. He did not have permission from his superiors to stay in California, but Father Salvatierra got it for him. Although Salvatierra regretted not having such an active procurator in Mexico, he foresaw how much a man of such great talent and such heroic vigor would contribute to the advancement of Christianity in that peninsula.

Chapter Seventeen

THE APPOINTMENT OF ANOTHER CAPTAIN. THE TRANSGRESSIONS OF THE INDIANS OF VIGGÈ

THE SCARCITY of provisions was not the only calamity which was suffered in that place. There were other quite considerable ones. Captain García, continuing disgusted with that life, disturbed the peace of all the colony with his restlessness; but, finally seeing neither that his bitter letters influenced the viceroy to remove him from subordination to the missionaries nor that the latter would permit him to employ the Indians in pearl fishing, as he was endeavoring to do, he agreed to leave that office by being discharged, as he was to the great pleasure of the missionaries.

In order that the soldiers might now live more happily under a leader appointed by themselves, Father Salvatierra let them have the liberty of naming a new captain, making their choice by secret votes. The Portuguese, Don Estevan Rodríguez Lorenzo, a good Christian, honorable, active, intrepid, moderate, and prudent, was elected by almost all the votes. He had entered California with Father Salvatierra in 1697, and he remained there until his death. During the forty-nine years that he lived in California he contributed much to the establishment of the Missions, to the spreading of Christianity, and to the peace of the soldiers and the Indians.

Shortly before this new captain was elected, the Indians of

Viggè, instigated by their *guamas* or medicine men, made the barbarous decision of destroying the Mission of San Javier and killing the missionary, despite several faithful Indians who opposed their intent. One day they came in a mob to the Mission, and, not having found Father Piccolo in it (because he had fortunately gone out), they discharged their fury on his little house, the small chapel, and the poor furnishings of each, destroying everything, breaking the crucifix into pieces, and shooting arrows at the face of the painted figure of the Virgin of Sorrows, who, they said, was the friend of the missionary. When Father Piccolo learned through a faithful Indian what had happened in his Mission, he went to Loreto, from where an officer left with some soldiers to punish that transgression; but the culpable ones had already fled over the most rugged mountains. In this way they escaped punishment; but soon after, importuned by the missionaries, they came humbly to Loreto to ask pardon, acknowledging their fickleness, which is so common among capricious men. That Mission was not long in being re-established advantageously, as we shall see later.

Chapter Eighteen

FATHER UGARTE ACCEPTS THE MISSION OF SAN JAVIER. HIS EXTRAORDINARY ZEAL

THOSE Indians seemed tranquil after their correction and well disposed to be obedient to the teaching of the missionary. Also, it was not deemed wise to abandon that place, the soil of which seemed the most adapted for agriculture because in Loreto they had been scarcely able to make a small tract of land useful for planting fruit trees and vegetables. Father Salvatierra, in front of the altar of the Virgin, now put in charge of that Mission Father Ugarte, because Father Piccolo had to leave for New Spain to transact business about California. Father Ugarte accepted the charge willingly and went there, accompanied by some soldiers; but for many days not an Indian appeared, either through fear or hatred of the soldiers. The soldiers continually caused trouble with their restlessness, because neither did they have Indians to serve them nor did he permit the soldiers to go and seek them, since he feared, rightly, that they would inspire more distrust in the Indians with their hostilities.

Finally Father Ugarte determined to withdraw the soldiers, placing himself in the hands of Providence. He spent one day in that solitude with his spirit disturbed alternately by the pious hope of martyrdom and by the natural fear of death. In the afternoon a boy approached his hut in the attitude of spying. After Father Ugarte approached the youth, he caressed him, gave him a gift, and sent him to tell his people that they could come with security because he no longer had soldiers.

When the savages were assured of this situation, they began to come little by little, and the practice of the doctrine was established again. But this great man, animated by a true zeal and not content with teaching them the mysteries of the Christian religion, tried to wrest from their hearts the fondness which they had for their medicine men and their ancient superstitions; and he took upon himself the arduous task of civilizing them, teaching them the trades and accustoming them to the works which social life requires. What he had to endure from some of the men who were accustomed to perpetual idleness and unchecked liberty can probably be imagined in some manner, but it cannot be expressed adequately.

Every morning after having held Holy Mass, which he had them hear, and after he had finished the Catechism and distributed *pozolli* to those who were to work, he took them either to labor on the church or the little houses which he was building for himself and for the neophytes; or he took them to the fields to clear off the thickets, carry away the stones, and prepare the soil for sowing or to make dams and ditches to irrigate the soil. He was not only the architect of the buildings but also the mason, carpenter, and everything. Neither admonitions, nor flatteries, nor the gifts of which he had made use would have been sufficient to remove habitual indolence from those brutish men if he had not encouraged them by his own example.

He was the first in the work, and the one who labored most.

In fact, he was the first in carrying the stones, in cutting the trees, in bringing and working the wood, in treading the mud, in digging out the soil, and in arranging the materials. He himself led the small flock which he had to pasture. He occupied himself, likewise, in all the trades, now with the ax in his hands removing the thickets, now with his pick breaking the rock, now with the hoe working the soil, which he was accustomed to do barefooted and barelegged. I cannot recall this without being affected and without recognizing the power of divine grace, when I see a gentleman brought up among the comforts of a wealthy house reduced to an insufferable and toilsome life; he was an erudite man, highly extolled in the schools and pulpits of Mexico, but buried in obscure and remote solitude—a man of lofty mind voluntarily condemned to converse with very stupid savages for thirty years.

After eating he took the Indians to say the Rosary; then he explained the Christian doctrine to them, and when this was finished he gave them something to eat again. As those barbarians were not capable of foreseeing the benefit of those efforts which deprived them of their idleness and liberty, so they found a thousand ways of tiring the patience of their charitable missionary, either by being absent, by not coming on time, by contemptuously opposing work, by making fun of it, or even by threatening him with death. There was no other recourse than to endure their impertinences, while discreetly getting them accustomed to an industrious life, yielding often to their weakness and at times mingling gentleness with firmness to make himself respected.

In the beginning they were very restless at the time of the Catechism, talking among themselves, making fun of what they were hearing, and often bursting out into loud laughter. He noticed that the principal reason for that mockery was his mistakes in speaking the language, and that the same Indians when he consulted them about the words or the pronunciation intentionally answered him with absurdities in order to have something to laugh at afterward in the Catechism. And for that reason from then on he asked only children about the language, for they were more sincere.

He tolerated these insults patiently, and at times he reproved the barbarians with some severity. On seeing that all this was of no use, he adopted a strange means but one opportune and suitable to the conditions and circumstances of the barbarians. As soon as he began to have anything to do with them he recognized their character readily; and he noticed that they did not esteem virtue, mind, or any spiritual or bodily gift, except bravery and strength, if they were not valiant and strong men. In order that they might respect his person and his doctrine he decided to give them a demonstration of the great strength with which he had been endowed by nature. Among the Indians who met at Catechism there was one who boasted greatly of his strength; and for that very reason he was most immoderate in his mockeries and laughter. One day when this barbarian was laughing unrestrainedly Father Ugarte grasped him suddenly by the hair and, lifting him in the air, kept him suspended for some time, shaking him three or four times.[156] This terrorized those barbarians to such an extent that they all fled instantly; but afterward they returned little by little and thereafter they always remained quiet and attentive during the doctrine.

On another occasion they told Father Ugarte that there were some brave wrestlers among them who wished to try their strength with him. "Well," he answered, "who is the bravest of all?" As soon as he was pointed out Father Ugarte took him by one arm and squeezed the large muscle of his arm so hard with his fingers that he made him give a terrible cry of pain. "Indeed," Father Ugarte then added, "he who cannot endure such a slight pain is not capable of fighting with me."

Nothing contributed so much to give credit to the strength of Father Ugarte among those barbarians as what he did with a lion. This kind of wild animal had multiplied greatly in that peninsula and they were doing as much harm to live stock as to men. Father Ugarte frequently urged the Indians to kill

[156] All writers attest Ugarte's great physical strength. Seizing unruly Indians by the hair and bouncing them up and down or swinging them about in a circle seemed to be effective. He even quieted a coarse jester in this way at one time during a service.

them, but without success, because, deceived by their medicine men (as has been said previously), they were invincibly persuaded that he who killed a lion would die.[157] There was nothing but experience that would convince them.

One day while Father Ugarte was traveling through the woods he perceived at a distance a lion which was coming toward him. Quickly dismounting and taking some stones in his hand he went to meet it; and when he had it within range he hit the animal a blow on the head with a stone, which knocked him to the ground. But he did not work so hard in killing him as in carrying him to the Mission (six miles distant), because he could not get the mule to consent to such a burden. To overcome this difficulty, he placed the lion in a tree which was in the road there and having mounted the mule he compelled her with his spurs and by striking her to pass near the tree, and on passing he caught the lion and threw it on the croup. The mule, curvetting furiously and then running quickly, took him to the Mission in a few minutes, where those barbarians could not doubt that deed, because the blood of the lion was still warm. Observing, after some time had passed, that the Father did not die and that no evil overtook him, they began to be disillusioned; and they devoted themselves thereafter to killing those very destructive wild animals.[158]

These and other notable deeds (the memory of which was retained even until our time among the inhabitants of that peninsula and among the Jesuits of New Spain, the story of which was published in the life of this great man printed in Mexico) instantly made the name of Ugarte famous. But a much greater glory was acquired among the true appraisers of merit through his great virtues, his apostolic tasks, and those services rendered to the Church of California, first as procura-

---

[157] The superstition that mountain lions must not be killed still lingers among certain Indians on the peninsula. For sketches of the habits and range of the mountain lion, see *Reports of the California Fish and Game Commission*, and *Report of the United States National Museum*, 1889, pp. 591–608.

[158] Hunters claim that a mountain lion will kill from two to three deer a week.

tor by collecting alms and by advancing the business of that colony with his zeal and industry and, secondly, as a missionary in establishing Missions, constructing buildings, clearing woods, opening roads, introducing agriculture and other crafts useful to the life in that uncivilized country, teaching those barbarians, civilizing them, and converting them into good citizens and excellent Christians.

And who can, in any measure, tell what he had to suffer from their coarseness? We shall cite a single example. After he had persisted greatly in teaching them he preached them a convincing sermon one day on the Inferno, explaining the fearful activity of the fire of that place and the atrocity and eternity of its torments. When he believed that he had derived much success from his sermon, he heard the Indians saying to each other that the Inferno was without doubt a better country than California, because if a perpetual fire were down there they would never have to suffer cold. A similar manner of thinking would have been enough to discourage the most ardent zeal; but it could not cool that of Father Ugarte.

He continued constant in his work, from which he finally gathered very abundant fruit. He developed a very pure and immaculate Christianity in the Mission of San Javier. The neophyte huntsmen were converted into agriculturists and artisans very well instructed in religion, temperate, and industrious; the absolutely untilled plains and the hills full of thickets and stones were changed into well-cultivated fields.

There he sowed wheat and corn and planted different kinds of garden stuff and vegetables. He planted a vineyard there, the first that was in that peninsula, and many kinds of fruit trees brought from Mexico. The excellent wine that was produced served for all the Masses which were said in that peninsula, and what was left over was sent to New Spain as a gift to the benefactors. The harvests of wheat and corn, although not sufficient for the consumption of an entire year, served for the greatest need and thus saved the expenses which were necessary in bringing those provisions from New Spain.

On account of the lack of rain in 1707, there was great scarcity of grains in Mexico and particularly in the fertile provinces of Sinaloa and Sonora. In California, where the rains are generally very scarce, grains were also lacking that year; but the industry of Father Ugarte supplied this lack in such a way that he makes the following statement in a letter of June 9, written to the royal *fiscal* in Guadalajara: "Thanks to the Master that for two months now we and all the soldiers and sailors have been eating good bread here from the harvest of our wheat, whereas the poor people of Sinaloa and Sonora are dying from hunger. Who would believe it?"

That incomparable man, not content with having supported the colony with agriculture and supplying it in large measure with the necessary provisions, also thought about clothing his naked neophytes, thereby making it unnecessary to have cloth come at great expense from Mexico. As soon as the sheep multiplied sufficiently he showed the Indians the time and the way to shear them, card the wool, spin it, and weave it; and he himself made the distaffs, spindles, and looms. But to make the Indians skillful, he had a good weaver, Antonio Moran,[159] come from Nueva Galicia under a contract of five hundred *scudi* annually, and he remained a long time in California to teach the Indians better and to perfect their manufactures.

Chapter Nineteen

THE PENURY OF THE COLONISTS. THE UPRISING AND THE PACIFICATION OF THE INDIANS

THESE achievements, which were not accomplished at once by Father Ugarte but only after some years of labor, would have been very valuable in the first years when the colony was more stricken. Near the end of 1701 nearly all the provisions in Loreto were gone. It was necessary, therefore, that Father Piccolo hasten to New Spain to solicit supplies and to make known by word of mouth to the govern-

---

[159] He was from Tepic, Mexico, and received an annual salary of $500 (Venegas, *Noticia de la California,* Vol. I, p. 32).

ment of Mexico and to that of Guadalajara what had already been uselessly presented in writing. He embarked on December 26, Fathers Salvatierra and Ugarte remaining at Loreto, which was in great need, until January 29, 1702, when the vessel "San Javier," loaded with wheat, corn, and other provisions, reached that port. But these things lasted a short time, because, as Captain Estevan Rodríguez states in his diaries, "the charity of Father Salvatierra in helping the Indians was so lavish that in a few days we were reduced to greater necessity."

The situation reached such an extreme in the spring, when provisions had come to be entirely lacking, that the missionaries as well as the soldiers were compelled to seek their food like the Californians (by fishing, in roots, and wild produce), Father Ugarte being the first in diligence and effort in searching for food for all. The letters written by the missionaries at that time, which contain the story of their labors, truly excite compassion.

Their destitution was aggravated by an uprising of the Indians, which was caused by the temerity of a soldier. He was married to a California Christian convert who, when June came, left her husband without his permission and at the suggestion of her mother to attend the dances and other amusements which the savages then carried on during the gathering of the *pitaje*. The soldier, disturbed by the flight of his wife, asked the captain for permission to go and look for her and to bring her back to Loreto and was granted permission to go for a certain time. He returned to Loreto without having found her; but a few days afterward, actuated by his affection, he left again without permission of the captain, accompanied by a Californian. He met an old Indian on the way and killed him with a bullet because he tried to dissuade him from that trip, telling him how dangerous it would be for him.

All the barbarians who were near by, and who were excited by the discharge of the harquebus and angry with the rash soldier, gathered quickly, killed him, and even wounded the Californian who accompanied him. The latter then fled hastily to Loreto and gave warning to the Spaniards. The captain, after having informed the missionaries who were then in Londò what had happened, so that by coming to Loreto in time they might place their persons in safety, set out with his small force against the culprits, who, knowing the miserable condition of the colony, tried to excite almost all the tribes to rebellion. The Spaniards, exhausted not less by hunger than by the roughness of the road, had some skirmishes rather than battles without much success except the killing of three or four conspirators. Father Ugarte had sown corn in Viggè and was expecting to raise his first crop; the culprits laid waste the field and killed some of the goats that furnished milk for the missionary. And they would even have demolished the chapel and the little house of the Mission of San Javier if they had not been protected by the soldiers and the faithful Indians. These disturbances lasted until the arrival of the vessel that came from Sinaloa with provisions and some troops. Everything then gradually became peaceful, the culprits making peace with the Spaniards by means of friendly Indians.

Chapter Twenty

ROYAL ORDERS. OFFERS TO ESTABLISH MISSIONS. TWO NEW MISSIONARIES. THE TRIPS OF FATHERS SALVATIERRA AND UGARTE

MEANWHILE, Father Piccolo, having left Loreto (as has been stated) on December 26, 1701, and having collected provisions in Sinaloa for the colony, went to Guadalajara, the capital of Nueva Galicia, where he obtained information about the three orders of the king which had been sent in favor of California. At the end of 1698 the viceroy of Mexico had informed the court of the undertaking of the Jesuits in that peninsula. This news was well received there, and a favorable reply was expected from it through the interest of the Condesa de Gálvez, the wife of the viceroy of Mexico, a very pious lady who had persisted in favoring the zeal of Father Salvatierra. But her death, which occurred that same year, and the grave illness which finally caused the death of King Charles II on November 1, 1700, delayed the success which it was hoped would be then attained.

When the pious youth Philip V[160] ascended the throne of Spain, notwithstanding the anxiety of the war which he was maintaining for the succession to the crown, he despatched orders in the first year of his reign, relative to California. He directed them to the viceroy of Mexico, to the *audiencia*, and to the bishop of Guadalajara, urging them never to neglect that enterprise but to promote and help it as much as they could and thanking those Jesuit missionaries for their apostolic tasks. He commanded also that they be given six thousand *scudi* annually from the royal treasury for the expenses of the colony of California, and that an exact account be sent to the court about the particular nature of California, the actual condition of the colony, and the means of enlarging it and facilitating its communication with New Spain.

Father Piccolo was entrusted with drawing up the account, which was attested by three eyewitnesses and printed shortly afterward in Mexico. The same Father then obtained, although with great effort, the six thousand *scudi* granted by the king; but he could not obtain the other things which he claimed were needed by the colony.

Then God touched the hearts of some gentlemen of Mexico in favor of the peninsula. The Marqués de Villapuente,[161] not less famous for his immense wealth than for his devout gener-

---

[160] He came to the throne at the age of seventeen. Although a fine soldier and extremely religious, he was easily influenced by those who won his confidence. It was during his reign that the French and Indian Wars took place in North America. Philip ruled until 1746.

[161] He was a man of great wealth, and is credited with endowing more Missions in California than any other person. One gift, made in 1735, represented several hundred thousand acres of rich land in the province of Tamaulipas and included all the improvements upon the land and the vast numbers of horses, mules, cattle, and sheep that roamed the range. Villapuente endowed the Mission of San José del Cabo with ten thousand pesos; he gave the same amount to each of the Missions of San José Comondù, to Purísima de Cadegomo, to Nuestra Señora de Guadalupe, to Santa Gertrudis, to Santiago de las Coras, and to Nuestra Señora del Pilar (Todos Santos). See Bolton, *Palóu*, Vol. IV (index).

osity in the many pious works of which he bore the cost in America, in Europe, and even in Asia, promised to endow three Missions in California; and Don Nicolás Arteaga (together with his wife, Doña Josefa Vallejo) took charge of the endowment of another.[162]

Father Piccolo went to California with this news, taking with him two new missionaries, Father Juan Manuel Basalduá,[163] of Michoacán, and Father Gerónimo Minutuli[164] of Sardinia. He embarked at the port of Matanchel in the "Virgen del Rosario," which had been bought at that time in Acapulco for the service of the colony and loaded with supplies and other things necessary for the presidio and the Missions. On crossing the Gulf of California, they were seized by such a fearful storm that shipwreck seemed inevitable, even after having thrown a great part of the cargo overboard; but after they had appealed with intense faith to the Blessed Virgin (the protectress of California), when all seemed lost, the wind ceased suddenly and the storm was ended; so they succeeded, fortunately, in reaching the port of Loreto on October 28, 1702, to the unspeakable joy of that distressed colony.

Father Ugarte embarked in December for Sonora, from where he brought some cows, sheep, goats, horses, and mules, and a good supply of provisions. Father Salvatierra had meanwhile penetrated into the interior of the peninsula with the purpose of observing better its inhabitants and soil; but he could do little because he had to journey on foot and because the roads were bad. Subsequently, with the help of horses, he left in March 1703, accompanied by the captain and some soldiers and neophytes, to explore the western coast of the penin-

---

[162] This was the Mission of Santa Rosalía de Mulegè, founded in 1705. Arteaga and his wife gave this Mission ten thousand pesos.

[163] He was sent to the Mission at Mulegè, but seven years later he returned to Mexico, where he was put in charge of the Mission at Guaymas.

[164] He returned to Mexico in December 1703 and went to work with Kino in Pimería Alta because of the more extensive field there and because of his health. He was sent to the Mission of San Pedro y San Pablo del Tubutama in Sonora, which was a few miles west of Dolores Mission. Later he served at the Missions of Santa Teresa de Caborca, and at Antonio del Uquibutama (Bolton, *Kino*, Vol. II, p. 136).

sula. He could not find any port or tillable ground; water was lacking entirely, although there were some good pieces of ground. In May he made another trip toward the northwest, but likewise unsuccessfully.

Chapter Twenty-One

THE FESTIVAL OF CORPUS CHRISTI. A CONSPIRACY AND THE PUNISHMENT OF THE CONSPIRATORS. THE KINDNESS OF THE MISSIONARIES TOWARD SOME SMUGGLERS. THE SCARCITY OF PROVISIONS

IN THE following month Father Salvatierra (because he wished to give a lofty idea of the sacrosanct mystery of the Eucharist to the catechumen and the neophytes on the festival of Corpus Christi)[165] called the missionaries to Loreto and celebrated there the festival and procession with all possible majesty and pomp, reviving the faith and devotion of the Spaniards and exciting the admiration and respect of the Indians. That service gave him an opportunity to explain to them the motives of the august ceremonies and the sacred happiness. But this was indeed soon followed by a great trouble because of the unfortunate news, brought by some Indians of the Mission of San Javier, that the abettors of the past conspiracy had united with other barbarians, made a night attack on the neophytes and catechumen of that Mission, and killed all of them with the exception of the few who had come to implore the protection of the Spaniards.

All those of the presidio were of the opinion that it was necessary to make an example of the barbarians in order to check their audacity and prevent their too frequent hostilities. The captain, accompanied by his soldiers and some faithful Indians, left the presidio very silently at midnight to pursue the culprits. They fled hastily in spite of the fact that they were

[165] A festival in honor of the Eucharist, observed on the Thursday after Trinity Sunday, which comes six weeks after Easter.

overtaken; nevertheless some were killed, among whom was one of the leaders. The captain, considering that following them over those rough mountains would be as dangerous as unsuccessful, returned to Loreto, determined not to let a similar crime go unpunished. With this purpose he threatened the catechumen who had escaped in the attack and compelled them to pursue the ringleader; and when they had finally caught him they brought him to Loreto. When he was presented to the captain, a trial was held; and, since it was evident not only through the depositions of various witnesses but by the confession of the culprit himself that he was the chief abettor, not only of that but of other conspiracies, he was condemned to capital punishment.

Fathers Salvatierra and Piccolo intervened, begging the captain to commute the death sentence to that of banishment. But the captain, firm in his determination, finally agreed, at the requests of the missionaries, that the execution should be deferred until the criminal was catechised and baptized. As this Indian was more acute than the others and had had some instructions in the mysteries of our religion, he was catechised quickly and accepted baptism voluntarily, through which he was converted into a new man in such a way that he desired death to pay for his crimes; and thus he died, well disposed and comforted by Father Basalduá. It was soon noticed how wise the decision of the captain had been, because the Indians were so humble and frightened that perfect tranquillity was enjoyed in each Mission for a long time.

A short time thereafter the misfortune of some smugglers compelled the poor missionaries to sacrifice to charity almost all the provisions which Father Piccolo had brought from Sonora. The viceroy[166] of Mexico, in order to avoid the harmful vexations and the frequent and serious extortions which pearl fisher-

---

[166] The duke of Albuquerque, Francisco Fernández de la Cueva Enríquez, held that office from 1702 to 1711, being the second viceroy to have this title. The failure of Enríquez to do more for California may be attributed to his constant fear that the War of the Spanish Succession might be brought to Mexico. He was also kept busy protecting the commerce of Mexico from the raids of pirates. This took considerable money.

men were accustomed to practice on the Californians, had strictly prohibited anyone from fishing for pearls without having first obtained a license from him and having shown it to the captain-governor of California. In spite of this some inhabitants of the coast of New Spain, incited by the hope of profit and assuring themselves impunity because of the distance from the government, after having equipped three large boats, went to the islands of the Gulf of California to carry on pearl fishing there; but a terrible storm destroyed one of their boats and carried the other two on the sands of the beach of Loreto, where the crew could scarcely save itself.

Shortly afterward fourteen men of those who had been shipwrecked in the first boat arrived in a small boat. All these people, numbering more than eighty persons, were maintained without charge by the missionaries during the four months that they remained there repairing the boats (until the close of 1703), when they returned to their country, taking Father Minutuli with them, because the climate of California did not agree with him.

The year 1704 was as unfortunate for that colony, which lacked little of being ruined. Provisions were for the most part very scarce; it was necessary to have them brought from Sinaloa or from Sonora and many times those trips could not be made on account of the foul winds or the poor condition of the boat. At other times the provisions were spoiled on the voyage because the ships sprang leaks with any storm whatsoever, or they were spoiled in the warehouse at Loreto by the excessive heat.

Chapter Twenty-Two

FATHER BASALDUÁ GOES TO MEXICO ON BUSINESS OF THE COLONY. THE ORDERS OF THE KING WITHOUT EFFECT

FATHER BASALDUÁ was sent to Mexico at the beginning of this year to discuss the business of the colony with the viceroy. Bearing in mind the reasonableness of his claims, and especially the fact that he knew that new orders of the king had arrived in the month of April regarding California, he expected success from this visit, but he was soon disappointed. Two Jesuit procurators[167] of Mexico had gone to Spain the year before and had presented a petition to the Catholic king in which they disclosed the actual condition of the Missions, the advantage which politics as well as religion could derive from them (if the missionaries were helped by His Majesty), and the harm which should be feared if that undertaking were abandoned. This petition was read in the Supreme Council of the Indies in the presence of the king, who, after having heard the opinions of the council and of the *fiscal*, issued five *cédulas* to Mexico on September 28 of that year.

In the first he commanded the viceroy to supply the missionaries of California annually from the royal treasury with the same stipend[168] which was given to the other missionaries of Sinaloa, Sonora, and Nueva Vizcaya, as well as with the cost of the bells, oil, vessels, and sacred ornaments which are accustomed to be given to the new Missions; that, with the unanimous advice of the army officers, the Jesuits, and other persons acquainted with that peninsula, a presidio be established with thirty soldiers and their commander on the coast of the Pacific Sea at the most northern point that might be possible, which would be as much for the security of that country as for a stopping place for the ships from the Philippine Islands; that a boat suitable for the transportation of all necessities to California be purchased; that he should try to send some poor families to that peninsula to increase the population; and that he should give the missionaries annually, besides the six thousand *scudi* already assigned at the end of 1701, another seven thousand and this should be done without any delay.

The other four *cédulas* were directed to the royal *fiscal* in Guadalajara, to the provincial of the Jesuits, praising his zeal for the promotion of the Missions of California, to Don Juan

[167] Fathers Bernard Rolandeguí and Nicolás de Vera (Venegas, *Noticia de la California*, Vol. II, p. 339).

[168] From the treasury at Guadalajara the California Missions were to receive $7,000, in addition to the $6,000 already assigned to this field (*ibid.*, p. 340).

Caballero, and to the Brotherhood of the Virgin de los Dolores in Mexico, commending their liberality in the establishment of the three Missions previously described by us.

In spite of these very strict orders and the opinion of the royal *fiscal*, who thought that they should be carried out punctually, the viceroy did not agree until the business was discussed in the Tribunal which was composed of the supreme judges, the officers of the king, and Fathers Salvatierra and Piccolo, who could not be present because of being one thousand two hundred miles distant from the metropolis.[169] And the viceroy not only was opposed to the prompt execution of these new commands but he did not allow Father Basaldúa those six thousand *scudi* which the king had commanded to be given since the end of 1701.

The reason for not executing these and other previous orders of the king which were favorable to California was (besides the one suggested above) the great and excessively expensive war of the succession to the crown of Spain which King Philip was then waging against the House of Austria and other allied powers. For this war all the treasures of America were scarcely sufficient. But precisely this was what obliged that pious monarch, in the midst of such disturbances and dangers, to show his zeal more and to extend his vigilance to remote and dark California.

Chapter Twenty-Three

FATHER PEDRO DE UGARTE, MISSIONARY. A CONFERENCE. FATHER SALVATIERRA'S SPEECH. THE DETERMINATION

FATHER BASALDUÁ, not expecting any success from his stay in Mexico, after he had had the vessel called "Rosario" calked, returned in it to Loreto, taking

---

[169] Mexico City, the largest city in Mexico, having now a population of 968,443. It is the most important financial, educational, and commercial city in the republic.

with him for those Missions Father Pedro de Ugarte,[170] a man not dissimilar in spirit to his great brother, Father Juan. At that time the colony was in great need, because for a long time the foul winds had not permitted them to go for provisions, as was usual, to Sinaloa and to Sonora. This need increased so much by the end of spring that Father Salvatierra thought it necessary to hold a meeting of the other missionaries and the officers of the presidio to determine whether or not it would be better to abandon California if they were no longer able to have the means of living in it. He was determined to remain there, although he might stay alone and at the evident risk of his life. This he had declared in his letter of February 8 to the royal *fiscal* of Guadalajara; but since he should not compel others to undergo such a heroic sacrifice, he wanted each one freely to choose the part which pleased him most.

Then after he had gathered them together, he spoke to them in this manner: "It is not necessary to explain to you the lamentable condition in which we are, because you see it; and you are tortured by hunger the same as we are. Our constant solicitude in obtaining provisions and all that is necessary for the colony is likewise known, and so none will be able to blame us for the present poverty. Subsequently, we have appealed to the government of Mexico, and in consideration of the strict orders of our pious monarch we did not doubt that we should find a remedy for our ills; but our hopes have been disappointed. Necessity urges too hard, and we do not know what to do. If we remain here without help we are exposed to death; if we abandon this country to seek relief elsewhere, we lose, in a moment, the success of our efforts. Therefore state your opinions freely."

Father Piccolo appeared absolutely indifferent in order that all the others might declare their opinions with entire freedom. But Father Juan de Ugarte openly opposed the idea of abandoning California, binding himself to seek fruits and roots in the mountains with which to support the soldiers of the presidio

---

[170] Born in Honduras (1660?), Ugarte came to California in 1704. He left seven years later.

until food was brought from Sinaloa and to remain alone[171] among the barbarians in case all the Spaniards left. In regard to the soldiers and sailors he was of the opinion that they should be given to understand that all who wished might go away, that discharge would be granted them, and that pay, in case it was due them, would be assured them.

All the missionaries approved and applauded this resolution. The captain and the officers, not content with approving it, declared that if the missionaries intended to leave California they would be the first to oppose them. There was not one either among the soldiers or the sailors who wished to make use of the liberty granted them; thus all determined unanimously to accompany the missionaries in their fate and to endure all hardships without complaining, as in fact they did.

Chapter Twenty-Four

THEY ENDEAVOR TO PROVIDE THE COLONY. THE VOYAGE OF FATHERS SALVATIERRA AND PEDRO DE UGARTE. THE DEDICATION OF THE NEW CHURCH OF LORETO. A NEW ORDINANCE OF THE PRESIDIO

WHEN the tempestuous winds which were hindering navigation had ceased, Father Piccolo left for Guaymas in the vessel "Rosario," as he had done so many other times; and at the same time he sent the "San Javier" to the port of Yaqui with letters for those missionaries. Father Juan de Ugarte, meanwhile, both by himself and aided by the soldiers and Indians, devoted himself to hunting everywhere for fruits and roots with which to satiate the hunger of the distressed colony. The poor Indians of San Javier, Viggè, and San Juan Londò performed the same service for the Spaniards.

Father Salvatierra, not desiring to forsake the propagation of Christianity in that country in the midst of such great trouble,

---

[171] This spirit was so often manifested by the early missionaries. It dominated the life of Father Junípero Serra, whose determination prevented the abandonment of the first settlement in Upper California at San Diego in 1769.

went in July to the coast of Liguig (or Malibat), a little more than forty miles distant to the south from Loreto, accompanied by Father Pedro de Ugarte, a Spanish soldier,[172] and two Indians, who were to act as interpreters, because the dialect which was spoken there was different from that of Loreto. He wished to establish a Mission in that place, and for that reason he went to inspect the soil and to prepare the minds of those barbarians. When they saw him coming they lay in ambush; and when they had him close they went out unexpectedly and shot their arrows at him. The Spanish soldier, holding his sword upright with one hand, fired a harquebus into the air with the other to frighten them. They in fact stretched themselves on the ground with their weapons; afterward they sat down with great coolness and silence to wait for their guests.

Father Salvatierra told them by means of the two faithful Indians not to be afraid, for they had come not to do them any harm but only to visit them and to bear them gifts as friends. The barbarians, laying aside their fear, approached Father Salvatierra, who treated them very kindly, giving them presents of some trifles which were valued by them and telling them that the missionary who had recently arrived in California to live with them, help them, take care of their children, and teach them the way to Heaven brought them those gifts as a sign of peace and friendship. They had their wives and children come in order to give proofs, mutually, of their confidence and gratitude.

The country was examined closely and was found good for the proposed Mission. But because Father Ugarte was not able then to undertake the building of the chapel and the houses and the cultivation of the soil, on account of the poverty of the colony, he was contented with gathering the first rewards of his Mission in the baptism of forty-eight children, with the consent and even at the petition of their mothers. When the missionaries had taken a tender farewell of the Indians, who had wished to detain them, they returned to Loreto, where two

---

[172] Francisco Xavier Valenzuela (Venegas, *Noticia de la California*, Vol. I, p. 348).

vessels loaded with provisions arrived at the end of August, to the great consolation of all those people.

Father Salvatierra had been called to Mexico [City] to attend the tribunal which was to be held in the presence of the viceroy and which was about the affairs of California. But before going he wished to celebrate the dedication of the new church built in Loreto. This was held on September 8 with great solemnity and with the baptism of many catechumen, although the ancient custom of the Church in conferring those baptisms on the eves of Christmas and Pentecost was usually observed in the Missions. Besides, it was necessary for him to make a new rule for the presidio, because the honorable Portuguese, Don Estevan Rodríguez Lorenzo, on account of the annoyances which some of his subordinates caused him, was so determined to give up the office of captain that all the reasonings and entreaties of the missionaries were not sufficient to dissuade him.

Don Juan Bautista Escalante,[173] the *alférez* of the presidio of Nacosari[174] in Sonora, a very brave man and one of considerable repute in the war against the Apaches, was therefore appointed captain. Wishing to become absolute master of California, as the captains paid by the king do in some presidios,[175] he caused the missionaries many disturbances and grave annoyances; but at the end of ten months the Portuguese, finally persuaded by Father Salvatierra, reassumed his office and held it until 1744, to the great advantage of that Christianity.

[173] A sergeant and a "soldier of great valor and credits" who had conducted campaigns against the Apaches. He accompanied Kino on his first expedition to the Gila River (Bolton, *Kino*, Vol. II, p. 107).

[174] In Sonora on the upper branch of the Yaqui River about twenty-five miles south of Arizpe. Today it is a town of six thousand people.

[175] Among the other more important presidios in the northwestern section of Mexico were Altar, Babispe, Bacoachi, Buenavista, Fronteras, Horcasitas (Pitis), Santa Cruz, and Tubac.

Chapter Twenty-Five

FATHER SALVATIERRA GOES TO MEXICO AND IS APPOINTED PROVINCIAL. HIS UNSUCCESSFUL VISIT AND PETITION TO THE VICEROY

FATHER SALVATIERRA, since he had given all the seasonable orders and had entrusted Father Juan de Ugarte with the spiritual and economic government of California, embarked on the first of October, accompanied by the Portuguese and by the *alférez*, who had also renounced his office. He landed at the port of Matanchel, whence he went to Guadalajara, where he discussed the interests of his Mission with those gentlemen, and particularly with his friend, the *fiscal* Miranda. And from there he went to Mexico [City] where he arrived at the beginning of November. At that time the provincial[176] of the Jesuits had died; and when the advisers had opened the sheet of paper which the father-general[177] was accustomed to send every three years so that it might be opened in such an event, they found in it that Father Salvatierra had been appointed provincial. He made all possible efforts to free himself from that charge, which of necessity separated him from his beloved Mission; but after he had been compelled to accept it, he wrote at once to the father-general, Tirso González, entreating him to confer that office on another and to permit him to go and end his days among the Californians.

As his zeal for California did not let him rest, as soon as he reached Mexico [City] he paid the viceroy a visit in which he disclosed the condition of the Missions; and he begged him urgently to command that the strict orders of the king be carried out. Although that gentleman showed him great esteem for his virtues and apostolic zeal and was convinced of the justice of his claims, he did not for that reason favor them.

---

[176] Manuel Pimeyro.

[177] Thyrso González was general of the Jesuits from July 6, 1687, to October 27, 1705. He was born in Spain in 1624, and became a Jesuit at the age of nineteen. He taught philosophy and theology in the College of San Bartolomé at Salamanca for twenty-one years.

Father Salvatierra, therefore, despairing of obtaining then what he desired, devoted himself to the fulfillment of his duty (visiting the colleges of the province), and he returned from it after Lent of the following year (1705). They made him wait then until the tribunal was notified by the king concerning the establishment of a new presidio in California and other points relative to it. And it seems that they should have met, under these circumstances, without other excuse for their consideration, because, besides the head of those Missions, the former captain, and the *alférez* of the presidio (all three very experienced in California), there were in Mexico many persons who, having made the journey from the Philippine Islands, had acquired some knowledge of the western coast of that peninsula where it was desired to establish the new presidio. But the tribunal did not meet, and Father Salvatierra was advised to present only a petition, which he did on May 25.

In it he stated to the viceroy the impossibility of the colony existing with only one boat, because experience had shown that the settlement could not be freed from the dangers of hunger even with three, and because of the inconstancy of the sea and the too frequent misfortunes of the boats. He made him see the very severe harm that would result if the presidio were made independent of the missionaries (as some inconsiderately wished), because then the officers, as well as the soldiers, neglecting their obligations toward the colony, would devote themselves wholly to pearl fishing as more profitable; and instead of defending the Missions and the missionaries and protecting the neophytes they would become enemies of each other, using the Indians as slaves and slandering the missionaries because they defended their neophytes, as happened frequently in the Missions of Sonora and Sinaloa.

He stated also that the independence of the captain was not even advantageous to the soldiers themselves in a remote country beyond the seas, because if he treated them badly they could free themselves from evil treatment only by desertion; whereas, if the captain were dependent on the superior of the Missions he would not dare harass them for fear of losing his office. Nor would it be difficult for the soldiers to complain in case of suffering any injury. Besides the fact that all these troops were paid by the missionaries, it did not seem unjust that they should be subordinate to them.

In regard to the royal command about sending some poor families from Mexico to California, he said that it could not be done until tillable soil was found in the peninsula so that they could be supported, because not even the small colony at Loreto could exist without assistance brought in from the outside. In reference to the presidio of thirty soldiers which they wished established on the western coast of California for the convenience of the ships coming from the Philippine Islands, Father Salvatierra declared that no one more than he desired the alleviation of those distressed sailors, and that he himself had gone to explore the coast with this purpose. But in order to attain it, it was not necessary for the royal treasury to make such an expenditure as would be required for maintaining the presidio, since the thirteen thousand *scudi* which the king had ordered to be given annually to the missionaries were enough so that the Missions, by advancing toward the west, could finally approach and establish one at some good port on that coast. There the ships could come and there the sailors tormented in great part by scurvy and *verben* could find relief in certain food.

At the end of the petition he explained the actual condition of the Missions, asserting that the country which was subjected in seven years to the obedience of the Catholic king by means of persuasion and kindness was the entire coast comprised between the port of Concepción and the place called Agua Verde; that is, a space of one hundred and fifty miles and almost as much more territory inland, in which was a population of one thousand two hundred Christians and a greater number of catechumen and gentiles, all friendly, obedient to the Spanish, and ready to take up arms in their defense; that among them there was such peacefulness that the missionaries traveled everywhere in security without soldiers; and that up to that time two hundred and twenty thousand *scudi* had been spent in that colony and on the Missions, all of which was donated by the liberality of benefactors, with the exception of the nine thousand [*scudi*] which had been taken from the royal treasury.

Father Salvatierra, seeing that neither this petition nor his other efforts were sufficient for obtaining what he so justly claimed, left Mexico [City] during the following month[178] for the purpose of making his visit as provincial of his Missions of California, taking again with him the Portuguese, Don Estevan Rodríguez, who, yielding to the petitions of that zealous missionary, consented finally to resume the office of captain. Scarcely had he left Mexico when the royal tribunal met. Despite the fact that Father Salvatierra, with other men acquainted with California, had to attend to learn of the decision, after eight months they wrote to the court that nothing had been done in the tribunal because Father Salvatierra had not been present. The order to give the thirteen thousand *scudi* annually to the missionaries of California was repeated by the king on August 13, 1705, and on July 26, 1708. But neither the urgency of the sovereign nor the entreaties of the Jesuits and the needs of California were capable of moving that viceroy to do anything in favor of those Missions during all the time of his rule, which was nine years.

At the close of 1710 the Duke of Linares[179] succeeded him. Although inclined to the Jesuits, like his illustrious ancestors, he did not favor the enterprise of California in the six years of his rule, because neither he nor the Jesuits had information about the new commands of the king, which were kept secret by those who did not favor the advance of Christianity in that peninsula. But what he did not do as a viceroy he did do as a private individual, because, when he had terminated his rule shortly after and when the course of his life was run in Mexico on June 3, 1717, he left five thousand *scudi* in his will to the Missions.

[178] June 1705.
[179] Fernando de Alencostre. He held the office from 1711 to 1716. He came from the family that united the royal houses of Spain, Portugal, and England; and he had been a vicar in Italy, viceroy in Sardinia, and an officer in the Spanish army. He endeavored to free Mexico from its commercial stagnation and from its political decay that he thought was imminent. He worked patiently to assist the Missions of California, giving large sums of his own money and getting contributions from rich people to found and maintain them. He gave one-third of his estate (all he could because his father

Chapter Twenty-Six

FATHER SALVATIERRA VISITS THE MISSIONS OF CALIFORNIA. BROTHER BRAVO IS EMPLOYED IN THEM. ORDERS FROM THE PROVINCIAL ON DEPARTING

FATHER SALVATIERRA left Mexico, as has been said, in June 1705 and reached Loreto in August, taking abundant provisions to that colony and cheering the Spaniards as well as the Indians with his presence, because he was equally loved by all. He had the consolation of finding the Missions in the best condition. Father Juan de Ugarte had prepared a considerable part of the land of his Mission for cultivation with great labor, removing the thickets and stones; and by penetrating into the interior of the country he had greatly increased the number of his catechumen and reduced several tribes of the barbarians to civilized life. Father Basalduá had also notably increased the Mission of Londò, attracting many Indians who had been wandering in the woods like wild animals. Father Piccolo was intrusted by the provincial with visiting the Missions of Sonora, because he could help the colony more easily from there, as he did do with great zeal and industry.

The provincial had brought a Brother from Mexico called Santiago Bravo,[180] a good religious, skillful, very industrious, and active. He had succeeded in making that trip with the intention of staying in California, if it were permitted him to serve in the callings suitable to his state. Having seen the glorious toils of those missionaries and knowing that they would

---

was living) and 50,000 doubloons to the Jesuits (Venegas, *Noticia de la California*, Vol. I, p. 374).

[180] An Aragonese. During the eight years that he was stationed at the Mission at La Paz he baptized 600 children and adults, gathered to the Mission 800 catechumen, and also won the friendship and confidence of hundreds of savages (Engelhardt, *op. cit.*, p. 172). He died May 13, 1744, at the Mission of San Javier, and was buried in Loreto. After his fourteen years of service as procurator, he was admitted to the priesthood (Venegas, *Noticia de la California*. Vol. I, p. 380).

appreciate being freed from the care of the temporal affairs of the colony in order to devote themselves more to the ministrations suitable to the apostleship, he petitioned the provincial and succeeded without difficulty in being employed to the great gain of California. He was, in fact, one of the most worthy men of that peninsula, where he worked with the greatest activity and exemplary conduct for thirty-nine years, fourteen as procurator of the presidio and the Missions, and twenty-five as a missionary, as we shall state later.

Father Salvatierra remained in California for two months, acting now as missionary in the ministries of catechising, confessing, and preaching; then as provincial in visiting the Missions and in the governing of the colony. When he left for New Spain, he entrusted three important orders to the missionaries. The first was that they establish two Missions, one in Liguig, an inland place about forty miles distant to the south from Loreto, and the other in Mulegè, also an inland place, one hundred and twenty miles distant to the northwest from Loreto. The second order was that they search in the interior of the peninsula for other places suitable for establishing new Missions; and, third, that they explore the west coast again for the purpose of finding a good harbor, consistent with the intentions of the king, where the ships from the Philippine Islands could make a stop.

Chapter Twenty-Seven

FATHER PEDRO DE UGARTE ESTABLISHES THE
MISSION OF LIGUIG

A FEW DAYS after his departure the missionaries carried out the first of his orders, Father Pedro de Ugarte leaving Loreto on the same day of the month of November for Liguig, and Father Basalduá leaving for Mulegè. Father Ugarte found the Indians in Liguig peaceable and safe; but he had to endure all the vexations of the new Missions, which are quite considerable when they are established among savages accustomed to idleness. At the beginning he had for shelter only the shade of the trees, and afterward he lived for a long time in a hut made of branches, while he sought the means of building a chapel or a little adobe house. He managed to win the good will of the Indians with kindness and with some small gifts, as much to induce them to help him in building as to inspire eagerness in them for the Christian doctrine, which he explained to them by means of some Indians from Loreto, because he had not yet learned the dialect peculiar to Liguig.

His efforts could not induce the adults to throw off their innate laziness, although he distributed *pozolli* to them daily; and for that reason it was necessary for him to employ the children, attracting them with subtlety and encouraging them with rewards. At times he laid wagers with them as to who could clear away the thickets most quickly or who could dig out the greater quantity of earth. At times, in order to tread the mud from which the adobe bricks were to be made he invited them to dance and jump on it, and he himself, with bare feet, danced and jumped with them. A man born of wealthy and noble parents was employed in tasks of that kind for the glory of God; and so he succeeded in building the proposed structures of the small houses and the chapel, the dedication of which was held with the help of the other missionaries.

After he learned with similar industry the dialect of the barbarians well enough, he devoted himself to catechising them, treating them kindly, making them gifts to oblige them to attend catechism, and using the children to instruct them, until with unspeakable work and with heroic patience and constancy he succeeded in reducing to the Christian life not only those of Liguig but all the neighboring tribes and many savages scattered in the mountains.

Father Ugarte had scarcely begun to take a rest when he almost lost the success of his zeal along with his life. When he had been called to confess a sick woman, he found that a *guama* (or quack) was using a reed, according to the superstition of foolishness of the Californians, to extract the evil with his breath from the body of the patient. Father Ugarte dismissed him with indignation and reproved his neophytes and catechumen because they had consented to such abuse. After he had administered the sacraments to the sick woman and attended her until death, he returned to his house, where some Indians came in a short time boasting of having killed the charlatan.

Pierced by the keenest grief, Father Ugarte severely condemned the cruelty of that greatly misconceived zeal, and in order to make them realize his indignation he turned his back on them. The murderers, instead of recognizing their mistake, swore secretly to kill their censurer; but having been informed of it in time by a child he called together the chief conspirators and, holding in his hand an old fowling piece, rusty and quite useless, which he had brought with him, he said to them: "Indeed I know that you want to kill me tonight; but understand that before you can execute your perverse design, I shall kill all of you with this weapon."

This alone was enough to frighten them in such a manner that all of one accord quickly decided to go away; and on account of this it was necessary that the zealous missionary should go on the following day to conduct them to the Mission, as he finally did, assuring them of the love he bore them, like that of a father who sought their welfare in everything. They returned there and esteemed him much more from that time on, because they knew that he was brave and did not fear them.

These perils of life are very frequent in the Missions of California, as in other new Missions in which nothing is sufficient to insure the security of the missionaries against the attempts of the barbarians. Thus the first offering which he who goes to establish Christianity among them should make to God is that of his own life.

Father Pedro de Ugarte continued in his apostolic tasks until 1709, when, weakened by much work, he was compelled to go to Mexico [City] to recover his lost health. But scarcely was his strength restored than he returned to California, and he persisted with new fervor in his ministry until, falling sick again, he was sent by his superiors to the Missions of the Yaqui River, from where he continued providing California with provisions, which he continually procured for her.

Chapter Twenty-Eight

FATHER BASALDUÁ ESTABLISHES THE MISSION OF MULEGÈ. JUAN DE UGARTE IS ENTRUSTED WITH THE CARE OF THREE MISSIONS

FATHER BASALDUÁ, on founding the Mission of Mulegè, not only endured the same toils that Father Ugarte did, but he had to open a long, bad road to make communication with Loreto less difficult. He established the Mission near the stream of Mulegè, two miles distant from the sea. Between the mountains and the sea there is a plain of some twenty miles, covered with mesquites (or acacias), which at first gave pasture only to the oxen; but when a dam was built afterward some part of the soil could be cultivated successfully. Father Basalduá stayed there for four years, working with great zeal. Because his health did not endure the work and the climate, he was sent to the Mission of Guaymas[181] in Sonora and afterward to that of Rahun[182] on the Yaqui River, where he continued helping California with the aid he sent her.

He was succeeded in the Mission of Mulegè by Father Piccolo, who, having returned from Sonora, increased the new Mission considerably with the conversion of many neighboring tribes. The Indians of Mulegè made themselves esteemed by their docility, by their skill in the Spanish language, and by the services which they performed for the missionaries, acting as interpreters, as catechists, and even as teachers in the Cochimì language. Among others who won praise, especially from the missionaries for the zeal with which they devoted themselves to the propagation of the Gospel, were two virtuous neophytes

---

[181] Situated about 270 miles south of Nogales, Arizona. Today the town has a population of about nine thousand, of whom about five thousand are Indians and one thousand are Chinese. Guaymas exports chiefly wheat, cotton, maize, copper, sugar, fish, tobacco, leather, and winter vegetables.

[182] At the mouth of the Yaqui River just south of Guaymas, being one of the five Missions founded on that stream in Sonora by the Jesuits (*Catholic Encyclopaedia*, Vol. XIV, p. 145).

George E. Lindsay

Fig. 19 – The mission site at Santa Rosalía Mulegé looking north. The church is built on an Indian settlement site and stands on an outcrop of a sill of volcanic rock that forces to the surface the ground-water of an extensive drainage basin, forming the oasis of Mulegé. The modern concrete dam replaces one constructed early in the mission period.

Fig. 20 – The mission church at Mulegé. The period of construction of this building complex is not known, but part at least must date from Jesuit times. It has had a resident priest most of the time since 1905 and so has received some maintenance.

George E. Lindsay

named Bernardo Dubavà and Andrés Comanajì of whom we shall speak later at greater length.

While the Fathers Pedro de Ugarte and Juan de Basalduá were occupied in establishing their new Missions, Father Juan de Ugarte was taking care of the three Missions, Loreto, San Juan de Londò, and San Javier de Viggè. This tireless and truly apostolic man did not rest; he worked and toiled continuously, now in the presidio admonishing, preaching, confessing, and attending the soldiers and the sailors; then in the Missions baptizing children, catechising adults, attending the sick, and assisting the dying; then in the mountains hunting up the savages to make them men and Christians; then, finally, in the fields, opening up roads, building irrigation ditches and dams, and preparing or cultivating the land. As he was beginning to gather harvests from his efforts in agriculture for the benefit of his neophytes, he persuaded these to be more punctual at church for the daily instruction of the catechism, Mass, Rosary, and sermon.

His interest in the education of the youth made him change his house into a seminary for children, where besides instructing them in the faith and in good habits he taught them handicrafts with singular patience and devotion. This school became very useful, not only to the Mission of San Javier, but also to the others in California.

He built another house for the girls, especially the orphans. There, in care of a matron of good character, they were taught all womanly duties, he being the teacher of all those crafts and duties. He also erected a hospital for the sick where the poor Indians were charitably aided with spiritual and bodily assistance.

Among the gentiles whom he converted to Christianity, were several *guamas* (or charlatans) who, as has been said already, are the most wicked and obstinate of all the Californians. One of them was induced to ask for baptism because he had seen the kindness with which his son was treated by Father Ugarte; but he wished to be baptized without being instructed first in the Christian religion. When he was finally convinced of the necessity of such instruction, he was catechised and baptized with the name of Domingo.[183] The grace of the Holy Spirit softened the heart of that barbarian to such an extent that, filled with joy and devotion in the forty days that he survived his regeneration, he did not wish to leave the house of the missionary and the church where he spent the days and nights in prayer. At last when he died, Father Ugarte held a very solemn funeral for him so that those people would become more attached to the Christian religion.

Another even more wicked *guama,* who spent much time inciting the gentiles and catechumen against the missionaries and their doctrine, and who was inspired by the Master, came to Loreto, where Father Ugarte was at the time, and, weeping, asked for baptism. It was denied him many times because of distrust; but he made so many petitions and gave such indications of sincerity and promised with so many tears to reform his life—even offering to stay always in Loreto in order to live in the sight of the Spaniards—that finally he succeeded in being instructed and baptized on December 7, for which reason he was given the name of Ambrosio.[184] He spent the first two days after his baptism in the church in continuous prayer; on the third day he fell ill; and shortly afterward he died, with great manifestation of piety and with clear indications of his preordination.

Chapter Twenty-Nine

THE UNSUCCESSFUL TRIPS OF FATHER JUAN DE UGARTE AND BROTHER BRAVO

FATHER UGARTE was not content with such great toil, for which three zealous missionaries would not have been sufficient, and he undertook, in November 1706, in fulfillment of the command from the provincial, to go and

---

[183] When an Indian was baptized and became a member of the Mission, he was given a Spanish name.

[184] December 7 is the day of Saint Ambrosio. The Spaniards celebrate not their birthday but their saint's day (*día del santo patrón*). That day determines the name of the baby.

explore the western coast of the peninsula. He asked the chief or general of the large and warlike Yaqui nation, established on the banks of the River Yaqui and reduced by the Jesuit missionaries to a civilized and Christian life since the preceding century, for forty men for this trip.

The general not only granted the forty select men but he himself took them to Loreto, from where Father Ugarte left on November 26, accompanied by them, the captain, and twelve soldiers of the presidio, and some Californians; and, going toward that coast, he closely examined a long distance of it without being able to find a good port such as was needed to serve as a stopping place for the ships from the Philippine Islands. The men as well as the horses were quite worn out on account of thirst, because potable water was scarce everywhere; and thus, not being able to continue the survey of that coast without risk, they returned to Loreto in a fortnight.

Another trip, which was taken by Brother Bravo in search of some places for establishing new Missions, was equally unsuccessful through a misfortune. He had left Loreto at the beginning of this year accompanied by the captain of the presidio and by ten soldiers and some Californians; he went toward Liguig and passed beyond on that coast. One of the soldiers found a bonfire in which some Californian fishermen had roasted fish a short time before, and especially some *botetti*,[185] the liver of which contains a very active and violent poison.

The fishermen, because they knew this, had eaten the flesh and left the livers on some shells. A soldier, seeing them, wished to eat them, and he invited three of his companions. A Californian who saw them called out at once, saying: "Do not eat, do not eat, because it will kill you." The soldier, scorning

---

[185] See note 140, Book I, p. 68, *supra*. Sometimes spelled "botates," and "botete," and called glove fish (*Spheroides lobatus*). It seems to be the *Tetraodon hispidus* of Linnaeus, or the *maki-maki* (deadly death) of the Hawaiian Islands, which is said to be poisonous (*United States Fish Commission*, Vol. XXIII, Part I, 1903, pp. 427–28). The livers of some sharks are poisonous, owing, evidently, to alkaloids that are developed in certain organs. The "botteti" is very harmful to pearl-bearing oysters, and continual effort is made to exterminate this fish (Herman Schnitzler's, *The Republic of Mexico*, p. 461).

this advice, began to eat and to share it with the other three. One of them ate a little; another only chewed it, but without swallowing it; and the last one only touched it, keeping it to eat later. The first of the four soldiers died in half an hour, the second shortly afterward; the third remained unconscious until the following day; and this one, as well as the fourth, felt weak and uncomfortable for many days. The two dead men were buried in Liguig, and the two sick ones were taken to Loreto; and so that expedition came to nothing.

Chapter Thirty

FATHER SALVATIERRA RENOUNCES THE OFFICE OF THE PROVINCIALSHIP AND RETURNS TO CALIFORNIA. THE MISSION OF COMONDÙ AND ITS MISSIONARY, FATHER MAYORGA

IN SEPTEMBER 1706 Father Salvatierra finally received in Mexico [City] the answer desired from the father provincial, Miguel Ángel Tamburini,[186] in which he accepted his resignation of the provincialship.[187] When freed from this office, he retired, to his great pleasure, for some days to the College of San Gregorio[188] in Mexico [City] to discuss with Father Alexandro Romano[189] (the procurator of Cali-

---

[186] Born in Modena, Italy, in 1648. After serving as a teacher of religion and philosophy for some years he was president of several colleges. At the death of Thyrso Gonzáles (1706), Tamburini was chosen to fill his place, and he held the office for twenty-four years. During this time the Missions of the Jesuits everywhere were advanced. When he died (1730) at the age of eighty-two, the Jesuits had 612 colleges and 57 seminaries in the various countries of the world.

[187] Bernardo Rolandeguí, who had been an agent of the government in Rome and in Madrid, was appointed in Salvatierra's place (Venegas, *Noticia de la California*, Vol. I, p. 399).

[188] Named after a college of the same kind in Valladolid, Spain, which was founded by King Alfonso the Wise, who ruled from 1252 to 1284.

[189] The first real business agent for the Missions of California. He was later made provincial (Venegas, *Noticia de la California*, Vol. I, p. 429). Romano purchased several large haciendas in Mexico for stock raising with the funds entrusted to him, and thereafter, for the time, the Missions were better supplied with provisions.

fornia in that court) the preparation of many things necessary for the presidio and the Missions, which should be sent to the port of Matanchel and thence to Loreto with Father Guillermo de Mayorga,[190] who had been newly appointed to those Missions.

Father Salvatierra decided to go to the port of Ahome in Sinaloa, one thousand and two hundred miles distant from Mexico [City], in order to thank those benefactors for the help sent to California; and he made all that trip by land, taking five Californians who had accompanied him on his last trip. Although these persons were well taken care of, all fell ill because of the difference of the climate and the food, which increased the troubles of that long trip for Father Salvatierra. After they had embarked at Ahome, one of them died shortly after leaving the port, but with such faith and with such acts of virtue that all were greatly uplifted. Then a storm descended upon them so violent that Father Salvatierra himself said in a letter that he had never found himself in similar difficulty and danger in the many trips which he had made by land and by sea. When the boat was given up to the wind and the waves by the sailors it was fortunately carried between islands and reefs to the island of San José, some ninety miles distant from Loreto, where, after the weather became calm, they arrived December 3.

After a few months Father Mayorga arrived also. He was so weakened with the fatigue of so many trips because he had come recently from Europe, and so indisposed because of the change in climate and food, that Father Salvatierra thought it necessary to have him return to New Spain; but he entreated him with tears to permit him to die in California whither the Master had led him. But instead of death, which he expected, he recovered his health in a short time; and after becoming accustomed to that climate and that coarse food he worked apostolically for thirty years in those Missions.

On the different trips made by the missionaries in the peninsula, seeking places to establish new Missions, they had found

---

[190] He arrived in California in 1707, and the next year he founded the Mission of Comondù. He died in 1736. His nativity is in doubt.

that of Comondù, sixty miles distant to the northwest from Loreto and situated in the mountains almost equidistant from both seas. Near a little stream which runs through that place, there were scattered several tribes of Indians, for the conversion of whom it was decided that one of the Missions (endowed by the Marqués de Villapuente) should be established there. With this purpose, Fathers Salvatierra and Juan de Ugarte, taking with them Father Mayorga, who was appointed to the new Mission, went to the same place at the beginning of 1708. They remained there with him for some days, helping him to tame the savages and to build two bowers from branches; one was for the missionary's room, and another was to be used as a church, while a good one was being built, which Father Mayorga finished later and dedicated with great solemnity.

With his great charity and his patience and with his constancy in the apostolic ministry he reduced all those barbarians to Christianity and gathered them in three towns called San José, San Juan, and San Ignacio. In San José, which was the principal town, besides the church and the parsonage, he built after the example of Father Ugarte three other buildings, to wit: a hospital, and two seminaries, one for the boys and one for the girls. He did not find any tillable soil in all the district of the Mission, except a little spot near San Ignacio, which he cultivated with great industry, and where he successfully planted vines. He continued working with much zeal, edification, and success until November 10, 1736, on which day his faithful soul went to receive from the Master, as may be believed, the reward for his toil and virtues.

Chapter Thirty-One

THE MISFORTUNES OF THE COLONY. THE DEATH OF FATHER KINO. HIS EULOGY

OTHER PLACES had been discovered in which Missions could be established. But this was not possible then, owing as much to the scarcity of missionaries as to the misfortunes which befell the colony. The vessel "San Javier," which had left Loreto in September 1709 with three thousand *scudi* to buy provisions in Yaqui, was carried one hundred and eighty miles above the port of its destination by a furious storm and was grounded on the sand. Some of the people were drowned; the rest saved themselves in the small boat; but after landing they were exposed to another not less serious danger because that coast was inhabited by the Seríes,[191] who were warlike gentiles and implacable enemies of the Spaniards. For this reason they hastened to bury the money and all the possessions which were on the boat; and after embarking again in the small boat they continued with a thousand dangers and hardships to Yaqui, from where they sent the news to Loreto. In a little while the Seríes came to the place where the Spaniards had buried those possessions, and they dug them up and carried them away. They even removed the rudder from the vessel, and they destroyed it in order to get out the nails.

As soon as Father Salvatierra learned of that misfortune, he left in the unseaworthy vessel, the "Rosario," and went to the port of Guaymas. From there he sent this vessel to the place where the "San Javier" was grounded, and he himself went with fourteen Yaqui Indians in that direction over a very bad road which absolutely lacked potable water, and for this reason they suffered great thirst for two days. During the two months which he lived there, exposed to hunger and hardships and to the great danger of all their lives (while the vessel was being repaired), he won the good will of the Seríes in such a manner that he not only recovered all the cargo of the boat which they had stolen but induced them also to make peace with the Pimas,[192] who were Christian neighbors of theirs and ene-

---

[191] Often spelled Seris, Ceris, Ceres or Heris. Sometimes called "Tiburones." They inhabit the Tiburón Island and a narrow adjacent strip along the mainland. They have been regarded as the most warlike tribe of Indians in Mexico, and, although they have been known since the time of Cortés, it was not until some forty years ago that any scientific knowledge was secured concerning them. For an extended description of these people, see the *Bureau of American Ethnology*, Vol. XVII, pp. 1–344.

[192] They dwelt along the coast north of Tiburón Island, and in the northern central section of Mexico, extending into Arizona.

mies whom they most hated. He baptized many of their children; he catechised the adults and inspired so much affection in them for Christianity that they immediately wanted a missionary to instruct them regularly and to baptize and govern them in all respects.

So the dominating sweetness of the character of Father Salvatierra, aided by the grace of the Master, triumphed over the ferocity of those barbarians who were so feared, not only by the other Indians, but also even by the Spaniards. He wept tenderly on seeing their unexpected docility and their good inclinations, thanking God for having had that much good come from the misfortune of the vessel; and he would have wished to remain always on that dry coast to finish that work so happily begun, but he could not desert his beloved California, where his presence was then even more necessary.

An epidemic of smallpox,[193] which was hitherto unknown in that peninsula, created such havoc at that time that many adults and almost all the children died, greatly increasing the work and the grief of the missionaries. Afterward other epidemics, originating from the kind of food eaten, deprived some Spaniards of the presidio of their lives and reduced the missionaries to the utmost degree. Father Piccolo was at death's door three times; Father Salvatierra twice, and Father Juan de Ugarte once. The Fathers Pedro de Ugarte and Basalduá were obliged to abandon the Missions through failure in health.

In the midst of this calamity another uprising of the neophytes was also feared, because the *guamas*, blaming the missionaries, scattered reports everywhere that the latter made the children ill with the baptismal water and the adults with the holy oil. The dire want which was suffered at the same time in New Spain also increased the calamities of California, because provisions were very scarce and very expensive.

To these misfortunes, produced by natural causes, were

[193] One of the many diseases of the white man brought to the Indian. Often one-third or one-half of the Indian population of a village or Mission would be carried off by this dreadful disease. In 1798 Governor Borica said this disease had not then reached Upper California. But a few years later it spread throughout all the Missions in that territory.

added others which originated from the malice of men. Father Francisco de Peralta,[194] who had reached California in 1709 and who was appointed to the Mission of Liguig in place of Father Pedro de Ugarte, was sent by Father Salvatierra in November 1711 to the port of Matanchel to have the vessel "Rosario" calked and another built. As that poor missionary had not had any experience in that kind of work, the rascals who were employed on it had an opportunity to deceive him. The repair of the "Rosario" cost some thousand *scudi*, but nevertheless it was so unseaworthy that a short time afterward it was carried ashore by a somewhat heavy wind and went entirely to pieces.

The new boat, which was built in eighteen months and at a cost of twenty-two thousand *scudi*, was not of a better quality. Notwithstanding, Fathers Clemente Guillen[195] and Benito Guisi,[196] appointed to the Missions of California, and Father Santiago Doye,[197] who was going to Sinaloa, embarked in it.

At the beginning they were carried by the wind to the cape of San Lucas, and from there to the islands of Mazatlán, a short distance from Matanchel. After they had set sail again after many deviations, they saw the shore of Loreto in the distance; but a storm suddenly carried them as far as the opposite coast of Sinaloa; and since the vessel was not able to withstand the violence of the wind and the waves they were finally shipwrecked, six persons along with Father Guisi being drowned. The remaining twenty-two saved themselves, part of them on the stern deck and part on the lower mast, which was floating.

[194] On his arrival in California he was sent to the Mission of San Juan Bautista to relieve Father Pedro Ugarte. Peralta served this Mission until 1713.

[195] Born in Zacatecas, Mexico, in 1677. He became a teacher of religion and philosophy in Mexico City, and arrived in California in 1713(?), where he labored until his death in 1748. He wrote *Noticias de la Misión de los Dolores del Sur de California, Alias S. Juan Talibat o Liqui y de sus pueblos Concepción, Encarnación, Trinidad, Redención, y Resurección.* Venegas used this manuscript.

[196] Little seems to be known of him. Engelhardt says (Vol. I, p. 285) that he died in 1711, but this is evidently a mistake. As to the date of his death, Bancroft (*History of the North Mexican States and Texas*, Vol. I, p. 427) agrees with Clavigero.

[197] He never worked among the Missions of Lower California.

While they were suffering in this manner and in so much danger on a very dark night, they occupied themselves in keeping the small boat afloat by bailing the water with two very small receptacles, because they had no others; and, embarking in it with only a piece of a sail, they gave themselves up to the sea until the coming of day. At that time, having seen land at a great distance, they started for it; and by dint of sail and oar they succeeded in reaching it after a day and a half of very toilsome navigation.

They landed on a barren beach where there was no fire nor any way of lighting one and where they could satisfy the hunger which tormented them only with raw oysters and snails and with wild roots and herbs. Finally, after other hardships they found refuge in the small city of Sinaloa (the capital of the province of the same name), from where Father Guillen made a trip of three hundred miles to Yaqui, where he embarked for California. On that short trip he had to endure another storm; but finally he reached Loreto in January 1714.

Among the misfortunes suffered in those years by the colony there should be related one which overtook it in 1711 in the death of Father Eusebio Francisco Kino, the pioneer and particular benefactor of the Missions. This great man was born in Triente, became a missionary in the states of Bavaria, and was a teacher of mathematics in the University of Ingolstad. In 1681 he went to Mexico, inspired by a vow which he had made during a dangerous sickness of which he was cured by the intercession of San Francisco Javier. In 1683[198] he left for California with the duties of a missionary and royal cosmographer, as has been stated above. In 1686 he returned to Mexico, and from there he left for the Missions of Sonora, the theater of his apostolic zeal.

It is not easy to state what he accomplished and what he tolerated in the twenty-five years[199] that he was there. Because he was continually on the move for the salvation of souls, he traveled more than twenty thousand miles; he learned several

---

[198] A misprint. Kino left California in 1685.
[199] Twenty-four.

languages; he proclaimed the Gospel to fifteen barbarous nations, among whom he baptized more than forty-eight thousand persons,[200] children as well as adults; he established several Missions; he built many churches; he taught the barbarians the crafts necessary for social life; he introduced Christianity into Pimería; and he was the first who explored the countries situated on the other side of the Red and Gila rivers. His works, although great and surprising, would have been without doubt much greater if, instead of the contradictions and calumnies which he suffered, he had been helped in his glorious undertakings as he insistently requested. He received from Heaven a peculiar gift for winning the love and respect of so many barbarous nations; and so he went in the midst of them as securely as among the most civilized Christians.

On his long and painful journeys he carried with him no other provisions than toasted corn. He never failed to say Holy Mass; nor did he ever sleep in a bed. He traveled conversing with God in prayer, or singing psalms and hymns. He died like a saint among his dear neophytes and to their extreme grief; and after his death several missionaries could not carry the burden of the apostolic tasks which he alone discharged.

[200] Kino personally baptized 4,500 Indians, and not the number given by Clavigero and by so many other writers. He wrote that he could have baptized ten or fifteen thousand natives if missionaries had been available to instruct them (Bolton, *Kino*, Vol. I, p. 89).

BOOK III

THE ESTABLISHMENT OF EIGHT OTHER MISSIONS. NEW TASKS, HARDSHIPS, HOSTILE RESISTANCE, AND DANGERS. THE EXAMPLES OF SOME CATECHUMEN AND NEOPHYTES. THE DEATHS OF FATHERS SALVATIERRA, PÌCCOLO, UGARTE, AND MAYORGA. THE CONSPIRACY OF THE PERICÙES; TWO MISSIONARIES MURDERED; THE LOSS AND RE-ESTABLISHMENT OF SOME MISSIONS

Chapter One

THE LACK OF VESSELS IN THE COLONY. THE INDIANS OF CADEGOMÒ AND KADAKAAMAN ASK FOR MISSIONARIES

THE UNFORTUNATE colony of California, after the loss of so much capital invested in vessels and provisions, was in a lamentable condition. The viceroy, the duke of Linares, touched by pity because of this, ordered that a vessel called "Nuestra Señora de Guadalupe," previously seized in Acapulco by the government as a prize, be sold to them for four thousand *scudi*. But this boat, although it appeared good at first sight, was worthless; and consequently it scarcely made two voyages before it was lost.

The same thing also happened to another, bought in Acapulco. There remained, therefore, in California, only the little "San Javier" for the transportation of provisions and all necessities, and for all the trips that it was necessary to make, now from one port to another of the peninsula and then to Sonora, Sinaloa, and Nueva Galicia. Because of this lack of boats, Father Salvatierra was unable to explore the islands and shores of the Gulf as far as the Red River in order to continue the conversion of the Series and Tepocas,[1] which he had begun auspiciously, or to establish new Missions on the peninsula.

In the midst of so many needs the missionaries had to decrease their apostolic work. On the other hand there was not one among them in those wretched years who did not reduce to civilized life many tribes of barbarians roving through the wilds. With this purpose Father Ugarte had made some unsuccessful trips to the south and Father Piccolo to the north.

---

[1] A branch of the Series, inhabiting a section of Sonora, some distance from the coast.

Many Indians of Cadegomò, a place ninety miles distant on the coast of the Pacific Sea, had come to Mulegè many times to request insistently that Father Piccolo visit them and bring a missionary with him to live among them always. In spite of not having recovered from a severe illness, he left for that place in 1712, accompanied by the captain of the presidio and some soldiers and Indians. And, having found a place twenty-four miles from the sea suitable for a new Mission, which he dedicated immediately to the Immaculate Conception of the Most Blessed Virgin (Purísima Concepción), he gathered there all the tribes of the vicinity, who entreated him earnestly to stay with them, offering to regale him with the best *pitaje* and presenting their children to him for him to baptize. In fact, Father Piccolo did baptize the little ones and treated the adults kindly, promising them a missionary to instruct them and help them in everything. But it was not possible to establish that Mission until the year 1717, Father Piccolo contenting himself, meanwhile, with going there sometimes to instruct and encourage those Indians in their good inclination; and they came frequently to Mulegè and continued to present their petitions.

The Cochimì Indians of Kadakaaman,[2] a place situated on the other side of the mountains one hundred and twenty miles distant from Mulegè, came frequently to make the same request. Father Piccolo went there also, on November 13, 1716, with three soldiers and some of his neophytes. The Cochimìes came out and received him with particular demonstrations of joy and respect, presenting him with *pitaje* and removing the rocks and all those hindrances which were in the road over which he had to pass; the children ran to him with as much love and tenderness as if he had raised them. In Kadakaaman many tribes from the adjacent places met, the women vying with each other in presenting their children to be baptized. Father Piccolo baptized fifty; but he found out then that those children were not the first rewards of that Christianity, because one of his neophytes named José, who was well instructed in the manner

[2] Sedgebrook.

of baptizing in case of necessity, had baptized during the spring of that year three dying persons, whose souls immediately fluttered to Paradise. Father Piccolo built a bower there to say Mass and a novena[3] to the Virgin for the conversion of that gentility; and he remained in that place until December with the purpose of winning their good will to a greater extent and making them more fond of the Christian religion. But the Mission, which afterward became one of the best in California, could not be established until the year 1728.

Chapter Two

FATHER SALVATIERRA VAINLY ATTEMPTS THE PACIFICATION OF THE GUAICURAS AND CONTINUES WORKING, ALTHOUGH HE IS ILL

FATHER SALVATIERRA, in 1716, undertook as his work the pacification of the Guaicuras, who (as much because of the hostilities which Admiral Otondo had committed against them thirty years before as because of the frequent vexations which they had suffered from the pearl fishermen who had arrived at their ports) were very ill disposed toward the Christians. After having embarked at Loreto, he went to the port of La Paz, accompanied by the captain, some soldiers, and several Indians from Loreto. He also took with him three Guaicuras who had been captured by some fishermen and who had been bought by him and treated very well in Loreto so that (by returning them to their relatives afterward) they might be witnesses of the kindness and sweetness of the missionaries toward the Indians.

When they reached La Paz they found some Guaicuras with their families, but the latter fled as soon as they saw the Spaniards. The Indians of Loreto followed them thoughtlessly, and the shouts of the Father and the captain were not sufficient to restrain them. The Guaicuras continued their flight; but

---

[3] A religious service that lasts nine days.

their women, not so swift in the race and being overtaken by the Christians, took a stand and began to defend themselves by throwing stones. The Christians, adding cruelty to impudence, abused them, and perhaps would have killed them if the captain and some Spanish soldiers had not arrived to defend them. The captain severely reproved the neophytes for behavior characteristic of their old barbarity which was contrary to the teaching of their missionaries, and he tried to reassure the offended Guaicura women and to treat them kindly. But they turned their backs disdainfully to follow their husbands.

Father Salvatierra was greatly annoyed. And, considering how vain any effort of which he might avail himself would be to make the fugitives return under those circumstances, he contented himself with sending them the three Guaicuras whom he had brought with him, after having made them gifts, caressed them, and entrusted them to tell their countrymen that neither he nor the Spaniards were to blame for what had happened, because they had come to seek their friendship. Father Salvatierra then returned disconsolately to Loreto.

Besides his labors and the grave annoyances which he had, especially in these last years, he was ill with a stone in the bladder. But in spite of this, he continued working as if he were well; and sometimes when the severity of the sickness did not permit him to rise from his bed, he did not fail, despite his illness, to look after everything.

Chapter Three

THE ARRIVAL OF FATHER TAMARAL IN CALIFORNIA. THE DEPARTURE OF FATHER SALVATIERRA FOR MEXICO AND HIS DEATH

In March of this year Father Nicolás Tamaral[4] arrived at Loreto, appointed to the proposed Mission of Cadegomò, or rather, Purísima Concepción. He

---

[4] Nicolás Tamaral was born in Seville, Spain, in 1687. He came to Mexico when thirty-one years old. He went to the peninsula in 1716, and later

brought Father Salvatierra a letter from the father provincial in which he stated that a new viceroy, the Marqués de Valero,[5] had reached Mexico, entrusted with some orders of the court relative to California, and that His Excellency, desirous of carrying them out and helping those missions, wished first to confer at length with him and ask him for some reports; and, therefore, it was suitable that he come as soon as possible to Mexico.

Father Salvatierra, despite his age and his serious sickness, left Loreto on the thirty-first of the same month, accompanied by Brother Bravo, leaving the superintendency of the presidio and the Missions to Father Ugarte. He reached the port of Matanchel after nine days of sailing; and from there he went on horseback to Tepic.[6]

This trip aggravated his sufferings from the stone [in the bladder] to such an extent that, not being able to continue the trip otherwise, he was carried on a litter by some Indians to the city of Guadalajara. Because his infirmities increased, he had to suffer a bitter martyrdom there for more than two months instead of the one which he had always desired to suffer for the faith of Jesus Christ; and knowing that his mortal life was going to end, he entrusted Brother Bravo with the business which should be carried on in Mexico [City]. He gave him the necessary instructions and commanded him to write to the missionaries of California that, aided by the little California children who had gone to Paradise, he hoped to attain powerful protection from the clemency of the Virgin for that budding Christianity; that they all place their hopes in God; and that he did not doubt that they would let themselves be deprived of life before they would abandon their children in Christ. He especially entreated the Brother and, by means of him, all those of California to pardon his bad example and all

---

founded the Mission of San José del Cabo, where he was murdered by the Indians. He wrote *Diario del reconocimiento de la Costa Setentrional de Cal'as*, a manuscript that Venegas used.

[5] Gaspar de Zúñiga, a cousin of the duke of Linares.

[6] A city now with a population of eighteen thousand, located in the state of Narayit.

the annoyances which he had caused them. The Brother wept bitterly, as did also some Californians who had come on that trip and whose extraordinary demonstrations of grief were such that they excited the pity of all who saw them or who knew them.

As soon as the dangerous condition of the man, venerated by all as a saint, was known in the city, public prayers for his recovery were held in many churches. But the Master wished to give rest, at last, to his faithful servant from so many labors and also the reward for such eminent services; and so, after having received the Blessed Sacraments and after preparing himself with the most fervid acts of all the Christian virtues, he calmly breathed forth his spirit on Saturday, July 17, at seventy-three years of age. The president and the supreme judges, the regular and the secular clergy, all the nobility, and an immense concourse of people attended his funeral, all vying in proclaiming his sanctity.

He was buried in the chapel of the Virgin of Loreto, which he had built in the church of the Jesuits; and his bones were placed afterward[7] in a separate coffin near the altar of the Virgin, whose devotion he had exalted in all the kingdom where even today his memory lasts.

Chapter Four

THE CLAIMS OF BROTHER BRAVO BEFORE THE GOVERNMENT. THE TRIBUNAL COMMANDS. A STORM IN THE PENINSULA

BROTHER BRAVO went to Mexico [City] immediately where he found the viceroy very well disposed toward California. On January 29, 1716, the king had sent a new order to California that they bestir themselves with all possible industry in carrying out the previous ones issued in 1708 concerning that peninsula; that particular care

---

[7] For an account of his death and burial, see Miguel Venegas, *Juan María de Salvatierra* (translated and edited by Marguerite Eyer Wilbur), pp. 218–32.

be taken of that colony; that an account be given the court of its condition then; and that, meantime, the form of government established there by the Fathers of the Society be not changed.

The Brother, after long private conferences with the viceroy, presented him with two petitions by order of His Excellency: In one he gave him a report of the country, harbors, inhabitants, presidio, and Missions of California; and in the other he explained the means which he believed most suitable for making the growth of the colony quicker and more permanent. He proposed, according to the instructions of Father Salvatierra, that a good seminary be established for the education of children; that fifty soldiers and their commander be paid from the account of the treasury; that a new presidio be established with them at the port of La Paz or at Cape San Lucas, according to the intentions of the court, where the ships from the Philippine Islands could take refuge without danger and find fresh food; that the colony be provided with a new vessel, since it no longer had any except the little "San Javier"; that the services of the captain, Don Estevan Rodríguez Lorenzo, be remunerated; and that the ownership of the salt marsh of the island of Carmen, from which neither the king nor private individuals derived any use, be ceded to the sanctuary of Our Lady of Loreto.

On September 25 the viceroy held a *junta* composed of two supreme magistrates, the royal *fiscal*, four other royal ministers, the provincial of the Jesuits, and Father Alejandro Romano and Brother Bravo, both procurators[8] of California.

---

[8] Another name for the business agent of the Jesuits. He lived in Mexico City. It was his duty to collect food, clothing, church furniture, equipment, etc., for the Missions in the peninsula. He received donations and kept the funds of the Jesuits properly invested. The procurator also went about the country talking to the young men attending college in order to get them interested in doing missionary work. Father Juan Ugarte was the first agent of the Jesuits in Mexico after they entered the peninsula. But he held this office for only one year. Father Alexander Romano continued serving until 1719, when Father Joseph Echeverría was made agent, because Romano was appointed *provincial* of New Spain. Ten years later Father Hernán Francisco Tompes was made procurator, and he served until May 1750 (Miguel Venegas, *Noticia de la California*, Vol. I, p. 427). The last procurator was Father Juan Armesto.

Not all which was requested was agreed to, and if the resolutions that were taken had been carried out they would have been very advantageous to California; but the *fiscal*, thinking that the heavy expenses which the royal treasury would have to bear in carrying out what had been determined might not perhaps be approved by the court, and that he would be responsible (since it was his duty to defend the interests of the crown), disclosed his fears to the viceroy and entreated him to suspend the proclamation of the decree.

The viceroy was likewise perplexed by his desire to fulfill the royal commands and his fear of displeasing the court. But the pious and magnanimous King Philip was very far from disapproving the first resolutions; for, induced by the spontaneous statements and requests which the Bishop of Nueva Vizcaya had made to him in favor of California, to whose diocese that peninsula was then believed to belong, he issued new and strict orders to the viceroy on January 29, 1719, recommending to him, with the most urgent expressions, the execution of his well-known commands with respect to the colony and the Missions of California.

Finally, the viceroy, in spite of his fears, ordered that the 18,276 *scudi* for the expenses of officers, soldiers, and sailors of the colony be given annually from the royal treasury to the procurator of California; that their debts be paid, which amounted to 3,022 *scudi*; and that a Peruvian vessel be bought for four thousand [*scudi*], also at the expense of the king. All was carried out; but the vessel had the same misfortune as so many others. It was lost the following year in the port of Matanchel because it was badly calked.

In the autumn of the same year (1717), while they were deliberating in Mexico [City] on the business of California, this peninsula suffered grave damages caused by a terrible hurricane of three continuous days, accompanied by the very heavy rains that are so rare in that country. All the houses and the churches made of adobe were destroyed; the dams were broken; and the fields were partly deprived of tillable ground and covered with rocks. Father Ugarte would have perished in the inundation of his Mission of San Javier if he had not climbed on a rock, where he was exposed to the rain without any protection for twenty-four hours; but what gives a better idea of the violence of the wind is the fact that in Loreto it carried away a boy named Mateo, who never was seen again either living or dead, in spite of search having been made for him. Two vessels of pearl fishermen which were on the coast of the peninsula were lost, with four men who were drowned, the rest being saved on two larger vessels which were well anchored and in a secure place. When these shipwrecked men arrived at Loreto after the storm they were well received and kindly treated by Father Ugarte. During the seventy years that the Jesuits remained in the peninsula there were many other very severe hurricanes, but none comparable to this one.

Chapter Five

FATHER SISTIAGA, MISSIONARY. FATHER TAMARAL APPOINTED TO THE MISSION OF CONCEPCIÓN

BROTHER BRAVO, after having thanked the viceroy and all those gentlemen of the *junta*, and after having bought all that he needed for the colony, returned to California, taking Father Sebastián de Sistiaga,[9] who was destined for those Missions. The appointment of this Jesuit seems to be a proof of the supernatural knowledge of Father Salvatierra. Father Sistiaga was a professor of belles-lettres in Mexico [City] when, induced by the Master, he informed his superiors of the desires which he had of being employed in the conversion of the Californians. The provincial did not consent to it at the beginning, nor could Father Salvatierra have had human knowledge of this when he was dying in Guadalajara, a city a little less than four hundred miles distant from Mexico [City].

Nevertheless, before dying he entrusted Brother Bravo,

---

[9] Spelled also "Sestaga" and "Sastiaga." He was a teacher in San Andrés College in Mexico before going to the peninsula. He returned to Mexico City in 1747, and nine years later he died at Puebla.

as soon as he reached Mexico [City], to tell Father Sistiaga to continue his petitions humbly in respect to California. Father Sistiaga was astonished at this, and he was persuaded that God had destined him to go to the Missions, in which he worked with much success for about thirty years.

Father Ugarte then had the supervision of the colony and the Missions and, at the same time, was missionary of San Javier Viggè; Father Mayorga, of Comondù; Father Guillen, of Liguig; and Father Piccolo, entrusted with the Missions of Loreto and Londò, had Father Sistiaga for a successor in that of Mulegè. Father Tamaral, a man of great spirit, who was to fertilize that evangelical field not less with his perspiration than with his blood, was appointed to the proposed Mission of Purísima Concepción.

Before establishing that Mission he stayed for some time in San Miguel, a place belonging to the Mission of San Javier in which he had the consolation of receiving two tribes of gentiles, who came to ask for baptism. These were supported by him, according to the custom of the missionaries, during the entire time that their instruction lasted; and afterward they were baptized. Encouraged by such auspicious beginnings, he undertook to open, as he did with considerable effort, first the road from San Miguel to Cadegomò, afterward the one from Cadegomò to the place of Purísima Concepción, and, finally, the one from Concepción to Mulegè. He stayed in Cadegomò a longer time for the purpose of catechising and baptizing the barbarians, as well as those of Codemino and those from the mountain of Vajademin. In Purísima (the place of that new Mission[10] which was thus commonly called) he found the land decorticated (let us so express it) by the furious storm of 1717. But with work and industry he succeeded in making tillable some sections of the country, which produced for him a quantity of corn sufficient to feed his neophytes. He guided the Mission

[10] When the first Missions were founded in Upper California this Mission sent to them seven broken mules, four good horses, twenty bushels of wheat, twenty-two leather bags, three sets of good leather harness, one hundred pounds of panocha, 450 pounds of figs, 200 pounds of flour, 575 pounds of raisins, and a quantity of pinole (Bolton, *Palóu*, Vol. I, p. 51).

for some years, the district of which was ninety miles of land, for the most part rough and rolling and inhabited by forty tribes of Indians of the Cochimì nation, thirty-three of which he instructed and reduced to a civilized and Christian life, and baptized almost two thousand persons. The heathen *guamas* conspired against his life many times; but God reserved this sacrifice for a different time and another place, as we shall see later.

Chapter Six

✣✣✣

THE PLANS OF FATHER UGARTE

FATHER UGARTE, always animated by heroic thoughts which befitted his magnanimity, decided at this time on the execution of two great enterprises. In the first place he wished to explore all the coast around the Gulf of California so that the Missions of Sonora, by advancing toward the north on one side, and those of California on the other, would finally come to be united in such a way that no tract of country that had not submitted to the Gospel would remain between them.[11] In spite of the discoveries of Fathers Kino and Salvatierra there were still many persons who doubted whether California was a true peninsula or whether there was a great canal between Loreto and the mouth of the Red River by which the Gulf of California was united with the Pacific Sea, since some ancient navigators flattered themselves upon having circumnavigated California. Father Ugarte also wished to explore the western coast of the peninsula in search of the port which was so desired by the king and again demanded by the viceroy for the ships from the Philippine Islands.

Now a large boat, strong and secure, which was not found in those seas, was needed to carry out these plans. It could not be ordered built in the ports of Nueva Galicia or in Sinaloa

---

[11] Ugarte was simply planning to carry out the dream of Kino and Salvatierra that some day a chain of Missions would connect the peninsula with Sonora by way of the Colorado River.

without being exposed to the dishonesty of the artful swindlers there. Father Ugarte therefore determined to build it in California itself, where there was a lack of wood, iron, rigging, pitch, and all the other necessary materials and tools, and also of a master workman to direct the construction and artisans to make it; but all the difficulties were overcome by his heroic fortitude and his marvelous industry. He had a master workman and some artisans come from New Spain; and he wished to bring even the wood from there, but when he found out from some of his neophytes that two hundred miles from Loreto toward the northwest there were very stout trees, he went to that place, escorted by the Indians and accompanied by the master workman.

In fact he found there a great quantity of large *guaribo*[12] trees, but in such deep ravines that it seemed impossible for the master workman to transport the timber as far as the port of Mulegè, ninety miles distant. "That is my responsibility," Father Ugarte then said, at whose enterprise almost all laughed, in spite of the fact that they so highly esteemed his intrepidity and ability.

After he had made suitable arrangements in Loreto, he moved to the ravines, in which he remained for four months, directing the cutting of the timber (which he often did); and he was aided for the most part by his neophytes and the neighboring tribes of gentiles, who, at the same time, were being domesticated, catechised, and disposed to Christianity by him. And a short time afterward a new Mission was established there. Later, when he had a long road opened and leveled down as much as possible as far as the port of Mulegè, he had the timber conveyed by oxen and mules, using the gentiles themselves to manage the animals. In Mulegè he gave such spirit to the work with his authority and manners that on September 14, 1719, a sloop was launched which was called "Triunfo de la Cruz."[13] In the opinion of all the well-

[12] See footnote 87, Book I, p. 47, *supra*.
[13] For an account of the building of this ship and the voyage of Ugarte, see *The Californian*, Vol. I, pp. 15–19.

informed, the boat was the most beautiful, the strongest, and the best made of the many which had been seen up to that time on the Gulf of California.

Chapter Seven

BROTHER BRAVO RECEIVES SACRED ORDERS AND IS MADE A MISSIONARY. THE ALFÉREZ OF THE PRESIDIO BECOMES A JESUIT

WHEN they were working on the upper decks and on the accoutrements of the sloop, California acquired a new vessel, a new procurator,[14] and a new missionary. The new missionary was Brother Bravo himself, who, after having gone to Sinaloa at this time to get provisions, found a letter there from the provincial in which he commanded him to go to Guadalajara to receive sacred orders from the bishop, since the father-general (advised by the superiors of Mexico) wished him to be employed as a missionary because of his great zeal for the conversion of the Californians.

The good Brother, although filled with confusion, obeyed promptly. Summoned by the same provincial, he went from Guadalajara to Mexico [City]. There he obtained a new vessel from the viceroy, since the one which had been bought two years before had been lost in the port of Matanchel. Besides this favor from the viceroy, he obtained another from the pious Marqués de Villapuente, who, desirous of the conversion of the Guaicuras, set aside capital for the endowment of a new Mission at the port of La Paz; and he wanted Father Bravo himself to be the founder. The latter willingly took charge of that arduous and dangerous undertaking; and when he had bought all that he needed then for the colony, he embarked at Acapulco in the new vessel given by the viceroy and went back to Loreto.

As the number of soldiers, sailors, neophytes, and catechu-

---

[14] Father Joseph Echeverría, who served until 1729.

men had increased considerably, so there was need of a greater quantity of supplies; and a procurator was necessary to care for acquiring and distributing them. Now that Father Bravo, assigned to apostolic offices, could not be occupied in temporal duties any longer, God provided in a singular manner. Don Juan Bautista Mugazabal,[15] the *alférez* of the presidio, was a man of such habits and ability that, from the time that he entered California, each one of the missionaries wanted him for a companion. Father Piccolo, whose companion he was for many years, asserted that the progress of Christianity in Mulegè was due in large measure to him.

Mugazabal, influenced by the examples of rectitude which he observed continually in that good religious, ardently desired to become a Jesuit, and he attained it without difficulty; but as the superiors considered, on the one hand, the great distance of Tepotzotlán,[16] where the general novitiate of the Jesuits of New Spain was (a distance of more than one thousand miles from Loreto), and, on the other hand, the need of California, they absolved him from the usual law, permitting him to do his two years of novitiate in that very peninsula under the guidance of Father Ugarte. In such a good school he became an exemplary and diligent religious and faithful administrator, as he showed in the forty-one years that he filled that office with much success and improvement.

[15] Born in Alava, Spain, in 1682, Mugazabal came to California in 1704. He was admitted as a lay brother to the Society of Jesus under the teaching of Father Juan Ugarte. Of him Father Engelhardt says that he was "the first religious novice, and the first to pronounce the simple religious vows on California soil" (Charles Anthony Engelhardt, *Missions and Missionaries in California*, Vol. I, p. 170).

[16] A college in the province of Misteca, Mexico.

Chapter Eight

THE MISSION OF LA PAZ AND ITS MISSIONARY FATHER BRAVO

IN THIS year[17] two new Missions[18] were established in California. The first at the port of La Paz had been vainly attempted by Father Salvatierra, and now it was endowed by the Marqués de Villapuente. When Father Salvatierra saw that his attempts were not successful, he said: "God keeps this enterprise reserved for the apostle," that is, for Father Ugarte, to whom he was accustomed to give this title. In fact, this great man was the one who, with Brother Bravo, established that dangerous Mission. In order to carry out the plan, he commanded Father Guillen to go by land from Liguig to that port for the purpose of having a road opened for the communication of that new Mission with Loreto; and he went by sea in his new sloop with Father Bravo and some soldiers and neophytes from Loreto. When they reached La Paz, all landed in a very orderly fashion, as they were in a hostile country; but although some armed Guaicuras appeared in the distance, as soon as they saw that the two missionaries, accompanied by a single Indian who was to act as an interpreter, were coming toward them, they sat down tranquilly to indicate their confidence. This attitude came from the favorable reports which the three Guaicuri prisoners had given them, whom Father Salvatierra had sent to their country bearing considerable gifts, as has been stated above.

The two missionaries tried to win the good will of those savages with kind treatment and presents, giving them some woolen clothing, some knives, and other trifles esteemed by

---

[17] In 1720.

[18] La Paz and Huasinapi (Guadalupe Mission). When the first Missions of Upper California were founded, the Guadalupe Mission gave to them 6,250 pounds of jerked meat, 250 pounds of beef tallow, 16 broken mules, 4 good horses, 10 sets of harness, and four leather bags (Bolton, *Palóu*, Vol. I, p. 51).

them, and assuring them that they had come to seek their friendship and that they should make peace with the barbarous inhabitants of the islands of San José and Espíritu Santo and with their other persecutors and tormentors. The Guaicuras showed great pleasure because of this; and, although on the first days they did not venture to approach the soldiers, they became less and less afraid afterward and appeared in throngs, even from very remote places. Cabins were built out of branches and roofed with straw for shelter for the men; the earth was leveled and cleaned off where the church and the houses were to be built; provisions and animals were taken out of the sloop; and the new Mission began to take form to the pleasure of the Guaicuras.

Notwithstanding the fact that Liguig is more than two hundred miles distant from La Paz, Father Guillen arrived with his followers after a journey of only twenty-six days. It was a very painful one because of the detours which he had to make to avoid ravines and other difficulties which he had to overcome on the way. Father Ugarte stayed three months in La Paz in which, by means of that divine grace which he had for making himself respected and loved by the savages, he won the friendship of the Guaicuras to such an extent that they repeatedly asked him to leave a missionary with them forever to instruct and to guide them. He also invited the savage inhabitants of the islands near by to come, and he persuaded them to make peace with the Guaicuras, their ancient enemies. The Guaicuras begged him to free them from the abuses of the pearl fishermen; and he assured them that under the protection of Father Bravo and the soldiers whom he was leaving there they would never again suffer similar evils.

After Father Ugarte returned to Loreto at the end of January, 1721, and Father Guillen to Liguig, Father Bravo stayed at the port of La Paz with some soldiers. His first concern was that of learning the language of the barbarians. This task was followed by the work of building the church and houses, cultivating the land, gathering the scattered savages from the woods, civilizing them, instructing them, getting them accustomed to a laborious life and the practice of Christianity, and establishing towns among them. That new missionary did all this with great zeal until the year 1728, when he was called to Loreto by his superiors to help Father Piccolo, now quite old and ill. In those eight years Father Bravo baptized more than six hundred children and adults; he left at the Mission eight hundred catechumen and many gentiles attached to the Gospel; and he established three towns, called the Virgin of Pilar, Todos Santos, and Ángel Custodio. In this way he made his talent and vocation for the priesthood of service to those barbarians.

Chapter Nine

THE MISSION OF HUASINAPI, OR RATHER OF GUADALUPE, AND ITS MISSIONARY, FATHER HELEN

WHILE Father Ugarte was occupied in establishing the Mission of La Paz, another was established at Huasinapi, a cold and unhealthy place in the mountains, one hundred and eighty miles distant to the northwest from Loreto. From the time when Father Ugarte went there to cut the timber for the sloop he inspired such an affection in the mountaineers of the Cochimì nation for the Christian religion that they frequently sent to entreat him to return to their mountains. After he had made another visit to be, assured of their sincerity, and when he was ready to embark for La Paz, he arranged that Father Helen,[19] a German Jesuit, who had reached California in April 1719 and had acquired some knowledge of the language in a few months, should go and establish the new Mission in Huasinapi. Accompanied by the captain and some soldiers of the presidio, Father Helen left at the end of the year 1720 for Huasinapi, where gathered the tribes which roved over the neighboring mountains. They were very happy to have a missionary among them.

---

[19] Spelled also "Hellen" or "Hyelen." He was educated at Prague, Germany. He left California in 1735 and spent the remainder of his life in Mexico, where he died (1757) at Tepotzotlán.

He started the work of the church and the houses immediately, the savages working on them on an equality with the soldiers as if they had been accustomed to the labor from childhood. Afterward Father Helen began to instruct them in the Christian doctrine; and their insistence was such in learning it that he could not free himself all day long from their pious solicitations in order to attend to other business. They repeated ceaselessly what they had learned; and every day they got up before dawn to say their prayers, the concert of which (so pleasing to God and the angels) made the missionary weep with tenderness. In a short time he found himself obliged to go continually through the mountains, summoned by the most remote tribes, to instruct the old and the sick, for whom delay might be harmful, and to baptize the children.

As soon as the buildings were finished, the captain returned with his soldiers to Loreto, leaving four who (he thought) were necessary for the security of that missionary who was in a country so far from the presidio and not yet subjected to the Gospel. Father Helen, continuing his apostolic tasks, held the first baptism of twenty adults with all the pomp and solemnity possible on Holy Saturday of 1721, and the second with equal solemnity on the eve of Pentecost.[20]

These examples encouraged the desire for baptism in other remote tribes. But Father Helen protested that he did not believe that they were capable of such surpassing grace if they did not bring him those little tablets, hair capes, deer hooves, and other similar things which they used in their superstitions. There was some difficulty in obtaining these conditions, because such things, as the material objects of superstition, were instruments of the deceit of their charlatans for procuring their living.

In fifteen years of continuous work and observation of these Indians, this missionary could not find among them any trace of idolatry, witchery, or pact with the Devil. He knew through experience that those who passed for witches were only true charlatans and impostors; but since the deceits of the latter were the greatest obstacle to the propagation of the faith, so after

---

[20] The Saturday that precedes Easter.

the example of other missionaries he demanded from those who asked for baptism that they bring him all the things which the *guamas* used to keep them in their blind heathenism. Finally he succeeded in having them bring him very many; and he had them all burned in a great bonfire on a day appointed for such a demonstration, to which he assembled all the Indians. The latter then showed the scorn in which they held those things by the stones which the men as well as the women and children threw at them.

The zeal of Father Helen took a much broader scope in the years 1722 and 1723, which were as lamentable to that peninsula because of the misfortunes which befell it as the two previous years had been happy ones on account of the establishment and the prosperous beginnings of the two Missions. In 1722 California was afflicted by the terrible scourge of locusts, which destroyed almost all the wild produce upon which the Indians lived; and if it had not been for the corn which they were given in the Missions, many would have perished from starvation. But as the corn was not sufficient to support them all, they devoted themselves to killing the locusts, not only to destroy them, but also to eat them. This food and others, equally harmful, caused an epidemic of malignant ulcers, which killed many. Father Helen, urged on by his fervid charity, walked ceaselessly over those rugged mountains, carrying spiritual and temporal aid to the sick and acting toward them as father, physician, nurse, confessor, and comforter.

Scarcely had this epidemic decreased when another very serious one of dysentery came, in which the missionary worked so hard that he contracted a dangerous hernia and an inflammation of the eyes so annoying and so severe that he was obliged to go to Loreto to get well; he returned to his Missions afterward, although he had not entirely recovered. The neophytes, seeing that he had sacrificed his rest and health for them, received him as an angel come from Heaven. He served, in total, one hundred and twenty-eight Christians whom that epidemic killed; in all the matters of soul and body he served a greater number who recovered, besides very many babies who were baptized by him and who fluttered away to Paradise. The same thing occurred in the other Missions, although not to such a degree as in that of Guadalupe or Huasinapi.

Father Helen availed himself greatly of the affection which the Indians bore him for the progress of Christianity, which was so rapid that there were in 1726 thirty-two converted tribes, one thousand seven hundred and seven individuals of which were Christians, besides the catechumen. Some of these tribes were added to the Mission of Mulegè, and others to that of San Ignacio, which was founded a little while afterward, because they were less distant from those places. Twenty tribes remained for the Mission of Guadalupe, scattered through the places in the mountains where there was potable water; but, finally, they were gathered by Father Helen into five villages where he built in each one a chapel for religious services, besides the houses.

In all the district of this Mission, no tillable land could be found. So the Indians were supported by the corn which was sent them from the other Missions, by fruits and roots which they sought in the mountains, and by the flesh of animals which were raised there. The neophytes of the Mission came to be the best-instructed and the most moderate and devout; this was due chiefly (after God) to the zeal of Father Helen, who devoted himself to the conversion of the barbarians in such a way that when he left the Mission by necessity he did not leave a single heathen in all that vast territory. But after fifteen years of such glorious endeavors, his complaints finally became so aggravated that his superiors compelled him (although he wished to die among his beloved neophytes) to move to New Spain in the year 1735, where he died in Tepotzotlán, near Mexico [City] in the year 1757, after a very pure life filled with toil.

Chapter Ten

THE COMMANDS OF THE VICEROY CARRIED OUT BY THE MISSIONARIES

Meanwhile the missionaries had bound themselves to carry out the new and strict orders of the viceroy about seeking a good port on the western coast of the peninsula. That could not be done by sea without large ships and considerable expense; therefore, they determined to make the explorations by land, as had already been done so unsuccessfully on so many other occasions by Fathers Salvatierra and Ugarte. With this purpose Father Guillen left in 1719 at the command of Father Ugarte, accompanied by the captain, some soldiers, and three companies of Californians, armed after their custom. But because it was known through the account of the voyages of Sebastián Vizcaíno that Magdalena Bay[21] was large, commodious, and secure for vessels, and was situated between 24° and 25°, they went in that direction and arrived only after a very distressing trip of twenty-five days.

In fact they saw that the bay was large enough and surrounded on all sides by mountains, which protected it from winds. But nowhere in the vicinity did they find potable water, or pastures, or firewood, or land capable of cultivation. So that neither the ships that arrived there could be provided with necessities, nor could the proposed colony be established there. Father Guillen wished to continue his explorations on those coasts; but since the captain and the soldiers were opposed to it, all returned to Loreto in fifteen days by another shorter route.

Father Tamaral, who had been particularly recommended by the viceroy to make the same explorations when he took leave of His Excellency in Mexico [City], went to that coast several times at that period and explored a great distance of it toward the north and almost all toward the south as far as Cape San Lucas without being able to find a suitable port for the much-desired colony.

[21] Latitude 24° 32'.

Finally, on November 19 Fathers Sistiaga and Helen left the Mission of Guadalupe, accompanied by the captain and some soldiers of the presidio; and, going as far as 28°, they explored a large stretch of that coast with exactness. On this trip, although otherwise unfortunte, they had the consolation of finding three suitable ports provided with water and firewood. It is true that the soil all along the coast seemed sterile to them and absolutely incapable of cultivation; but, being the largest, the most secure, and the most abundant in water of these ports and not too far from the village of San Miguel, belonging to the Mission of San Javier, the vessels which put in that bay could receive the necessary fresh supplies there.

Chapter Eleven

THE UNDERTAKING OF FATHER UGARTE AND THE INFORMATION ACQUIRED WITH IT

BEFORE Father Sistiaga made that trip to the western coast of California in 1721, Father Ugarte put into practice the daring plan of sailing over all the Gulf to clear up the doubt of the union of California[22] with the continent of New Spain. The space of the sea over which he was to sail was small. But the frequent storms (the more to be feared because they were so severe), the violence of the tide on those coasts, the multitude of islands and shoals, the narrowness of the canals, the impact and the opposition of the currents, the lack of ports in which to find shelter and take fresh food, the unhealthy climate of the northern part of the Gulf, and the

---

[22] Doubt still existed in the minds of many that California could be a peninsula. The slow spread of geographical knowledge at that time is illustrated by the fact that, although it had been nearly two hundred years since Ulloa had reached the head of the Gulf and ascended the Colorado River for many miles, navigators and explorers still expressed their belief that California was an island. Ulloa, Kino, and many others were positive that the country could not be an island; yet it was not until 1746 that the king of Spain issued a decree declaring California to be a peninsula.

caustic quality of those waters made the voyage much more troublesome and dangerous than if it were over the ocean.[23]

Then when the sloop, the "Triunfo de la Cruz," together with the small boat, the "Santa Barbara," which had been built with the sloop, was made ready, Father Ugarte left Loreto on May 15. Six Europeans who were very skilled in navigation (especially the pilot Guillermo Strafort)[24] and thirteen Californians went in the sloop; eight Indians went in the small boat, to wit: two from the Philippine Islands, one Yaqui, and five Californians. They sailed toward the north as far as 28°, and from there they crossed the Gulf in five days to the port of Santa Sabina in Sonora with the intention of continuing their voyage as far as the mouth of the Red River, after they had provided themselves with water and provisions.

Misfortunes began in this port. Because Father Ugarte had accidentally got wet on landing, he was attacked by such severe pains in the thighs, legs, and feet that he could neither stand nor sit. When they landed there they did not see an Indian but only a cross planted in the sand of the beach, which they approached, and, kneeling, they embraced it and kissed it.

Scarcely had they done this when many Serì Indians, who had gone into ambush, appeared and showed themselves friendly. Such demonstrations from these barbarians, mortal enemies of the Spaniards, were the results of the requests of Father Salvatierra, who besought them, when he was among them in 1710, to give a kind reception to the vessels from California which might put into port there. And in order that they

---

[23] It will be noted that Clavigero comments upon almost every trip across the Gulf as being long and hazardous. The difficulties and the dangers incident to crossing the Gulf from the mainland greatly delayed the progress of the Missions and the settlement later of Upper California. More than two months were spent by Otondo in 1683 in getting across this Gulf. The Jesuits in five years (1712–1717) lost a ship a year from storms in these waters. In 1768, when preparations were being made to plant the first settlement in Upper California, it took the two supply ships, the "San Antonio" and the "San Carlos," nearly three months to make the voyage from the port of San Blas to La Paz.

[24] He was an Englishman. Bancroft calls him "Strafford," and Venegas, "Estrafort."

might recognize them, he instructed them to observe whether they bore the hoisted standard of the cross; and that if they wished to be further assured they should present that holy wood to the navigators, and if it were adored by them it was not to be doubted that they came from California. This advice was necessary because the seas were infested with English pirates.[25]

Then when the Series had noticed the said countersigns among these navigators, they received them in a friendly fashion; and when they saw Father Ugarte on board the sloop, they did not wait for him to land to do him reverence, but, diving into the sea, swam to the sloop and climbed on it, embraced his feet, kissed his hands and face, and made other demonstrations of affection and respect. After Father Ugarte had caressed them and made them presents, he availed himself of them by sending a letter to a missionary of the neighboring country; and he had them fill the barrels of the sloop with water, which they did with great diligence and haste.

They entreated Father Ugarte to go to an island near by to visit their relatives. And he agreed to go in order to gain their affection more, while the provisions were coming for which he had asked the missionary in his letter. Then having set sail on the following day, dawn found them in a very narrow, tortuous strait, full of shoals, on one of which the sloop ran aground; and surely it would have been destroyed if those men, so skilled on the sea, had not got it out of danger with the greatest care and industry. They sailed three days through that perilous strait, momentarily fearing being lost, until they reached the island for which they were looking.

At first the islanders took up arms and began to shout loudly to prevent landing; but when their countrymen, who were on the sloop, had advised them that a missionary was coming in it

---

[25] Piracy had been not only a sea sport but a regular and often profitable business for centuries. When Spain extended her possessions in the New World, built up a lucrative sea trade, and found much gold and silver, the English, Dutch, and French pirates and privateers infested the waters surrounding the Spanish colonies. On one occasion the Dutch pirate, Peter Heyn, in command of thirty-one vessels, captured a Spanish fleet and procured a cargo valued at $15,000,000. English pirates were particularly active in the Spanish waters about 1700.

to visit them, they at once laid aside their weapons. And fifty men came out on thirteen rafts to the boat to greet him and to beg him to land on their island, where they had a house in which to lodge him. Father Ugarte was so distressed by pain that every movement, however slight, was unendurable to him. Notwithstanding this, in order to please them, he had the sailors and the Californians carry him to shore, where he was received by the savages drawn up in two lines, one composed of men and the other of women, and then they carried him to a cabin made of branches and having two doors. There all the natives of the island met to do him reverence, first the men and afterward the women, entering one by one, inclining their heads for the father to put his hand on them, and going out by the other door.

Afterward, when all had surrounded him, he showed them, in spite of his pain, as much kindness as it was possible for him to do; and he urged them to move to the Mission of Pópulo[26] (which was two or three days' journey distant from the beach of the neighboring continent) and to have a Christian catechist among them, so that after they had been well instructed they could be baptized.

Father Ugarte did not stay long on the island, because it was urgent that he return to the continent to make provision for food for continuing the voyage. Then he embarked for that place; and since no port existed there where refuge could be had, it was necessary for the sloop to anchor in an insecure place, because a storm had carried away the anchor and destroyed the bow mast, although it was of very hard wood. Father Ugarte ordered those in the small boat to explore that route which they were to follow, and some men were to land to observe the coasts. Both groups informed him that there was no port on all that coast, that the country was sterile and lacked water, and that the tide everywhere was very violent. All of this coincided with the observations made in those places by Fathers Kino and Salvatierra. The small boat was high and dry in a violent ebb tide of the sea, and it lost part of its calking.

---

[26] Santa María del Pòpulo Tonichi, founded in 1628 and located on the San Miguel River just a few miles north of Horcasitas.

Now Father Ugarte, thinking that he could not continue the voyage on the Sonora side without rashness, determined to do it on the opposite side of California. With this purpose, after having ordered the boats repaired and the provisions which he could get on that shore put on board, they set sail on July 2; and after they had crossed the Gulf in three days, which is only one hundred and twenty miles wide in that part, they landed on the beach of California; and although there was no port, they anchored and sent the canoe (or bark) to the shore. The Indian inhabitants of that coast presented themselves armed and, drawing a line on the sand, threatened any one who might pass it. But the sailors, having won them easily with some trifling gifts and various demonstrations of friendship, not only were well received but were also recommended to other Indians of those coasts. So they traveled securely overland for almost thirty miles.

When they returned to the sloop, they continued their voyage, always going north and coasting along in search of some port where protection could be had if a storm came up. They did not find it; but when they had doubled a cape, they discovered a small inlet where they thought they were safe from the south wind which was then blowing. There the currents were so violent and the sloop was rocked so much it seemed as if it were in a heavy storm. The pilot, desirous of discovering some place where the sloop would be more secure, embarked in the canoe with five sailors and went everywhere sounding the depth of the inlet as far as the end of the bay. There they landed, and having left the canoe on the sand they went to certain savages who were at the foot of a mountain and presented them with some trifles which they had received from Father Ugarte for this purpose.

While they were visiting with them, a furious, big wave, accompanied by a fearful roar, came and carried away the canoe, dashed it against a rock, and broke it lengthwise in two pieces. The six sailors promptly ran with the savages; but as they had neither materials nor tools at hand to overcome that misfortune, necessity taught them the way to supply them. They used two nails removed from an oar and the sounding rope to fasten the two pieces together; and to calk the boat they made use of the hemp of a cable (instead of oakum) and mud instead of pitch. In spite of their industry the water leaked in great quantity through the crack, all their efforts not being enough to stop it. Nevertheless, they could not help but embark; and, after crossing that short but dangerous space, they finally reached the sloop.

Father Ugarte meanwhile had sent other men in the small boat to examine the shore. But after having coasted along for more than sixty miles, they found no port. Then, after they had lifted anchor and gone toward the north (some time later), they noticed a great diversity in the color of the water; at times it appeared ash-colored, then black, and more frequently red. This made them infer that they were not very far from the mouths of the Red River. Then they approached the coast of Pimerìa in order to avoid the shoals which they feared there. In the middle of the Gulf, which is very narrow in that place, they observed that the water was muddier; and, near the shore, they found eight, ten, and more fathoms of water. Finally they cast anchor at the mouth of the Red River which is on the Pimerìa side; and there they saw two great floods which bore tree-trunks, entire trees, fragments of cabins, and similar things.

As soon as the sailors saw the flood receding, they wished to go up the river. But the prudence of Father Ugarte did not permit it. When he observed toward the north the same clouds which he had seen two nights before and which had caused the floods, he foresaw that another storm was to come; and in fact, it did, and those who had wished to navigate the river would have irreparably perished in it.

Leaving that place they passed in front of the first mouth of the river, and after a little they cast anchor in four fathoms of water. From there they saw in the distance another mouth, which is on the California side, and they saw the continuation of the land of that peninsula clearly as far as the river and that there was no strait which separated it from the continent. Father Ugarte desired to land on the shore where the Gulf ends in order to make his discovery more positive; but neither did his severe complaints permit him nor could the sloop approach on account of the many shoals and the heavy swells, which came and dashed against the beach with extraordinary impetus.

Notwithstanding this, the pilot embarked in the small boat and approached land in various places as near as it was possible for him in order to observe the shore better and to make a hydrographical map of the Gulf afterward. Besides, the ocular observations of those shores, the many shoals, and the great violence of the tide were sufficient for one to infer that the Gulf terminated in that place and that the waters were enclosed there and shut off from all junction.

Since they had attained the principal purpose of that dangerous voyage, and since (on the other hand) some of the crew were sick because of the unhealthfulness of the deadly climate, and since the vessels were in such danger, the decision was made to return to California. After lifting anchor they resumed their trip on July 16. The small boat went coasting along the peninsula in order to land whenever it was necessary. The sloop went down the middle of the Gulf, veering now to the one coast, then to the other in order to avoid the many islands and shoals. Scarcely had it passed the island of Tiburón with great difficulty when the contrary currents, as rapid as a river, made it go back in six hours as far as it had advanced in a week.

After they had entered the narrow and very dangerous channels of Salsipuedes Islands,[27] they succeeded, although with the greatest effort, in passing the first and the second island, but they could not sail by the third in twenty days of continuous endeavors. Because of this they anchored and landed when they found a suitable shelter in one of those islands. This had become absolutely necessary because only five of the entire crew were well, all the rest being either ill from scurvy or from their skin being stripped off and burnt by the caustic water of the

---

[27] Meaning "get out if you can." In 1844 when the Frenchman Duflot de Mofras came to this place, he said, "sors si tu peux (find your way out if you can)", and in 1875 when an American naval officer was caught in the strong current there, he reported that "sailing vessels found it almost impossible to make any headway" (*United States Bureau of Navigation, Publication 56*, 1880, p. 113).

northern part of that gulf. Father Ugarte had protected himself from the water, since it had been so harmful to him; he was not even touched by scurvy. But in addition to his other complaints, another new and strange one attacked him, that is, a burning from the lower to the upper part of his abdomen, so great and so feverish that when his shirt was removed from his body, it tore away his skin, dripping with blood.

All were persuaded that the decision to take shelter on that island had been a consequence of the paternal protection of God; otherwise, shipwreck would have been inevitable in those straits on account of a heavy storm which arose in a little while. They remained in the port four days, during which time the sick were somewhat restored by the land air; but Father Ugarte, on the contrary, became so much worse that he decided to go in a canoe to the coast of the Series. This determination terrified all the crew to such an extent that he found himself obliged to promise them that he would not desert them, even though he was sure that he was to die on that voyage.

Then after they had fervidly commended themselves to the Master they set sail on August 18 and with a favorable wind finally got out of those islands. They sailed toward California, quite consoled on seeing themselves freed from so many dangers, when they were surprised near the port of Concepción by a new storm, accompanied by terrible thunder and lightning, heavy rain, and such darkness that it seemed night at noonday. What frightened the sailors most was to see themselves threatened by a dreadful hurricane that was descending upon them in a cloud scarcely two miles distant. Father Ugarte asserted afterward that on all that very dangerous trip there had never been such a day of fear as that. Finally, freed from this last danger, the sloop put in at Port Concepción; and from there all went to the Mission of Mulegè, part by sea and part by land, where they were well treated and kindly restored to health by Father Sistiaga. When they had recovered they went to Loreto in the sloop about the middle of September, four months after they had departed thence; and there they found the small boat, which happily had arrived a few days before.

This voyage served not only to settle the much-discussed

question about the union of California with the continent and to refute the opinion of those who pretended that ships from the Philippines could make trips through the strait which they imagined was between California and Sonora, but it also served to acquire clearer knowledge of that sea and its coasts, and to correct the many common errors about the situation of the islands, the shoals, and the direction of the coasts. Father Ugarte drew up an exact account of the voyage and sent it to the viceroy, with the log of the pilot, Strafort, and with the hydrographic map of that gulf and its coasts, drawn by the same pilot.

Chapter Twelve

THE PRUDENT ZEAL OF THE MISSIONARIES IN THE SPREAD OF THE GOSPEL. THE MISSION OF THE VIRGEN DE LOS DOLORES, AND ITS MISSIONARY, FATHER GUILLEN

THESE undertakings, carried out to serve the will of the king and his ministers, did not diminish in any way the individual zeal of each of the missionaries to make safe the advancement of Christianity in his respective district. Contact with the different nations of the peninsula had made them acquainted with the diversity among them. It had been observed that the Cochimìes, the inhabitants of the most northern countries, were more intelligent and docile, more peaceable and faithful, less vicious and less dissolute, and therefore much better disposed to receive the Gospel and to subject themselves to a civilized and Christian life. On the contrary, it had been noticed that the Pericùes and the Guaicuras, the inhabitants of the southern countries, were more lazy and idle, more fickle and ungrateful, more tricky and taciturn, and above all more licentious than the other savages, and that their tribes lived in continual dissension and war, with which they mutually destroyed each other.

For this reason it seemed that the light of the Gospel should be carried first to the docile barbarians of the northern countries; but the missionaries thought that the conservation of the others was more necessary, since the tranquillity of some Missions already established depended on it. The Uchitas, who lived between Loreto and La Paz, endeavored to hinder communication between those two Missions, with different hostilities directed against the Christians who went from one to another. The Guaicuras of La Paz were troubled frequently by the Pericùes, their ancient enemies. Besides, the fierce Indians of the islands of San José, Espíritu Santo, and Cerralvo, although they had made peace with the Guaicuras at the request of Father Ugarte, had begun their hostilities again; and three times they had had the daring to pillage the Mission of Liguig while the missionary was absent. It is true that the captain of the presidio went with some soldiers to punish them, killing three or four, making eleven prisoners, and taking fourteen canoes from them; but these punishments, although they checked them for some time, did not entirely hinder their raids. Therefore there was no other remedy than to subject them to the yoke of the Gospel.

With this purpose they tried to establish two Missions in that year in the midst of those barbarians. Father Guillen, the missionary of Liguig, was appointed to the first, which was dedicated to the Virgin of Dolores. As the Indians of Liguig had become reduced to a very small number by sickness and were exposed frequently to the raids of so many heathen enemies, the decision was made to add them to another Mission. Father Guillen then gave himself up to the new tasks and dangers of that arduous enterprise, having to construct new buildings, collect, civilize, instruct, baptize, and guide the new savages. That new Mission was founded during the month of August of the said year on Apate beach, one hundred and twenty miles south of Loreto. But afterward, for the sake of the comfort of those Indians, it was moved to Tagnuetìa, a place in the mountains almost twenty miles distant to the west from that beach.

We are unable to say particularly what Father Guillen had to endure and do in the establishment of that Mission and in the twenty-five years that he had charge of it. But it is known with what unspeakable work he got the barbarians who were scattered in the woods out of them and congregated them in nine villages, three of which were added to the Mission of San Luis Gonzaga, which was established there in 1747[28] at the expense of the very noble Mexican, Don Luis de Velasco, the Count of Santiago. It is also known that in spite of the territory of his Mission being so large (it extended from one sea to another), he did not leave any Indian in it who was not a Christian or at least a catechumen. His apostolic tasks were more wearisome because of the excessive sterility of all that land, with the exception of a small stretch of the shore of Apate, where a little corn was sown. This Mission of the Virgin of Dolores served as a refuge for the missionaries and neophytes in the rebellion of the Pericùes in 1734, of which we shall speak later.

Chapter Thirteen

THE PORT OF LAS PALMAS IS ALLOTTED A NEW MISSION, AND FATHER NÀPOLI IS APPOINTED TO GUIDE IT

THE OTHER Mission was to be established in the country of the Pericùes, the most southern country of California. Father Ugarte greatly desired this; and, therefore, before undertaking the trip to the Red River, he commanded Father Ignazio Maria Nàpoli,[29] an Italian who had come to that peninsula a few months before, to go there.

---

[28] No doubt a misprint, since both Bancroft and Engelhardt give 1737 as the date of founding.

[29] According to the Gordon manuscript, Nàpoli founded the Mission of Santiago in 1720. Bancroft and Engelhardt state that Nàpoli arrived in the peninsula in 1721. He seems to have served at Santiago until 1726. Later he went to Sonora on account of ill health, but returned to the peninsula and went through the Indian Revolt (1734–1737), part of this time working with Father William Gordon to pacify the Indians.

Fig. 21 – The mission church at San Luis Gonzaga. The building must be of Jesuit construction since the mission was abandoned shortly after the Jesuit expulsion. Father Baegert is given credit for building it. During the late nineteenth century, when San Luis Gonzaga was a regional trading center, the facade was refinished.

George E. Lindsay

Fig. 22 – Rear view of the mission church at San Luis Gonzaga.

After having given him all the necessary instructions that as soon as the vessel loaded with provisions arrived from New Spain he should take all that he needed of them and go in the same boat to the port of La Paz, and from there to that of Las Palmas, the place selected for the new Mission, Father Nàpoli arrived at La Paz on August 2, 1721, where the neophytes of the Mission, kneeling to kiss his hands, received him with a thousand demonstrations of respect and took him, the captain, and the four soldiers who accompanied him to the church, in the door of which Father Bravo was awaiting him. From La Paz they went by land, leveling down a road for communication between those two Missions; and they reached the port of Las Palmas on August 24.

No Indian appeared during the first four days. Near the evening of the fourth day, when Father Nàpoli had gone out to examine the beach and when he was far from the tent in which the others were under cover from the sun, he saw coming toward him a troop of absolutely naked savages led by a *guama* taller and stouter than the others, with his body painted red and black and poorly covered with a cape made of locks of hair, and with some deers' hooves hung at his belt, a feather fan in one hand and in the other a drawn bow and arrow, uttering fearful howls, to which the others answered with threatening cries and movements.

Father Nàpoli believed beyond a doubt that they were coming to kill him. And so, lifting his heart to Heaven, he commended himself to God and made Him a fervid offering of his life; but in order to dissimulate his natural fear by following the advice given to him by Father Ugarte, and fortified by the sign of the cross, he went to meet them. By making signs he reproached them as well as he knew how for their perverse intention. After taking from his pocket some trifles which by chance he carried with him, he distributed them among them; and having gradually inspired their confidence he had them come to the tent, where he gave them food, treated them kindly, and gave them presents again. By means of an interpreter they gave assurance that they would soon be back with other countrymen of theirs whenever they would remove the mules and a dog which they had seen there. Not being accustomed to those animals, they were afraid of them. On the following day at least fifty persons came in different groups and presented the missionary with wild fruits and roots on which they were accustomed to sustain themselves; and in recompense they were given some *pozolli*, some common cloth, some knives, and other similar little gifts.

After having explored the country and found some tillable soil and the necessary supply of water, the place was cleaned off where the church and the dwellings of the Mission were to be built and the construction was begun immediately. But the Indians who had begun to come daily disappeared suddenly one day, for which no reason could be given. Father Nàpoli went out with one soldier and the interpreter to look for them and, having met some, learned from them that the true cause of their flight was their ancient hostility to the Guaicuras. Since they had seen that the missionary had come to their country accompanied by some Guaicuras from La Paz and by Father Bravo, who was believed by them to be their chief and leader, and since they had observed afterward that the Guaicuras kept going to La Paz and soon returned, and that the missionary and soldiers were erecting buildings after having explored the country, they suspected that the missionary and the soldiers had allied themselves with all the Guaicura nation in order to fall upon them suddenly, and that they were constructing the houses in order to carry on hostilities with more security. It is to be believed that these suspicions were suggested to them by the *guamas* to hinder the introduction of Christianity. It was very difficult for Father Nàpoli to convince them; but finally he succeeded.

Chapter Fourteen

HOSTILITIES IN LA PAZ. FATHER NÀPOLI MOVES HIS
MISSION AND NAMES IT SANTIAGO APÓSTOL

WHILE these two missionaries were devoting themselves to establishing that new Mission, forty savages from the island of Cerralvo landed at the port of La Paz and, finding the Mission without a missionary or soldiers, attacked a tribe of Guaicuras. They killed five baptized children, two heathen women, and one man; they carried away a Christian youth and robbed the others of their poor household goods; they would have pillaged even the church and the parsonage if they had not feared that the Guaicuras would fall upon them in a greater number. As soon as the captain of the presidio learned of this attempt, he went to the island with some soldiers. The islanders fled to the most rugged places; and although he killed only two or three, the rest were much frightened by the firearms.

The captain returned to Loreto and Father Bravo to La Paz. Father Nàpoli continued his labors in the establishment of the new Mission, which was moved in 1723 to a more convenient place farther away from the sea; but there a misfortune almost made him lose all the success of his efforts. He had already erected the walls of the new church and placed the beams on them to make the roof. Then one day after he went out to confess a sick person, there came one of those furious hurricanes which are accustomed to bring desolation to that unfortunate country. The Indians took refuge in the church; but the violence of the hurricane was such that it destroyed the building over them, some being killed, others wounded, and all the rest frightened.

Father Nàpoli came quickly and extricated those who were alive from under the ruins in order to relieve their misfortune in all possible ways and to baptize those who were dangerously hurt, since all were now catechumen. Although all saw the charity and compassion with which he hunted for those who were injured, a conspiracy among the relatives of the dead was suddenly formed against him because they blamed him for that misfortune. But it was soon dissipated, because the very ones who had escaped fortunately from the danger protested that no one had obliged them to enter the church but they had taken refuge in it of their own free will.

A new church was built afterward in another better location[30] and called Santiago Apóstol,[31] a name which that Mission took. He also constructed the other necessary buildings and began to cultivate the land successfully; but no reward was reaped from the seed of the Gospel sown in the hearts of those fickle, lazy, and dissolute savages. Although Father Nàpoli devoted himself with great fervor during the five years that he was there and baptized about four hundred children, he was unable to baptize more than ninety adults because they did not give indications of persevering in the faith and in good customs. In 1726 he was sent by his superiors to the Missions of Sonora, and in Santiago Apóstol he had as a successor Father Lorenzo Carranco,[32] who was to fertilize that vineyard of the Master with his blood.

Chapter Fifteen

THE MISSION OF SAN IGNACIO DE KADAKAAMAN. ITS MISSIONARY, FATHER LUYANDO

THE COCHIMÌ Indians, very different from the Pericùes, appeared each day better disposed to Christianity. At the end of 1706 it was greatly desired to estab-

---

[30] About forty miles from La Paz, and some five miles from the coast (Bancroft, *History of the North Mexican States and Texas*, Vol. I, p. 447). Some think that Father Taraval founded this Mission (Engelhardt, *op. cit.*, Vol. I, p. 210).

[31] This Mission was endowed in 1719 by Villapuente.

[32] Carranco was a Mexican Jesuit, born in Cholula. He was educated at Puebla and at Tepotzotlán, Mexico. He wrote "Cartas al P. Juan Antonio de Oviedo, Provincial de la N. E. Sobre la necesidad de enviar Obreros Evangélicos a los pueblos de la Costa del Sur" 1729, MS in the Library of the University of Mexico.

lish a Mission at Kadakaaman (an inland place) located in the mountains at 28° latitude north and seventy miles distant toward the north from the Mission of Guadalupe, which was then the most northern one. But the scarcity of missionaries and the establishment of other Missions which were considered more necessary frustrated that plan until the year 1728.

Father Juan Bautista Luyando,[33] a Mexican Jesuit, not only allotted a part (in the renunciation) of his patrimony to the establishment of that Mission but also offered to his superiors to go in person to establish it. In fact, when he was sent to California he left Loreto with nine soldiers at the beginning of the year and reached Kadakaaman on January 20. He was received by the Indians with great demonstrations of rejoicing, and in a few days almost five hundred persons from different tribes met with him. Catechism was begun immediately, all applying themselves with extraordinary ardor to learn the Christian doctrine. Many had been already well instructed by Father Sistiaga,[34] who had gone a few months before from Mulegè, one hundred and twenty miles distant, to prepare them for the new Mission.

With such good inclinations baptisms[35] were begun in a short time. But that great concourse of catechumen, although they filled the new missionary with consolation, were on the other hand very burdensome, because he had to support five hundred persons for six months; consequently, in order to economize somewhat on food and to ask for new supplies from Loreto, he discharged seven soldiers who did not seem necessary and remained with two. These and their companions, seeing Father

[33] Luyando was born of a noble family, and before he arrived in the peninsula he had given liberally to found Missions.

[34] Sistiaga and Father Helen had been among these Indians some years before and had taught them to raise grain and vegetables.

[35] As early as 1716 baptisms had taken place among these Indians, and 419 had been baptized before the actual founding of the Mission. Bancroft thinks that July 7, instead of Christmas, may have been the day of the founding, before which thirty-six marriages had taken place there (*History of the North Mexican States and Texas*, Vol. I, p. 448). This writer is also inclined to believe that Father Sistiaga was the founder of the Mission, because his signature is found on the earliest records.

Luyando so busy in the instruction of the catechumen, had begun the building of the church and the parsonage with the help of the Indians, who were quick to do all that was commanded of them. They had put the church in such condition that by Christmas Day of that same year the dedication of it, consecrated to San Ignacio from which the Mission took its name, was held with great solemnity.

Scarcely had two months passed after the arrival of Father Luyando at Kadakaaman, when an entire tribe of gentiles presented themselves to him from a very distant country to ask for baptism with great importunacy. "I shall gratify you very willingly," the missionary told them, "provided you learn the Christian doctrine first and bring me the superstitious instruments which your *guamas* make use of to keep you in error." They replied that they already knew the doctrine, and that they brought those things with them which were of use to the *guamas* in their deceits and which were to be burned, since they were aware that they could not be baptized without fulfilling these conditions.

Father Luyando was surprised and wanted to know how they had learned the doctrine, since they were from a country so distant from the Missions and had never seen any missionary. He learned from these good men that they had been instructed by a Christian child whom they had had brought to their country for that purpose. In fact, he found them so well instructed in the doctrine that, after three weeks employed in perfecting their instruction, he baptized them all.

The divine providence of God was also lovingly bestowed upon a young heathen woman, deaf and dumb from birth. She made herself noticed by all in her devotion and perseverance in accompanying the Christians and catechumen in the services of mass, catechism, and the rosary, litanies, and processions, being the first to present herself in everything. Whenever some were baptized, she knelt among the other catechumen and, placing her hand on her head, sought baptism persistently. Father Luyando had endeavored, as much by himself as by availing himself of others, to make her understand in a manner with signs the mysteries of the Christian religion; but being

Fig. 23 — San Ignacio, the central settlement and the mission church surrounded by date gardens and vineyards.

Hugh Manessier

Fig. 24 – The mission church at San Ignacio. Although the mission was operated by the Jesuits for nearly 40 years, the imposing church was built under the administration of the Dominicans during the 1780s.

Homer Aschmann

not yet satisfied he did not venture to baptize her until one day, seeing her kneeling as she was accustomed to do, and considering on the one hand the innocence of her life and the desire which she showed of being a Christian, and persuaded on the other hand that by reason of her lacking the usual human knowledge (she could be considered as a small child), he finally baptized her.

She was very happy, and not being able to express it with her voice she indicated it with leaps and other singular demonstrations of happiness, looking up and pointing to Heaven, as if she wished to give all to understand that now she could go to Paradise. After she was baptized, she almost never went out of that cabin which then served as a church; and scarcely had two months passed when she died with many indications of her predestination.

These events encouraged the new missionary not only to work in the instruction of those who came to Kadakaaman but also to look everywhere for new catechumen. On a certain occasion when he was summoned from a very distant place to aid a neophyte bitten by a snake, he went on horseback, accompanied by a single neophyte, and found a numerous tribe of gentiles. As they had never seen horses they were greatly frightened by that one; but Father Luyando, with his good manners and some little gifts which he made them, inspired such affection in them for his person that (not wishing to be separated from him) they did not let him sleep all night. He stayed there also on the following day for the purpose of inducing them (as he did) to move to Kadakaaman to be instructed in the Christian religion.

The docility of the Cochimìes, together with their acuteness and their politeness, contributed greatly to the progress which the Mission of San Ignacio made in spiritual matters as well as in temporal ones. That soil is one of the best which California has for agriculture, as much because of the quality of land as because of the abundance of water. Father Sistiaga had opportunely prepared a part of it for the sowing of grain and corn; and the first harvest that Father Luyando raised was almost a hundred *fanegas*. But in the fourth year he raised fully a thousand, because the cultivation was increased with the help of the Indians, who worked willingly, seeing that all the produce was for them except the small quantity which served as food for the missionary and the two soldiers who protected it.

Father Helen, the missionary of Guadalupe, had brought them seeds of squash and other vegetables and had taught them the way to cultivate them. This was of use to Father Luyando in making a garden of imported plants and of the slightly useful ones which grow wild in the soil of the peninsula and in planting a vineyard of five hundred grapevines. These plantings were so useful to the Mission that its neophytes were among the richest ones. Besides, he put a large number of cattle and sheep in suitable places so that by multiplying they would be a support of the Indians themselves. Finally, they were gathered into various villages; and in each one a chapel was built so that they could say their prayers daily and so that the missionary could say Holy Mass when he came to visit them. Of these buildings Father Luyando was not only the architect but also the mason and day laborer, after the example of the other missionaries.

Chapter Sixteen

THE NEW MISSION OF SAN IGNACIO IS AFFLICTED

ALTHOUGH this Mission had enjoyed such prosperity from its beginning, it did not escape those hostile resistances and reverses which are accustomed to accompany the works of divine glory. One night eight gentiles killed a catechumen next to the house of the missionary, for no other reason (as it was believed) than that the latter esteemed him very much for his good disposition toward Christianity; and it was necessary to tolerate this offense in order not to cause greater disorders. Not wishing to leave this act unpunished, in the following year God deprived (in an epidemic which followed) all the guilty ones of life.

The Indians of one of the tribes appeared so obstinate that

in spite of the repeated urgings and invitations of the missionary and the example of the other tribes, they did not wish for two years to come to Kadakaaman to be instructed in the Christian doctrine. And their old people maintained their obstinacy for seven years; but finally all gave themselves up to the grace of the Master. It is very natural that the old people should be more difficult to be converted, because their age is less susceptible to instruction and their vices have stronger and deeper roots. This was observed continually in those Missions (as well as in others), especially if the office of *guama* belonged to the senile age, because then their obstinacy was supported by a lust for gain.

When Father Luyando had finished the first sermon which he addressed to the Cochimìes, telling them of the attributes of God, the mysteries of the Trinity and the Incarnation, the reward of the righteous in Heaven, the punishment of sinners in Hell, the hatred which the Devil has for men, and how he made use of the *guamas* to deceive them, a loud noise was heard and such a commotion in the audience that the missionary feared that they wished to kill him. The cause of this disturbance was due to a famous *guama* who was there and who had acquired superiority over all because of his spirit and ability, although he was not very old.

When the sermon was ended and the audience dismissed, the *guama* assembled all the Indians in a secret place and delivered to them another talk against that of the missionary, giving as many reasons as he could to contradict him, the principal one being that they had not seen what the missionary was telling them. But, on the contrary, that they had seen *Fehual*, who was the directing spirit of human actions, and had heard him speak on many occasions, as was testified to by all the *guamas;* and that, as children, they had learned no other doctrine than what *Fehual* taught them. Finlly, he added that *Fehual* was very angry, since the Christians had entered that country, and, for this reason, he had driven away all the deer.

This talk made a great impression on those barbarians because, in fact, deer had not been seen there since the establishment of the Mission of San Ignacio. But some neophytes who were more enlightened because they had been brought up in Loreto, and were, consequently, more respected, opportunely arrived from Mulegè. They asserted that in those thirty miles which they had walked before reaching Kadakaaman they had seen seven deer. Therefore, they should infer that the *guama* was an impostor. The Cochimìes believed them, and the *guama* was confused, but not changed.

Father Luyando reproved him many times for the dissolute life which he led until he induced him to seek baptism, after he promised to change his ways. He was not only baptized, but the position of governor (inspector of the Indians) was conferred on him, perhaps to compel him, with this honor, to be more moderate.

Nevertheless, he was not long in returning to his more ungovernable vices; and when neither private warnings nor public censure were enough to correct him, Father Luyando assembled all the Indians one day, and, in their presence, he severely reprimanded the governor for all those scandals. And afterward he added that since the guilt was more serious in him than in a private individual he should suffer at least the same penalty as the other culpable persons. All were silent, with the exception of a more zealous and daring neophyte named Tomás who confirmed in a loud voice what the missionary was saying; and after encouraging the others, he took hold of the Indian governor to whom the usual punishment of lashings was applied after he had been deprived of his office.

He changed his ways, and for some time he concealed his anger, but in a short time he tried to get all the nation to rise against the missionary, and several times he tried to kill him; neither the one nor the other had any effect. After a few months God freed Father Luyando from such a fierce persecutor and the latter from perdition; he was the first victim of the epidemic which followed, dying very repentant and kindly nursed and comforted by his Father in Christ.

The reform of another *guama* was more easily attained. He had asked for baptism many times and had become a catechumen, but without giving up his vices. Also, at the same time, he deceived a Christian woman and went away with her to the woods. When the two were caught by some neophytes and taken to the Mission, Father Luyando contented himself with reproving the catechumen for his crime and threatening him with punishment. In fact, he soon deserved it on account of new offenses for which he did receive punishment, although light.

Nevertheless, he resented it so much that he ran away at once, venting his anger in threats against the missionary; and, going to a place where the goats of the Mission were grazing, he killed a black one, telling the shepherd that he killed it to avenge himself on the missionary, who wore a habit of the very same color, and that what he did then to the goat he would soon do to its owner. As restlessness was very contagious among the barbarians, an effort was made in every way to put hands on this seditious man.

In fact, he was captured by his own countrymen, taken to Kadakaaman, and held as a prisoner one night. On the following day a trial was held with great pomp in which the two soldiers of the Mission and the Indian governor acted as judges. When the criminal appeared in the presence of all the village, verbal criminal proceedings were entered against him; and, while weeping, he openly and frankly confessd his crimes. He was sentenced by the judges to be punished by a lashing. They began to carry out the sentence at once; but scarcely had two or three blows been given him, when Father Luyando, who had purposely not wished to take part in the trial, appeared. He ordered the punishment stopped and begged the judges to pardon the criminal, whose reform was not doubted. The judges allowed themselves to be convinced, and, in this way, the criminal was under obligations to the Christian benevolence of the missionary. He changed his way of life from that moment, and after he had been baptized he became a good Christian.

With the very same stratagem Father Luyando won another seditious old man who had not ceased to declaim everywhere against him and against those of his nation who had permitted themselves to be deceived by a foreigner who had come to abolish the ancient customs of the country and the usages of their ancestors. This one, also indebted by gratitude, became a Christian and was truly such until his death.

Chapter Seventeen

THE PROGRESS OF THE MISSION. THE FERVOR OF A GENTILE

IN THE MIDST of these events, now prosperous and then adverse, the Mission of San Ignacio was now growing daily, and to this progress the natural goodness of the Indians contributed not a little. In fact, they were so good that they warned the missionary of all that was reprehensible that they observed in their countrymen so that he might correct them; and even the culpable ones presented themselves to him of their own free will to ask him for punishment for their faults, although they might be secret ones. Father Luyando availed himself of this fine attitude in order to persuade them to construct those roads which led from Kadakaaman to each one of their respective tribes, which was very important for good government. In order to encourage them in this work, he promised them prizes, and he extolled those with praises who accomplished the most. Hence there arose among them a useful emulation that showed that they were not stupid nor insensible to the stimulus of fame.

One tribe, having observed that the other had excelled it in the work on their road (for which they would deserve greater praises), decided to disturb their undertaking. As they had understood that letters were of use to talk with the absent and to send them directions from distant places, they made some scrawls on a piece of paper in imitation of our characters and sent a messenger with the paper and a verbal order of the missionary to those of the other tribe telling them to suspend their work and open the road in another place. The latter became suspicious and returned the messenger with the paper, saying that the missionary would never have sent that paper to those who did not know how to read. But the messenger, instructed by those who had sent him, returned after saying that the missionary sent the letter not so it could be read but only to serve as a sign of the verbal order which he brought them. Nevertheless, they arranged that some of them should go to Kadakaaman to hear from the mouth of the missionary himself what he wished; and in this way they discovered the deceit of their rivals.

The great plague which occurred during 1729, instead of retarding the progress of that Mission, was very advantageous to it, because it took the lives of some of those *guamas* who were most opposed to Christianity. Although some adults and many children died, those who survived showed more affection for our faith from then on, because they had seen with their own eyes the benevolence of their missionaries in taking spiritual and corporeal aid to the sick, working night and day, and suffering infinite difficulties in behalf of their health. The *guamas* scattered among the gentiles the report that all those who were baptized had died; and for that reason some hid their children from the missionary who wished to baptize them, because they were in danger; but this report was contradicted by the neophytes, who observed that among an equal number of sick Christian and gentile people more gentiles died; and it could not have been otherwise, because the Christians had the advantages of houses and more healthful food and medicine which the gentiles lacked.

Among the Cochimìes who embraced the Christian religion at that time a gentile of the Hualimea tribe on the shore of the Pacific Sea became particularly worthy of remembrance and admiration. Although he had never seen a missionary and lived very far from all the Missions, he had acquired some knowledge through some Christians of the mysteries of our faith and the necessity of baptism for salvation. He became the preacher of his countrymen, urging them incessantly to go to Kadakaaman to be instructed and baptized, and promising them that he would be the first to become a Christian.

The *guamas* and the old people contradicted him, affirming the scattered rumors that the ones who died were the ones who had been baptized. He defended himself with good arguments and the dispute became so heated that they went from words to blows. Finally he determined to go to Kadakaaman with his family, assuring his relatives that he wished to be baptized, although it might be certain that he had to die on the same day. In fact, he left, accompanied by his family and some others who wished to follow him; and when all had arrived at the Mission, they were received by Father Luyando with the esteem and love which were befitting such great fervor. His small children were baptized that very afternoon on account of the fear of smallpox, which was already beginning to play havoc; and the adults were enrolled among the catechumen on the following day as much to have them instructed from that day as to be supported at the expense of the missionary all the time that their instruction lasted, according to the practice of those Missions.

In a few days a small daughter of the fervid catechumen died and his wife and his brother fell ill. Father Luyando was afraid that this misfortune would be a strong temptation for them to oppose the faith; but, on the contrary, they became more insistent in being instructed and more desirous of baptism, after the example of their leader. The latter was baptized first, taking the name of Cristóbal,[36] which was so suitable for him; and the others followed afterward. As was usual in those Missions, all stayed for some weeks after their baptism, during which time the good Cristóbal gave such examples of righteousness that the missionary did not cease to thank God; and he held him up to the rest of the neophytes as a model of the Christian life.

On leaving for his country he promised the missionary that he would spare no industry nor effort in reducing to Christianity all those of his tribe and even the neighboring ones. In fact in a few days he returned, bringing a multitude of his relatives to make them Christians; and in this way he attracted the others gradually, even the old people and the *guamas*, who could not resist the potency of divine grace which communed with them through the voice of Cristóbal. The conversion of

---

[36] Meaning "Christ-bearer," because St. Christopher carried Christ, in the guise of a child, across the river where he carried pilgrims across as a penance. This day is celebrated on July 25.

this tribe hastened the spread of the Gospel over all the coast toward the north.

Chapter Eighteen

THE MISFORTUNE OF THE MISSION. THE DETERMINATION MADE AND ITS SUCCESS

FATHER LUYANDO's consolation was embittered by a great tribulation which afterward brought considerable advantages to the Mission. The fierce savages of some northern countries, in indignation against Christianity, suddenly fell on a Christian tribe, killed a girl and an old man, and routed the remainder, who became terrified and fled to Kadakaaman. The Christians of some tribes prepared to avenge that offense. But Father Luyando, fearing that an endless war might be kindled by this scheme, dissuaded them from their determination, urging them to endure those injuries patiently like good Christians. He thought that this example of generous patience on the part of the neophytes would contribute to making their enemies fond of Christianity; and with this purpose he sent them some messages and some gifts.

But experience made him see that, in such circumstances, that was not the way to win those barbarians. They were persuaded that the messages and the gifts were the effects of fear which their weapons had created in the missionary and his neophytes, and for this reason they became more insolent and daring; they attacked another Christian tribe, driving it out of the place where it was living and robbing it of its poor goods; and they threatened to do the same in Kadakaaman.

When Father Luyando saw that his neophytes were terrified, because he had only two Spanish soldiers with him and because he was not able to have the troops of Loreto come quickly on account of the distance of more than two hundred miles, he took the advice of Father Sistiaga as the person best informed about that country and those peoples.

This father was then guiding the Mission of Guadalupe during the absence of Father Helen, and he went to Kadakaaman at once; he decided there, in conference with Father Luyando, that first of all the protection of God should be implored in a pious novena to the blessed Trinity in the presence of all those people and that afterward a small but well-armed party of neophytes should be sent against those savages, not to destroy them but to catch them and punish them. With this purpose all the Christian tribes of the Mission were assembled; and preparations for war were begun with great show and gossip (after the fashion of the country), as much to encourage the timid neophytes as to terrify the conceited enemies. A great quantity of bows and arrows were made; many lances never before seen in the peninsula were made; some were set with knives instead of being tipped with iron, and the points of others were hardened in the fire. The two Spanish soldiers, aided by the Indians, made as many as three hundred leather shields. Even the women had to work making these preparations, fitting the leather soles which were to serve as sandals for their warriors, toasting the corn for their provisions, and weaving nets in which to carry it.

When the preparations were ended a review of the troops was held, and there were almost seven hundred warriors. But since there were not provisions for all, three hundred and fifty were chosen from different tribes. It had been previously the custom among these barbarians that, in order to go to war, each tribe should name its captain, who commanded it with absolute independence of the others.

This must have been very harmful to them on account of the division of opinion which was inevitable among so many chiefs. In order to avoid similar disorders the Indians were advised that the troops would march under the command of only two captains, both of whom were clear-sighted and brave and each of whom had a knowledge of the country; and both would agree in their plans; one was to be elected by them, and the other by the missionaries. The Indians elected the one who had the best reputation among them; and the missionaries, for their part, named the Indian governor of Kadakaaman, an apt young man, reared by Father Ugarte and educated in Loreto. The instruction was then given to the captains not to kill any gentile except in self-defense. This instruction was carried out promptly, as we shall see.

After the troops had received the blessing of the missionaries at the church, they marched against the enemy, carrying the insignia of the Holy Cross as a standard. The captain-governor sent out his scouts beforehand and, when he was informed by them that the enemies were encamped on the slope of a mountain, he approached them by night; he made a circle around them and closed in on them gradually and very silently in order not to be heard. On the following morning all at once and with fearful shouts, according to their method of fighting, they fell upon the enemies, who at first took up arms to defend themselves. But when they saw that their forces were very inferior, all surrendered except two who were able to escape. After thirty-four men were captured without difficulty and were well tied, they were taken to Kadakaaman.

The victorious army went to church to render thanks to God for having won that victory without bloodshed and without even shooting an arrow. On the following day Mass was said with the greatest solemnity possible as a thanksgiving to the most blessed Trinity. After all the people were assembled in a suitable place, a court was established in which the two Spanish soldiers and the Indian governor took their seats as judges. After the prisoners had appeared there and their case had been investigated, they were found guilty of murder and theft. The judges, who had an understanding with the missionaries in everything, declared that the offenders should be taken to Loreto (since they were subject to the death penalty), because no one but the captain of the presidio could condemn them to such punishment. The criminals, greatly overcome by their fate, were thrown into prison; but the new and uncultured Christians were rejoicing at the deaths of their enemies. Then the missionaries who had remained home in the meantime went to see the prisoners to console them and assure them that they would escape death; and, not content with bearing them this new cheer, they made them many presents, and afterward they severely reproved the neophytes for their condemnable happiness, giving them some useful advice about Christian charity.

On the following day the court was opened again at the public requests of the missionaries, who brought some Indians with them to beg the judges to revoke their sentence and not to condemn the prisoners to death nor send them to Loreto. When the latter appeared again before the court, they were sentenced, not to die but to suffer a great number of lashes; in fact, they began there to carry out this punishment on the principal criminal. But after a few lashes, the missionaries appeared again, interceding in the presence of the judges that the punishment of that criminal cease and that all the rest be pardoned. So it was done, the most eminent of the victors being content to appropriate some weapons of the vanquished.

The success of this Christian moderation was very great, because the neophytes were better instructed and the gentiles were then very fond of the missionaries and their religion, which commanded love for the enemies. The latter were purposely detained for some days, so that, after noticing the good order of the Mission and the kindness and gentleness with which the neophytes were treated, they, too, might be induced to embrace Christianity. In fact, they begged the missionaries to baptize them, together with their children whom they had brought with them; but in order to test their constancy and to quicken their desires, the missionaries did not comply at first. Then they left disconsolately to return to their country; but scarcely had they gone half way than they returned to beg that at least their little ones be baptized.

All were in fact baptized except the son of the principal murderer. He left again, very sad; but in a little while he returned weeping to the missionaries to tell them to kill him if they wished, providing his son might be baptized. The missionaries, who had refused baptism to this child only to prove the constancy of the father, finally baptized him, and the savage left happy. In a few months all the prisoners returned to Kadakaaman, bringing their families, all their relatives, and even their old people who could not walk because of their weakness, to be instructed in the Christian doctrine and to recive baptism, as was done to the great joy of all.

This was not the only reward of that victory. The report

of it which was scattered over almost all the peninsula laid low the pride of the gentiles, inspired in them a lofty idea of the religion which the foreigners were preaching, and hastened their conversion in the following years. But Father Luyando, after four years of such laborious life, found himself compelled by his serious ailments to leave the Mission which he had founded with his own property and with his own zeal and efforts.

Chapter Nineteen

THE DEATHS OF FATHERS PÌCCOLO AND JUAN DE UGARTE. THE CONDITION OF THE MISSIONS

WHILE Christianity was spreading so fortunately toward the north, California had two great losses in the deaths of the two oldest and most renowned missionaries, Father Francisco María Piccolo and Father Juan de Ugarte. Father Piccolo died in Loreto on February 22, 1729, at the age of seventy-nine years, and after forty-six years of apostolic service in the Missions of Tarahumara, Sonora, and California. Father Ugarte, so well deserving of this peninsula, died on December 29, 1730, at his Mission of San Javier. The thirty years which he had lived in California were worth a century if one considers what he did there in the service of God and in behalf of that country and those nations. The lives of these two men (so beloved by God) were published in Mexico in private memoirs, and the menology of that province makes honorable mention of them.

The Missions of the southern part did not get along so well as those of the North. Their neophytes were annoyed frequently by the many gentiles who were still there, and some, because of their inconstancy, became displeased easily with the Christian life and disturbed those who were living tranquilly in the faith. In 1723, when the Missions of La Paz, Dolores, and Santiago were newly established, it was necessary that the captain-governor of the peninsula visit that country with soldiers to inspire fear and check their restlessness. He did the same thing in 1725 and in 1729. The missionaries had no other means of preventing the evils which they feared than that of increasing the Missions in that country. Their desires were favored by the inexhaustible liberality of the Marqués de Villapuente and by his cousin and sister-in-law, Doña Rosa de la Peña.[37] The Marqués offered the capital for one Mission which was to be founded near the cape of San Lucas, and Doña Rosa for the other, which was to be established at the port of Las Palmas, where that of Santiago had been before.

The procurator of California in Mexico then was Father José de Echeverría, who, having learned that a boat of that colony had been lost with the provisions which it was carrying, went to Sinaloa in October 1729 to buy a new boat and to seek new provisions. When he was occupied in this business, he received a letter from the provincial informing him that the father general, Miguel Angel Tamburini, had appointed him visitator-general of all the Missions belonging to the Mexican province.

As he wished to begin his visit with California, he went to Loreto, and from there to the seven most northern Missions of that peninsula. The progress of these Missions gave him so much pleasure and such sentiments of piety and virtue that he spoke in the following way in a letter which he wrote a little afterward and sent from Loreto to Mexico: "All the inconveniences and efforts of this trip can be endured willingly in order to have the consolation of seeing the fervor of this new and happy Christianity. Tears cannot be restrained when one hears the divine praises from the mouths of those poor Indians who did not know God a short time ago. Thanks to His infinite mercy there are not only more than six thousand baptized persons in these seven Missions today but I believe that there is not among them a child who cannot now speak Spanish and who has not learned the Christian doctrine well."

---

[37] Doña Rosa de la Peña gave ten thousand pesos.

Chapter Twenty

THE MISSION OF SAN JOSÉ DEL CABO; FATHER TAMARAL IS APPOINTED TO IT

WHEN the *visitator* had returned to Loreto, he embarked there to go and visit the southern Missions and to establish the two proposed Missions among the Pericùes, namely, that of San José on the cape of San Lucas and that of Santa Rosa at the port of Las Palmas. Father Tamaral, who had already established that of Purísima very successfully, was appointed to the first; and at the second, Father Sigismundo Taraval was to be employed but he had not yet arrived from Mexico. Then, Father Tamaral embarked there with the *visitator*, going first to La Paz, where the missionary, Father Guillermo Gordon,[38] a Scotchman, was, and afterward to Santiago, where Father Lorenzo Carranco had succeeded Father Nàpoli four years before. From here they went to the cape of San Lucas, the southern terminus of the peninsula, and there they selected a place near a small lagoon which seemed most suitable for the establishment of the new Mission of San José which, from then on, they called San José del Cabo,[39] to distinguish it from San José del Comondù. As usual they built two bowers, one to serve as a church and the other as a dwelling place for the missionary; both were roofed with reeds and straw and made of palm leaves, which were very abundant there.

In the three weeks which the *visitator* remained there, scarcely twenty families of gentiles appeared. When these were

---

[38] Not much is known of Father Guillermo Gordon. He was born in Scotland in 1697, and became a Jesuit in 1717. He wrote *Historia de la Missiones Jesuitas en la California baja desde su establecimiento hasta 1737* (Carlos Sommervogel's *Bibliothéque de la Compagnie de Jésus*, Vol. III, p. 360). Father Gordon probably arrived in the peninsula before 1730.

[39] Cabo is now the site of a small seaport, having a population of about 4,000. It is at the extreme end of the peninsula, about 125 miles from La Paz. The town today is one of the best fishing centers in the peninsula, and it exports many kinds of vegetables, at times shipping 200,000 crates of early tomatoes a year to the United States.

asked where the others were whom the captain of the presidio had seen in such great numbers the year before, they answered that all had died in an epidemic. This answer was not true (as will be seen soon) because scarcely had the *visitator* left with the soldiers who were accompanying him when the Indians began to come in numerous bands. They declared afterward that the true reason for their hiding was that, having waged some hostilities against the neophytes of Santiago and La Paz, they feared that the soldiers had come to punish them.

After Father Tamaral had consecrated the first fruits of that Mission in the baptism of a large number of infants, he celebrated Holy Saturday of that year (1730); and, having enrolled may adults among the catechumen, he began to seek for a location more suitable for the Mission, because the place where it had been established at the beginning was very warm and swarming with mosquitoes and other harmful insects. And it must have been unhealthy, because it was enclosed between two mountains. After he had found a place six miles from the sea, he moved the Mission; he built the house and the church; he gathered into two villages the different tribes of the barbarians whom he got out of the woods; and he devoted himself with such zeal to their conversion and instruction that in the first year he baptized one thousand and thirty-six infants and adults.

This is so much the more to be marveled at since those savages were the least disposed to embrace Christianity. Besides what we have said about this in another place, that which this zealous missionary wrote in his letter to the Marqués de Villapuente will aid us to know them better. He says: "It is exceedingly difficult to persuade them to leave aside the great number of wives whom they have, because the feminine sex is very numerous among them. It is enough to say that the most ordinary men have at least two or three wives. This is the most invincible obstacle for the men as well as for the women. It is so for the women because they do not find anyone who wants them when they are repudiated by their husbands; it is so also for the men because the greater the number of their wives so much the better are they served and provided with all necessities. They recline in perpetual idleness in the shade of the trees, and their wives work, hunting in the woods for wild roots and fruits upon which they sustain themselves, and trying to take the best that she finds to the husband to win his affection above his other wives. It is therefore a miracle of divine grace that these lazy men, brought up to a bestial life, consent to content themselves with only one wife, to look for food for themselves and their children, and to lead a rational life."

Chapter Twenty-One

FATHER TARAVAL REACHES CALIFORNIA. HE GOVERNS OTHER MISSIONS, AND HE ESTABLISHES THAT OF SANTA ROSA

FATHER SIGISMUNDO TARAVAL,[40] appointed to the proposed Mission of Santa Rosa, reached Loreto in May 1730. He was a native of Lodi, a city of Lombardy, where his father, Don Miguel Taraval, was lieutenant-general of the armies of His Catholic Majesty. When this gentleman returned to Spain, he took with him his son who became a Jesuit at the age of eighteen years in the province of Toledo. When he was studying philosophy in Alcalá,[41] he was urged on by the desire of working in the conversion of the gentiles; and he went to Mexico with the permission of his superiors; when his studies

---

[40] Father Taraval was born in 1700, in Lodi, Italy, as stated above in the text, and at the age of eighteen he became a Jesuit while a student at the Ocaña College at Toledo, Spain. He finished his studies after coming to Mexico. In 1730 he was sent to the peninsula, and was given the important task of writing a complete history of the activities of the Jesuits there. It is believed that the records of Taraval were used chiefly by Father Andrés Burriel in his *Noticia de la California*. It was published in Madrid anonymously in 1757, and based upon the manuscript written in 1739 in Mexico City by Father Miguel Venegas, to whom is usually ascribed the authorship of the history (Charles Edward Chapman, *The Founding of Spanish California*, p. 56).

[41] Located in a small village in Spain near the city of Seville. It was founded in 1499 by Francisco Ximénez de Cisneros, who was then prime minister of Spain; and later the institution was known as the College of San Ildefonso.

were finished, he was sent from there to California. He worked with much zeal for twenty-one years in the different Missions of this peninsula, being engaged in study (as he had always been) all the time that his occupations left him free. In 1751 he went to reside in Guadalajara, the capital of Nueva Galicia, where he was always consulted during the twelve years that he stayed there by all sorts of persons on account of his great wisdom and erudition in theological and canonical matters. At his death, which occurred in 1763, he left a large number of works in manuscript form, of which I saw twelve volumes[42] in the library of the Jesuits in that city and from which I had some copied.

As there were some serious difficulties to overcome in order to establish the Mission of Santa Rosa at the time of his arrival in California, he was sent first to that of Purísima, which Father Tamaral had left. Afterward, in 1732, he was entrusted with guiding that of San Ignacio, while its missionary, Father Sistiaga, acted as *visitator* of all the other Missions. A few months after his arrival at Kadakaaman, some Indian inhabitants of some islands of the Pacific Sea presented themselves to him and begged him to go to their country to visit and make their relatives Christians. Determined to please them, he first sent some scouts to get acquainted with the disposition of those islanders; and, meanwhile, he made a few preparations for the trip. After he had left Kadakaaman, he traveled for six days on the coast as far as a cape where the islands were seen; the nearest one was about twenty miles distant.

Since he did not have a boat with which to navigate that space, he built a raft with the wood which was there. The first island, called Afeguà ("island of the birds"), is very small; it is scarcely half a mile long, barren, lacking in water and uninhabited; but there are a great number of birds there. For this reason the Indians gave it that name. Besides the known bird

---

[42] In 1757 Father Andrés Burriel published in Madrid *Noticia de la California*, the materials of which it is thought came from these volumes, which were also used extensively by Venegas. In his history Burriel defends the work of the Jesuits and shows the importance of extending northward the Missions in the peninsula and on the mainland.

species Father Taraval found two new ones on it. The first includes certain birds, all black, somewhat larger than a sparrow, which go to sea by day hunting for their food and by night come to their subterranean nests which they build to the depth of three or four feet. The other species includes certain large birds that are the size of a duck, black on the back and white underneath, with a curved beak, and toes armed with thick claws for fishing, in which they are engaged as much by day as by night when the sea is rough; but when it is calm, they withdraw to the island. They also live under the ground in holes from ten to twelve feet deep. Hunting these birds attracts there the Indians of the continent and even those of the Huamalguà Island at times.

Huamalguà (Foggy Island) is a little more than twelve miles distant from Afeguà, and both are situated at 31° latitude North, as Father Taraval calculated it. Huamalguà is a triangular island, the greater side of which is a two days' journey from one cape to the other; and in the middle of it there is a very high mountain. It abounds in springs of fresh water, deer, rabbits, birds of different species, and especially seals. The deer are smaller than those of California, and they have a thicker skin. Among the rabbits there are some entirely black and covered with a softer fur than that of the beaver.* There are otters also. The mescal, which serves as the staff of life to the Indians, is juicier than that of California. Many kinds of shells are found on the beach; and among them are dark blue ones much prized for their singular beauty. The sea is frequented by many small whales, for which the Indians fish with wooden pronged forks only because they want their tendons, which they dry for making strings for their bows.

From the summit of that mountain Father Taraval saw two small islands toward the west and at a distance of from twenty-four to thirty miles, and in another direction three more inhabited only by otter and seals which the Indians sometimes go and hunt. At a long distance toward the north he observed other

---

* It may be believed that those quadrupeds which Father Taraval took for rabbits and deer were of other different species.

larger islands which he believed (not without reason) were probably those which make the channel of Santa Barbara, beginning with that of Santa Catalina.

The inhabitants of Huamalguà were few. It was not hard to induce them to move to Kadakaaman to be instructed and baptized, with the exception of one *guama*, who was opposed to the idea to such a degree that all had determined to leave him alone on the island—not even his wife wished to stay. But when he saw all were going, he decided to accompany them, although unwillingly. After they had embarked on their rafts they found themselves forced by a storm to take refuge on the island of Afeguà, where they remained for some days, sustaining themselves on mescal. When the sea became calm they approached the peninsula, and coasting along the shore they saw many seals on some shoals.

The *guama*, who still showed very much annoyance and who wished to kill a seal, jumped into the sea and swam to the shoals; but on returning to his companions, because the seals had disappeared, he was caught by a shark. With extraordinary efforts he managed to free himself from the teeth of that terrible creature; but when the shark caught him again with greater force it sank with him and he was never seen again. The loss of this unfortunate man caused Father Taraval great regret, but it served to make the gentiles sincere in their good intentions. After their arrival at Kadakaaman they were well instructed and baptized; and, renouncing their native country, they willingly joined the Mission.

The conversion of these islanders was not the only result of the fervor of Father Taraval in the months which he governed the Mission of San Ignacio. In the beginning of 1733, at his kind invitation, three tribes of gentiles came from very distant places—two from inland countries and the other from the eastern coast near the cape of San Miguel, situated at 29° and 30′ latitude North—and the latter came in its entirety, even without leaving behind the old and the sick. Father Taraval received them lovingly; he instructed them all and baptized some of them; all the rest were baptized later by Father Sistiaga, who, having returned to Kadakaaman from his laborious visit, continued working, aided by Father Fernando Consag[43] during the following years with no less success than zeal.

Father Taraval, who was now freed from the care of the Mission of San Javier through the return of Father Sistiaga, left in the same year to establish the new Mission of Santa Rosa among the Pericùes, the establishment of which had been frustrated until then by some difficulties. Finally it was founded, not at the port of Las Palmas (as was desired) but in the village of Todos Santos, a mile and a half distant from the Pacific Sea. This village, which belonged formerly to the Mission of La Paz, had been inhabited by Guaicuras; but, having been depopulated afterward as much by epidemics which deprived many of their lives as because others went elsewhere to live, several tribes of Pericùes with whom Father Taraval made the beginning of his Mission were established in it after 1731.

He found these gentiles very well disposed because of the visits which the missionaries of La Paz, Santiago, and San José del Cabo made them. At the beginning he had to endure serious opposition on the part of some Indians who were obdurate in their bestial life; for this reason he did not wish to discharge the three soldiers from Loreto who accompanied him. But he worked so hard and he devoted himself in such a way to winning their affection that in less than a year he baptized the greater part of the infants and the adults of his district; and it was on account of their affection that he escaped with his life in the general rebellion of that nation.

---

[43] Often spelled "Konscak," "Konsag," and "Konschak." He was born in the city of Varazdin, Austria, in 1703. He left Spain for Cuba in 1730, and three years later he arrived in California. He made many trips about the peninsula, seeking desirable places where Missions might be established. It is said that while he was on these journeys he carried only a "walking stick and a piece of canvas." After serving in the peninsula for twenty-eight years, he died at the Mission of Bajorca in 1759. For an interesting sketch of his life see M. D. Krmpotic, *Rev. Ferdinand Konsack, S.J., 1703–1759, an early missionary in California*. Father Consag wrote *Historia de las misiones de Californias, nombradas: los Dolores del Norte y la Magdalena*.

Chapter Twenty-Two

INDICATIONS OF GENERAL REBELLION AGAINST THE MISSION
ARIES. THE KINDNESS AND SINGULAR GENEROSITY OF
FATHER TAMARAL TOWARD CERTAIN
NAVIGATORS

THE FIRST sparks of this fire were noticed at the end of 1733 and at the beginning of 1734. The Indian governor of Santiago was a neophyte called Boton, born of a mulatto* father and an Indian mother. Boton's office had been given him by Father Carranco because he had more ability than the rest and to compel him to lead a more moderate life; but in spite of this he gave himself up without restraint to the same vices which had been characteristic of him before becoming a Christian. Because neither private warnings nor public rebukes were sufficient to correct him, he was finally deprived of the office and publicly punished. Angered by this affront, Boton conspired secretly against Father Carranco and would have been successful in killing him (as he intended to do by trying to attract some malcontents to his party) if that missionary, aware of his criminal design, had not taken all possible precautions to prevent it.

The restlessness and disorders, nevertheless, continued until that depraved man, angered by living with the Christians, went away to Yeneca, a place where lived a tribe of gentiles whose chief was a mulatto named Chicori.[44] He was as corrupt and wicked as Boton; and, not content with the many wives whom he possessed, he had stolen a Christian girl from the Mission of San José. For some time Father Tamaral had overlooked this crime to avoid other greater troubles; but, after having an

---

* Mulatto means one who is born to, or descends from, a European and an African, or the contrary.

---

[44] Chief of the ranchería of Yeneca, a village not far from San José del Cabo. He was deposed for his misconduct and publicly whipped by Father Carranco.

occasion to go to Yeneca, he talked to Chicori with gentleness, complaining of the abduction. He replied arrogantly that since the Christian woman was his wife he was right in having taken her away. Father Tamaral answered him thus: "If she were your wife, neither would you have left her such a long time at the Mission to be instructed nor would you have consented to her being baptized."

Afterward he reproached him for his licentiousness and urged him to embrace Christianity, following the example of so many Pericùes. But instead of being compliant Chicori became more obstinate in his heathenism and vices and planned for an occasion to kill the missionary and to get all the nation to rise in rebellion against the other missionaries.

Such were the resolutions of Chicori when Boton came to find him at Yeneca, after he had incited some Indians of Santiago to sedition. As Father Tamaral had not yet noticed the machinations of these wicked men, so he went fearlessly to Santiago for the purpose of helping Father Carranco to calm the disturbances there; but when he wanted to return (because all seemed peaceful), some faithful Indians of Santiago warned him that Boton and Chicori were waiting for him on the way with two armed bands of their followers to kill him.

This news was found to be true by other Indians who were sent purposely to investigate the road. And so Father Tamaral, in order not to expose his life to such evident danger, sent word by another road to his neophytes to come armed to accompany him to San José. On seeing such an armed host approach, the conspirators fled. But afterward, fearing that the Christians might unite against them, they pretended that they repented of their wicked plot and asked for peace, which was granted them at once, although to last only a short time as will be seen later.

Scarcely had Father Tamaral reached San José, when some Indian fishermen came from Cape San Lucas to tell him that a large ship had been seen in the distance near the coast. It was from the Philippine Islands and was going to the port of Acapulco; but being very much in need of water the captain had decided to land at California. He put in at the port of San

Bernabé, a short distance from the cape of San Lucas; and, as he feared that the country might be hostile, he sent soldiers[45] ashore to obtain water.

As soon as Father Tamaral received the news, he ordered that all the fresh meat and fresh produce of the country that they could succeed in getting for the navigators be brought to San Bernabé; and he himself went to offer them his services and those of his neophytes. So the captain of the ship as well as the crew were greatly consoled on finding such a good reception where they had feared hostilities, and on obtaining fresh food where they scarcely hoped to have water. Many of the crew, who were ill with scurvy, began to get relief just by eating the fresh food. When they sailed again, after having given infinite thanks to the diligent and kind missionary, they went to Acapulco; and from there to Mexico, where the kind and opportune reception which they had found in California was made known. The captain of the ship informed the viceroy[46] of it, and the latter ordered that in the future all ships from the Philippine Islands should put in at the port of San Bernabé. The governor of those islands issued the same command when he received the information.

When the ship sailed from the port of San Bernabé, the captain left three sick men, entrusted to the kindness of Father Tamaral, who were not in a condition to continue the voyage on account of the seriousness of their illness. They were Don Juan Francisco Baitos, an infantry captain, Don Antonio de Herrera, who also had a good post on the ship, and the Augustine Father, Friar Domingo Horbigoso, appointed to the office of procurator-general in Mexico from his province in the Philippine Islands.

All three were taken to the Mission of San José. They were

---

[45] At this time there were only six soldiers in the southern section of the peninsula. Father Taraval had three of them at Santa Rosa; Father Carranco had two invalid men at Santiago; and only one soldier was stationed at La Paz. Father Tamaral at San José had no guard (Bancroft, *History of the North Mexican States and Texas*, Vol. I, p. 454). The first person murdered in the revolt was one of the soldiers of Father Taraval.

[46] The archbishop of Mexico, Juan Antonio de Vizarrón Eguiarreta.

treated by the missionary with as much kindness and gentleness and served with as great ardor and assiduity as that of a mother toward the dearest of her children. Not content with making liberal gifts for their recovery of everything that he had in his Mission, which could be useful to them, he had some things brought from the neighboring Missions.

Captain Baitos and the Augustine, Father Horbigoso, recovered their health completely; but Herrera, who was out of danger on leaving the ship, was attacked afterward by a new misfortune which aggravated his principal illness of *verben*[47]; and he died after having made his will and received the sacraments.

Father Tamaral held his funeral rites with the greatest pomp possible; and later, in the presence of Captain Baitos and the Augustine Horbigoso, he made an exact inventory of all that Herrera had taken from the ship, and he gave it all to them. In spite of the many efforts which they made, they could not get him to accept anything, either as a recompense for the expenses of the illness and the funeral or as a sign of gratitude for his great services. When they had reached Mexico [City], they praised the goodness of the apostolic missionary in that place with extraordinary encomiums, and Father Horbigoso gave a public testimony of this with warm commendations of the Jesuits.

Chapter Twenty-Three

REBELLION BREAKS OUT AND SPREADS THROUGH THE SOUTHERN PART

THE NURSING of the sick did not distract Father Tamaral from the care of his Mission. He, as well as the other neighboring missionaries, thought that the first sparks of the rebellion kindled by Boton and Chicori were extinguished because everywhere the attitude of the Pericùes seemed peaceful. But those two wicked men were concealing,

---

[47] A nervous disease, probably similar to beri-beri, and caused by a lack of certain food values.

under an apparent tranquillity, a fatal conspiracy which finally broke out in the autumn of 1734, resulting in the destruction of four Missions[48] and in the consternation of all the Christianity of the peninsula.

The motive of this conspiracy was none other than the hatred of those savages for the Christian religion, because it deprived them of the many women whom they had for their comfort and pleasure; and, as was explained afterward, the conspirators, themselves, confessed it. The first groups which followed the conspirators were another tribe of gentiles who lived along the southern coast between the Missions of Santiago and San José.

From there the flame spread to all the five Missions of the southern part, but with such secrecy that the missionaries did not even suspect it. When the conspirators saw that their party had grown very strong (since many neophytes had also joined them without failing to attend the daily services of the Mission for that reason), they decided to begin the execution of their perverse designs with the killing of the few soldiers who were there and whose firearms inspired such fear in them.

There were only three soldiers at Santa Rosa, two at Santiago, and one at La Paz; but as those cowardly traitors did not dare attack even two or three soldiers at one time, so they kept waiting for the opportunity to kill them one by one. In the early part of September when they had met one at Santa Rosa alone in the woods, they killed him cruelly; and, wishing to hide their crime or cast the blame on Father Taraval or on one of the two soldiers who remained, they sent word to the missionary that the soldier had met with an accident and consequently that he should go and confess him or send another soldier to have him carried to the Mission. But Father Taraval, suspecting and surmising their crime and their machinations because of the confusion of the messengers and because of other indications, wished neither to go nor to send the soldier; and in a little while he found out for certain what had happened. A few days later they found a way to kill the only soldier[49] at La

[48] La Paz, Santiago, San José, and Santa Rosa.
[49] Manuel Andrés Romero (see Venegas, *Noticia de la California*, Vol. II, p. 461).

Paz, who was taking care of the temporalities of that Mission during the absence of Father Gordon, who had gone to Loreto to get provisions.

At that time a soldier came from Loreto to San José with the purpose of keeping Father Tamaral company and also of bleeding[50] him, because he had become ill from the work at that new Mission. This soldier had observed some signs of the conspiracy in the territory of Santiago, and he saw others in that of San José; he warned the missionary about it, telling him that it was necessary for him to seek safety, because his life among the barbarians was in manifest danger. Father Tamaral, animated by divine grace, which was leading him to a glorious death, succeeded in dissipating his fear; but dreading to remain in the hands of the savages where he would have undoubtedly perished if he had stayed there, he went to La Paz by another road.

On entering the village, he gave the accustomed salute, firing one shot; but no one answered him. He approached the house of the missionary and called to the soldier in a loud voice; but not hearing an answer or finding any Indians from whom to get information, he entered and saw some traces of blood and the knapsack of the dead soldier with everything that he had within it scattered over the floor; and not doubting the tragic death of his companion by virtue of such evidence, he fled hastily to the Mission of Dolores, where he gave an account of all that he had observed to Father Guillen, who was then superior of all the Missions of California.

Father Guillen, who already had some information through his neophytes, wrote immediately to the three missionaries of Santiago, San José, and Santa Rosa, commanding those missionaries to join him at once. In a few days he received a letter from Father Carranco in which he gave him warning of the conspiracy which had been almost disclosed by the Pericùes; and he asked him for his orders so that he could obey them promptly.

[50] Until the latter part of the nineteenth century the best physicians practiced bleeding. President George Washington, in 1799, was "bled" three times, losing two quarts of blood, and died after being blistered "to rawness," presumably with mustard.

The danger of the two missionaries compelled Father Guillen to write to them again, but neither these letters nor the first ones reached their hands, because the conspirators had closed all the approaches.

Because Father Carranco thought that Father Tamaral was in great danger on account of being alone and without soldiers, he sent him an escort of those of his neophytes who seemed most faithful to him for the purpose of bringing him to Santiago, where the two by coming to an understanding would determine what was suitable for such a difficulty. But Father Tamaral did not consent. On the contrary he answered bravely that those fears arose from the cowardice of the neophytes; that he did not find any indication of revolt among his people; that he trusted in God, whom he served in life and death; that Divine Providence would dispose of him as it wished; and that he was not worthy of martyrdom, the divine grace he had desired for so long a time and for which he had prayed God during all his life. Nor did he think that he should abandon his Mission under the circumstances, especially after his neophytes had given such great proofs of their faithfulness in past disturbances.

This letter was found afterward among the destroyed effects of Father Carranco. When the neophytes returned to Santiago, they met some bands of conspirators who asked them whence they came. They answered that they had gone to San José to escort Father Tamaral to Santiago, because Father Carranco learned from the boy whom he had in his house that they wished to kill them all. The conspirators wished to begin their hostilities with Father Tamaral, who was the most defenseless, and then continue afterward through the other Missions until they drove out all the missionaries from the peninsula if it were possible. But seeing that Father Carranco was aware of their intentions, they determined to strike the first blow at him in order not to give him time to escape or to have soldiers come. They frankly communicated their intentions to those of Santiago; and, forgetting the faithfulness which they owed to God and their Father in Christ, these united with the conspirators. And so having combined with them, they took the road to Santiago.

Chapter Twenty-Four

THE GLORIOUS DEATHS OF FATHERS CARRANCO AND TAMARAL. THEIR CORPSES ARE MUTILATED, AND BURNED WITH THE CHURCH FURNISHINGS

WHEN THE barbarians had reached that village on Friday (the first of October at sunrise), they inquired first whether the two soldiers who guarded the missionary were there and when they had found out that they had gone to the mountain shortly before to bring two oxen to provide meat for the catechumen, the children, the old people, and all those who were supported at the expense of the missionary, they approached his house. But not having the daring then to present themselves to him, they made some of the neophytes, who had gone to San José to bring Father Tamaral, enter the house. Father Carranco had said Holy Mass a little while before and had retired to his bedroom to pray when the Indians found him on his knees.

He arose to read the letter which they brought from Father Tamaral; and while he was carefully reading it a rabble of the mob entered. Two of them immediately took hold of him, forced him outside of the house, and held him hanging by his habit, while the others shot their arrows at him. Lifting his eyes and his courage to Heaven, and with fervid desires, he offered God the sacrifice of his innocent life for his faults and for those of his children in Christ; and afterward he fell dying to the earth, while he invoked the sacred names of Jesus, Mary, and Joseph.

Then, with cudgels and by throwing stones, they ended by depriving him of the little life which remained to him. And those unfortunate barbarians became more cruelly enraged against him when they saw him unable any longer to defend himself. Thus Father Lorenzo Carranco, born in the city of Cholula of the diocese of Puebla de los Ángeles, ended his day. The menology of that province makes mention of his glorious death; and his portraits were kept until 1767 in the colleges of

San Gerónimo and San Ignacio in Puebla de los Ángeles where he had been a student, and in the College of Tepotzotlán where he had spent his novitiate.

When the savages were performing their cruelties on the corpse of the father, his serving boy bitterly wept over his death. When one of the rabble saw him, he said to the others: "Since this boy regrets the death of his dear Father so much, let him go and accompany him," and, picking him up by the feet, they killed him cruelly by dashing him with fury against the walls of the house and the rocks.

Aroused by the noise, all the Indians of every age and both sexes of that village came running. And, although some greatly regretted the inhumanity toward a man who had done so many kind things for them, nevertheless, either through fear of the conspirators or because of their natural fickleness, they joined the murderers; and while the wood was being prepared for the fire in which they were going to burn the corpses, they dragged along that of the missionary; and after they had divested him of his clothing so they could make use of it, the women as well as the men committed the most execrable and abominable insults on him in order to avenge themselves for the zeal with which he had tried to divert them from their brutal licentiousness.[51]

---

[51] Father Taraval testifies to this murder as follows: "Sigismundo Taraval of the Jesuits, Rector of the Missions of the south of the islands of Californias, Vicar and ecclesiastical Judge for the venerable Cabildo of Guadalajara, New Galicia, the new Kingdom of Leon, Nahiarit, Californias, Coahuila, etc., I assert not only as an eyewitness but through the efforts made according to sacred precepts that the venerable Fathers Lorenzo José Carranco and Nicolás Tamaral died at the hands of the Pericùes in their hatred of the holy faith and so that this may be evident I signed it in this Mission of Our Lady of Pilar at La Paz in Californias, August 12 of 1737. Sigismundo Taraval" (MS in Bancroft Library, University of California).

This Indian revolt is told in a detailed and vivid style in a valuable manuscript, the authorship of which is still a matter of some controversy. It was advertised in London (1888) for sixty-three pounds by Quaritch, an English book dealer, who seems to have found the manuscript, and he sold it for seventy pounds. It was purchased by Edward Everett Ayer of Chicago, and is now in the Ayer Library of that city. The city Library in Los Angeles and the Lummis Library of the Southwestern Museum in that city each have a typewritten copy of the priceless manuscript. This manuscript is written in the first person. It is a diary kept from month to month, beginning at La Paz

Then, in the midst of these insults and mockeries, the two corpses were thrown into the fire.[52] At the same time they pillaged the church and the house of the missionary; and, keeping what might be useful to them, they threw the Cross itself, the images of the saints, the altar, the missal, the sacred utensils, and other things pertaining to divine service into the bonfire, in this way making evident the reason for their anger against the minister of God.

The corpses and the church furnishings were still burning when two mounted soldiers reached Santiago, leading the two oxen which they had gone to bring for the provision of the Mission. These were not soldiers of the presidio of Loreto but

---

in 1734, and ending at Santiago in 1737. It furnishes an important link in the complete history of Lower California, and continues the account of the Missions where Venegas left off after the murder of Fathers Carranco and Tamaral. The events of this revolt, Quaritch says, "are described with a singleness of purpose and a simplicity of manner beyond our description, reminding the reader of De Foe's magical narration." When discovered by Quaritch, the manuscript was found to be mutilated. Five leaves have been cut from the front of it, and nine from the end of the diary. There is no name by which the manuscript may be identified. Some have thought that the name of its author must have been on one of the pages taken out, but the author states that he did not sign the manuscript. He says (paragraph 177): "I shall keep quiet what I can keep quiet which will not hinder the narration or the marvellous woof of Divine Providence, which has been marvelled at and is marvelled at in it [this history]. *I shall suppress my name for His credit.*" Father William Gordon is usually given credit for writing this diary, which contains 360 pages that are 8½ inches by 6 inches in size. Says Quaritch concerning its authorship: "We know from comparing the text with certain statements of Clavigero that the writer was the Hispano-Scottish Jesuit, W. Gordon."

[52] Father Nàpoli gathered up the ashes and the burned bones of the two men, according to the Gordon manuscript. This statement is followed by a eulogy on Father Carranco which differs in only a few words from the eulogy of Carranco written by Father Taraval, and by the eulogy on Father Tamaral, which is almost an exact copy of Taraval's eulogy of Tamaral. The third eulogy is that of Father Mayorga. The eulogies of these three men, as written by Father Taraval, are in the Bancroft Library. These three eulogies, undoubtedly written by Taraval, in the Gordon manuscript represent the only clear, scholarly, and beautiful Spanish in the entire document. Taraval could not have written the manuscript, if judgment is based on his vocabulary and style of composition. For a discussion of this controversy, see the *California Historical Society Quarterly*, Vol. VIII, pp. 374–77.

mestizos* of New Spain who acted as soldiers and carried no other weapons than their knives. As soon as they arrived, the rebels surrounded them and ordered them to dismount and kill the oxen, because the vile executioners who had performed such cruelties fearlessly on their benefactor and on an innocent child did not dare to kill those animals. The soldiers obeyed by compulsion; but scarcely had they killed the oxen than they also were killed by a cloud of arrows, and their bodies were thrown into the fire.

Now that the rebels no longer had anything to do at the Mission of Santiago, they set out promptly in larger numbers to that of San José del Cabo. They arrived there on the morning of October 3, after Father Tamaral had already said Holy Mass. Many insurgent Indians of the same Mission (armed and in a throng) entered the house of the missionary and arrogantly asked for different things, with the purpose of finding some pretext, in the refusal of the missionary, to become infuriated against him. One kept asking him for corn, another for a blanket, another for a knife, and for other things likewise.

Father Tamaral penetrated their perverse intent at once, and to quiet them, he said to them: "Wait, dear sons, I shall try to please you with all that there is in the house." Seeing that they were not succeeding in their intent, they did not want to seek another pretext. The same ones who had taken possession of Father Carranco threw themselves upon him, knocked him to the floor, and, dragging him by the feet, took him outside to shoot him with their arrows; but all the conspirators crowded around him; they decided to decapitate him, as in fact they did with one of those knives which he was accustomed to distribute to them for their needs.

When this exemplary and tireless missionary was dying, he fervidly commended his spirit and his flock to God. He was born in Sevilla in 1687. He went to Mexico in 1712 and from there, in 1716, to California, where he worked for eighteen years, establishing two new Missions. His memory is also hon-

* Those were called *mestizos* who were born of a European father and an American mother, or the contrary.

ored in the menology of the Mexican province. His death was followed by the same insults and profanations that took place in Santiago; and his corpse was also burned with the furnishings of that church, although here they made greater merriment because their sacrilegious triumph had been doubled.

Chapter Twenty-Five

THE INSURGENTS TRY TO KILL FATHER TARAVAL. THEY ATTACK THE NEOPHYTES OF SANTA ROSA. FATHER GUILLEN VAINLY INFORMS THE VICEROY ABOUT EVERYTHING

THE BARBARIANS could not be content while there was a single missionary in their nation. After they had killed those of Santiago and San José they tried also to kill the one at Santa Rosa; and with this purpose they sent an embassy to the Guaicuras of La Paz, urging them on in that cruel undertaking. But Father Taraval, having learned in time through some of his neophytes who were eyewitnesses of the deaths of the other two missionaries (although he wished to have the same fate as his companions), nevertheless believed that he was obliged under the circumstances to save his life and those of his soldiers; and in order to prevent the sacred things from being profaned by these sacrilegious people he went immediately to the Mission of La Paz, accompanied by two soldiers, and taking the sacred vessels and all that belonged to divine worship away with him. He also took out of the church at La Paz all the sacred furnishings that could be desecrated; and from there he went in a canoe to the island of Espíritu Santo, where he remained until he had received the help of soldiers and provisions from Loreto.

He moved to the Mission of Dolores with all his followers as much to insure that Mission, which was also threatened by the insurgents, as to confer with Father Guillen, the superior of all the Missions, about the means of re-establishing peace and about the four destroyed Missions. As soon as the conspirators found out that Father Taraval had escaped, they vented their ill-will against the neophytes of Santa Rosa and, falling upon them suddenly, killed twenty-seven. A long war which caused them mutual havoc, as in the time of their gentility, arose between them from this action.

As soon as Father Guillen knew about these disturbances and misfortunes, he wrote to the archbishop-viceroy of Mexico, giving him an account of what had happened. He explained to him the danger of destruction in which the other Missions were, together with all the Christianity of that peninsula (if the example of the Pericùes were imitated by the other nations, as was greatly feared), and entreated him that a new presidio should be established in the southern part, as had been desired for some time and as he had requested many times, not less to protect the lives of the missionaries and neophytes from the machinations of the gentiles than to give refuge to the ships from the Philippine Islands, which were to put into port there during the years to follow. But neither the violent deaths of the two missionaries, the soldiers, and so many neophytes and catechumen, nor the loss of those Missions, nor the imminent danger of the others, nor the proposed advantages for the ships from the Philippines appeared reasons sufficient to that gentleman for making an extraordinary expenditure, although it had been arranged for by the Catholic king in a *cédula* sent to the Marqués de Casafuerte,[53] his predecessor[54] in the office of viceroy, when there were then no such urgent reasons for establishing that presidio.

He contented himself by giving a courteous reply to Father Guillen, expressing to him how much he regretted the misfortunes of California, urging him to appeal to the court and offering to support his just claims in the presence of the king. But neither his compliments nor his promises helped the calamities which were suffered then or those which were feared.

[53] Juan de Acuña, who held office from 1722 to 1734. He was a Creole, and was born in Peru.

[54] See above, footnote 46. One of the very few viceroys buried in Mexico.

Chapter Twenty-Six

THE REBELLION CONTINUES. MEASURES PUT INTO EFFECT TO CHECK IT

THE SPIRIT of the rebellion was spreading; and also some disturbance was beginning to be felt in the district of Dolores, which would probably have become more serious if the captain of the presidio, on receipt of the first news which was received in Loreto about the disorders of the Pericùes, had not arrived there on time with some soldiers. He desired to go after the enemies to punish them (as in other times) but, considering their large forces and the small number of his soldiers, he did not wish to expose himself foolishly; and he wisely determined to establish himself in the Mission of Dolores in order to maintain the peace of its district and to prevent the communication of the conspirators with the Indians of the northern Missions.

Notwithstanding this, the rumor of what had happened in the southern part was extended little by little from one tribe to another until it reached the Mission of San Ignacio more than six hundred miles distant from that of San José del Cabo. A seditious murmur began to be scattered there among some who were displeased with the Christian life; they said to each-other that it was necessary for all to join together in order to free themselves entirely from the foreigners who had come to abolish the ancient customs of the Californians, and that if the Pericùes had done this the Cochimìes could attain it better, for they were greater in number and braver. The principal Indians of the Missions did not take part in that uprising; on the contrary, they made their constant faithfulness known and gave warning to the missionaries, who wrote at once to Loreto asking for more soldiers for their security, since those who acted as guards in the Missions were greatly dismayed.

In fact, the news of the two soldiers who had been killed by the Pericùes frightened those of the other Missions to such a degree that their letters received in Loreto made one believe that the Cochimìes were determined to imitate the fatal example of the Pericùes. For this reason Father Guillen, since he did not have soldiers to send to the missionaries, commanded all under the precept of holy obedience to abandon their respective Missions immediately and retire to Loreto with the purpose, at least, of placing their lives in safety. Without the Indians noticing it, the missionaries obeyed, because they kept absenting themselves in succession from the Missions accordingly as the letters of the superior kept arriving. The necessity for such a plan was quickly recognized, without which perhaps the Missions would have been lost forever, because the fickle minds of the savages, although calmer and less stupid and vicious than the Pericùes, had really changed considerably with the example of the latter.

After the missionaries had retired to Loreto, Father Guillen wrote again to the archbishop-viceroy at the beginning of 1735, stating the lamentable condition of that Christianity. Father Bravo, the missionary of Loreto, sent a boat to Yaqui with letters for the governor of Sinaloa and for the missionaries of that country, in which he related to them the unfortunate events which we have mentioned and the danger in which they were. And he entreated them to send sixty[55] Indian warriors and some soldiers with firearms to defend the lives of the missionaries. In order to check the Pericùe insurgents a great many troops were needed, especially if they succeeded (as they were trying to do) in forming a confederation with the other two nations of California.

Father Guillen's letter reached Mexico [City] on April 13 and was handed at once to the archbishop-viceroy by the provincial of the Jesuits. But the provincial, seeing that he could not obtain the desired help for the urgent needs of California with either that letter or the two petitions which he presented to that gentleman, resolved to write without delay to the Catholic monarch himself, from whose zeal, which was shown in so

[55] In the Gordon manuscript it is stated that forty soldiers came from the mainland and thirty came from the presidio in Lower California, also that Father Nàpoli was the one asked to come because he was so greatly beloved by the Indians.

many orders sent in favor of the Missions, he did not doubt that he would get help. The letters of Father Bravo were much more successful; for no sooner had the faithful and warlike Yaquis received the news than more than five hundred men, armed after their fashion and ready to sail for California, presented themselves at that port. Because the boat could not carry so many soldiers, sixty of the bravest, who went at once to Loreto, were chosen; and from there they went to the Mission of Dolores, where the captain of the presidio was at that time. When they arrived at that port the northern Missions had been re-established in their former peacefulness with singular demonstrations on the part of the neophytes.

As soon as the principal neophytes noticed that the missionaries had gone away with the soldiers and had taken the furnishings of the churches, they regretted it very much. And having come to an understanding they determined to go all together to Loreto to recover their dear missionaries. So they entered Loreto in a very orderly and numerous procession, carrying all the crosses of the Missions on their shoulders and asking, tearfully, that the missionaries who had baptized them and brought them up in the Christian life would not condemn them to perdition. They insisted that they wished to live and die in the religion of Jesus Christ which they had adopted, saying that it was not just that all should suffer the punishment deserved by only some few malcontents, whom they were ready to catch and hand over to the captain-governor to be punished, and adding that they were under obligations to take care of the lives of the missionaries and to defend them in any event; and, lastly, that if the missionaries did not wish to return to their respective countries they had decided to remain in Loreto, because they could not live without their priests.

The missionaries on hearing the affectionate expressions of their neophytes could not restrain their tears at such a sight. But in spite of this, they let some days pass to be better assured of their sincerity. Finally, being sure of their good intentions, they returned with them to the abandoned Missions in which they were received triumphantly by all the other neophytes and catechumen. A light punishment was imposed on the culpable;

only four of the Mission of San Ignacio were exiled for some time so that they might not contaminate the others.

When the Yaquis had reached the Mission of Dolores, many faithful Californians, besides the captain and the soldiers of the presidio, were stationed there to resist the conspirators. The captain decided to leave a competent garrison there to check all disturbances and to go with the rest of the troops to encamp at the port of La Paz, as a place suitable for receiving provisions from Loreto and for making raids into the country of the Pericùes. He sent there by land part of the troops with the horses and another division by sea with the provisions. The latter arrived first, and, having landed in good order, they took an advantageous position and all the necessary precautions in order to be able to resist the enemy.

These efforts were not in vain because they were soon attacked in the night with considerable system by the conspirators, some on both sides being wounded in the fray. They continued being disturbed in this way until the division which was coming by land arrived. Then the enemies, terrified at seeing so many soldiers with firearms and horses, did not dare to appear. Some Indians of La Paz presented themselves, saying that they had always been faithful to the missionaries and for that reason had been persecuted by the rebels. But it was soon learned through them that the reason for the new attack of the conspirators was the hostilities which they had shown to some men belonging to the ship from the Philippine Islands, which had been at the port of San Bernabé a short time before.

Chapter Twenty-Seven

HOSTILITIES SHOWN THE SHIP FROM THE PHILIPPINE ISLANDS. THE CAPTAIN GIVES AN ACCOUNT OF THEM TO THE VICEROY. THE COMMAND OF THIS GENTLEMAN TO THE GOVERNOR OF SINALOA

As THOSE sailors who had been there the year before had been so well received by Father Tamaral, and as they had so fortunately recovered there, they put into the same port this year, hoping to find a very much greater abundance of fresh food, because that missionary was thought to be better provided. But on approaching land they did not see those signals which the latter should have placed on the beach as they had agreed, nor did they observe any people. Notwithstanding this, the captain sent thirteen sailors in a small boat to inform the missionary of their arrival. While some of them remained in the small boat to guard it, the others went to the settlement of San José; but on the way they were suddenly attacked and killed by a large number of conspirators who were lying in ambush and who went immediately to do the same thing with those who had remained with the small boat.

The captain of the ship, suspecting what had really happened on account of the delay of the sailors, sent another boat with armed men. On approaching the shore they saw a great number of Indians who were destroying the small boat in order to carry away the iron; they fired on them, killing some and wounding others, made four prisoners, and put the remainder to flight. When these men had returned to the ship, the captain discovered that instead of having procured fresh food, which he needed chiefly for the very many who were there ill with scurvy, he had lost thirteen sailors and the small boat. He set sail for Acapulco and from there went to Mexico [City], where he presented the archbishop-viceroy with the four Pericùe prisoners, relating to him all that had happened.

It seems that these statements were more effective than the great number of reports which had been made up to that time, because that gentleman was finally persuaded to give some help in the disorders of California. He commanded the governor of Sinaloa to go at once with troops to the peninsula in order to check the insolence of the savages and to punish the leaders of the conspiracy; but he informed him that, although it might be fitting that he work in agreement with the captain-governor of California if he had need of him, he should not, on the other hand, be subordinate to him, and by no means was he to be subordinate to the guidance of the missionaries. The governor of Sinaloa wrote to Loreto, informing them of his commission so that they might send him the boat for transporting his troops, and commanding that the hostilities begun against the Pericùes at the port of La Paz should cease.

The captain of California had made some raids into the country of the Pericùes, with little success because he did not find anyone with whom to fight, since the conspirators, avoiding every combat, kept in hiding. Subsequently, by virtue of the new commands, he retired to the Mission of Dolores to stay on the defensive in that place until the coming of the governor. In a short time the latter arrived at Loreto, where he was received by the missionaries with the honors which were due him and the courtesies which befitted him.

But he soon made it clear that he was not devoting himself to any other thing than paying attention to the wishes of the viceroy, having no regard for the advice which the missionaries, who were men well acquainted with that country and the people, gave him. He began to carry out his commission, availing himself of the means which seemed to him most conducive to the end proposed. He spent two years there with varied fortune and much annoyance, because the results which he promised himself did not measure up to his capacity.

Chapter Twenty-Eight

THE DEATH OF FATHER MAYORGA. THE GOVERNOR FOLLOWS THE ADVICE OF THE MISSIONARIES IN HIS OPERATIONS, AND TRIUMPHS OVER THE CONSPIRATORS

MEANTIME, Father Mayorga, a person dear to God and men, after having established the Mission of San José de Comondù in 1707 and managed it for more than twenty-nine years to the great benefit of the Indians there, died on November 10, 1736. This venerable man bewailed the destruction of the Missions and the loss of the Indians' souls for the salvation of which he had renounced his native land and had imprisoned himself in the deserts of that peninsula. Every day he made some private complaisance to God to induce him to take pity on those souls; and in the midst of these pious sentiments he rendered his fervent spirit to the Master.

There were not lacking those who attributed the sudden change in the attitude of the governor to the fervor of his prayers. After the governor had remained obstinate in his unsuccessful designs, and as soon as that exemplary missionary died, he began to do what the missionaries had advised him from the beginning; that is, that instead of proposing terms of peace to the Pericùes or of pursuing their scattered groups, he should try to engage them in a general and noisy battle. In this way he might succeed in humbling them with less loss on his part; otherwise they would neither submit, nor would they show gratitude for clemency, except after having known by experience the superiority of their opponents in bravery, discipline, and weapons.

Following this advice the governor then pursued the conspirators so closely that he forced them to a regular battle, in which they were defeated and then fled ignominiously. But as their pride had been increased greatly for two years with their resistance against the forces of the governor, so they did not want to surrender with that defeat; on the contrary, they renewed their hostilities, although in weak attacks, until the governor found a way of engaging them in another battle. Being defeated as in the first battle, they came to him humbly asking pardon and peace and placed themselves at his disposal. The governor refused to hear them until they promised to divulge the names and hand over to him the leader of the conspiracy and the murderers of the missionaries and the soldiers.

All were delivered promptly to him, and he was satisfied in ordering them exiled to the coast of New Spain. But it seems that God wished to punish their many and atrocious crimes more severely, because when they wished to take possession of the boat in which they were going to the place of their exile the soldiers who were guarding them were obliged to fire on them and killed the greater part of them. Among the few who escaped with their lives were the two who first dared to lift their sacrilegious hands against the missionaries. One of these, without receiving sacraments, was killed within a few months after exile; and the other, who had climbed a tall palm, fell unfortunately on the rocks below and died instantly.

Chapter Twenty-Nine

THE NEW PRESIDIO IS NOT AGREEABLE TO THE INTENTIONS OF THE KING. THE VICEROY REVOKES HIS ORDERS, WHICH ARE CONTRARY TO THE FORMER

WHILE that war was being carried on in California, the Catholic king, induced by the remonstrances of the Jesuits, sent a strict order to establish the proposed presidio quickly for the security of the Missions in the southern part of the peninsula. He had notified the viceroy, the Marqués de Casafuerte, some years before to do this. The archbishop-viceroy gave this commission to the governor of Sinaloa, declaring that the captain and the soldiers of the new presidio should be subordinate neither to the missionaries nor to the captain of Loreto, but only to the viceroy. At the beginning it was desired to establish the presidio at the port of La Paz; but, in consideration of the ships coming from the Philippine Islands, it was finally located at San José del Cabo, where ten soldiers were quartered with the captain and the other officers, and another ten were stationed at the Mission of La Paz, and as many more at that of Santiago.

The governor of Sinaloa conferred the office of captain of the new presidio on Don Bernardo Rodríguez de Larrea, the son of the famous captain of Loreto, Don Estevan Rodríguez Lorenzo. Surely no one was more worthy or more suitable than he. Born and raised in California with his good father, he had that piety and religion, that prudence and bravery, and that knowledge of the country and of the Indians which were required under such circumstances and for such an office. But as he was accustomed to respect Fathers Salvatierra, Ugarte, and Piccolo, he deferred more to the missionaries than their enemies wished, and for this reason he was soon removed from office and replaced by another who knew better how to accommodate himself to the humor of the viceroy. The procurator of the Missions in Mexico stated that, since the singular independence of those officers and soldiers was opposed to the intentions of the king, who had expressly commanded the viceroy not to change the form of government established by Father Salvatierra in California in any way, these remonstrances were not considered.

The presidio was maintained in this manner for eighteen months. But the disturbances that its independence occasioned were so grave and the complaints presented to the viceroy were so numerous that he could not help but revoke his orders and conform to the arrangements of his predecessors. He removed the captain of the new presidio and advised him that he could be only a lieutenant, subordinate with his soldiers to the captain of the old presidio of Loreto; and that the captain, as well as the other officers, soldiers, and sailors, should be subordinate in everything, as before, to the superior of the Missions. This revocation of his own orders by a viceroy who was not partial to the Jesuits is enough to justify the system of government established in California by Father Salvatierra.

Chapter Thirty

THE FOUR DESTROYED MISSIONS ARE RESTORED. THE ATTEMPT ON THE LIFE OF FATHER WAGNER. THE PUNISHMENT OF THE GUILTY

WHEN peace was restored in the southern part of the peninsula, after the punishment of the conspirators and after the establishment of a new presidio, the superiors appointed new missionaries there so that (with their efforts) they might rebuild the destroyed Missions in that country which was washed with the perspiration and the blood of their dear brothers. In fact, they succeeded, although with great effort, in re-establishing the four Missions of La Paz, Santa Rosa, Santiago, and San José, in gathering those strayed sheep [Indians] into their ancient folds, and in returning them to the healthful pastures of the Christian doctrine.

When the governor of Sinaloa had concluded his charge, he returned to his province. But on leaving California he ordered that a garrison of eight or ten soldiers from Loreto be established on each of the two frontiers of San Ignacio and Dolores, and that all those soldiers who were in the other Missions guarding the missionaries should go and stay in the presidio, convincing himself that the soldiers were no longer necessary, since the Indians were quiet. But experience soon proved that although there might be only one soldier, he was not useless in those Missions (as it seemed to that governor who knew little about the character of those Indians), since not a year passed in the absence of the soldier who had been in San José de Comondù without some serious disturbances arising in the Mission.

Father Mayorga had been succeeded there by Father Francisco Javier Wagner,[56] a German, who followed in the footsteps of his predecessors and devoted himself with much zeal to making his neophytes live in a Christian manner and in trying particularly to free them from the deceptions of the *guamas*. Among the latter there were some who continued practicing their barbarous healings and their usual impostures after being converted to Christianity and after their baptisms. It happened many times that after a missionary had administered the blessed sacraments and other spiritual and corporeal aid to a sick person, the *guama* stole in secretly (either of his own volition or called by the relatives of the patient himself) to apply to him fumigations or other ridiculous and unconducive remedies which they used in the time of their gentility; and he urged him to abjure what the missionary had taught him.

Father Wagner could not be at peace with these harmful charlatans; and he tried as much as possible to discredit them with his neophytes. For their part these deceivers hated him to the extent that they often conspired against his life. But they did not dare to declare themselves against him for fear of the people who loved and respected him.

One night when the missionary was at the door of his house enjoying the open air, a *guama*, availing himself of the darkness, shot an arrow at him with such force that he drove it into a stone of the wall at a distance of only four or five fingers'

---

[56] Father Wagner arrived in the peninsula in 1737, and died in 1744. He wrote *Noticia de la Misión de S. José de Comondú y de sus Cuatro Pueblos*, which manuscript Venegas used.

width from the head of the missionary. Some neophytes who were near, hearing the slight whistle of the arrow at such an hour and suspecting what it really was, ran up quickly to defend their dear shepherd of the flock and, taking a light, found the arrow stuck in the wall. One of the most influential neophytes immediately sent a messenger to Loreto to give warning of the trouble. Since the captain was not able to come in person to Comondù, he ordered his son Bernardo, who was the lieutenant of that presidio, to go with some soldiers and Indians of Loreto, after having instructed him what he was to do and authorized him to administer justice.

The lieutenant went with the greatest celerity. He began to make investigations about the person who had committed that offense against the missionary; but all protested that they did not know him, until the very arrow which was shot by the *guama* and kept by another Indian was shown them; then some recognized who had made it.

When this person was questioned by the lieutenant, he declared that, although he had made that arrow, he had never used it, because another Indian, Juan Bautista, had asked him for it and he had given it to him without knowing for what purpose he wanted it. Then they hunted for Juan Bautista, but he had fled as soon as he had heard of the excitement after his offense. The lieutenant ordered that he be searched for everywhere; and after some days he was found and brought before him. He confessed his crime and was condemned to death; his corpse was hung up as a warning to the rest.

Various others who were culpable in the affair were condemned to floggings. When the lieutenant had finished his work, he returned to Loreto. But in three weeks he had to return to Comondù because those who had been punished renewed their disturbances. With the exile of three of the most culpable ones quiet was restored, and peace was never disturbed in the future.[57] These and other similar examples made the captain-governor of that peninsula station a soldier again to guard each missionary, despite the orders of the governor of Sinaloa.

[57] The Gordon manuscript has recently been translated and edited by Marguerite Eyer Wilbur.

Chapter Thirty-One

A NEW REBELLION OF SOME TRIBES OF THE PERICÙES. THE PUNISHMENT OF THE LEADERS PUTS AN END TO THE DISTURBANCES OF THAT NATION

A SHORT time afterward four tribes of the Pericùe nation who lived between San José del Cabo and Santiago, rebelled again, despite the new presidio. The first of their hostilities was inflicted on a poor herdsman of the Mission of San José. While he was sleeping peacefully in his cabin, ten of the main conspirators entered suddenly and killed him inhumanely by crushing his head with a heavy rock. Afterward they shot arrows at the herdsman who took care of the goats of the presidio; but he saved himself by running away and gave warning to the missionary and the soldiers. The latter became greatly alarmed, especially one night when they noticed that all the Indians of both sexes had gone from the village of San José and slipped away to the mountains. Then it was feared that the conspiracy was general; but after the missionary made an investigation he found out that the cause of the sudden flight of his neophytes was the rumor intentionally spread among them by the conspirators themselves that the soldiers of the presidio had agreed to kill all of them in one night; believing this report readily, they had tried to place their lives in safety by escaping.

The missionary exerted himself to remove this idea from their minds, making them see that the conspirators had wished to intimidate them with this false rumor in order to get them to the mountains and thus induce them to rebellion and cause their destruction. He assured them that the soldiers would not do them any harm if they remained faithful and quiet; and he begged them especially to trust him who loved them as a father and sought their welfare in everything. When the Indians were reassured in this manner not only the inhabitants of San José returned to that village but all the other neophytes and catechumen belonging to the Mission also placed themselves under the protection of the soldiers and sheltered themselves from the insults and offenses of the rebels. The same thing happened in the other two Missions of Santiago and Santa Rosa, where, for the same reason, all the faithful Indians took shelter in the main villages; but meanwhile the rebels remained masters of the roads and no one could go from one Mission to another without danger of falling into their hands.

The captain of the presidio of the cape [San Lucas] (because at that time the viceroy had not yet revoked his orders relative to independence) asked the captain of Loreto for help, entreating him particularly to send him many faithful and well-armed Indians in order to pursue the rebels in the ravines and rough places. For this he could not avail himself of the Pericùes, who, instead of pursuing the rebels to catch them, would give them warning so they could escape. The captain of Loreto sent him some soldiers with a sufficient number of Guaicuras, who were enemies of the Pericùes and reputed to be the most courageous among them. Accompanied by these auxiliary troops and his own soldiers, the captain began to pursue the enemies to subdue them; but the latter, not being able to face him, fled in every direction; and when they saw themselves pursued closely they hid themselves in the roughest and most inaccessible places.

In spite of this some were killed and some were made prisoners, among whom were the eleven leaders of the rebellion and the guiltiest ones. Seven of them were exiled from the peninsula, and the other four were condemned to death, which they suffered after having been prepared as Christians. All the rest of the conspirators presented themselves voluntarily, submitting to the punishment of floggings to which they were condemned in order to avoid death which they feared and deserved. In this way the disorders of that restless nation ended; and all those who had fled, through fear of the rebels, to the principal villages of those Missions returned securely to those places where they had lived before.

BOOK IV

NEW ORDERS OF THE CATHOLIC KING IN FAVOR OF CALIFORNIA. TRIPS TO THE RED RIVER. THE EXTRAVAGANT CLAIMS AND DISTURBANCES OF THE PERICÙES. THE EULOGY OF SOME WORTHY MEN OF CALIFORNIA. THE ESTABLISHMENT OF THE LAST FOUR MISSIONS AND THE SUPPRESSION OF OTHERS. THE CONDITION OF THAT CHRISTIANITY IN 1767. THE SYSTEM OF GOVERNMENT OF THE MISSIONS AND PRESIDIOS. THE EXPULSION OF THE JESUIT MISSIONARIES

Chapter One

PHILIP THE FIFTH CONSULTS HIS COUNCIL. ANSWERS. THE CÉDULA OF THE KING. THE PROVINCIAL INFORMS THE KING ABOUT THE MISSIONS OF SONORA AND CALIFORNIA. THE CÉDULA OF FERDINAND THE SIXTH

CALIFORNIA, distressed by the revolutions of the intractable Pericùes, was consoled at that time by the zeal of the magnanimous and religious monarch, Philip V. Not content with having commanded that a new presidio be established for the defense of the southern Missions of that peninsula and with having ordered, in 1742, that all the expenses involved in the war against the rebels be paid from the royal treasury, and desirous of increasing the kingdom of Jesus Christ as much as possible rather than his own, he consulted his Supreme Council of the Indies[1] as to the most efficient means that could be employed to render the peace of California durable and to make the advance of Christianity greater and more rapid.

The council after mature deliberation answered his majesty thus:

1. Since the solid conversion of the Californians to the faith

---

[1] A court of appeals in Spain where cases from the *audiencias* in the various colonies were presented for final settlement. It was established in 1524 by King Charles V, and was composed of eight lawyers, two secretaries, a *fiscal*, a lieutenant-chancellor, a high chancellor, and a president. To attend to the heavy correspondence that came to the king a large force of clerks, scribes, bookkeepers, and reporters was needed. For a complete list of the *audiencias* from 1526 to 1893, see Charles Henry Cunningham, *The Audiencia in the Spanish Colonies*, pp. 16–18. The *audiencia* at Guadalajara was created February 15, 1548, being the sixth established by the king. It was composed of a president, a *fiscal*, and four *oidores*.

of Jesus Christ was the basis and the foundation of the happiness of the peninsula it should be continued by the Jesuit missionaries who had begun it and who (it added) *have worked so successfully among those peoples and among many other nations entrusted to their care all over America.*

2. The fortified settlements of the Spaniards and the presidios of soldiers should continue being established at those ports that were suitable and large; and in the center of the peninsula another should be established where the missionaries could take refuge in case of rebellion of the Indians. This plan would have been very useful if the barrenness of that peninsula had permitted its execution, and if the colonists had been composed of families that were well-behaved and not evil-doers, bandits, or idlers, taken from the dregs of the people,[2] as they usually are.

3. To facilitate the advance of Christianity in that peninsula, it would be desirable that the Jesuit missionaries push their Missions forward toward the north and that others of the same Society enter the peninsula on the northern part or by the Red River and, by taking a contrary direction, come and meet the first ones. This was what was so much desired by the missionaries because of the advantages which they expected from it. And Fathers Salvatierra, Kino, and Ugarte had directed their great efforts to the same purpose. But time and patience were needed to attain it. According to the rules of prudence Missions could not be established at the Red River without first having subjected to the Christian religion those nations who lived between that river and Sonora in which the missionaries of this last province were then working.

4. It would also be fitting for the quickest spread of Christianity in the Missions of California as well as in those of Sonora which bordered on the gentile nations that the missionaries be doubled so that one might take care of the neophytes and catechumen gathered in the Mission, and the other might be employed in search of the gentiles in order to attract them to

---

[2] Many of the same base type of people were sent from Mexico a century later when Upper California was colonized.

the faith; and that there should also be soldiers in them, subject to the missionaries themselves, to defend their persons and to accompany them whenever it might be necessary.

This measure of doubling the missionaries in similar Missions was put into practice as much as possible in Sonora as well as in California; but as the Missions entrusted to the Jesuits in the Mexican province were more than one hundred, it was not so easy to have such a great number of missionaries or to find the means of supporting them.

These and other opinions expressed to King Philip by those learned counselors made it clear that they were animated by the same zeal as the sovereign and that they had given all the attention possible to the business. The king subsequently sent a long *cédula* on November 13, 1744, which was directed to the Count of Fuenclara,[3] the viceroy of Mexico, and which was so detailed and strict that it seems that the king had nothing so much at heart as the conversion of the Californians.

After having explained it at length and approved the judgment of his council with extraordinary praises of the zeal and efforts of the Jesuit missionaries, he commanded that the viceroy devote himself to carrying it out with the greatest activity. His majesty stated, among many other things: "In 1702 I commanded that the missionaries of California be aided with everything that might contribute to their relief and to the attainment of their holy purpose; and in 1703 I commanded that the missionaries who were already in California, as well as those who might go there subsequently, should be furnished annually without delay and in ready money the same stipend (or alms) which is accustomed to be given the other missionaries of their Order for their support. This has not been done up to the present time, nor has anything been spent in those Missions at my expense, while the fifteen Missions which are at present in California are maintained without the least expense to my royal treasury but with the increased alms of pri-

---

[3] Pedro Cebrián y Agustín, the fortieth viceroy, who served from 1742 to 1746. He was forced to leave his office because of ill health. It was during his term that a galleon, the famous treasure ship, the "Covadonga," was captured in the Pacific Ocean by an Englishman.

vate persons obtained through the zeal and diligence of the Society of the Jesuits. Now since the means proposed by my council are so inexpensive and, on the other hand, so useful, it would be fitting for them to be put into execution, as well as those which are considered most suitable by the Jesuits who are most experienced in that province and from whom I have asked reports[4] through their provincial, for which I am waiting."

In fact, during the following year (1745) the father-provincial, Cristóbal de Escobar, sent his majesty an extended and exact report about the Missions of Sonora and California in which, after he had explained about the climate, the quality of the soil, the situation and extension of those countries, and the number and actual condition of those Missions, he showed the impossibility of establishing settlements of Spaniards in the barren countries of California; he suggested the most suitable means for the promotion of Christianity and for the proposed continuation of both chains of Missions through the north.[5]

With this in mind he proposed, among several other useful projects, establishing a presidio of one hundred soldiers on the banks of the Gila River to check the daring of the cruel Apaches, whose frequent raids on Sonora and Pimerìa were the greatest obstacle to the advance of Christianity in that place. He also informed his majesty that the three hundred *scudi* assigned for the support of each missionary were not sufficient for those who were in the most remote Missions of Pimería, since more than half of this sum was spent in the transportation of those necessities which were brought from Mexico over a trip of more than one thousand seven hundred miles. He could have added also that, despite the strict and repeated commands of his majesty and those of the preceding monarchs, a considerable part of these alms was spent in gifts which it seemed necessary to make to those who paid it in order to obtain it.

When this report reached Madrid, Philip V had already

---

[4] For comments on this report, see Charles E. Chapman, *A History of California: The Spanish Period*, pp. 32–34.

[5] Irving Berdine Richman, *Mexico under Spain and Mexico, 1535–1847*, pp. 42–61, gives the plans for such a chain of Missions.

died. Ferdinand VI,[6] his worthy son and successor, dispatched a *cédula* on December 4, 1747, which was directed to the viceroy[7] of Mexico, and in which he inserted that one of his father already cited; and he sent him a copy of the aforesaid report so that, by having examined it and having conferred with learned persons (without waiting for a new order), he might carry out what he found most convenient for the promotion of Christianity in those countries so distant from the court. And he notified him also to interpose his authority on the bishop of Nueva Vizcaya in order to induce him to accept the surrender which the previously mentioned provincial of the Jesuits made of the twenty-two Missions in the provinces of Topia[8] and Tepehuana[9] for the purpose of using those missionaries who were no longer necessary to the said Missions in the conversion of the northern gentiles. Since Christianity was well established and rooted in those places, they could be ruled by secular priests like the other old parishes of that diocese.

Chapter Two

THE EFFECT OF THE CÉDULA. THE COMMAND OF THE PROVINCIAL. THE TRIPS OF FATHERS CONSAG AND SEDELMAYER

THESE *cédulas* served only to make evident the piety and zeal of the monarchs, because nothing of all the things that were proposed by the council and the provincial took effect, except the outlined surrender of the

---

[6] He died the same year he took the throne, and his father again became king.

[7] The Count of Revillagigedo, Juan Francisco de Güemes y Horcasitas. He had been a military officer in Cuba and had become wealthy by what was considered illicit trade in tobacco. He held office until 1755.

[8] On the west coast of Mexico. Father Melchor founded the first Mission there at the village of Tepocas in 1699 (*United States Bureau of Ethnology*, Vol. XVII, p. 60).

[9] See footnote 104, Book II, p. 148, *supra*.

twenty-two Missions. The father-provincial,[10] in order not to omit any effort on his part that might contribute to the attainment of such a desired end, commanded Father Fernando Consag, an able missionary of exemplary life who was then the colleague of Father Sistiaga in the Mission of San Ignacio, to make a new voyage to the Red River, sailing along the coast to explore the ports and beaches of the eastern coast of California which no one had examined carefully up to that time. This voyage was made at the expense of those Missions, each one contributing what it could.

Four boats were equipped in the small port of San Carlos, situated beyond 28°; and on June 9, 1746, Father Consag embarked, accompanied by some soldiers, several Californians, and a sufficient number of Yaquis,[11] who are the most skilled of all those Indians in seamanship. He sailed along the coast, observing beaches, ports, islands, and reefs with the greatest diligence. They landed frequently to explore the country; and at two or three places the savage inhabitants wanted to attack them as enemies, taking them for pearl fishermen by whom they were accustomed to be troubled. But they avoided their hostilities, now with kind words and then by frightening them without doing them any harm.

When they had reached the end of the Gulf, all those who got wet with its caustic waters felt the harmful effects which had been experienced before on the voyage of Father Ugarte. They reached the mouth of the river on July 14 and stayed there until the twenty-fifth; they examined those three islands which are in it; and they tried to go up the river, but they could not overcome the rapidity of the current with oars. When some of the crew had landed on those little islands, they almost drowned; they were surprised suddenly by two opposing currents, one from the river swollen from the rains, and the other from a surge of the sea. One of the boats, afterward overturned by the violence of the waves, was lost with almost all the cargo. But the crew which was in it was saved, although

[10] Father Juan Antonio Balthasar.

[11] An Indian tribe that dwelt, for the most part, in Mexico between the Yaqui and Mayo rivers, and about twelve leagues from the coast.

with difficulty. Besides this, scurvy, which was so harmful then in those seas, was already beginning to be felt; therefore Father Consag, since he had carried out the command of his superior, set out on the return trip for the port of San Carlos from where he had embarked, examining the places along the coast which he had not been able to observe when he was going to the river. After he had returned to his Mission, he wrote a very detailed log of his voyage and drew a map of the coast. Both were published in the third volume of the *History of California*,[12] printed in Madrid.

Father Santiago Sedelmayer,[13] an industrious German missionary of Tubutama[14] in Pimería, made three trips (as his part) to the Red and Gila rivers in the years 1744, 1746, and 1750, which, besides giving him the occasion of adding four hundred and nine new catechumen to his Mission, served to makes the course of the rivers, the surrounding countries, and the different nations of gentiles which inhabit it better known.

Chapter Three

THE MISFORTUNES OF THE MISSIONS OF THE SOUTH AND THE DECISION TAKEN THERE. THE LOSS OF FIVE WORTHY MEN OF CALIFORNIA AND THEIR EULOGY. THE NEW GOVERNOR OF THE PENINSULA

WHILE those devoted missionaries were wearing themselves out in similar trips for the purpose of spreading Christianity toward the north, the Missions

---

[12] See footnote 40, Book III, p. 279, *supra*. Taraval contributed to this history.

[13] He worked chiefly among the tribes on the Gila River, erecting at least seven Missions. From 1736 to 1740 he visited among the Pima Indians on the Colorado River, but founded no Mission there (*Catholic Encyclopaedia*, Vol. XII, p. 100).

[14] An Indian village and Mission located on the Altar River in Sonora, the full name being San Pedro del Tubutama. It was one of the most prosperous Missions in that section. Kino supervised the building of the church there (Herbert Eugene Bolton, *Kino's Historical Memoir of Pimería Alta*, Vol. II, p. 136).

of the South were becoming depopulated on account of the epidemics sent by God (as may be believed), in punishment of the wickedness of the Pericùes. The several epidemics which came in 1742, 1744, and 1748 made such havoc on that nation that scarcely a sixth part of them escaped death. The labors of the missionaries during those unfortunate years cannot be fully stated, since they were occupied all day and a great part of the night in giving spiritual and corporeal aid to the sick.

The Uchitas, who were a branch of the Guaicura nation, suffered a similar loss at that time, and even greater in proportion than the Pericùes. When the Uchitas had taken up arms against other Christians and had continued stubbornly in their hostile undertakings, the lieutenant of the captain-governor of the presidio of San José declared war on them as enemies and killed many of them; others died afterward in the epidemics. Thus their number kept decreasing, until in 1767 only one single member remained alive.

Therefore, since the number of the neophytes of the southern Missions had decreased so much, it was necessary to reduce the number of the Missions. With this purpose in view it was arranged that the Pericùes, who resided in the Mission of Santa Rosa, should go and stay at Santiago and be added to that Mission; and likewise the few at the Mission of San José who survived the repeated calamities of their nation should be sent there. It was ordered also that the place of La Paz, the country which was lacking in water, should be abandoned and that those tribes of the Guaicuras who inhabit it should go together with their missionary to that of Santa Rosa, now depopulated. Since the principal village of this Mission was called Todos Santos,[15] that Mission took this name.

This arrangement was useful to the neophytes—they went to a place better than that which they inhabited—and it was useful also to the rest of California, because, with the suppression of those two unnecessary Missions, the two missionaries who were spared could be used with more advantage in the northern Missions.

[15] "All Saints."

California suffered greatly at this time not only from the war with the Uchitas and from the epidemics which depopulated the southern countries but also from the loss of five men of importance who were well deserving of the peninsula; namely: Father Bravo in 1744, Father Tempis and the captain-governor in 1746, Father Sistiaga in 1747, and Father Guillen in 1748—all worthy of our memory and our praise.

Father Jaime Bravo, an Aragonese, reached California in 1705 in company with Father Salvatierra and remained there for thirty-nine years, working as a missionary and as procurator to the great advantage of the Missions and leading a life no less laborious than exemplary. He established and guided the abolished Mission of La Paz for eight years; he built a large church in Loreto, the house of the missionary-procurator, and a good boat which served that colony for twenty-five years. He died May 13, 1744, at the Mission of San Javier whither he had gone hoping to get well with that climate. His body was taken to Loreto and buried in the church which he himself built.

Father Antonio Tempis was born[16] in Bohemia. He went to Mexico in 1736, and during the same year was sent to California and was appointed to re-establish the Mission of Santiago, previously destroyed in the rebellion of the Pericùes. Led on by their hatred of Christianity the Pericùes had demolished the church and the houses, and laid waste the fields; but they surrendered, although obliged by the force of arms rather than induced by the desire of the Christian life. Nevertheless Father Tempis with his great charity, his incomparable sweetness, and the extraordinary and constant examples of his life caused them to become so fond of the doctrine of Jesus Christ that they were reduced to good habits and to the occupations of civilized life so well that in three or four years that Mission, in spiritual as well as in temporal matters, was put in a better condition than it had been before it was destroyed.

Because he knew that there is nothing more important than a good education to improve a people, he took particular care

---

[16] Austria, in 1703. Father Tempis was educated at Prague and became a distinguished scholar. He came to the peninsula when thirty-three years old and died at the Mission of Santiago in 1746.

of his children, whom he always kept near him and in his sight; he instructed them frequently; he corrected them as a father; and he had them do some labor suitable to their age and strength in order to get them accustomed to work. Zeal for the glory of his Creator compelled him to make all possible efforts to eradicate all kinds of sins; but this zeal was so tempered by prudence and gentleness that no one had any reason to complain of him. Although he was so insistent in seeking the good of others and so compassionate toward all, he showed particular protection and tenderness for the sick, feeding them, taking care of them, consoling them, and helping them with all the aids necessary to the health and the soul of each one; he did this with such devotion that it seemed as if the one receiving his attention was the only neophyte commended to his spiritual care.

This great charity was more evident in the epidemics which so afflicted the southern Missions. At that time he worked to excess. Sometimes, although he was ill and so weak that he could not stand, he had himself carried by his neophytes to places many miles distant from Santiago to help the sick; and at times he dragged himself along to help others near by. The extent of his heroic patience in tribulations was reduced by him to this laconic expression, which he always had on his lips: "All work is for the love of God."

This saying became not less familiar to the soldiers who accompanied him than to his neophytes, who availed themselves of it profitably in any adversity, however slight. The radiant examples of his life won for him the reputation of a saint among those who witnessed them and who also related extraordinary things of him, which the populace considered as miraculous. But as we do not believe them at all superior to the forces of nature, we do not doubt that they were probably some divine gifts from Heaven, attained by the merit of this faithful servant of God. Finally, after ten years of truly apostolic tasks, Father Tempis died, piously, at his Mission of Santiago[17]; and

[17] He served only at the Mission of Santiago, and here he wrote *Noticia de la fundación y estado de la misión de Santiago de Californias y de sus Pueblos Santa María y San Borja.*

three years later, in 1749, a short account of his blameless life was printed in Mexico.

Father Sebastián de Sistiaga, one of the most industrious and famous missionaries of California, was born in 1684 in Tepozcolula, a place of some importance in the province of Misteca of New Spain. In the Jesuit Society, which he entered while still young, he made himself esteemed not only for his integrity but also for his fine mind. When he was a professor of belles-lettres in Mexico in 1718 he was appointed by his superiors to California in the manner elsewhere stated. During those twenty-nine years in which he guided, in succession, the Missions of Mulegè and San Ignacio he converted a very considerable number of barbarians and spread the doctrine of Jesus Christ from one sea to another with unspeakable hardships.

All the barbarians who came to the Missions to be instructed in the faith were supported, according to the early custom of California, at the expense of the missionaries during the time that their instruction lasted. Whenever Father Sistiaga lacked provisions to feed the catechumen he took a little sack of corn and dried meat for his food and set out to look for the savages in their own retreats, perhaps forty or fifty miles distant from the Mission; and there he stayed more or less time, according as it was necessary, preaching, catechising, baptizing, confessing, and leading, as regards the existence of the body, a life similar to that of the savages, without a house and without a bed, exposed day and night to the open air, and deprived of all the comforts of life. With this manner of living he was accustomed to sleep always dressed. Thus he was quite ready to get up, as he did every day two hours before daybreak, to engage in the practice of prayer and prepare himself for Holy Mass.

Making some apostolic excursion at times through the woods in company with some of his neophytes, and inspired by zeal and with kindled face, he used to break into these calls: "Come, all of you, come to the faith of Jesus Christ. Oh! If I could only make all of you Christians and take you to Paradise." His heart was so freed from earthly things that when the waves of the sea during a storm had cast many mother-of-pearl on the beach of his Mission and when these were presented to him by the Indians, he ordered them returned at once to the sea without even wishing to open them. But his rare delicacy of conscience occasioned him such a tempest of scruples that (being almost useless through them for the duties of a missionary) he was, to his regret, obliged to leave the Missions. The superiors sent him to Mexico [City] and afterward to the Puebla de Los Angeles, where I had the good luck to know him in the last year of his life and to be present at his blessed death, which happened on June 22, 1756.

Father Clemente Guillen was a native of Zacatecas, a city of New Spain. After he had become a professor of philosophy in Mexico [City] he was sent by his superiors to the Missions of California, where he arrived in 1714, after having been shipwrecked and having suffered other very serious mishaps, and where he remained for thirty-four years, working gloriously until his death. He established the Mission of the Virgin of Dolores in the country of the Guaicuras, the most barren part of that peninsula; and in the twenty-five years which he governed[18] it, he converted, with great hardship, the larger part of those fierce barbarians. In 1746 the superior of those Missions, seeing him very weak with years, work, and sickness, freed him from the charge of that Mission, sending him to Loreto to rest. But even there he continued working as much as it was possible for him; and he gave a rare example of devotion, because, when an old Indian woman whose language the missionaries did not understand arrived at that Mission from a very remote land, he set about learning the language, at the age of seventy years, with the sole object of instructing that poor woman; and in this heroic practice of charity death overcame him in 1748.

Don Estevan Rodríguez Lorenzo, of whom mention has been made so many times in this history, was a native of Algarve, a country under the crown of Portugal, from which he went while he was still a young man to Seville[19] and thence to

---

[18] During this time Father Guillen wrote *Noticias de la Misión de lo Dolores del Sur de California, alias S. Juan Talibat o Liquí; y de sus Pueblo Concepción, Encarnación, Trinidad, Redención y Resurrección.* This manuscript was used by Venegas.

[19] One of the most historic cities of Europe, having a population of

Mexico, where he was *major-domo* for some years of an estate belonging to the Jesuit College of Tepotzotlán. In 1697 when Father Salvatierra, the former rector of that college, undertook his first voyage to California, the *major-domo* (Rodríguez) was engaged to accompany him in the status of a soldier after he had been made to understand the inconveniences and dangers that were incident to that undertaking. In 1701 he was made captain-governor by the votes of his companions whom Father Salvatierra selected to make the appointment; he filled this office with great approbation for more than forty years, winning the esteem of the missionaries and the respect of the soldiers and the Indians with his good conduct.

He added to great bravery a constancy superior to the greatest difficulties, rare prudence, the highest integrity in the administration of justice, and, above all, exemplary piety, good habits, and great zeal for the glory of God. He devoutly attended Holy Mass daily and all the other religious exercises which were practiced in the church of Loreto. The missionaries confessed themselves debtors, in a great measure, to him for the progress of Christianity in California.

Whenever a new Mission was to be established, he would accompany the missionary with some soldiers to the appointed place and remain there with him for some time, not only to defend the missionary against any offense whatsoever from the barbarians toward his person but also to help him in opening the road, preparing the tillable ground, and constructing the rude buildings which served in the beginning as the church and dwelling. He was the first in all those works, inducing his soldiers and Indians by his example to do likewise. And so the tasks were ended very soon; otherwise, without him, it would have necessitated considerable time to complete them.

He often gave proof that the attraction of wealth was not capable of deflecting his honesty or inducing him to commit any act that might seem unlawful or unbecoming of him. Once

---

400,000 in the eighth century. Today it is scarcely half this size. In 1026 Seville became the capital of the Moorish kingdom, and when Spain was united it became the capital of the nation. Shortly after the discovery of the New World, Seville became one of the chief commercial centers of the world.

when he arrived at the island of San José, the Indians offered him a great quantity of pearls for the sword which he wore at his belt; but he absolutely did not wish to make that bargain (although highly advantageous to him) because he considered it disgraceful for a soldier to despoil himself of his weapons for any gain whatsoever. In 1744, after he became useless for service in the militia by reason of his blindness, the superior of those Missions obtained from the viceroy a communication that his office devolve on his son, Don Bernardo Rodríguez de Larrea. But he could not get that worthy soldier, who was an octogenarian and blind and who had served the king for forty-seven years with such faithfulness, even the miserable pension which is given any disabled soldier whatsoever to live on during the rest of his life. It is true that he did not need it, because he was sure of having an abundance of all that was necessary from the piety of his good son and from the charity and gratitude of the missionaries. Finally he died like a good Christian, on November 1, 1746.

Don Bernardo Rodríguez inherited the Christian and military virtues but not the robustness of his father. Some complaints from which he suffered became so aggravated in the six years which he governed California that he died in 1750. He was succeeded by Don Fernando Javier de Rivera y Moncada,[20]

[20] When the first expedition was sent to Upper California by the viceroy in 1769 to found a Mission there, Rivera was placed in command by Governor Portolá and commissioned to collect livestock among the Missions of the peninsula to take along. Beginning at Loreto, Rivera went north asking the various settlements for supplies. He collected one hundred and forty mules broken to work and forty-eight good horses. Assembling these animals and some cattle at Vellicatá, an Indian village about one hundred miles south of the present city of San Diego, he started north on May 24. With him went three muleteers, about forty Indians, and twenty-five leather-jacket soldiers, so called because they wore thick jackets made of cow hide, without sleeves, which protected them from the deadly arrows of the Indians. Father Juan Crespi, famous traveler and diarist, also accompanied him. When Portolá left San Diego to find Monterey Bay, Rivera accompanied him. On their return, after a fruitless attempt to find this bay, Rivera was sent from San Diego to Vellicatá in May 1770 to get some cattle. He returned with one hundred and sixty-four head.

Later he was placed in command of the presidio at Monterey, Upper California, much against the wishes of Father Junípero Serra, who had recom-

who had served with approbation in the peninsula and who afterward conducted himself in his new office as a worthy successor of that celebrated Portuguese.

Chapter Four

THE APOSTOLIC TRIPS OF FATHER CONSAG. THE MISSION OF SANTA GERTRUDIS AND ITS MISSIONARY, FATHER RETZ

FOR a long time the establishment of new Missions toward the north had been desired but had been prevented by the revolutions of the Pericùes and, partly, by the scarcity of missionaries. While waiting for them to come from Mexico, Fathers Sistiaga and Consag had made various trips from their Mission of San Ignacio, not less to make the savages favorably disposed to receive the Gospel than to seek places suitable for establishing new Missions. After Father Sistiaga retired from California in 1747, Father Consag, for his part, continued that laborious enterprise and so exerted himself that in 1751 he had already converted, catechised, and baptized five hundred and forty-eight Indians of those who were to belong to the proposed new Mission; but he could find no place suitable for establishing it except a location more than eighty miles distant from San Ignacio toward the north which had only a single spring of water and that so scanty that it did not suffice to irrigate the soil there which is capable of cultiva-

mended to the viceroy the appointment of José Francisco Ortega. Rivera came from Sonora to the Mission of San Gabriel with some soldiers and there met Juan Baptista de Anza, who had come overland from Mexico with a few soldiers. The two men had a quarrel, and Rivera would then give no order to establish a Mission and a presidio on the bay of San Francisco. These were not founded until two years later. In June, 1781, while Rivera was leading a party of colonists from Sonora to Upper California, escorted by twelve soldiers, the Indians attacked them at Yuma, Arizona, and he and every soldier with him were killed. The women and children were made captives. For the great importance of this event, see Chapman, *A History of California: The Spanish Period*, chapters xxvi and xxvii.

tion. But, as another better place could not be found and since the Mission was necessary, he decided to establish it in that place.

The pious Marqués de Villapuente, on making the donation of capital for the founding of the Mission of San José del Cabo, had declared that whenever that Mission was deemed unnecessary he wished the money to be used in the endowment of another Mission in the Cochimì country which would be dedicated to Santa Gertrudis.[21] The situation foreseen by that illustrious founder had arrived, since that Mission which had been at San José until the year 1730 had been moved from there because the Pericùes had decreased so much and because its people had been added to the Mission of Santiago, although thirty miles distant.

But Father Consag, before establishing the new Mission, wanted to make another longer trip than the previous ones, in order to penetrate as far inland as possible toward the north in search of places to establish new Missions. With this purpose in mind he left San Ignacio in May 1751, accompanied by the new captain, Don Fernando de Rivera, a sufficient number of soldiers, one hundred neophytes, and many animals loaded with provisions and water. The reason for taking such a numerous following with him was to avoid the disasters which otherwise might have happened, because if they had to travel over unknown countries and among barbarians who had no information about Christianity, the natives, on seeing a few strangers enter their lands, would inevitably have attacked them, and misfortunes would have occurred on the one hand or the other; on the contrary, their number being large, no one would dare to commit any hostile acts against them. Moreover, in that mountainous and roadless country many men were necessary to open up roads and prepare them for travel.

Father Consag set out in the direction of the mountains which face the Pacific Sea, because it had been observed that streams were less rare on that side than in all the country of the

---

[21] See Bolton, *Palóu*, Vol. I, p. 52, for the aid this Mission gave those in Upper California.

peninsula known up to that time. But after he had traveled in circles for two months and gone inland as far as 30° or more, he could not find any place with sufficient water for a Mission. After approaching 30° on a path where they intended going, they saw a branch of *pitajo* pierced with arrows which told how the barbarians threatened to use (in that manner) those who dared to pass beyond that boundary. But our travelers went forward without paying attention to those threats; and the barbarians did not venture to commit any hostilities against them. On the other hand, they received them as friends; and, greatly astonished on seeing horses, they begged the captain to permit them to lead the animals to graze near that place where their relatives lived so that they might see them also.

The captain consented in order to please them, and the barbarians never wearied of studying those large and beautiful animals, so docile to the will of man. This unfortunate and very expensive trip was not useless, although what was sought was not obtained; it served to reconcile the savages, to make them like Christianity, and to open the door of Heaven with baptism for the babies who were dangerously sick and who in fact died.

After Father Consag returned to San Ignacio, he sent some of his neophytes, already accustomed to work, to the place destined for the new Mission so that they could build the church and the necessary houses under the direction of a celebrated blind Indian called Andrés Comanajì, who was also known by the name of Sistiaga, having been thus named from his teacher and father in Christ, Father Sebastián de Sistiaga. Comanajì had been the first catechist in the Mission of Mulegè, and he held the same office later with the greatest praise in the Missions of San Ignacio and Santa Gertrudis until the expulsion[22] of the Jesuits. His exemplary integrity, the zeal which he showed for the conversion of his countrymen, the particular charm which he had for explaining to them and making them understand the mysteries of our religion, his constancy in their

---

[22] The order for the expulsion was issued by King Charles III in 1767, and in January 1768 the Jesuits left Lower California.

instruction, and his unalterable patience in enduring the restlessness of the children and the rudeness of the catechumen whom he taught made the name of Andrés famous and won for him the esteem of the missionaries and the soldiers and the respect and veneration of the Indians. He frequently strengthened his blameless soul with the holy sacraments; and all the time that he was not engaged in the catechism or in providing the necessities of life he was in the church praying with great devotion.

It is not to be wondered at that a blind man should have been director and architect of those buildings, because they were so crude that they did not need the rules of architecture. His skill was such that his touch was substituted for the lack of sight. The frame of those rustic buildings was of wood, and the walls were of mud and small stones; the roof was also of wood and of twigs or canes covered with reeds. The four very heavy timbers which were set upright in the four corners of each room were forked, like those which supported the roof, and to them they tied the cross beams of the walls (as well as the twigs or cane of the roof) securely by means of leather thongs; so in these buildings neither plumb-bob, nor hammer, nor nails, nor lime was used. These were the best buildings that were constructed at the Missions in the beginning, usually only cabins or mere bowers. But when the Missions acquired stability with the passing of time, the neophytes began to shake off the laziness of savage life and secured better materials for building; and then good churches and more comfortable dwellings were constructed.

When the buildings of Santa Gertrudis were finished, Father Jorge Retz,[23] a German who had been at the Mission of San Ignacio from the year before and who had learned the Cochimì language, went to establish that Mission in the summer of 1752. Each one of the missionaries, according to the regular practice in the country, contributed what he could for the new establishment by giving some goats, sheep, horses, mules, and any

[23] Born in Conflanz, Germany, in 1717, Father Jorge Retz became a Jesuit at the age of sixteen. He served at Santa Gertrudis Mission until the expulsion, and was superior of the peninsula Missions from 1756 to 1762.

Fig. 25 – The mission church at Santa Gertrudis. It is likely that this stone structure dates from Dominican rather than Jesuit times.

George E. Lindsay

Homer Aschmann

Fig. 26a — The site of Mission San Borja, looking west. Local residents say that the adobe ruins on the near side of the stone church include the Franciscan church; they may, however, be of Jesuit origin. The stone buildings were constructed by the Dominicans.

Hugh Manessier

Fig. 26b — The mission church at San Borja. This is the most northerly of the stone missions.

quantity of provisions. With this help, which the missionaries gave mutually, many needs were satisfied and the progress of the Missions was hastened. Father Retz began his with six hundred neophytes, catechised and baptized by Father Consag; but as these gave information to the gentiles (their neighbors) about the new religion, the necessity of baptism for salvation, and the kind treatment of the missionaries, they began to come in troops of thirty, fifty, or seventy persons asking for baptism.

In a few years Father Retz, assisted by the tireless Andrés Comanají, the catechist, had as many as a thousand and four hundred neophytes under his care. As soon as one of the catechumen was baptized, the missionary, according to the custom long before introduced into the peninsula, gave him a little cross, which he was asked to wear always hanging from his neck so that it might serve him as the insignia of his faith and always incite him to the memory of redemption.

Only agriculture was lacking to make the Mission strong and prosperous, but all that soil was very gravelly and devoid of water. Nevertheless scarcely two months had passed after the establishment of that Mission before a small spring was found in a place not very far from it; and almost a mile below it a small tract of land was found which was suitable for cultivation, to which water was taken by a narrow ditch made in the solid rock. Near this another small field was made with earth carried from another place and spread over the stones, as was customary in that peninsula, using all the economy possible in order not to lose any of the little water. Besides some fruit trees they had planted a vineyard also, which gave good wine in due time.

In a few years the cultivated fields produced all the wheat and corn that the Mission needed. But to get this result it was necessary to sow the two seeds successively in the same land. The sowing of grain was done in October, and the harvest was reaped in May; this was followed by the fertilization of the land and the new ploughing for planting the corn in June, which was gathered at the end of September; and then the same earth was worked again in order to sow the wheat the following month.

The method of keeping the wine was also singular. Since hogsheads were unknown in California and Father Retz could not have those large earthen jars which were used in the other Missions, he decided to make use of some of those very large rocks which are abundant in that country. He had them hollowed out like sepulchers and covered with boards painted with pitch. The wine was poured in, and it kept well in such vessels.

The success of this Mission revived the ardent zeal of Father Consag. Not even on the voyage which he made to the Red River in 1746 had he been able to find any place suitable for establishing a Mission on all the eastern coast of the peninsula. Nor during the trip of 1751 could he find one in that part of the mountains which face the Pacific Sea. Therefore he needed to look only in that part of the same mountains which face the Gulf. With this purpose the missionary himself undertook a third trip in the spring of 1753; it was no less toilsome and no more successful than the second. He went inland as far as 31°; but he did not find anything but immense stony tracts which were very hard on the horses.

Chapter Five

+++

THE DIFFICULTIES ARE OVERCOME WHICH HALTED THE ADVANCE OF THE MISSIONS TOWARD THE NORTH. FATHER CONSAG DIES. HIS EULOGY

CAPITAL was needed to endow the Missions and places to establish them so that they might advance toward the north, as the missionaries desired. And while there was no hope of either, God moved the spirit of a remarkable and very noble benefactress. She was the Duchess of Gandía, Doña María de Borja,[24] who thought, after having found out about the sterility of these countries, the poverty of

---

[24] See footnote 128, Book II, p. 156, *supra*. Antonia Lanza also endowed the Mission of San Borja (Bolton, *Palóu*, Vol. I, p. 205).

the Indians, and the apostolic works and tasks of the missionaries through a servant of hers who had been a soldier in California, that she could do nothing more pleasing to God than to spend her wealth in helping these Missions. She arranged, therefore, in her will, that after taking out of her unencumbered properties the large pensions which she left to her domestics during their lifetimes all the remainder should go to the missionaries of California, together with the principals from these pensions after the deaths of the legatees, and that a Mission should be founded in the peninsula consecrated to the honor of her very famous ancestor, San Francisco de Borja.

The sum of money acquired by this will in favor of the Missions amounted, in 1767, to sixty thousand *scudi*; and almost as much more was to be received after the deaths of the pensioned domestics, besides some heavy debts which were expected to be collected. Many Missions could be endowed in California with such an immense capital; and in fact they would have been founded if the Jesuits had not been compelled to leave the peninsula during the said year.

Then it was necessary to overcome the other obstacles relative to the place for establishing the proposed Mission; but the Master desired that it should be overcome in 1758, because Father Retz, having found out from some of his neophytes that there was an abundant spring in a place called Adac, which was almost three days' journey distant from Santa Gertrudis toward the north, sent some persons in whom he had confidence to see it and observe the soil. In fact they found the spring on the slope of a hill a short distance from the port of Los Angeles on the eastern coast. There they noticed that the water gushed out hot and with a sulphurous odor, that in cooling it lost all that odor and became drinkable, and that, although it was not so abundant as those Indians had said, it was sufficient to irrigate the tillable soil which was there.

Father Consag had approached quite near the spring of Adac on his last trip, but he neither saw it nor had any information about it. Since he was superior of California when this place was discovered, he greatly desired to establish that new Mission for which he had worked so diligently; but he did not succeed in this regard, because he died in September 1759, at the age of fifty-six years.

He was a native of Austria where he entered the Company of the Jesuits. After having gone to Mexico, he was sent by the superiors to California in 1732. During the first five years of his residence there he successively guided several Missions which lacked missionaries; and during the other twenty-two years he was at the Mission of San Ignacio, first in company with Father Sistiaga and afterward alone, taking care not only of numerous converts but also of the gentiles who should have belonged to the Mission of Santa Gertrudis, six hundred of whom he converted, catechised, and baptized.

It is not easy to number the miles which this indefatigable man traveled on his continual trips to the lands of his Mission, on the many journeys made among the gentiles, or to that of the Red River, and on the visit which he made as superior to all the Missions of the peninsula; and what is most remarkable is that he was almost always sick. When he halted on his trips to rest his companions and the animals, he would get on his knees and pray, overlooking the repose of the body for that of the soul. In fact, on account of his exemplary virtues and apostolic tasks, the name of Consag deserves to be placed among those of the illustrious men of California.

Chapter Six

THE LACK AND THE CONSTRUCTION OF SHIPS. THE DEATH AND THE EULOGY OF BROTHER MUGAZABAL

For a long time the peninsula had needed boats for the transportation of necessities for the presidio and the Missions. The sloop "Lauretana," ordered made by Father Bravo, was in such bad condition because of the continuous trips of so many years that it was feared it would become useless in a little while. The boat "San José" (bought at the expense of the royal treasury), besides being very small, was made of such bad wood that it needed to be calked frequently. For these reasons the viceroy,[25] by virtue of the statements made to him by Father Juan Armesto,[26] previously a missionary of California and then procurator of the Missions in Mexico, had commanded that a boat be built in Realejo, a port of Nicaragua. This cost the king more than nineteen thousand *scudi*, besides the expense of its conveyance to Acapulo. From here it left for California at the expense of the missionaries, but before arriving, it was destroyed by a storm on the rocks of Purùm near Cape San Lucas. The crew, which saved itself on the land near by, was taken to the Mission of Santiago and supported for two months by the missionary, Father Francisco de Escalante.[27] Thus this boat, instead of being useful, brought loss to the Missions.

When the viceroy was informed of this misfortune he permitted a new boat to be built in California at the expense of the royal treasury. With this purpose Father Lucas Ventura,[28] the procurator of the Missions in Loreto, had a considerable quantity of cedar wood brought from Matanchel; and for the curved timbers which were needed for the construction, he had some mesquites, or acacias, cut at Londò, which wood is very hard and suitable for such work.

The master-workman was an Indian from the Philippine

[25] The Marqués de las Amarillas, Agustín de Ahumada, who held this office from 1755 to 1760. He was a distinguished soldier, having won fame in the wars with Italy. He died in Mexico City. The absence of graft during his administration may be judged from the fact that the government had to pay his wife's transportation to Spain (Herbert Ingram Priestley, *The Mexican Nation*, p. 185).

[26] Born in Cristóbal, Spain, in 1713, Father Juan Armesto came to Lower California in 1748. Five years later he was sent to Mexico City to act as procurator there. His place at Loreto was filled by Father Juan Javier Bischoff, a Bohemian Jesuit, who came to the peninsula in 1752. Armesto died in Bologna in 1799.

[27] Born in Jaen in 1724, Father Francisco de Escalante became a Jesuit at the age of twenty, and died in the place of his birth in 1806.

[28] Born in Aragón, Spain, in 1727, Father Lucas Ventura came to Lower California in 1757. From this time until the expulsion of the Jesuits his name is found on the register of the Mission of Loreto (Bancroft, *History of the North Mexican States and Texas*, Vol. I, p. 470). He died in 1793. He wrote *Historia Natural de Californias* while living in Italy. This history has been printed.

Islands named Gaspar de Molina, who had given no proof of his skill in this art even in the years that he had been at times in California and at times in Sinaloa; nevertheless he constructed a large, strong, sailboat, well-proportioned and fast, and in fact as good as the most excellent shipwright could have made. It cost more than eighteen thousand *scudi;* but the procurator did not want to expend more than ten thousand on the account of the king and also in consideration of the expenses borne by the royal treasury on the boat lost a short time before.

Father Ventura, encouraged by the success of this enterprise, wanted the same Indian (Molina) to build at the expense of the missionaries another boat slightly smaller than the first but equally perfect; and he did build it just as he wanted it. These two boats, the best that there had been in California, were turned over to the royal commissioner[29] when the Jesuits left the peninsula.

[29] Gaspar Portolá, born in 1723 in the village of Balaguer in the Pyrenees Mountains in Catalonia. At the early age of eleven years he began his military life and a few years later joined the royal army. At twenty-one he was appointed *alférez*, and about ten years later he became lieutenant in the army. He served in this capacity for more than twenty years, seeing active service in Portugal and in Italy. When he arrived in Mexico, he was sent to the frontier presidios in Sinaloa and in Sonora. The visitor-general of Mexico, José de Gálvez, selected Portolá to go to Lower California and collect the Jesuits when the order for expulsion came from the king.

The next year Portolá was ordered by Gálvez to establish two Missions and two presidios in what is now the state of California. One site was to be at the bay of San Diego and the other at Monterey Bay. For this purpose supplies were collected from the Missions in Lower California. Portolá sent two ships to the bay of San Diego, while he and Captain Rivera came up the Peninsula, each leading separate units. All the forces were united at San Diego on July 1, 1769. Eight days later Portolá started north to locate Monterey Bay. He took with him Fathers Crespi and Gómez, fifteen Indians, two servants, Captain Rivera, Sergeant Ortega, who commanded twenty-five soldiers, Lieutenant Fages, who had six Catalán soldiers, and Miguel Costansó, a map maker. In October they reached the bay of San Francisco. They were the first white men to see this great "inland sea."

They returned to San Diego, having failed to find Monterey Bay. After a rest of a few weeks, Portolá again marched north to look for this bay. This time he found it; and, after a Mission and a presidio had been founded there, he left by boat for Mexico City. He was made governor of the state of Puebla in 1779, and later became a lieutenant-colonel in the Spanish army. Portolá never returned to California. A new governor was sent to Puebla in

During the same year (1759) in which the boat previously built at Realejo was lost, the Mission of Dolores also lost a boat which it used for the transportation of necessities. On account of the great sterility of that land, the Mission needed all the provisions that could be brought in from elsewhere. When a certain question had excited the Indian rowers on a trip which the boat was making, the master of the boat, who was a Sinaloan Indian of very good habits and helpful to the Mission, managed to pacify them; but he received his death as the reward of his kindness, because one of the contenders, indignant at him, killed him with a blow of a stone on his head; and to avoid due punishment he agreed with the other nine or ten companions of his (all Guaicuras) to circulate the report that the boat had been broken to pieces on a reef in the midst of a fierce storm and the master had been drowned because he was not so good a swimmer as they.

To gain credence they purposely destroyed the boat and scattered the fragments, the sail, the rigging, and the cargo here and there; but when this news reached Loreto the captain-governor, suspecting what had really happened, went to the Mission of Dolores, and there he made investigations such that he discovered the truth. All the Indians openly confessed to the act; and for this reason he condemned the murderer to death and punished the others with lighter penalties. But Father Lamberto Hostel,[30] who guided that Mission from then on, did not wish to have a boat, depriving himself of that convenience in order not to expose his neophytes to similar misfortunes; and he had all the necessities brought to him by land, although from very distant places and over bad roads.

More lamentable than those losses was that which California suffered in 1761 in the death of Brother Juan Bautista Muga-

---

1784, and Portolá returned immediately to Spain. See *Sunset Magazine*, October 1909, pp. 337–51; also *San Francisco Call*, October 3, 17, 1909 (supplement).

[30] A German Jesuit born in Münster, Germany, in 1706, Father Lamberto Hostel came to California in 1745. He wrote *Noticia y Descripción de la Misión de S. Luis Gonzaga y de sus Pueblos, S. Juan Nepomuceno y la Magdalena*. Venegas used this manuscript.

zabal, who had been very useful not less in his personal services than with the examples of his saintly life during those fifty-seven years that he lived there. He was a native of the province of Alava in Spain; from here he went to California in 1704. He was first a soldier there, and afterward an *alférez* until 1720, always leading an irreproachable life. During that year he became a coadjutor of the Jesuits, and, having learned the science of the saints in the school of that great master, Father Juan de Ugarte, he became a perfect religious. He was entrusted for almost forty years with the warehouse of the Missions and the presidio established at Loreto, with the payment of the soldiers and sailors, with the boats, the purchase of necessary supplies, and their conveyance to all the Missions.

Besides this, he also acted as sacristan of Loreto and sometimes as catechist, conducting himself in such callings with diligence, humbleness, modesty, and devotion, as he did in all the practices of religious life. His constancy in prayer for so many years had worn away the bricks of the church floor on which he had been accustomed to kneel; but neither this continuous application of his mind to the things of Heaven nor his laborious work as agent of the affairs of the Missions and presidios nor the discipline, cilices, and fasts (with which he frequently tormented his body) nor the unhealthfulness of that climate prevented him from reaching eighty years of age; he served the Master faithfully until his last breath, and left the pleasant fragrance of his virtues after his death.

Chapter Seven

THE MISSION OF SAN FRANCISCO DE BORJA AND ITS MISSIONARY, FATHER LINK

THE AFFAIRS of the proposed Mission of San Francisco de Borja, meanwhile, were not forgotten. Father José Rotea, who reached California in 1759, was appointed to establish it; but as that of San Ignacio was left unoccupied during that year by the death of Father Consag, he was invested with its guidance, since the Missions already established would not be abandoned to found new ones. Father Retz, nevertheless, after having reduced to Christianity almost all of the gentiles of the vast territory of his Mission, devoted himself also to reducing many tribes of those who were to belong to the new Mission. He also had a road opened that joined the two Missions, and he had the necessary buildings constructed in Adac; to wit, the church, the dwellings of the missionary and the soldiers, a warehouse, and a hospital. He also worked the small amount of land there which was capable of cultivation, and he sowed corn.

All this was done before Father Wenceslao Link[31] (a native of Bohemia) appointed to guide the Mission, went to that place. He arrived in California in the beginning of 1762, stayed some months at Santa Gertrudis, learning the Cochimí language, and in the summer of the same year moved to Adac, accompanied by some soldiers. He made a beginning of his Mission with three hundred neophytes who were converted, catechised, and baptized by Father Retz; and soon afterward many gentiles from the surrounding countries began to come to it with the intent of becoming Christians.

But in a new Mission situated in a barren country, it was not possible to support so many catechumen, besides the soldiers and all those who were employed in the service of the same. It is true that the territory of Adac abounds in hares, rabbits, and other species of game; but as to vegetation, it had only *pitaje*, mescal, palms with tasteless dates, and a great quantity of those trees as strange as they are useless, called *milapà*, which we have described in Book I. Timber and firewood were also lacking, and pastures were not found. And so some of those sheep and goats which were taken there at the beginning died right away and the rest became so thin that it was necessary to take them out of that country so they would not die.

Since this Mission had no way to exist, it was necessary that the others help it, according to their custom. The nearest Mis-

---

[31] Born in Austria in 1736, Father Wenceslao Link became a Jesuit in 1754, and eight years later arrived in Lower California. He wrote a history of the Mission there in Latin, and his *Nachrichten von Californien* also describes the Mission life of the peninsula. He died in Vienna in 1772.

sion was that of Santa Gertrudis, which was ninety miles away; and it had almost nothing that it could give. The Mission of Guadalupe, about two hundred and forty miles distant, sent it dried meat. It received the other provisions and all it needed for divine worship (as well as clothing for the missionary, soldiers, and neophytes), for agriculture, and the other things of prime necessity, from Loreto, which was more than three hundred miles distant. These things which were sent from Loreto went by sea as far as the port of Los Angeles (twenty-four miles from Adac) in a boat which was given that Mission by the procurator of Loreto to use in this transportation; but as this voyage was dangerous on account of the frequent storms and the violent and contrary currents of the islands of Salsipuedes, and as the Californians were not skilled in navigation, the command of the boat was given to an upright Indian of Sinaloa, called Buenaventura de Ahome, who served the Mission also in other offices with the greatest diligence and faithfulness all the time that he was not at sea.

Father Link selected some apt young men from among his neophytes to learn seamanship by sailing in company with this one from Sinaloa, just as he had others learn agriculture under the direction of a soldier who understood it. In the first year he cut a small crop from the little amount of corn which Father Retz had sown at the proper time; but having discovered and cultivated another small tract of tillable land and having followed in both pieces of land the practice (already used in the Mission of Santa Gertrudis) of sowing wheat and corn in succession in the same field, he harvested a much greater quantity, although not so much as he needed for the consumption of the Mission. He had planted a small kitchen garden in which several plants had grown from the seeds which he had brought from Mexico, and he waited until they were a little larger in order to transplant them; but he lost all of the plants through the stupidity of the Indians, because he had to carry the sacred viaticum to a soldier who was seriously ill. He ordered his neophytes to sweep the street and scatter herbs on it; and not finding better ones than those in the kitchen garden of the missionary, they pulled up all these and scattered them on the street. Father Link, on leaving with the blessed sacrament, noticed that he was walking on the fruit of his own labor; but he made a voluntary sacrifice of it to the Creator.

Almost eighteen months after the Mission was established they had not been able to find pastures in all that territory. When the captain-governor had come there and had insisted on looking for them again, he finally found a level place with water and sufficient grazing for eight hundred head of stock on a hill twenty-four miles distant from Adac. Scarcely had the other missionaries received notice of this discovery (so advantageous to the Mission) than they sent horses and cows there, and from then on they had fresh meat. When the animals were taken to this place in December 1763, snow, which had not been seen in all the rest of California, was observed on those hills. In Adac fresh fish also could be eaten, because fish are abundant in the port of Los Angeles; but Father Link deprived himself of this food in order to spare his neophytes the work of bringing it to him.

The prosperity of the Mission of San Francisco de Borja in temporal affairs was not comparable to what it had made in the progress of the Christian religion. After having been established with three hundred neophytes, it had increased notably, because the gentiles came in troops to be instructed and baptized; and in all the time that the Mission existed (until the expulsion of the Jesuits) catechumen were never lacking there. Father Link, seeing that the church which had been built in the beginning was small and poorly constructed, built another larger one. Almost thirty families of neophytes, besides the soldiers, lived continually in the village of Adac. There were, moreover, catechumen who were in actual instruction and a tribe of neophytes who had their homes in another place. Each week one of the outside tribes stayed there, as much to renew its instruction, to hear Mass, to receive the sacraments if they asked for them, and to engage in other acts of devotion as to cultivate the soil or to be trained in other duties in order that they might get used to work and avoid laziness, so harmful to good habits. On Sunday the tribe which had been there during the week went away and another came to be occupied in the same manner.

Chapter Eight

THE MISSION OF SAN FRANCISCO DE BORJA BECOMES RESTLESS, AND A REMEDY IS APPLIED THERE

THIS MISSION had to endure much opposition in the midst of its success, as happens to all the works for the glory of God. One tribe of savage gentiles who lived in a place ninety miles distant to the northeast from Adac, seeing that Mission established and that their countrymen went to it (in competition) to become Christians, and being unable to endure this new religion which checked their pernicious liberty and corrected their ancient habits, barbarously resolved to persecute, without giving quarter to anyone, all those who had embraced Christianity or who wished to accept it. Since they knew that the gentiles who lived between them and the neophytes had declared that they wished to become Christians, they fell armed on the nearest tribe and afterward on the others in succession, killing many and putting the rest to flight. The latter, having taken refuge among the Christians, threw everyone into consternation.

Father Retz, advised by Father Link, was of the opinion that they should take a stand against the barbarians and terrify them so that in the future they would not dare to begin similar hostilities; for otherwise (their vanity and pride having increased with that destruction) they would not cease to do all possible damage to the Christians. Not content with giving this advice, he ordered that a troop of his neophytes be well armed, so that after joining those of Adac and the soldiers they might go out to meet the enemies.

When this advice had been accepted and the small army equipped, an order was given to its leader to conduct himself on that expedition in such a way that without killing any of the enemies he might catch them all and conduct them to Adac as prisoners. This they did promptly because, having learned about the place where the enemies were camping, they approached very silently, and, falling on them suddenly, they caught them and tied them, without shooting an arrow or firing a harquebus; they burned their huts or bowers and took possession of their meager household goods. Led to Adac in triumph, they were imprisoned in the soldiers' house, whose corporal, acting as judge, informed the criminals that by using Christian clemency he had condemned them only to the punishment of floggings, although they were nevertheless deserving of the death penalty. This punishment was applied only to the twelve most culpable ones, with the same preparation exercised before in a similar case in the Mission of San Ignacio and by availing themselves of the same subtlety which Fathers Sistiaga and Luyando had used so successfully. Scarcely had eight or ten lashes been applied to each one of the criminals when Father Link came out and begged the judge to have the punishment stopped; and he agreed (informing the criminal) that if it were not for the mediation of that saintly Father, the minister of the All-Highest, he would have been treated with greater severity.

When this act of justice was terminated, the criminals were returned to their prison, whither the missionary went to feed them and delivered to them some useful exhortations. During the first days those Indians appeared excessively indignant and impatient; and one of them was so angered that he seemed frenzied or mad; but with the continuation of the punishment for seven or eight days and with the paternal advice and good offices of Father Link, they became more gentle and humble. As soon as they received the punishment for their offenses they were given liberty; and they went to their country with little desire of repeating their hostilities. Attracted in this way by the good order which reigned in Adac, by the peace and tranquillity which the Christians enjoyed there, and by the kindness with which they had been treated by the missionary, or (better said) induced by the power of the divine grace of God, they returned after some time with their families and relatives and with various other gentiles who had joined them to ask insistently for baptism. This they received after being well instructed and after giving sufficient proofs of the sincerity of their conversion.

A short time after that Mission was established, a *guama*,

who greatly regretted the damage which the conversion of his countrymen caused his interests, determined to dissuade them from Christianity by means of fear. To attain this end one night he lighted a great bonfire in Adac, and then he started to howl horribly around it. The bystanders on hearing those howls and on seeing the different and extraordinary colors which appeared in the flames, either through a true effect of the fuel or through the mere illusion of their exalted imaginations, became so afraid that they fled to the house of the missionary to put themselves under his protection. Father Link, informed of the event and with a whip in his hand, intrepidly approached the *guama;* but the latter fled without daring to wait for him. The neophytes, laying aside their fear, esteemed their missionary more from then on, because he had shown courage; and the *guama,* sincerely converted and baptized after some time, lived subsequently as a good Christian.

Chapter Nine

THE DEATH OF FATHER NEUMAYER. THE VOYAGE OF FATHER LINK

ON AUGUST 30, 1764, two years after the establishment of the Mission of San Francisco de Borja, Father Carlos Neumayer,[32] a German, died in the Mission of Todos Santos. He had been for some years in the Mission of Topia,[33] from which he was sent to those of California in 1745, always leading a truly apostolic life in each place, fearlessly facing the dangers of life in order not to fail his duty, and never sparing any work that might contribute to the glory of God and to the spiritual and temporal welfare of his neophytes. He acted as a day laborer, working the soil with his own hands; as a fisherman, standing in the water at times half-

---

[32] Father Carlos Neumayer came to the peninsula in 1745 and died at Todos Santos in 1764.

[33] The Mission of Topia had been founded on the mainland at the Indian village of Tepocas in 1699 by Padre Melchor Bartiromo.

way up his legs; as an architect, a mason, and a carpenter, building the church and the little dwellings of the Indians with his own hands; as a tailor, cutting and sewing their clothes; as a doctor and nurse, taking care of the sick and applying the remedies himself even to the most loathsome sores; finally, he did everything with all to win everybody for Christ. The needy and the distressed came to him as to a father, hoping to find help and consolation in his well-known charity. He died like a saint after having given great examples of patience in his last illness.

Two months before, two new missionaries, Father Victoriano Arnés[34] and Father Francisco Javier Franco,[35] had reached California. The latter was sent to Todos Santos to help Father Neumayer in his last illness and to succeed him in the guidance of that Mission. Father Arnés was appointed to San Francisco de Borja to aid Father Link while a place was being found in which to establish a new Mission.

Thus Father Link, having someone to substitute for him, was able to be absent for some days during the year 1765 to make a little voyage which he considered useful for the spread of Christianity. Since some of his neophytes who lived on the Gulf coast told him that they had observed fires on the island of Angel Custodio, twenty-four miles distant from the coast of California, he believed that some gentiles lived there to whom the Gospel had not been announced. He embarked, therefore, at the port of Los Angeles and went in that direction, accompanied by some soldiers and neophytes.

This island extends from southeast to northwest, beginning at about 30° 20′, and ending beyond the parallel of 31°. Its length, according to the map made by Father Consag, is about fifty miles, but its width does not exceed six. Father Link traversed a considerable part of it on foot without being able to find any inhabitants, animals, or water; and so all the rest of the

---

[34] Little is known of Father Arnés. He was born in 1736 and arrived in Lower California when twenty-eight years old.

[35] Born in 1738, Father Franco came to the peninsula in 1764. He and Father Arnés were the last Jesuits to go to Lower California before the expulsion.

country seemed to him. He would have liked to have examined it all, but a lack of water compelled him to give up the undertaking.

On returning to the port of Los Angeles they were much exhausted from thirst and annoyed by the very strong, foul winds, which drove them toward the island several times; and once, after having torn the sail, the wind overturned the boat in such a way that had it not been for the skillfulness of the master, the Sinaloan (Buenaventura de Ahome), and a soldier who righted it, surely all would have been drowned. Finally the weather grew calm, and they made the port of Los Angeles. Father Link was persuaded that the island was uninhabited and that the fires seen by his neophytes had been lighted by some Californians carried there on their rafts, or perhaps by some pearl fishermen who had come from Sinaloa.

The trip which Father Link himself made the following year by land to the Red River was not so unsuccessful. But before talking about it, it is necessary to cast a glance at the southern Missions, which it will perhaps appear we have forgotten for a long time. They ought to have as much consideration in this history on account of their repeated misfortunes as the northern Missions because of their fortunate progress.

Chapter Ten

A NEW CALAMITY FOR THE SOUTHERN MISSIONS. THE INIQUITOUS CLAIMS AND COMPLAINTS OF THE PERICÙES

THE EVILS occasioned in the southern part by the rebellion of the Pericùes and by the epidemics which reduced the population to a sixth were without doubt considerable. Afterwards (1748) the working of a silver mine was commenced, which was a new calamity for those Missions and a new source of disturbances and anxieties.

Don Manuel de Ocio, a former soldier of the presidio of Loreto, had been discharged from the militia to make a fortune in pearl fishing, from which, in fact, he became wealthy. But, observing later that the fishing was not very profitable, he devoted himself to working a silver mine at a place in the peninsula called Santa Ana, which was thirty-six miles from the Mission of Santiago. And with this purpose he brought workmen from New Spain; but as he did not also bring a priest to take care of them, it was necessary that the missionary of Santiago make a parish for them, going there frequently to say Holy Mass and to administer the sacraments.

This work was increased in 1756 when they began to work the mine of San Antonio, which was still more distant from the Mission. These services were performed by him only for the welfare of those souls and without the slightest temporal profit. Instead of receiving any recompense from it, generally he had to take food not only for himself and the two neophytes who accompanied him but also for some of the poor workmen.

In spite of this the superior of the Missions, fearing that the enemies of the Jesuits might make a pretext of slandering them for that very thing which was done solely for charity, urged Ocio so much that he compelled him to seek a priest in Guadalajara to secure the licenses necessary to make a parish at the mines. But as the latter became disgusted in two or three years and returned to his country and as another could not be found who wanted to succeed him, it was necessary for the missionary of Santiago to take up that toilsome burden again.

Since the workmen lacked provisions and did not have any place to obtain them, they could not help going to the Missions of Santiago and Todos Santos, which were the nearest, to provide themselves. The missionaries refused to sell them their provisions, because they needed them for their neophytes. In order to compel Ocio by this means to abandon the mines, which were slightly profitable to him and very harmful to that new Christianity, they certainly should not have yielded but have compelled him to seek elsewhere for necessities without harm to the Missions, since he had plenty of money. But the entreaties were such and the urgings of the men so importune that the missionaries yielded to them, granting not the entire quantity of provisions which they asked for but only a part. They gave provisions to the very poor for nothing, and also they sold them at just prices to those who had money with which to buy. Afterward they used the revenue from the sales in divine worship or in the purchase of clothes for their neophytes, because the missionaries considered themselves not the owners but the administrators of the property of the Missions, in spite of the fact that this was the fruit of their work and their industrious economy.

Notwithstanding this, they could not escape the shots of slander; but, whatever the part might have been which they took, how could they have avoided slander? If they sold the corn and other produce of the Missions to the laborers of the mines, the enemies of the Jesuits would have said that the missionaries of California had turned merchants, just as they said when the missionary of Santiago (conforming to the will of the viceroy and the precepts of charity) furnished fresh food to the ship from the Philippine Islands, which annually put into port at San Bernabé.

If all the provisions which were asked of them had been given for nothing, they would have said at least (and not without reason) that they were regular fools, for they were impoverishing their Missions and depriving their neophytes of necessities by giving them to those worthless strangers. And never would it have been believed that there was a dearth of charity, as it was accustomed to be said. In short, if they had absolutely refused to supply the provisions, their enemies, without doubt, would have proclaimed that the missionaries of California, with their avarice, opposed the income of the royal treasury by hindering the working of the mines. Such is the contrast which is ordinarily noted between the interests of God and those of the world.

These were by no means the greatest troubles which the mines caused those missionaries. The workmen, who were drawn from the dregs of humanity and were generally demoralized, soon began with their suggestions to awaken the natural restlessness and the bad inclinations of the Pericùes. These men kept telling them that the Indians of Mexico paid taxes to the king and supported their parish priests but, on the other hand, enjoyed complete liberty and went where they pleased, the parish priests there permitting them to do what they liked provided they took communion at Easter. Each Indian had his field which he cultivated according to his desire, selling the produce at the mines or in some city, accordingly as it turned out more profitable to him.

These stories, filled with falsehoods and accompanied by bad advice, led the foolish Pericùes to the most extravagant and iniquitous pretensions. They contended that the Mission lands should be distributed to them, which, although uncultivated before, were cultivated now by great industry, continual work, and at no little expense to the missionaries. Each one of them wanted to have authority to cultivate his field as he liked and to sell the produce where he wished, notwithstanding the fact that the missionaries should continue to support all the women, the children, the old people, and the sick of the Missions as they were doing and also that the missionaries should provide beasts of burden to those who wished to go to another place to sell their produce. Not content with this they wanted the liberty to travel whenever they felt like it, not only through all the Missions of that peninsula but also to the countries across the sea, including Sinaloa, Culiacán, and Nueva Galicia. And for this purpose they asked that the boat of the Mission of Santiago be placed at their disposal, which had been bought for more than eight hundred *scudi* that had been taken from the endowment capital and which was to be used to transport necessities to the Mission.

Among these irrational claims of theirs that which referred to the division of the lands would have been very just and advantageous, not less to the Missions than to the Indians themselves, if the latter had worked the land well by themselves and kept the produce. But it is certain that men recently taken out of savage life and accustomed to supporting themselves with fruit which the trees offer them of their own accord excessively abhor the labor of agriculture and, paying little attention to the future, waste the provisions of many months in a week. They never shake off their laziness, if they are not encouraged in industry and kindly compelled to work. Nor would they ever have been able to enjoy the products of agriculture a whole year if the missionaries had not guarded them well in a warehouse so that they could keep distributing them with prudent economy.

As to the right of going wherever they wished, which at first sight seems due to the natural liberty of man, they asked for more than was permitted them in the time of their gentility. Then, in spite of the fact that they roved and wandered without towns or houses, they were confined in such a way in the district of their own nation that neither the Pericùes could go to the country of the Guaicuras nor the latter to that of the Cochimìes. And, what is still more remarkable, it was not even permitted one tribe to set foot in the territory of another of the same nation.

But after having received Christianity, they could go at their fancy through all the territory of their own Mission (which was very vast) and also to the adjacent countries. In order to go to the distant Missions they had to ask permission of their respective missionary, who readily granted it to them whenever there was a just reason or when some grave difficulty was not feared. Otherwise these trips, especially if they were of long duration, caused much harm to the Indians who made them, to their families, and to the Missions. It was a regularly observed custom there that the missionaries supported the strange neophytes all the time that they lived in their Missions and took care of them as if they belonged to their flock.

Another origin of restlessness and complaints among the Pericùes was the scarcity of women. It is truly a strange thing that in the time of their gentility polygamy was very common among them, and that the feminine sex, much more numerous than the masculine, diminished after some years to such an extent that there was scarcely one woman for ten men. It may be believed that the epidemics of the previous years were the cause, which perhaps might have wrought greater havoc on the weaker sex. This excess of the number of men over that of women was common to some northern Missions; but there it was not so difficult for the men to find wives in other Missions near by in which the feminine sex had not diminished so greatly.

Some young men of Loreto who could not get married because of the lack of sweethearts went with the permission and recommendation of their missionary to look for them among the Yaquis. The latter, on seeing them well dressed and of good habits, had no difficulty in giving them their daughters, who, after moving to Loreto with their husbands, lived there contented and like good Christians. But neither the Yaquis nor any others would have yielded their daughters so readily to the rebellious Pericùes, who were universally disparaged because of their disturbances and uprisings.

The missionary of Santiago made all possible effort, although in vain, to supply the need of the Pericùes and to satisfy their vexatious and arrogant demands. With this purpose he wrote to the missionaries of Sinaloa, but he obtained nothing. By means of the same missionaries he asked the governor of that province (since he was waging war on the Seris) to send the young women of that nation whom he might capture to California in order to marry them to the Pericùes. The governor agreed to it, but he did not succeed in capturing any. And thus the missionary was disappointed in his plan.

Chapter Eleven

THE UNLAWFUL MEETING OF THE PERICÙES. THE OUTCOME OF THEIR DELIBERATIONS AND CLAIMS

WHEN the arrogant Pericùes saw that their extravagant claims were not listened to in California, they secretly held a meeting in which they deliberated on presenting them to the government of Guadalajara or to that of Mexico [City]; and they asked also that their missionary be taken away from them and that a priest of the secular clergy be given his place, promising to support him and pay taxes besides to the king. A more foolish and pretentious claim cannot be imagined, since some men who could not support themselves and their families believed themselves capable of defraying such expenses.

In order to carry out their proposed ultra-marine voyage, they went by night with the greatest secrecy to the anchoring ground where the Mission boat was and where the anchors, sails, oars, and other necessities were kept in the warehouse, and, taking possession of all and providing themselves with water, twenty of them embarked and set sail immediately. The accomplices of this wicked deed kept it so secret that there was no rumor of it until after it was done; neither did the missionary even have a suspicion of it, nor the soldiers, nor the governor of Santiago, who (although a Pericùe) was an honorable man and would have opposed the perverse design of his countrymen if he had found it out in time.

The navigators, after having crossed the Gulf, reached the coast of Sinaloa near the Mission of Ahome, which was then guided by Father Antonio Ventura. Informed of the reason and the circumstances of their voyage, he rebuked them severely for the disturbances with which they had made themselves hateful to God and men, for their temerity in taking possession of the Mission boat like thieves, and for their ingratitude toward their missionaries, who had toiled so much for their welfare. After he had thus calmed them, he kept them with him, supporting them at his expense for almost six months; but three of them had gone inland toward the presidio of Montesclaros,[36] where they presented their complaints to the lieutenant of the governor of Sinaloa, who had already begun to make a report, despite the fact that the business of California did not belong to him in any way. He was prudently dissuaded from doing so by Father Ventura. The procurator of Loreto, informed by this missionary, sent a boat to the port of Ahome to get those fugitives and take them to Loreto, as in fact was done. That captain-governor wished to punish them as they deserved, but, yielding to the entreaties of the missionaries, he granted them pardon; and this impunity encouraged the guilty ones to repeat the offense, as we shall soon see.

After the turbulent Pericùes had returned to their country,

[36] Built on the Fuerte River in Mexico in 1610, and named after the viceroy, Juan de Mendoza, the marquis of Montesclaros, who served from 1603 to 1607.

they did not give up their foolish claims. So, in a little while, they presented them with their accustomed arrogance to Father Ignacio Lisaxoain,[37] the visitator-general of the Missions, who answered them that he could not grant them their requests while there were definite orders from the viceroy[38] of Mexico and from the king of Spain not to change in any way the government established in the peninsula.

As they were obstinate in their determination, they were not long in undertaking another escape with the same intent as the first. The missionary of Santiago, in order to prevent it, had had the sails and all the other equipment of the boat taken away, and he kept them well guarded near him. But one night they found a way of opening the door of the room where these things were kept, and, taking out what they needed, they carried them with great secrecy and quickness to the port; they went to the coast of Sinaloa as they did the first time. There, after having abandoned the boat (which was lost for this reason), some who were never heard of again went to Durango, the capital of Nueva Vizcaya. The others went along the coast to Tepic,[39] a place in Nueva Galicia, about forty miles distant from the port of Matanchel; and three of them went inland

[37] Father Lisaxoain founded the Mission of Guaymas on the mainland in 1751. When the Indian revolts spread throughout Pimería Alta, he made a long report to the viceroy, commenting on the "inhuman cruelty" which the Pápagos, the Pimas, and the Seríes had inflicted upon the Spanish inhabitants of the region. Father Lisaxoain never worked in Lower California, but he became visitor-general of the Missions there (Engelhardt, *The Missions and Missionaries of California*, Vol. I, p. 269).

[38] The marquis of Cruillas, Joaquín Monserrat, who served from 1760 to 1765.

[39] Now the capital of the state of Nayarit, and having a population of 18,000. It is surrounded by a good grain-growing country, and has become a center of the coffee and tobacco trade. This small village became a place of international interest in 1840. In that year an American, Isaac Graham, who was a noted trapper, was accused of leading a revolt against the Mexican government in Upper California. He and thirty-eight Americans and Englishmen were arrested and sent to Tepic in chains, as Graham said, "like a tub of lard." The authorities of the United States and England intefered, and after some delay all the men were released. Graham returned to California some years later. This incident served to create more intense interest in California, and to cause much doubt that Mexico could continue to hold that country.

as far as the city of Guadalajara, where they stated their claims and complaints to one of the supreme magistrates.

The latter received them very willingly, because they were against the Jesuits; and, instead of sending them to the viceroy (as he should have done), who could give instructions to them with greater ease and issue suitable orders more quickly, he informed the court of Madrid where he hoped to gain favor by furthering the designs of the enemies of the Jesuits.

As soon as the three Pericùes had stated their complaints, they returned to their companions who had begun to feel the effects of poverty, after having scattered in the vicinity of Tepic, and to learn, very much to their cost, that it is necessary to work in order to live and that it would have been better for them to have stayed quietly in their native country, enjoying the charity of their missionary.

Don José Manuel de Escobar, the priest of Guainamota (the village nearest the port of Matanchel), who was stirred by his pastoral zeal, managed to gather up the wretched strangers who were wandering about scattered here and there; he urged them to return to their native country, and he promised to secure their transportation on a boat to Loreto. They themselves needed no urging to decide on that departure. The severe hardships which they had suffered on the trip and sojourn had greatly distressed them and had even deprived some of life. The unfortunate death of one of them caused great pity and sorrow to that good priest. He had been called to confess the Pericùe who was ill in a woods very distant from Guainamota; and, although he made every effort to arrive on time, he did not find anything but the bones of that unfortunate man, since the wild animals had devoured him either dead or dying.

When the much-desired boat from California reached Matanchel, the unlucky fugitives embarked in it and were taken to Loreto; and from there they went to their native country two years after their escape with few desires of making another, although they did not receive the punishment merited the second time. The Mission of Santiago, like that of Dolores, remained deprived of its boat which was so necessary for the transportation of everything that was sent from Loreto to it and to Todos Santos. The missionary did not wish to buy another because his turbulent neophytes might avail themselves of it for another escape. So the necessary provisions, which were sent to him before by sea, were sent to him afterward on pack mules over a bad road of three hundred miles, the shipments being delayed in this way, and the trouble and expenses being increased. Although the Pericùes were little desirous of transmarine trips, they did not desist from their claims; again they presented them, this time to Father Carlos Roxas,[40] the visitator-general of the Missions, who arrived there at the beginning of 1766. But they were rejected by him likewise.

Chapter Twelve

THE JESUITS SOLEMNLY RENOUNCE THE MISSIONS AND A GREAT INHERITANCE

AT THAT TIME Francisco Zevallos, the provincial of the Jesuits in Mexico, basing his opinion on powerful reasons and afterward on mature deliberation, made a solemn renunciation in the presence of the viceroy[41] of all the hundred-odd Missions which were under the charge and the direction of this religious (especially those of California), promising the Catholic king, in the name of all the province, that the Fathers would be engaged in other laborious missions among the gentiles wherever His Majesty might wish to make use of their persons.

As this business was of great importance, the viceroy called a *junta*[42] of the supreme magistrates, the *auditor de guerra*, and the royal *fiscal* to consider it; and in it, it was decided that the

[40] Father Roxas had served among the Missions in Sinaloa and in Sonora since 1742. He never served in the peninsula.
[41] Carlos Francisco de Croix, who served from 1766 to 1771.
[42] A gathering of experts called by the viceroy to advise him on important state matters. Most of the men called in a *junta* were usually connected with the administration of the government; all were subordinate to the viceroy. The *junta* might meet without being called by the viceroy, but he had power to veto its actions and even to suspend it. No plan of major importance was ever undertaken by the viceroy without consulting this important body.

opinion of the bishops and governors in whose districts the Missions of the Jesuits were situated be obtained. The bishops at once opposed the acceptance of this renunciation; and the governors, at least the greater part of them, thought the same thing. The viceroy refrained from making any decision in the matter; but it was believed that he would send the renunciation and the reports of the bishops and the governors to the court.

As soon as the missionaries of California were informed of this, they endeavored through their procurator in Mexico [City] (in case the viceroy did not accept the general renunciation) to have him accept it at least in regard to the two southern Missions of the peninsula in which there were little success and great and continuous efforts and troubles, especially since the mines had begun to be worked there. It would not be so difficult to find someone who wished to take charge of them as it would be for the other Missions, because all who did not know them believed them to be rich. But not even this could be attained, despite all the petitions which the procurator presented to the viceroy.

A matter that was much more commented upon was another renunciation which was made by the Jesuits themselves during the following year, 1767. Doña Josefa de Argüelles y Miranda,[43] a Mexican lady not less pious than she was rich, left to the Missions of California and to the College of Guadalajara[44] at her death her great wealth, which, according to common opinion, amounted to six hundred thousand *scudi*. Such a considerable capital would have greatly hastened the advance of Christianity in the peninsula, but those Jesuits, fearing that they might greatly irritate the enemies of their Order, and so beset with calumnies in Portugal, France, and other states in Europe, solemnly renounced that inheritance before the Mexican government. Their enemies were astonished at the beginning, but afterward they attributed this resolution to their astute politics.

[43] She had already given two hundred pesos to the Pious Fund to support the Missions in Lower California (Chapman, *A History of California: The Spanish Period*, p. 182).

[44] In the state of Jalisco, founded in 1659.

Chapter Thirteen

OTHER PLACES ARE SOUGHT FOR THE ESTABLISHMENT OF NEW MISSIONS, AND THIS COMMISSION IS ENTRUSTED TO FATHER LINK

NEITHER these renunciations made by the superiors nor the troubles caused by the restless Pericùes cooled the zeal of the missionaries. They desired to promote Christianity toward the north with new Missions; but places had not been found where they could establish them, with the exception of Calagnujuet,[45] which was ninety miles distant from the Mission of San Francisco de Borja and situated between the mountains and the Gulf. This place was discovered at the end of 1753 by Father Consag, but the lack of potable water seemed a great obstacle, since there was only that of a small stream, which had a harsh and astringent taste because it contained copperas. And for this reason it was rightly believed harmful to the health, although the Indians used it.

Therefore, it was necessary to make new investigations, and the superior assigned this task to Father Link, whom he ordered to try to explore all that country as far as the Red River. The captain-governor wanted the missionary to go, accompanied by the lieutenant of Loreto and by fifteen soldiers to prevent hostilities, which were rightly feared on that trip, because on the last one which Father Sedelmayer had made, when the barbarous inhabitants of the banks of the Red River wanted to take away the horses forcibly from the soldiers who accompanied him and when the latter were not able to dissuade them from their intent, they found themselves compelled to make use of weapons, killing some of them; and, since the barbarians had become hostile to the Spaniards for this

---

[45] Located about four miles from the Bay of San Luis and about twenty-six leagues northwest from the San Francisco de Borja. Here Governor Gaspar Portolá stopped to rest in May 1769 on his way to plant the first settlement in Upper California. It is still a mining camp. See *Sunset Magazine*, December 1906, pp. 153–54.

reason, it was feared that now they might want to avenge themselves. This number of soldiers increased the expenses of the trip, to which all the Missions from Loreto to San Francisco de Borja contributed by sending provisions and animals to carry them over those unknown countries, where it was not possible to be provided with them.

When the preparations were made, Father Link left Adac in February (1766), accompanied by the lieutenant, the fifteen soldiers, and a good number of neophytes. He went toward the north, between the mountains and the Pacific Sea. They traveled for some days over a land not so hilly and rough as the rest of the country of the Cochimìes but so barren and arid that there was scarcely drinking water for the travelers and the animals. After continuing they found abundant pastures with a stream and several springs, although the water was not sufficient to irrigate sown fields; it was enough to water a considerable number of cattle, which could be maintained there.

This place was called San Juan de Dios, perhaps because it was discovered on March 8, on which day the holiday of that saint is held. In order that the location might be useful, it was necessary to find another place at a little distance where the proposed Mission could be established. This was found twelve miles farther on where there was an ample stream from which the tillable land that there was on both sides could easily be irrigated. There were also many pines, *guaribos*, and other kinds of trees which were useful for building and which were lacking in all the other Missions of California except the southern ones. This place, situated at about 32° and called "Guiricatà" by the Indians, seemed to our travelers one hundred and eighty miles distant from Adac, although it was by the shortest possible way.

As they continued their trip to 33°, or a little more, they observed that from San Juan de Dios toward the north the country appeared less unpleasant because it had a greater abundance of water and vegetation; and its inhabitants were more affable and less timid. It is true that they fled the first time because of the fear which that strange people who were entering their country caused them, and especially because of the horses, which they had never seen before. But as soon as the neophytes of the retinue assured them that they had not come to do them any harm, they returned without timidity; they approached our travelers confidently; they answered all their questions amicably, showed them the places where there was potable water, and accompanied them part of the way.

After one of the barbarian tribes had taken to flight on seeing the party, the widow of an eminent Indian of this same tribe, without being afraid or moving from the place where she was, called them, telling them to come and see if the men were truly friends, as they seemed to be. Becoming assured of this, she treated her guests with such courteous manners that she seemed not brought up in the wilds, but in some city. The cape of skins which she wore and which was newer and more beautiful than those of the other women, the noble air which she displayed in all her actions, and, above all, the deference and respect with which all those of her tribe treated her, persuaded our travelers that she was probably the ruler of these Indians.[46] This was all the more surprising since the feminine sex in the rest of California is degraded.

Another tribe of barbarians there exhibited valor superior to that of the other Californians. When they saw some soldiers who had preceded their companions approaching, they took their bows, drew their arrows, and stopped fearlessly opposite, without manifesting any dread of their weapons or their horses. Since the soldiers were not able to calm them by talking to them, because they did not know their language and because it was forbidden them to use their weapons, they took the part of retreating until an interpreter arrived and stated to the barbarians that they had not come to do them any harm. This was enough to pacify them and persuade them to treat the strangers as friends. It seemed to Father Link, as well as to his followers, that all the savages of those countries were well disposed to receive Christianity. They listened attentively and respectfully to the exhortations which the missionary made

---

[46] This supports the gynecocentric theory regarding the relation of the sexes. For a scholarly treatment of this subject, see Lester F. Ward, *Pure Sociology*, pp. 291–302.

them; and he had the consolation of opening the doors of Heaven to two dying infants and to a very old woman who soon passed away.

Some cabins of hewn wood were seen in that country, which makes it appear evident that its inhabitants are more active and industrious than the other Californians. But the cabins were deserted, and for that reason it was believed that they had been built by the Indians not to be inhabited permanently but only to take refuge there in time of cold weather. Snow is not unusual there in the winter, but our travelers saw snow fall in April.

As soon as the visitors believed that they were in the latitude of the Red River, they traveled toward the east to pass over the mountains and to descend to the mouths of that river; the mountains were so precipitous and rough that the horses could not climb them. They turned aside from there to find another better way, and they struck a very great sandy stretch; and because they lacked water and feared that the horses might become useless from too much hardship they decided to give up the enterprise at that time and to undertake it the following year; they returned to Adac. The diaries[47] of Father Link and the lieutenant were sent to the viceroy.

Chapter Fourteen

THE MISSION OF CALAGNUJUET AND THE MISSIONARIES APPOINTED TO IT

THERE was, therefore, no other place suitable for the establishment of the proposed Mission except that of Guiricatà, situated at about 32°; but it was one hundred and eighty miles distant from Adac, and it would have

---

[47] They record the first land exploration made in the extreme northern part of the peninsula. Link's diary was also sent to the king of Spain just at the time when he was considering expelling the Jesuits (Engelhardt, *op. cit.*, Vol. I, p. 259).

been isolated, leaving many gentiles in between, who could hinder communication between those two Missions; or, at least, they would have made the transportation of provisions from one to the other difficult and dangerous. In order to avoid such inconveniences, the missionaries had never tried to establish a Mission there until after they had made all the barbarians who lived between it and the nearest one Christians.

Consequently they could not help but establish a Mission which would serve as a stopping place to the one which they wished to establish in Guiricatà. In fact, they founded that one in October 1766 at Calagnujuet, a place situated at 30° 40' on the slope of a high mountain called "Jubai," ten or twelve miles distant from the Gulf. In spite of this location being considered useless in the beginning for the founding (as in reality it was on account of the bad quality of the water), yet it was preferred for that establishment because there was not a better one in all that great space which intervenes between Adac and Guiricatà, and it was believed then that the mineral water would be of use at least to fertilize the soil which might be cultivated.

Fathers Victoriano Arnés and Juan José Diez,[48] who had learned the Cochimì language for this purpose, were appointed by the superior to establish the Mission. They came accompanied by ten soldiers. The captain-governor thought that a lesser number would be insufficient to protect the lives of the missionaries, because the Mission was on the frontier of the barbarian gentiles and hence distant from the presidio. More than fifty neophytes belonging to that territory, although baptized in the Mission of San Francisco de Borja, accompanied them. Among them was one named Juan Nepomuceno, who was very well known in those countries and much feared and respected by the barbarians for his great bravery; on him the post of governor, or guardian of the Indians of Calagnujuet, was conferred.

Besides the house for the soldiers only three buildings were constructed. One served as a chapel, the other as a storehouse

---

[48] A Mexican Jesuit, born in 1735, Father Diez had arrived in Lower California in 1766. He also served at the Mission of Borja and at Purísima. He died in 1809.

for provisions, and the third as a parsonage. As there was only one wooden door for the buildings, it was allotted to the storehouse, where it was more necessary. The poverty of this recent Mission was such that the missionaries needed to use all the economy possible in order to be able to maintain themselves and the soldiers and catechumen. Since the water was not drinkable, except by the barbarians who were accustomed to eat and drink whatever was put before them, it was necessary to carry water for the missionaries and for the soldiers from some wells a mile and a half distant from that place.

As this Mission was very far from the others which could furnish it with supplies, transportation was rendered difficult and the missionaries tried to get at least a part of their subsistence out of the soil. Therefore, they sowed wheat, which grew easily; but after they had begun to irrigate it (as it is necessary to do in California), the earth turned white in a short time, being covered with the copperas which the mineral water of the stream left there. And so all was spoiled. Besides there were absolutely no pastures for the horses which the missionaries and the soldiers needed, nor any for some sheep which had been sent by Father Link.

In spite of this poverty, the Mission kept on prospering in what pertains to religion, because as soon as the barbarians of those countries saw that the Mission was established they began to go to it in great numbers to be instructed and baptized. The scarcity of provisions did not permit having many catechumen at one time; but the missionaries devoted themselves to their instruction with such diligence and application that they prepared them for baptism more quickly than in other Missions. And as soon as they had baptized and discharged one crowd, another entered to be instructed in a like manner. In this way in a few months they baptized more than two hundred adults and little ones.

But whether through work or want Father Diez became so ill that it was thought he could not live; and on this account he was sent to Adac and afterward to Guadalupe. But after he recovered there, he was appointed to the Mission of Purísima. Father Arnés not only had the sorrow of being deprived of the help of his companion but also the trouble which the offenses of some wild gentiles caused him. The inhabitants of Cagnajuet, which was a place seventy miles distant to the north from Calagnujuet, seeing that many of the young women who had previously served their pleasures were going to become Christians, refusing to condescend to the men's lascivious desires, and becoming indignant with Christianity which was the cause of this, considered attacking the Mission by night and killing the missionary and the soldiers. But not daring to do this by themselves, they invited two other tribes, principally that of Guiricatà, which was very large.

This tribe did not consent, because Father Link had been kind to them and treated them well on this trip; they protested honorably that they did not want to use their weapons against those who had done them no injury. With this answer those of Cagnajuet desisted from their project of assault, but at the same time they determined to continue their hostilities on all the neophytes who came into their district. In fact, they wanted to kill one neophyte who went there by accident; and if it had not been for a gentile relative of his, who defended him, he would certainly have perished at their hands. The governor, Juan Nepomuceno, found out this news before it reached the ears of Father Arnés. This very brave neophyte, who seemed to communicate his intrepidity to those whom he had about him (without saying anything to the missionary) immediately sent six determined and well-armed men to Cagnajuet. He had instructed them previously what they were to do.

When Father Arnés discovered this he was astonished at their temerity, and he became very solicitous about the outcome of the enterprise in which six men had to contend with a large tribe. His astonishment was increased when he saw those six men appear in a little while, bringing some families from Cagnajuet as prisoners.

They had made their attack by night with such impetus and determination that they had routed the barbarians, who were half asleep and terror-stricken; those who did not have time to save themselves by flight were led like lambs to Calagnujuet. After Father Arnés had secretly agreed with the corporal of the soldiers, who was to act as judge in the case, he sent a message to the public so that all might hear it (principally the prisoners), entreating them earnestly to be content with inflicting a slight punishment on the leaders of the offenders, pardoning the rest, and granting to all the liberty of returning to their native country. The corporal made a false show of yielding to the entreaties of the missionaries, and, after having ordered only eight lashes applied to the chief offender, he gave them all liberty. Because they believed themselves debtors to the missionary for that favor, they came to him and thanked him; and after reproving them for that iniquitous design of pursuing, as enemies, those who did not do them evil, he explained some principles of Christianity to them, and especially the need of baptism for saving their souls.

They appeared persuaded to such a degree that they enrolled immediately among the catechumen and began to be instructed; and although they went away to their country when scarcely a week had passed, either to free their relatives from the uncertainty in which they probably were in regard to them or because they hoped to be more conveniently instructed in that place to which the Mission was going to be moved (as it was nearer Cagnajuet), they were finally catechised and baptized with many others of their tribe.

Chapter Fifteen

THE MISSION IS MOVED TO ANOTHER PLACE WITH THE NAME OF SANTA MARÍA, AND IT IS THE LAST ONE THAT THE JESUITS ESTABLISH IN CALIFORNIA

SINCE Father Arnés had suffered great inconveniences in Calagnujuet, and since he saw that it was impossible to live in that very barren place, which was lacking in everything, he devoted himself to looking everywhere for another more tolerable one; and after many trips he found it near the small stream of Cabujakaamang during May in 1767. This place, situated at about 31°, is some fifty miles dis-

Fig. 27 — Ruins of the mission church at Santa Maria. This was the last and most northerly of the Jesuit missions. At its rugged and barren site it never prospered. The extant ruins are almost certainly of Franciscan or Dominican construction since the Jesuits occupied the site only a little more than a year.

Homer Aschmann

Fig. 28 — Ruins of the mission church at San Fernando Velicatá (Guiricata). The site was discovered by the Jesuit Father Link and selected for a mission, but the expulsion intervened. The Franciscan Father Serra founded the mission in 1768, but the building probably was built by the Dominicans.

Homer Aschmann

tant to the northwest from Calagnujuet and more than one hundred to the north-northwest from Adac. Its soil was not so barren as that which they had left; it was equally lacking in fruits, pastures, and wood, but the small amount of water in its stream was very good. There were also, at that place, some palm trees with red wood which were good for building; and the scarcity of fruits was compensated, in a way, by the abundance of good fish in the Gulf, which is scarcely twelve miles distant.

The church and the dwellings of the missionary and the soldiers, which were built there, were wretched cabins of wood covered with palm leaves. The Mission was given the name of Santa María, dedicated to the Mother of God and in memory of the Duquesa de Gandía, the remarkable benefactress of the Missions at whose expense this one was founded[49] and others which were about to be established. The missionary, in order to omit no effort that might be advantageous to his Mission, cultivated a small field near the stream; and in it he sowed wheat and cotton.[50] Both crops were in good condition in January 1768 when the Jesuits were obliged to abandon the Missions.

Father Arnés, in the midst of the poverty and the troubles which some of the soldiers who were discontented in that remote solitude caused him, devoted himself diligently to the conversion of the savages; and in the few months which he remained there, he did not lack catechumen.

This Mission of Santa María was the last which the Jesuits

---

[49] Duquesa de Gandía guaranteed five hundred dollars yearly from capital that she bequeathed to this Mission (Engelhardt, *op. cit.*, Vol. I, p. 262).

[50] Cotton was grown also at the Missions of San José Comondù, Purísima de Cadegomo, Santa Rosalía de Mulegè, and San Ignacio, and at San Fernando Vellicatá (*California Historical Society Quarterly*, Vol. VI, p. 161; see also Bolton, *Palóu*, Vol. I, pp. 163, 172, 185). When the Missions were founded in Upper California, efforts were made to grow cotton, but with little success. Peter Lassen grew some cotton on his ranch near Mount Lassen in 1847, but it was not until 1919 that cotton-raising in the state assumed commercial importance. Since then cotton culture has spread rapidly throughout the Imperial and San Joaquin valleys. Today there are about 300,000 acres annually planted to cotton, of which more than three-fourths are confined to the San Joaquin Valley. Tulare County usually has the largest acreage of any of the numerous counties growing cotton.

established in California; for when it was a question of founding others, a royal order put an end to the apostolic tasks of the missionaries. But before relating this event it is necessary to describe briefly the status of the Missions, the military government, and the political and economic condition of the peninsula.

Chapter Sixteen

THE NUMBER AND THE LOCATION OF ALL THE MISSIONS. THE NUMBER OF NEOPHYTES. THE NUMBER OF SUPERIORS WHOM EACH MISSIONARY HAD OVER HIM. VISITS RARE AMONG THE MISSIONARIES

THE MISSIONS established by the Jesuits in the seventy years which they were in California were eighteen in number. But the four of Londò, Liguig, La Paz, and San José del Cabo were abandoned because the number of their neophytes had decreased notably; they were added to other Missions. And so the ones existing at the beginning of 1768 were only fourteen, one of which was among the Pericùes, four were among the Guaicuras, and nine were among the Cochimìes. Here is the location of them and the number of neophytes belonging to each one,[51] beginning with the most southerly one.*

I. The Mission of Santiago, situated at about 23°, is twenty-four miles from the Gulf. To it the village of San José del Cabo belonged, where the second presidio of soldiers was, thirty-six miles distant from Santiago. In both villages there were almost three hundred and fifty neophytes.

II. The Mission of Todos Santos, or Santa Rosa, located

---

* What we say about the location of the Missions should be understood about the principal villages, where the missionaries resided.

[51] For additional information regarding the Missions at that time, see Engelhardt, *op. cit.*, Vol. I, p. 304; also Bancroft, *History of the North Mexican States and Texas*, Vol. I, pp. 574–76.

with a slight difference in the same latitude as the cape of San Lucas, is a mile and a half distant from the Pacific Sea, and it had only ninety neophytes.

III. The Mission of the Virgen de los Dolores is located at a place called Tagnuetìa at 24½°. In this village and in the other small villages belonging to it there were about four hundred and fifty neophytes.

IV. The Mission of San Luis Gonzaga is twenty-four miles distant to the west from the village just named, and had other small villages and three hundred and ten neophytes.

V. The Mission of the Virgen de Loreto is situated near the sea at 25½°. This village was the capital of California; in it lived the captain-governor, and in it were the main presidio and the general warehouse. The missionary there was at the same time the procurator of all the Missions. Its inhabitants, including neophytes, soldiers, and sailors and their families, were more than four hundred.

VI. The Mission of San Francisco Javier is situated in the same latitude as that of Loreto, which is twenty-nine miles distant to the west. In this village and in other small villages belonging to San Javier there were four hundred and eighty-five neophytes.

VII. The Mission of San José de Comondù, where there were three hundred and sixty neophytes, is situated at about 26°.

VIII. The Mission of Purísima Concepción, where there were one hundred and thirty neophytes, is situated at a little more than 26°, almost to the west of Comondù.

IX. The Mission of Santa Rosalía de Mulegè, where there were three hundred neophytes, is at 26° 50' on the coast of the Gulf.

X. The Mission of Nuestra Señora de Guadalupe, located at 27° in the mountains, had among its villages five hundred and thirty neophytes.

XI. The Mission of San Ignacio, or Kadakaamang, located almost at 28°, had seven hundred and fifty neophytes.

XII. The Mission of Santa Gertrudis (at about 29°) was comprised of small villages and had about one thousand neophytes.

XIII. The Mission of San Francisco de Borja (at 30°) had with its small villages one thousand and five hundred neophytes.

XIV. The recent Mission of Santa María (near 31°) had three hundred neophytes and thirty catechumen.

Hence it is deduced that there were only seven thousand inhabitants in a country which has a length of some five hundred miles and a width of now thirty, then fifty, then seventy miles; multiplying the length by the medium width of fifty miles, we have twenty-five thousand square miles, which gives approximately three and one-half square miles for each individual. The population had been very scarce also in the time of their gentility, because neither the savage life which they led, the continuous wars with which they alternately destroyed each other, nor the scarcity of provisions of that arid soil permitted the barbarians to multiply rapidly. It is certain that after the introduction of Christianity the number of the gentile inhabitants decreased greatly, especially in the southern part, in which the number of Pericùes who were there when the Gospel was proclaimed to them was reduced afterward to a tenth part, and in spite of the fact that since their conversion their wars ceased, they were better fed, and their lives were more regular.

It is not easy to assign the reason for such a result. It is known only that epidemics have caused it; but why were these epidemics not so fatal to them when they were lacking every remedy and assistance? Why did they not die in greater number when the epidemics worked jointly with hunger and war?

These fourteen Missions comprised three districts; to wit, that of the North, that of the South, and that of Loreto located between those two. In each district there was a missionary rector whom the others obeyed; and all the missionaries of the three districts were subject to the visitor of the peninsula, who was one of the missionaries themselves, appointed by the provincial every three years; and during this time he was expected to visit all the Missions, watch over the conduct of the missionaries, and give an account of it to the provincial. Besides, those Missions, as well as all the others belonging to the province of Mexico, were visited every three years by the visitator-general. In this way each missionary had over him five regular superiors; to wit: the rector, the visitator of the peninsula, the visitator-general, the father-provincial, and the father-general.

The missionaries were so distant from each other (because it could not be helped) that every time they visited to confess, console, or help each other in their illnesses or in their dangers they had to make long journeys, often over bad roads. The missionary of Santa Gertrudis was eighty miles distant from the nearest neighbor; he of San Francisco de Borja was almost ninety; and he of Santa María was more than a hundred. They rarely visited each other, as much for this reason of distance as for not leaving the Missions in which their presence was very necessary. So then, the missionaries, educated for the most part in large cities and accustomed to deal with cultured people, were now confined to those vast solitudes and compelled to converse only with men recently taken out of the barbarous life, or at best with ignorant and crude soldiers.

Chapter Seventeen

A DESCRIPTION OF THE CAPITAL OF EACH MISSION. HOW TIME WAS DISTRIBUTED FOR THE NEOPHYTES. THEIR FERVOR

THE PRINCIPAL town of each Mission where the missionary lived was a village in which, besides the church, the parsonage, the storehouse, the soldiers' dwelling, and schools for boys and girls, there were several little houses for those families of the neophytes who lived there regularly. The other places, more or less distant from the principal one and in which the rest of the neophytes who belonged to the same Mission lived, regularly lacked houses and their inhabitants lived exposed to the open air, according to their ancient custom. There were some twenty villages in the peninsula, all built by the missionaries at great expense.

The churches of the Missions, although poor for the most part, were maintained with all the cleanliness and neatness possible. The one at Loreto was very large and well furnished; that of San José de Comondù, built by Father Francisco Inamma,[52] had three naves; and that of San Francisco Javier, built with an arch by Father Miguel del Barco,[53] was very beautiful. Each church had its choir of musicians, and each Mission had its school where some selected children learned to sing and to play different instruments, as the harp, the violin, the violincello, and others.

The ecclesiastical festivities and performances were held with all possible show and pomp. The neophytes attended them with such silence, modesty, and devotion that they yielded nothing in their conduct to the most religious peoples of Christendom.

The missionary said Holy Mass daily, which all the neophytes of the village and all those who were in it attended. In the church itself they repeated the Christian doctrine; and they sang a canticle in praise of God and the Blessed Virgin which the Spaniards called *alabado*[54] because it begins with that word Afterward the *pozolli*, that is, that corn mush which all the Indians in Mexico use for breakfast, was distributed to them. On work days after breakfast they went to the field to work, because, being supported entirely by the Mission and receiving the produce of their labor, it was just that they should be engaged in it; and to be diverted from idleness and accustomed to a busy life was useful also to their spiritual and physical health. But their work was very moderate, because the few

---

[52] An Austrian Jesuit, born in Vienna in 1719, Father Inamma became a Jesuit at the age of sixteen. He arrived in Lower California in 1750. For his many interesting experiments on rattlesnakes, see Appendix A, p. 560.

[53] Little is known of Father Barco. It is thought that he was born in Milan, Italy, in 1706. He came to Lower California in 1744, and was made visitor-general in 1750 (Bancroft, *History of the North Mexican States and Texas*, Vol. I, pp. 465, 482). Father Barco wrote *Noticia y Estados de la Misión de S. Javier en California y de sus Pueblos, Sta. Rosalía, S. Miguel, S. Agustín, S. Pablo y los Dolores*. He died in Italy in 1790.

[54] It is still used by the Indians of California and by the Mexicans. In the service it was repeated three times. It is: "Alabado sea el Santísimo Sacramento del Altar! Bendita sea la Limpia y Purísima Concepción de Nuestra Señora María Santísima sin mancha de pecado original!" (Engelhardt, *op. cit.*, Vol. I, p. 139).

tasks which were necessary to be done were divided among many persons.

At noon they returned to the village to eat. Their meal consisted of a great quantity of *pozolli* (corn cooked in water), which was much prized by them; in some of the richer Missions which were more abundant in cattle a meat dish was added and another of vegetables or fruits. After a long rest they returned to the field, and the work ended before sunset; they gathered in the church at the ringing of the bell to say the rosary and to chant the litany to the Virgin and the *alabado*. When this was finished they ate and retired to their houses. When there was nothing to do in the field each one was occupied at his own work.

The same distribution was observed with the strange tribes belonging to the Mission when they were living in the village. But when they were in their respective places they repeated the Christian doctrine[55] in the morning, said some prayers, and chanted the *alabado*; afterward they went to the woods to seek their sustenance; and when they returned in the afternoon they chanted the litany before going to their rest. Each one of these tribes was under the charge of a faithful neophyte of good habits, who took care that these pious exercises should not be omitted and that there should be no disorder; also he rendered an account of everything to the missionary. In the new Missions each week two outside tribes stayed with the missionary and were maintained by him in order to be better instructed in the Christian doctrine and to be strengthened in the faith; and when they went away two other tribes came. In the old Missions two outside tribes came every Saturday and stayed there all Saturday and Sunday and went away on Monday. During the principal feast of the Mission and during all of Holy Week all the tribes gathered at the capital.

The missionary preached to his neophytes every Sunday and

---

[55] Constituted as follows: Sign of the Cross, the Lord's Prayer, the Hail to Mary, the Apostle's Creed, the Confiteor, the acts of Faith, Hope, Charity, and Contrition, the Ten Commandments of God, the Precepts of the Church, the Seven Sacraments, the Six Necessary Points of Faith, and the Four Last Things of Man. The teaching of these religious principles was uniform throughout the Missions. These principles indicate the laborious task which the padre had in inducing the Indians to memorize them.

holiday, and sometimes during the week; and he went promptly where he was called to administer the sacraments to the sick, for which purpose he had to go to places thirty, forty, and sometimes sixty miles distant.

In administering the Eucharist the missionaries used great circumspection, giving it only to those who became capable of it through instruction and who were worthy through their firmness in the faith and through a truly Christian life. Among those were many who, not limiting themselves to the precepts of annual communion, received the sacrament even on some holidays, preparing themselves diligently and leading a life which frequently required to be sustained with the sacrosanct body of Jesus Christ.

As education is the foundation and the basis of civilized and Christian life, almost all the boys and girls of the Mission from six to twelve years old were educated at the principal village in the presence of and at the expense of the missionary. During this time they were instructed in what pertained to religion and good habits; and they learned the crafts of which their tender age was capable. The children were in separate houses, the boys under the care of a trustworthy man, and the girls under that of an upright matron.

The indefatigable zeal of the missionaries, aided by divine grace, could not fail to produce very abundant fruit. That peninsula, buried previously for so many centuries in the most terrible barbarity, became almost entirely Christian in the space of seventy years in such a manner that from the cape of San Lucas near 23°, to Cabujakaamang at 31°, there was not a single man who did not know and worship the true God; but what is much more valuable, a Christianity was founded there so pure and immaculate that it seemed like that of the original church.

With the exception of some of the Pericùes who (on account of their bad inclination and the evil examples and insinuations of the workmen of the mines) caused many disturbances and troubles for the missionaries, all the neophytes of California led a pious, innocent, and industrious life. Almost never were those scandalous disorders which are so common even in the most Christian cities seen among them. If anyone incurred any offense whatsoever, although it were secret, he was the first to accuse himself and to ask for punishment; and after having suffered it he thanked the missionary for his paternal correction by kissing his hand. This custom, so beneficial spiritually and unknown to our Christians, was common in California.

Chapter Eighteen

THE EXPENSES WHICH THE MISSIONARIES INCURRED FOR THE WELFARE OF THE MISSIONS. THE DUTIES OF THE TWO PROCURATORS OF CALIFORNIA. THE RIGHTS AND THE AUTHORITY OF THE CAPTAIN

THE MISSIONARIES, besides the daily care of their churches in what pertained to religion and good habits, had also the maintenance of the flock entrusted to their care. This was, without doubt, the most vexatious part of their ministry. Since it was not suitable that the Californians after their conversion should continue that indecent nakedness in which they lived before and since they did not have a way to obtain the cloth necessary to cover themselves, it was requisite that each missionary clothe all his neophytes. With this object they kept sheep, cultivated cotton in some places, provided the Missions with looms, and taught the art of weaving to their neophytes. But because the cloth which was made there was not sufficient to clothe so many poor people it was necessary to have it brought from Mexico at the expense of the Missions.

The richest Missions (those which had the most abundant crops of corn and a sufficient number of cattle) maintained all their neophytes. Those which did not have such a quantity of either one or the other for supporting all the neophytes, fed only the soldiers who were kept there for the security of the missionaries, the catechumen during the time that their instruction lasted, the neighboring neophytes of the principal villages of the Mission, all the children of both sexes from the age of six to twelve years, and all the feeble and sick, to whom medicines were also furnished. It was necessary for the missionaries to have horses for their inevitable trips as well as for the trips of the soldiers who were with them.

Besides, the expenses of all the buildings of their Missions, the sacred vessels, the sacerdotal ornaments, the furnishings of the church and the sacristy, the farming utensils, and all those crafts which were carried on there, fell on the missionaries.

No one will consider that the capital of ten thousand *scudi* which was required for the establishment of each Mission in California was excessive for so many and for such great expenses. And especially no one would think thus, if individual expenses are added to general expenses; that is, those for the transportation of things necessary in California from Mexico to the port of Matanchel, a journey of over one thousand and six hundred miles, and then from Matanchel by sea to Loreto.

The boats which the Missions used for such transportation were twenty in number, large and small, of which six were built or bought on the account of the royal treasury, and the remainder at the expense of the Missions themselves, on which the repair of the boats also fell whenever it was necessary.

In the early years the sailors who served on the boats, and the captain and the soldiers who were there for the security of that recent Christianity, were paid by Father Salvatierra. Afterward six thousand *scudi* were assigned from the royal treasury for this purpose. But since this sum was very much less than the expenses, it was necessary that the Missions continue to support the major part until 1719, when eighteen thousand *scudi* began to be given annually by the order of King Philip V for the expenses of the presidio of Loreto and the sailors; to this sum another twelve thousand were added in 1736, when a new presidio was established in the southern part.

These thirty thousand *scudi*, which were paid out of the royal treasury from then on to the Missions, were for the salaries of the captain, two lieutenants, sixty soldiers, ten sailors, and some of the other officers of the boats. Since forty sailors were necessary for manning the two boats of California, the remaining thirty sailors were always paid by the Missions. The salary of each soldier was four hundred and fifty *scudi;* but the king allotted the same for the captain as for the private; wherefore, that sum was doubled at the expense of the Missions, and thus they paid him nine hundred *scudi*, besides the gifts of wheat, meat, and wine which the missionaries gave him.

Pious King Philip V had provided, likewise, that the missionaries of California, like those of the other missionaries, be paid from his treasury, giving each one three hundred *scudi* for his support, besides providing the churches of the Missions with bells, sacred utensils, sacerdotal ornaments, images, oil, and wax. But that royal order was never carried out in California. The expenses of the missionaries, as well as those of their churches, always came out of the funds created by those Missions themselves.

These resources consisted of estates situated in New Spain and bought with the donations of benefactors and with the sums from the endowments of the Missions. A procurator of California who lived in Mexico [City] took care of these funds; he was also entrusted with dealing with the viceroy and with the supreme magistrates about the business of the Missions; with drawing out the thirty thousand *scudi* from the treasury for the soldiers and sailors; with providing a new boat for California whenever there was need for it; and with buying and sending all the necessities for the missionaries and their churches, for the soldiers and sailors, for the boats, and even for the Indians. The first procurator was, as has been said before, the famous Father Juan de Ugarte. He, as well as his four successors,[56] served this office with great zeal and industry and to the great advantage of the Missions.

All that was sent from Mexico was usually taken to the port of Matanchel, and from there it was transported in a vessel to Loreto, where another procurator lived. This man was a missionary at the same time; and, besides the work of catechising, baptizing, preaching, confessing, and other similar duties, he was in charge of the temporal affairs of the peninsula. He received the cargo of the boats; he sent to each missionary what

[56] These were: Father Alexander Romano, who served until 1719; Father Joseph Echeverría, serving until 1729; Father Hernán Francisco Tompes, serving until 1750; and Father Juan Armesto, serving until the Jesuits were expelled.

belonged to him; he paid the soldiers and sailors their salaries, either all in cash or part in clothing or in other things, just as they wished; he took care of the general warehouse of the peninsula, and he sent the boats at the right time to the ports of New Spain; the larger one went to Matanchel and sometimes to Acapulco to receive the goods which were sent from Mexico [City], and the other to Yaqui or to another port of Sinaloa to bring food or cattle. As it was not possible for one man to attend to so many things, especially since the number of the Missions and the soldiers was increased, the procurator was aided in the care of the temporal matters by a brother coadjutor who had much to do with the distribution of the provisions to the soldiers, sailors, and Indians.

The captain was not only the commander of the seventy soldiers who were in the two presidios of Loreto and San José del Cabo, but he was also the governor and judge of the peninsula and the supreme commandant of all those seas. And for that reason the principal vessel of California had the honor of being the admiral's ship and had the colors hoisted in all the ports of the Pacific Sea except that of Acapulco when the ship from the Philippines was there.

Fishing for pearls was not permitted in those seas without first showing the license of the viceroy to the captain, whose duty it was to collect the tax which is paid to the king from the pearls which are fished for. This he did with the greatest faithfulness and without any profit to himself. He was likewise authorized by the viceroy to seize boats and to make prisoners of their masters whenever they fished without licenses, or when they did not pay the decreed tax, harassed the Californians, or caused any serious disturbance.

Chapter Nineteen

PEARL FISHING IS PROHIBITED. THE DISTRIBUTION AND THE DUTIES OF THE SOLDIERS. THE AUTHORITY OF THE JESUITS OVER THEM. THE RESIDENCE OF THE CAPTAIN IN LORETO. THE EXEMPLARY HABITS OF THAT VILLAGE

IN SPITE of the fact that the captain had this superintendency over pearl fishing, he could not engage in it. In all the seventy years that the Jesuits were there, pearl fishing was never permitted to the captain, to the soldiers, to the sailors, or to any one of those who went to serve there in any capacity. This is a point on which neither Father Salvatierra nor his successors ever wished to yield, in spite of the slanders and calumnies of their enemies and the petitions and complaints of the soldiers themselves. Father Salvatierra, although very charitable toward all, was nevertheless so severe in maintaining the interdict on the fishing that, when he found out that some soldiers and sailors whom he had sent to Sinaloa to bring provisions had gone to fish for pearls he dismissed them all as soon as they returned. It seemed very harsh and unendurable to the soldiers that they should be denied permission to take advantage of the only valuable thing that there was in that country (in other ways so poor) where they served in the midst of so many dangers, when (on the other hand) permission was readily granted to those of Sinaloa and Culiacán and to anyone else who wanted to enrich himself, thus reserving the wealth of that peninsula to strangers while the poverty, work, and dangers were reserved for its inhabitants.

But Father Salvatierra used to answer that he paid not fishermen but sailors; that when they had been employed in that capacity a contract had been made with them that they were never to be employed in fishing; that if they were not content with their life and wished to become wealthy with that trade (as they flattered themselves they could do), each one of them was free to leave his post as a soldier and go and ask the viceroy for permission for the fishing which he so much desired. In fact, many became licensed for that reason and were afterward disappointed.

As regards the missionaries (as much because of their office as because of their institution), they were very far from thinking of pearls; but in order that they might be less so, the superiors had forbidden them, under the precept of holy obedience, to fish for pearls, to have them fished for, or to buy them from anyone. And this precept was never broken. Of all the inhabitants of California pearl fishing was permitted only to the Indians for their own use; but they did not value it very much.

The soldiers were distributed in two presidios and in the Missions. There was one in each Mission; but in the last one, because it was on the frontier of the barbarian gentiles, there were three or four, just as they were needed. Those who were at the Missions shared the jurisdiction of the captain to a certain degree. They could punish the less serious crimes, provided it were with the consent and the direction of the missionary. This punishment was reduced to six or eight lashes or to a few days in prison; but when it was a question of a crime that deserved the penalty of banishment or death, they simply apprehended the criminal and reported with him to the captain, whose duty it was to sentence him.

Whenever the missionary was absent to confess some sick person or was engaged in other spiritual duties, the soldier took his place in taking charge of the storehouse, in distributing food to the neophytes and catechumen, and in directing the labors of the field and other similar things. But this was not done gratuitously by him because, besides being paid by the missionary, he was richly recompensed in proportion to his services and to the means of the Mission. Therefore, he had to spend almost nothing of the four hundred and fifty *scudi* which the king assigned to him. At times he made the dinner for himself and the missionary, but at other times, the missionary made it for the two.

The soldiers by their bad behavior often increased the troubles of the missionaries; but, on the other hand, it was necessary to tolerate them. Father Ugarte was accustomed to apply to this situation that verse of Martial: *Nec tecum possum vivere, nec sine te.*[57] But when their ardor for pearls had cooled off or had entirely passed, and when the captain had tried with the greatest care to send to the Missions those of better habits who were more honorable and industrious, the missionaries then began to breathe.

It was the duty of the superior of the Missions to appoint the captain and admit or discharge soldiers. Although this was approved by the viceroy of Mexico and by the Catholic king as most convenient to the government of the peninsula, the Jesuits nevertheless, in order to free themselves from those serious troubles which the use of that authority caused them, renounced it in 1744, contenting themselves from then on with recommending to the viceroy the person who seemed most suitable to them for the office of captain, so that he might appoint him and leave to the captain himself the authority of admitting and discharging soldiers as he thought best.

The captain-governor lived in Loreto, as much because there it was easier to hinder contraband trade in pearl fishing, to send commands, or to move to any other part of the peninsula where it might be necessary, as because the principal presidio, the soldiers, the procurator of the Missions, the general warehouse, the boats, and the sailors were there. This wretched village, which did not deserve the title of capital except in comparison with the other villages of the peninsula, which were much more wretched, was worthy of respect on account of the exemplary devotion and purity of the habits of its people. Every day at dawn, as soon as the harquebus shot was heard which the soldier fired who was on guard at the barracks, the praises of God began to resound in the barracks, as well as in the rest of the houses; and some went at once to church to visit the Real Presence and to dedicate the work of that day to Him. At the time of Mass, almost all went to hear it; and at evening the Indians gathered there to say the rosary and to chant the litany to the Virgin, the soldiers doing the same thing in the barracks at the same time, and all the others in their houses; but on Wednesday, Friday, and Saturday all did it at church.

[57] I can live neither with you nor without you.

On Sunday afternoons the people left the church in a procession, singing, as far as the barracks, the Christian doctrine and meeting the soldiers there. All returned together to the church, in which they heard the sermon of the missionary. He also preached on Saturdays to the Indians only; and on Thursdays he catechised the children, with whom the catechist did the same thing all week. On the first Sunday of every month and during all the holidays of the Blessed Virgin, the procession of the rosary was held in the afternoon with music. The veneration which those good people rendered the church was so great that no one passed in front of it without kneeling, although the doors might be locked. They often strengthened their souls with the holy sacraments, especially on the first Sunday of each month and on the holidays of Christ, the Blessed Virgin, or some of the saints. There were some persons of both sexes who, not limiting themselves to observing the Ten Commandments exactly, aspired to a more perfect life with prayer, with the mortification of the senses, and with the practices of the Christian virtues.

Chapter Twenty

THE ROYAL ORDER FOR THE EXPULSION OF THE JESUITS FROM SPANISH DOMAINS. THEIR SUCCESSORS IN THE MISSIONS OF CALIFORNIA

SUCH was the condition of that village and the peninsula when the Catholic king gave the order to expel the members of the Company of Jesus from all his domains.[58] This order took effect on June 25, 1767, in the

[58] On June 24, 1767, the viceroy, Marqués de la Croix, summoned to his office in Mexico City the archbishop of Mexico and several high officials of the government to discuss a confidential report from the king. Croix brought before them a sealed package. On removing the outside cover, he found another upon which was written, "Under penalty of death, you will not open this letter until at midnight on the 24th of June." Opening the letter, the viceroy found the order from King Charles III, commanding that the Jesuits be sent out of all Mexico. It read: "I invest you with my whole authority

towns of Mexico.[59] In regard to California the viceroy commended the execution of this order to a Catalán captain by the name of Don Gaspar Portolá; and at the same time he ap-

and royal power that you shall forthwith repair with an armed force—*a mano armada*—to the houses of the Jesuits. You will seize the persons of all of them and despatch them within twenty-four hours as prisoners to the port of Vera Cruz, where they will be embarked on vessels provided for that purpose. At the very moment of such arrest you will cause to be sealed the records of said houses, and the papers of such persons, without allowing them to remove anything but their prayer-books and such garments as are absolutely necessary for the journey. If after the embarkation there should be found in that district a single Jesuit, even if ill or dying, you shall suffer the penalty of death. Yo el Rey" (Bancroft, *History of Mexico*, Vol. III, pp. 438–39).

The next day Croix made public the following edict: "I make known to all the inhabitants of this country that the King, our Lord, on account of past occurrences, and in order to fulfill the first obligation with which God has granted him the crown of preserving intact its sovereign prerogatives, and of keeping his loyal and beloved people in subordination, peace, and justice, and for other very grave reasons which he conceals in his royal heart, has vouchsafed to command, upon the advice of his royal council and by decree issued on the 27th of last February, that the religious of the Company (of Jesus), priests as well as coadjutors or lay-brothers, who have made the first vows, and the novices who desire to follow them, shall be banished from all his dominions in Spain, the Indies, the Philippine Islands, and the other adjoining countries, and that all the property of the Company in his dominions shall be seized. His Majesty, for the sake of uniform execution everywhere, having authorized exclusively the Conde de Aranda, President of Castilla, and having committed to me its execution in this realm with the same plenitude of power, I have assigned this day for the announcement of the Supreme Sentence to be expelled in their colleges and houses of residence in this New Spain, and likewise for the publishing of it to its people with the warning that all subjects of whatever dignity, class, or condition they may be, strictly obliged as they are to respect and obey the ever just resolutions of their sovereign, must venerate, assist, and execute this one with the greatest exactitude and fidelity, because His Majesty declares that the disobedient or the remiss in co-operating with its fulfillment incur his royal indignation, and I shall see myself compelled to use the utmost rigor and military force against those that in public or in private for this purpose may have conferences, meetings, assemblies, talks, or discussions by word or in writing; for the subjects of the great monarch who occupies the throne of Spain must henceforth know once for all that they are born to keep silent and to obey, but not to discuss nor to judge the lofty affairs of government. Mexico, June 25th, 1767. El Marqués de Croix." See Engelhardt, *op. cit.*, Vol. I, pp. 272–73.

[59] The Jesuits were requested to gather at Mexico City. The noted Don José de Gálvez, whose services as visitor-general in Mexico are so closely related to the early history of the present state of California, was commissioned

pointed him governor of that very famous peninsula and ordered fifty well-armed men to accompany him in order to compel the Jesuits by means of terror to leave those Missions which they themselves two years before had renounced of their own free will but which they kept then only because their renunciation had not been accepted.

This commissioner [Portolá] embarked at the port of Matanchel in three small boats with the fifty soldiers and fourteen Franciscan Observants[60] who were going to succeed the Jesuits in the Missions of the peninsula. The boats were scattered by a storm; and the one of the commissioner, unable to go straight to the port of Loreto on account of foul winds, as he had been commanded by the viceroy, put in at the port of San

---

to care for the exiled Jesuits and to conduct them safely to Vera Cruz. Regarding the journey, Father Engelhardt says:

"On the 28th the religious, who had been collected at the capital, were placed in coaches and guarded by soldiers as though they were dangerous criminals, whereupon began the weary journey to Vera Cruz. At Guadalupe Don José de Gálvez, who had charge of the prisoners, allowed a stop to be made so that they might for the last time pay homage to the Patroness of Mexico at her famous shrine. After they had recommended the people of the country to their heavenly Queen, the journey was resumed. Meanwhile great crowds surrounded the coaches and gave vent to their grief in various ways. As the road to Vera Cruz was not intended for vehicles, the Jesuits were compelled to make much of the way on horseback or on foot, which caused intense suffering to the aged and the sick. Their arrival at Jalapa resembled a triumphal entry, though it was attended by so much bitterness. Streets, windows, balconies, and roofs were crowded with people, who showed in their faces what they dared not express in words. The troops found it necessary to force a passage with the butt-ends of their muskets" (Engelhardt, *op. cit.*, Vol. I, p. 274).

The physical suffering of the Jesuits must have been intense. Before leaving Vera Cruz thirty-four died. The remainder sailed for Havana, Cuba, where, under the kindness of the governor of the island, Antonio María Bucareli, who is also closely connected with the history of the state of California, allowed them to remain for a month that their health might be improved. Before landing in Italy several others died. There they were given a home and poorly supported, provided they did not criticize the actions of the king in expelling them. For a list of exiled Jesuits from Mexico and from the peninsula, see Bancroft, *History of the North Mexican States and Texas*, Vol. I, pp. 578-80.

[60] For the names of these Franciscans and a list of the Missions on the peninsula to which they were sent, see Englehardt, *The Missions and Missionaries of California*, Vol. I, pp. 289-305.

Bernabé, where he landed at the end of November of this year. Those missionaries knew nothing of what had happened to the Jesuits in Mexico, because during all those months no boat which could have brought the news had put in at the ports of California.

The commissioner went by land from the port to Loreto, accompanied by twenty-five of his soldiers; and the captain[61] of the peninsula was by chance in the southern part when the former arrived. In the long and secret conferences which the commissioner had with the captain, the former became disillusioned in regard to the errors which the enemies of the Jesuits had infused in his mind about the imaginary power of the missionaries; and he was convinced that in order to make them leave all their Missions and all their colleges and possessions a simple letter from the viceroy in which he might have intimated the royal order to their superiors would have been sufficient.

When the commissioner reached Loreto, he had Father Benito Ducrue[62] called, who was at that time the missionary of Guadalupe and the superior of those Missions; and, while Ducrue was there in company with three other Jesuits[63] he intimated to them the decree of the king, to which they submitted respectfully. At the request of the commissioner the superior wrote to all the other missionaries, giving them the news about it and notifying them to continue in their ministry until the arrival of the religious who were sent by the commissioner to make an inventory of each Mission; and after this was done, they were asked to gather at Loreto, bringing with them noth-

[61] Fernando Rivera y Moncada; see footnote 20, *supra*, p. 326.

[62] A German Jesuit, Father Ducrue was born in Munich in 1721. He became a Jesuit at the age of sixteen, and arrived in the peninsula in 1748. It became his sad duty to inform all the missionaries in the peninsula to prepare to leave. He wrote the story of the expulsion of the Jesuits from Lower California and of their journey to Europe, which Bancroft says (*History of the North Mexican States and Texas*, Vol. I, p. 478), "must be regarded as a standard work on the subject," as regards California. Father Ducrue returned to his native land where he died in 1799. Slowly the padres came to Loreto. Father Retz was suffering from a broken leg, and his neophytes carried him on their backs from Santa Gertrudis.

[63] Lucas Ventura, Francisco Franco, and Juan Villavieja (Bancroft, *History of the North Mexican States and Texas*, Vol. I, p. 480).

ing but their clothes and other necessary trifles, and only three books, one of devotions, one of theology, and one of history. The commissioner also urged them to preach to their neophytes exhorting them to keep calm and faithful during the absence of their former missionaries and to do likewise under the guidance of the new ones who were soon to arrive.

After the missionaries had promptly carried out what the superior and the commissioner required of them, they started out on their way to Loreto. When the neophytes saw those who had brought them up in a Christian life and who had toiled so hard for their welfare depart, they wept unrestrainedly; and the missionaries, turning their eyes to their beloved children in Christ whom they had brought into light with such pain and whom they were now leaving so distressed, could not hold back their tears.[64] When they took leave on embarking, the soldiers and even those who had come with the commissioner were moved to compassion, and they knelt in the presence of the latter to kiss their feet and bathe them with their tears.

The sixteen Jesuits[65] who were in the peninsula, including a Brother who had charge of the warehouse of Loreto, set sail[66] on February 3, 1768,* to go to the port of San Blas, a short distance from that of Matanchel.[67] And from there they made

---

* Fifteen priests and one Brother left California and fifteen priests and one Brother died there.

---

[64] As the Jesuits embarked at Loreto for their long journey to Europe, Father Baegert wrote in his *Nachrichten*, which was published in 1773: "I wept not only then but through the journey, and even now as I write tears fill my eyes" (Engelhardt, *op. cit.*, Vol. I, p. 277).

[65] For a list of the Jesuits who served in Lower California, together with some data about them, see Engelhardt, *op. cit.*, p. 285. Bancroft, *History of the North Mexican States and Texas*, Vol. I, p. 482, gives the same lists, with the exception of one, Father José de Echeverría. He arrived in the peninsula in 1730. With only a few exceptions these two historians agree relative to the length of time that each Jesuit served in Lower California. Engelhardt (*op. cit.*, p. 284), says, "fifteen Jesuit Fathers and One Jesuit lay-brother left the peninsula as exiles." According to Father Baegert, of those expelled eight were Germans, six were Spaniards, and two were Mexicans.

[66] From Loreto.

[67] They landed at Matanchel after four days of sailing. Here they were despoiled of a few personal effects that Portolá had allowed them to keep, and

a trip of more than eight hundred and fifty miles by land to the port of Vera Cruz,[68] whence they embarked again to be taken to Europe.[69]

When the missionaries withdrew from the Missions the soldiers stayed in them to maintain good order and to prevent the desertion of the neophytes until the Franciscan[70] Fathers arrived. These, after a painful passage of eighty days, put in at the port of San Bernabé[71] a few days before the Jesuits weighed anchor from that of Loreto.

then they were reshipped to San Blas. After a brief rest of four days in squalid quarters, they were placed on horses and mules and escorted, under guard, across Mexico.

[68] The trip to Vera Cruz was made in forty-four days under intense suffering. On April 13 the Jesuits embarked for Europe. At the same time that Portolá collected the padres in Lower California, the Jesuits were removed from the Missions in Sinaloa and in Sonora and assembled at Guaymas, where they were kept, as Father Baegert said (*Nachrichten*, pp. 299–301), in "cattle sheds for nine months." Then they were shipped to Matanchel and marched to Vera Cruz. Of the fifty who sailed from Guaymas only thirty lived to reach Europe. For a detailed account of the expulsion of the Jesuits, see Peter M. Dunne, "The Expulsion of the Jesuits from New Spain," in *Mid-America: An Historical Review*, January, 1937, pp. 3–30.

[69] The abrupt ending of Clavigero's story of the expulsion of the Jesuits has always caused comment. Regarding the despotic actions of Charles III Clavigero remains silent. Being a Jesuit he probably feared the wrath of the king should he criticize his policy.

[70] The Franciscans were the first of the religious orders to arrive in Mexico, under the authority of the king. Three padres, Juan de Ayora, Juan de Tecto, and Pedro de Gante, landed at Vera Cruz in August 1522. By July 1524 there were seventeen Franciscans in Mexico, and they began building churches, hospitals, and schools. The first school organized by this order, which was placed under the care of Father Gante, had a capacity of a thousand Indian children (Priestley, *The Mexican Nation*, pp. 97–99). Later (1536) the Franciscans opened a college (Santa Cruz) for the instruction of the Indian boys at Tlaltelolco. The college began with an enrollment of seventy students and offered courses in rhetoric, music, Latin grammar, medicine, and philosophy. Among the able teachers were Fathers Bernardino de Sahagún, a noted writer and historian, and Juan Focher, a distinguished scholar from the University of Paris. Schools were also started for Indian girls. They were taught chiefly the domestic arts and "the responsibilities of matrimony" (*ibid.*, p. 152). The Franciscans finished the first Mexican church in 1525.

[71] For the arrival of the Franciscans in the peninsula and their distribution there, see Bancroft, *History of the North Mexican States and Texas*, Vol. I, pp. 482–87; Engelhardt, *op. cit.*, Vol. I, pp. 289–313; and Bolton, *Palóu*, Vol. I, pp. 3–29.

We do not know how slowly they went to the Missions.[72] The only news brought in letters from Mexico at that time is that scarcely did the new missionaries see with their own eyes that California was not what they wished to have believed than they left the Missions and the peninsula and returned to their monasteries,[73] proclaiming everywhere that that country was uninhabitable and that the Jesuits should have been very thankful to the king for having taken them out of that great poverty. Afterward, some priests and friars went there; but, being unable to subsist in that country, Dominicans were sent there from Spain.[74] We do not know what these religious have done,[75] but we hope that their zeal is efficiently aided to maintain the faith of Jesus Christ among the Californians and to spread it among those very numerous peoples who are to the north so that all may know, worship, and love their Creator.

[72] The Franciscans remained in Lower California until 1772, when the king transferred them to Upper California, where they had already established four Missions. These were San Diego de Alcalá, San Carlos Borroméo, San Antonio de Padua, and San Gabriel Archangel. By the time that Clavigero had finished this history, the Franciscans had established six more Missions in Upper California. They were: San Luis Obispo de Tolosa, San Francisco de Asis, San Juan Capistrano, Santa Clara, San Buenaventura, and Santa Barbara. This order founded only one Mission in Lower California. When Governor Gaspar Portolá was marching north through the peninsula in 1769 to found a settlement at the bay of San Diego, he stopped just north of the Mission of Santa María at the Indian village of Vellicatá, and there the padres established a Mission. Father Junípero Serra preached to the Indians on that occasion. For the story of the transfer of the peninsula Missions from the Jesuits to the Franciscans, and from this order to the Dominicans, see Bolton, *Palóu*, Vol. I, pp. 169–213, 223–55.

[73] On this point Clavigero was misinformed, probably for a definite purpose.

[74] Two hundred Dominicans volunteered to come from Spain, but only twenty-six were accepted. They landed at Vera Cruz. Of these, four came from Andalusia, eight from Aragon, and thirteen from Castille. One was too sick to come.

[75] When California was divided in 1772 and the Dominicans took charge of the fourteen Missions on the peninsula, they possessed 6,220 sheep, 3,403 goats, 2,792 mules, 2,196 cows, and only 55 pigs. On May 12, 1773, eighteen Dominicans landed at Loreto and were assigned to the different Missions. For a careful study of the work of the Dominicans in Lower California, see Peveril Meigs, *The Dominican Mission Frontier of Lower California*.

Appendix

Appendix A

EXPERIMENTS AND OBSERVATIONS WHICH FATHER INAMMA,[1] A GERMAN JESUIT MISSIONARY IN THAT PENINSULA, MADE ON THE SNAKES OF THAT PENINSULA

THE REASON for these experiments was the extravagant opinion of another German missionary who maintained with scholastic subtleties that the illness caused by the bites of vipers and other poisonous snakes did not come from some harmful fluid transmitted to the blood, as is commonly believed, but only from the structure of the viperous tooth, which is very harmful to the limb bitten. In order to refute conclusively this very improbable opinion, although it had been believed by reason and experience, it was enough simply to state what Galen[2] relates about certain quacks of his time who let themselves be bitten by vipers without feeling any serious discomfort because they had been careful to stop up with a certain paste or with wax the holes of the fangs, through which they transmit the poison to the blood. Even before Galen, the ignorant Africans knew this, among whom they call those who busy themselves in sucking the poison from serpents' bites before the whole of the blood is infected *psylli*. But Father Inamma, in order to convince his companion, took the trouble to perform experiments and to explain them in a well-constructed letter from which we shall take some notes.

He made his experiments and observations on twelve live snakes, and all were of the genus *Crotaliferi* or rattlesnakes. These have a large head, a flat nose, and their jaws seem swollen because of a movable bone, which they have outside the upper gum on each side. Their ears are placed near the nostrils, that is, immediately above the two said bones.

---

[1] Father Inamma was an Austrian Jesuit, born in Vienna in 1719. He came to Lower California in 1750, and remained there until the Jesuits were expelled, at which time he was stationed at the Mission of San José.

[2] Born in A.D. 131, Galen was one of the most celebrated scientific writers and philosophers of Greece. He went to Rome when thirty-four years of age, and soon won fame as a physician and surgeon. Rejecting the theories of medicine of his time, he set up his own system, which was universally accepted for more than a thousand years.

Their tongues are round, but divided in two parts toward the end; they are cartilaginous and a dark red color, similar to coagulated blood, which they keep in transparent membranes, like sheaths; but when they become angry, they take them out of the sheath and stick them out of the mouth, vibrating[3] them with unbelievable velocity. When Father Inamma cut off the tongue of one snake within its very mouth, he could not draw even a drop of blood out of it. The tail, which is three or four fingers long, according to the size of the snake, is formed of rattles, which are made up of some little rings of a horny substance, movable and joined together by means of joints or articulations composed of three little rings each. If these rattles are separated from the body of the snake they do not sound, but sound only when it moves them, particularly when it flutters violently for biting.

It is deduced from the observations of Father Inamma that these snakes have three kinds of teeth; to wit: the first are canine-like curved fangs, concave and pierced, hollow near the root as well as in the convex part near the point, and designed to wound and to transmit the poison through the holes to the blood. The second, of canine-like curved fangs, but not pierced, are of use to the snakes for making their prey fast; and the third are upright incisors which it uses for masticating its food.

There are fourteen of the first kind, four of which are situated in the two hollows of the two movable bones, which have been mentioned. These four, the largest of all, are the weapons of the snake. When it does not use them for biting, it has them hidden within a membrane, in an almost horizontal position, with the ends turned toward the throat; but when it wants to bite, it raises these bones, unsheaths them, and erects the fangs. These are not so firmly inserted in their hollows that they cannot be drawn out easily, and, for that reason, the snakes often lose some fang on biting; but this loss is replaced in a short time because it has others near them within a livid membrane, in both parts of the gum. Each one of these two membranes contains five fangs, similar in all respects to the four principal ones, but smaller and different from each other in size, because they grow one after another. When the snake loses one of the principal four, it is replaced by another of those contained in the livid membrane; and it is joined to the hollow of the bone, where the lost tooth was, with a certain mucous substance which seems designed to form its root.

This was observed faithfully by Father Inamma. Each one of these creatures has, therefore, fourteen curved, sharp fangs; two in each movable bone, and five in each livid membrane. Only in one reptile did our observer find sixteen. The fangs of the second class are situ-

---

[3] It can scarcely be said that the rattlesnake really vibrates its tongue.

ated near the end of the nose, in the upper as well as in the lower part; and they also have the ends turned toward the throat. The teeth of the third class are placed in two rows in the lower jaw.

Now as regards the experiments, Father Inamma made many to demonstrate the falsity of the opinion of his companion. He made use of the teeth recently pulled from a snake, and of others when dry, to wound some animals in various places on their bodies; and he made their wounds deeper and more severe than the snakes are accustomed to make them. In spite of this the wounded animals did not undergo any bad change, with the exception of three roosters, two of which had some swelling that soon went away. The third was on the point of dying because the wound was so great, since he pierced it through a thick vein; but it recovered within two days without any remedy being applied. Nor was any remedy applied to either of the other animals on which he performed the experiments.

Afterward he inflicted wounds with the tooth dipped in the very poison of the snake; and he observed that considerable sickness was caused, but it was not comparable to that which the snakes themselves made. He wounded a rooster in this manner in the leg with a tooth, and, not being content with that, he even smeared the wound with poison. This immediately caused a great swelling; and on the following day all the flesh around about it became green, this color spreading afterward over all the leg as far as the joint-articulation of the toes; then the skin began at once to wrinkle up as if the leg were shrinking away. But after some days, the wrinkles, the green color, and the swelling disappeared; and the rooster became perfectly well without any help.

With a penknife dipped in the poison he made a wound in the same position on another rooster; and this wound, since it was larger and deeper, produced a more considerable effect, because, besides the swelling of the entire leg, the wound became ulcerated and oozed pus for some weeks. An eruption of about half an inch in diameter appeared, the skin separated from the flesh, and a growth appeared between the two, which was cut out when it had dried. Afterward the swelling went down, the pus ceased, the wound healed, and the rooster remained entirely well.

It may be believed that the reason why the poison used in this way does not do so much harm as that which the snake uses is probably because, by passing immediately from the teeth to the wound and being introduced into it violently, it maintains the necessary fluidity to be well mixed with the blood; and on the contrary, when it is taken out of the mouth of the snake, it thickens quickly with the air; and so, instead of mingling with the blood, it sticks, for the most part, at the mouth of the wound.

In order to make it evident that the poison transmitted to the blood in any way whatsoever causes death, Father Inamma caught a large dove and made it swallow four or five drops of that fluid, which he had caught in a small shell when the snake ejected it. When Father Inamma had done this, he left the house in the performance of his duties (I do not know what); and when he returned three-quarters of an hour later, he found the dove dead; and he noticed that it had thrown out a turbid and foamy liquid from its beak.

In order to obtain some quantity of poison for the purpose of observing it and for making experiments on animals, he irritated the snake. And he had an animal approach and provoke the snake to bite, but endeavoring that it should not carry out its intent, because they eject the poison not only when they bite but also when they make any violent effort to bite. On a certain occasion, when he was extracting a tooth from a snake with a penknife, it threw out the poison through the other tooth with such abundance and force that it not only bathed his hand, but even part of his arm; and after he had extracted all the four teeth, which it uses for wounding, it continued sending forth that fluid from the hollow of the movable bones where the teeth are situated.

These experiments of Father Inamma show that the greatest or the least sickness, which the snakes cause, and the greatest or the least quickness in producing it depend on the size of the wound, the quantity of poison transmitted, the constitution of the wounded animal, and the condition of the wounded part. If the snake does not drive its teeth into the flesh, but only scratches the skin and does not inject the poison into it, no swelling or any other evil results. If it leaves poison in the scratch, it does not cause death, although it produces considerable sickness. A puppy wounded in this manner on the joint-articulation of a paw had a considerable swelling and spent two days in continual whining, after which he became perfectly well. If the bitten part is all composed of bones and skin with little blood, as in the feet of birds, the wound is very painful but not fatal. A rooster bitten on the toe by one of the snakes of Father Inamma had a great swelling in the entire foot; the wound became ulcerated and produced a very bad-smelling pus; afterward the wound wrinkled up, and all the skin became dry; and finally it lost the toe. Eleven months had already passed without the swelling going down completely, when the rooster disappeared, having gone away from the poultry-yard or having been caught perhaps by some wildcat or coyote.

If the snake drives its teeth into the flesh of any animal and transmits the poison into the blood, it indubitably causes death, provided some efficient antidote is not applied quickly. Thus a dove bitten on the breast died in two hours; a kid bitten on the lip, in an hour and a half; and at Cademino, a place in the Mission of Purísima, an Indian woman who was wounded on a foot died in a day and a half, because Father Inamma, who was the missionary then, was absent and the Indians did not apply any remedy until some hours had passed. On the contrary, an Indian of Comondù, who was bitten on the large toe, was cured perfectly because Father Inamma helped him immediately with suitable remedies. It is true that another, likewise bitten on the foot, bled through the mouth and soon died in spite of the remedies which the same missionary applied to him; perhaps the latter was bitten not by a rattlesnake but by another of those snakes which the Mexicans call *Aheujactli*,[4] and which are more venomous and make the blood flow through the mouth, nostrils, ears, and even through the eyes.

Although Father Inamma dissected several snakes, he does not venture to say where they keep the poison. But the analogy between them and vipers is so great in the structure of the fangs as well as in the manner of injecting the poison that what we know about the latter can probably be asserted about the former, judging from the exact experiments of Dr. Mead;[5] that is, that the poison is separated from the blood in the two glands which are found back of the eyes and above the muscles used to lower the upper jaw, which facilitate the separation and the exit of the poison by pressing the glands with their movement. These two large glands are composed of many small ones, all contained in a common membrane and each one having its secretory vein. The venom, thus separated from the blood, passes from these small veins to a large one, and from here to the little elevations of the gums which cover the large, strong roots of the four main fangs. The snake, by pressing this small elevation when erecting its teeth to bite, makes the poison pass to the cavity of the teeth through the hole which these have near the root, and from there forces it through the opening which these same teeth have at the ends.

The remedies used in California for the venom of snakes and other animals are partly internal and partly external. The most usual and efficacious internal one is *teriaca umana*, or human excrement, which they make the bitten person drink, when it is fresh and dissolved in water. This drink, although loathsome, is taken without repugnance because of love of life; besides, since the people bitten are almost frantic because of confusion and fear, they are not accustomed to notice what is given them, as an Indian bitten by a snake confessed to Father Inamma after his recovery.

The most usual external remedies, besides the ligatures which are usually made to retard the spread of the poison, are lizard's fangs and snake-stone. The fang of the lizard receives much credence in all of

[4] Perhaps a name given to a traditional snake.

[5] A celebrated physician, born in England in 1673, Richard Mead graduated in medicine at Padua. In 1702 he wrote *Mechanical Accounts of Poisons*.

New Spain, because it is considered as a most efficient counter-poison. It is applied to the wound which is made larger with it so that the counter-poison may work better. Those who have used this remedy say that many times the tooth bursts with the activity of the venom which it extracts. That which is called snake-stone is nothing else than a deer horn which is burnt to a certain degree. This is applied like the fang to the wound and remains like it, adhered to it. Those who have applied snake-stone regularly assert that it extracts the poison until, not being able to extract more, it becomes loosened by itself. In order to use it again, they first purify it of the poison with which it has become saturated by placing it in hot water. As soon as it reaches the bottom of the water, it begins to throw off toward the surface a certain foam, which it does not cease discharging until the water is changed two or three times. Then it is entirely purified.

The Indians of the Philippine Islands, who were the first who prepared and used this antidote, do it this way. After they have crushed the deer horn, they make a pyramidal heap of it on the bare ground, placing an alternate layer of rice-hulls and another of pieces of horn. On a calm night they set fire to the hulls, which, burning little by little, set fire moderately to the horn. Afterward they give the shape they wish to the little burned pieces, usually making them round and the shape of a lentil; they polish them with the rough leaves of a shrub called *Is-is*,[6] and finally they give them luster with tanned leather. When they have become black, smooth, and lustrous with this process, they are sold as stones. In Mexico they are commonly known by the name of "Chinese stones" because the general public call the Philippine Islands China; but the Mexicans now know the manner of preparing that horn.

Vallisnieri[7] says that what is related about snake-stone is a fiction of the Indians who are very astute in deceiving Europeans, that he was not deceived by many experiments, and that he discovered that those over-esteemed stones were only ox bones burnt and well polished. But if those which he used were only ox bones, it is not strange that his experiments were not successful. M. San Bomare,[8] in the article, *Pierre d'Serpens*,[9] which contains some errors, speaks with scorn about snake-

[6] Confined chiefly to the Oriental islands, being so named from its resemblance to the corals.

[7] An eminent Italian naturalist, Vallisnieri was born in Módena, Italy, in 1661. He was widely known as a physician, and became the first professor of practical medicine at Padua. He died in 1730.

[8] A French naturalist, M. San Bomare was born in Roúen in 1731, and died in Paris in 1807. He published a work on mineralogy in 1794, and a dictionary of natural history in 1800.

[9] *"The Serpent's Stone."*

stone; but he states that he had neither seen it nor knows what it is; because if he had known it, he would have spoken about it in a different manner, since in the article, "Cerf,"[10] he states that *the horn of this quadruped is abundant in volatile salt and is an excellent counter-poison.* Father Vaniere,[11] in his excellent poem entitled *Praedium Rusticum*, describes snake-stone in Book 3 in this manner:

> Est lapis Eoo nuper delatus ab orbe,
> Subniger, et levior, serpentum nomine dictus
> Quem si tecum habeas secura innoxius angues
> Jam poteris tractare manu. Serpentis ad ictum
> Applicitus lapis in sese trahit omne venenum
> Quod removet vel aqua mersus, vel lacti tepenti.
> Quin et mortiferam lapis idem sugit ab altis
> Vulneribus tabem, plagaeque tenacius haeret,
> Ebrius exhausta sanie, dum labatur ultro.[12]

---

[10] "Deer."

[11] A French Jesuit, Father Vaniere was born in Languedoc in 1664. He taught in several of the French colleges, and enjoyed a wide reputation for his Latin poems. He died in 1739.

[12] "This blackish and quite smooth stone recently brought from the Orient is called serpent-stone. If you have it with you, you will at once be able to handle snakes unharmed with a careful hand. The stone, applied to the snake-bite, draws all the poison into itself, which it gives up when immersed in either tepid water or milk. Indeed the same stone both sucks the death-dealing poison from deep wounds and clings very tenaciously to the wound until, filled with the venomous humor which it has drawn out, it is loosened of its own accord.

Appendix B

Here we write the Lord's Prayer in the three dialects of the Cochimí language, so one may see how great the diversity is which exists among the dialects of a single Californian language.

The *Pater Noster* in the Cochimí language in the dialect of the missions of San Francisco Javier and San José de Comoñdù:

Pennayù nakaenambà, yaà ambayujùp miya mò, buhù mombojuà tammalà gkomendà hi nogodognò de muejueg gkajim: pennayulà bodognòg gkajim, guihì ambayujup mabà yaà Kaeammet è decuinyi mò puegign; yaàm buhula mùjua ambayujupmò de dahijua, amet è no guilugui, ji pafkajim. Tamadà yaà ibò tejuèg guilugigui pamijich è mò, ibò yanno puegin: guihì tammà yaà gambue jula Kaepujui ambinyijuà pennayula dedaudugùjua, guilugui pagkajim: guihì haà tagamuelà huì ambinyyjùa hi doomò pueguegjuà hi doomò pogounyim; tameugjua, guihì ufi mahel Kaeammet è dicuin yumò, guihì yaà huì mabinyì yaà gambuegjùa pagkaudugum. Amen.

The *Pater Noster* in the Cochimì dialect of the missions of San Francisco de Borja, Santa Gertrudis, and Santa María:

Cahaì apà, ambeìng mìa, mimbang-ajùa val vuit-mahà: amèt mididuvajuà cucuèm: jemmujuà, amabàng vihì mièng, ame tenàng luvihim. The-vàp yicuè timiei: digùa, i banganàng gna cahittevi-chip nuhiguà aviuvehàm, vi chip iyeguà gnacaviuvèm: cassetasuàng mamenit-gnakùm, guang tevisièc gna cavignahà. Amen.

The *Pater Noster* in the dialect of the missions of San Ignacio:

Ua-bappà amma-bang miamù, ma-mang-à-juà huit maja tegem: Amat-mathadabajuà acuem: kem-mu-juà amma-bang vahi-mang amat-à-nang la-uahim. Teguap ibang gual guìeng-a-vit-à-jua iban-à-nang pac-kagit: maht-pugijuà abadakegem, machi uayecg-juà pac-kabaya-guem: Kazet-à-juangamuegnit-pacum: guang mayi-acg packabana jam. Amen.

Index

INDEX

Acacia, 48, 53, 210
Acaponeta, 135
Acapulco, port of, viii, 19, 120, 285, 335; ships at, 376; vessels from, 119
Acapulco, town, 19, 28 n., 123, 128, 132, 225
ACEVEDO, GASPAR DE ZÚÑIGA, 128 n.
ACUÑA, JUAN DE, 296 n.
Adac, 342, 343, 358, 361; buildings, 339; location, 333; population, 341
"Adam's Tree," 58
adultery, 105
Afeguà Island, 280, 281, 282
Aheujactli, 393
AHOME, BUENAVENTURA DE, 340, 345, 346
Ahome Mission, 362
Ahome, port of, 215
AHUMADA, AUGUSTÍN, MARQUÉS DE LA, 335 n.
alabado, 370, 371
ALARCÓN, HERNANDO DE, 20 n., 125
Alaska, 136 n.
ALBUQUERQUE, CUEVA ENRÍQUEZ, Duke of, 194 n.
ALENCOSTRE, FRANCISCO DE, Duke of Linares, 153 n.; career of, 205
alférez, 202, 336 n., 338
Algarve, 324
Altar River, 180 n.
ALVARADO, PEDRO DE, 126
anabà, 39
Anàhuac, 89
Ángel Custodio Island, 20, 345
Ángel Custodio, village of, 241
Ángel de la Guardia, 20, 69
ANZA, JUAN BAUTISTA DE, 16 n.; expedition with Rivera, 327 n.
Apache Indians, 16 n., 201, 316
Apate, 255, 256

ARGÜELLES Y MIRANDA, DOÑA JOSEFA DE, 356
Arizona, 124 n., 125 n., 148 n., 210 n., 217 n.
Arizpe, 201 n.
ARMESTO, JUAN, S.J., 231 n.; procurator, 335, 375 n.
ARNÉS, VICTORIANO, S.J., 72, 361, 345, 363, 365; trips of, 364
arrowtree, 55
ARTEAGA, FRANCISCO DE, S.J., 177 n.
ARTEAGA, NICOLÀS DE, 153 n., 192
ARTEDI, PETER, 67
asigandù, 39
audiencia, 122, 151, 154, 191; described, 313 n.
avocado, 42 n.
AYER, EDWARD EVERETT, 292 n.
AYORA, FATHER JUAN, 385 n.
AZEVEDO, IGNACIO DE, S.J., ix

BAEGERT, JACOBO, S.J., 4, 36 n., 85 n., 87 n., 88 n., 93 n., 103 n., 385 n.; and Clavigero, 110 n.; grieving of, 384 n.; story of *guama*, 114 n.
bagre, 67, 70
BAITOS, JUAN FRANCISCO, 286, 287
Bajorca Mission, 283 n.
BALTHASAR, JUAN ANTONIO, S.J., 318 n.
BANCROFT, HUBERT HOWE, 18 n., 103 n., 119 n., 123 n., 128 n., 132 n., 140 n., 146 n., 159 n., 164 n., 180 n., 219 n., 260 n., 261 n., 335 n., 370 n., 381 n., 382 n., 383 n., 385 n.
Banderas Bay, 119 n.
BARCO, MIGUEL DEL, S.J., 4, 44 n., 144, 370
BARTIROMO, MELCHOR, S.J., 344 n.

399

BASALDUA, JUAN MANUEL, S.J., 207, 210; in Mexico, 195; money for, 197; work of, 192, 206
batamote, 50
Berkeley shellmound, 26 n.
birds, 77–78; islands of, 280; new, 281
BISCHOFF, JUAN JAVIER, S.J., 335 n.
Boats, 156, 170, 174, 200, 217, 237, 239, 241, 245, 251, 253, 280, 285, 286, 318, 340; "Agueda," the, 123 n.; best, 336; captured, 166–67, 301; construction of, 219; cost of, 335, 336, 349; "Covadonga," the, 315 n.; destroyed, 337; "Lauretana," the, 334; lost, 247 n., 250, 276, 301, 318, 353; "Nuestra Señora de Guadalupe," the, 225; "Nuestra Señora del Rosario de Torrentuguí," the, xiv, 192, 197, 199, 217, 219; number of, 374; poorly built, 170; purchase of, 196; "San Antonio," the, 247 n.; "San Carlos," the, 247 n.; "San Fermin," the, 170, 176; "San Francisco Javier," the, 170, 179, 182, 188, 199, 217, 225, 231; "San José," the, 170, 334; "Santa Barbara," the, 247; "Trinidad," 123 n.; "Triunfo de la Cruz," the, 236, 247
Bologna, xiv, xv, xvii, 335 n.
BOLTON, HERBERT EUGENE, xix, 27 n., 28 n., 124 n., 125 n., 129 n., 130 n., 135 n., 139 n., 140 n., 156 n., 171 n., 179 n., 180 n., 192 n., 221 n., 234 n., 328 n., 365 n., 385 n., 386 n.; bibliography of Kino, 148 n.; discovery of manuscript, 143 n.
BOMARE, M. DE, 65, 67 n., 69, 70, 71, 72; article by, 394
BORJA, DOÑA MARÍA DE, 332; donations of, 333
BORJA, SAN FRANCISCO DE, S.J., 156, 333
BOTON, Indian governor, 285; conspiracy of, 288; deprived of office, 284

BRAVO, BROTHER, xviii, 233, 239, 240; business of, 229; missionary, 237; petitions, 230–31; services of, 206–7, 213
BRAVO, SANTIAGO, S.J., 258, 259, 298, 334; letters, 998–99; mission of, 239–40; work of, 240–41, 321–22
Brotherhood of Dolores, 153, 196
BRUCE, JAY, 79 n.
BUCARELI, ANTONIO MARÍA, 382 n.
BUCHANAN, JAMES, vii
BUENAVISTA, MARQUÉS DE, 153
BUFFON, C. DE, 81, 82, 83
BURRIEL, ANDRÉS MARCOS, S.J., 3, 279 n.

CABALLERO, JUAN, 168
Caborca, 179 n.
CABRILLO, JUAN RODRÍGUEZ, 20 n.; discoverer of state of California, 127
Cabujakaamang River, 364
Cadegomò, 226, 234
Cagnajuet, 364; location of, 363
Calagnujuet, 72 n., 363, 364, 365; location of, 357, 361
California, Gulf of, 15, 16, 120, 123, 179; crossed by Cortés, 121; difficulties in, 246, 247; Iturbi in, 134; pearls in, 28; Ugarte in, 246–54; Ulloa in, viii, 22 n.
California, name of, 16, 17, 122
California, state of, vii, 16 n., 79 n., 87 n.; grasshoppers in, 64 n.; Missions in, 172 n.
CALVERT, CECILIUS, x
CAMPOI, JOSÉ RAFAEL, S.J., xiii, 17 n.
CAÑAS, LUIS CESTÍN DE, 136–37
CARAVANA, JUAN (NICOLÁS), 156 n., 160, 161
CARBONEL, ESTEVAN, 136
CÁRDENAS, LÓPEZ DE, 125 n.
cardón, 36, 37, 56, 57
CARDONA, TOMÁS, 134 n.
Carmelites, 130
Carmen, island of, 20, 30, 31, 160, 231

400

CARRANCO, LORENZO, S.J., 260, 277; conspiracy against, 284, 290; eulogy on, 293 n.; letter of, 289; murdered, 291, 292 n.; sketch of, 260 n.
CASAFUERTE, MARQUÉS DE, 296, 304
CASANATE, PEDRO PORTEL DE, 137
CASTILLO, ANTONIO DE, 134
CASTRO, AGUSTÍN, S.J., xvii
cat's-claw, 49 n.
cattle, 93, 156 n., 326 n., 373; from Sonora, 179 n.; sent to Salvatierra, 148 n.
cédulas, 196, 296, 315, 316, 317
CERMENHO, RODRÍGUEZ, 132 n.
Cerralvo, island of, 19, 87, 255; savages from, 259
Cerros Island, 20
Chacala, port of, 139, 140, 170
CHAPMAN, CHARLES E., 16 n., 122 n., 128 n., 136 n., 152 n., 156 n., 279 n., 316 n., 327 n., 356 n.
CHARLES II, King of Spain, 17, 138, 139, 191
CHARLES III, King of Spain, xiv, xv, 329 n., 385 n.; expulsion order, 380–81
cherimoyer, 43
Chiametla, 121, 131, 134
Chichimecas, 52
CHICORI, Indian chief, conspiracy of, 287; girl stolen by, 284; resolution of rebellion, 285
Chihuahua, vii, 36 n.; tribes in, 155 n.
China, ix, 394
Chinese, 210 n.
"Chinese stone," 394
Chinipas, headquarters of Salvatierra, 149 n.
cholla, 57
Cholula, 291
ciruelo, 38
Civil War (United States), vii, viii, 28 n.
CLAVIGERO, FRANCISCO JAVIER, S.J., 15 n., 18 n., 26 n., 28 n., 40 n., 44 n., 82 n., 103 n., 111 n.,

140 n., 149 n., 219 n., 293 n., 386 n.; and Father Baegert, 110 n.; birth of, xii; comments of, 247 n.; death of, xvi; education of, xii–xiii; lacked information, 132 n.; Preface of, 3–12; silence on expulsion, 385 n.; writers, ridiculed by, 5–12; writings, xiii–xvii
Cochimì Indians, 23, 35, 48, 51, 53, 56, 57, 86, 97, 98, 112, 114, 144, 241, 260, 269, 297, 350; character of, 254, 263; deceit of, 111; holidays, 102; language of, 87, 88, 155, 210; location of, 87, 110; Missions among, 366; number of, 87 n.; preacher to, 269–70; religion, 110–11; skill in killing hare, 100; welcome to Piccolo, 226; women of, 97, 111
Colima, 19 n., 36 n.
colleges, 153 n., 203, 231 n., 385 n.; Alcalá, 279; French, 395 n.; Jesuit, 151 n.; Nice, 149 n.; Ocaña, 279 n.; Padua, 393 n.; San Andrés, 233 n.; San Gerónimo, 292; San Gregorio, 152 n.; San Ignacio, 292; San Ildefonso, 279 n.; San Pedro y San Pablo, xiii, 153; Tepotzotlán, 160 n., 292, 325; Valladolid, xii
colombella, 67, 69, 70
Colorado River, 15, 16 n., 22 n., 28 n., 125 n., 235 n.; Missions on, 179 n.
Columbia River, 68 n.
COLUMBUS, CHRISTOPHER, viii, 71 n.
COMANJI, ANDRÉS, 211, 329, 330, 331
Comondù, Mission San José del, 277; founded, 216, 302; location of, 216
Company of Jesus, *see* Jesuits
Compostela, 125 n., 170
Concepción, port of, 253
CONSAG, FERNANDO, S.J., 93, 331, 338, 357; death of, 334; inland trip, 328–29; log of, 319; map of, 345; sketch of life, 283 n.; voyage of, 318; zeal of, 332

401

copal, 54
COPART, JUAN BAUTISTA, S.J., 140 n., 155, 158
Coras Indians, 141, 142
corcho, 49–50
CORONADO, FRANCISCO, 125, 126
CORTÉS, HERNÁN, viii, ix, xi, 11, 17, 19 n., 123, 125, 126, 129 n., 146 n., 217 n.; at Vera Cruz, viii; death of, 124; in Lower California, 121; letters of, 139; plans of, 119; recalled, 122
CORTÉS, JACINTO, S.J., 137 n.
COSTANSÓ, MIGUEL, 336 n.
cotton, 365, 373
Count of Miravalles, 153
CRESPI, FATHER JUAN, 326 n.
CROIX, CARLOS FRANCISCO DE, 355 n.; edict of, 381 n.; sealed package, 380 n.
Cuba, 283 n., 317 n.
Culiacán, 31, 74, 124, 126, 134; founded, 121 n.
CUNNINGHAM, CHARLES HENRY, 313 n.

dammià, 34
DAVIDSON, GEORGE, 20 n., 130 n.
deer, 79, 80–81, 102, 115, 186 n., 281; dispute about, 265–66; killed by Indians, 99
DÍAZ, MELCHOR, 125 n.
DIEZ, JUAN JOSÉ, S.J., 72 n., 361 illness of, 362
DIOS, SAN JUAN DE, 358
dogs, 78, 93, 258
Dolores, Virgen de los, 254–56, 324, 367
Dominicans, 386
dorados, 67, 70
DOS, VICENTE, 15 n.
DOYE, SANTIAGO, S.J., 219
DRAKE, SIR FRANCIS, 17 n., 28 n., 46 n., 127, 131 n.; on Pacific Coast, 128; voyage of, 127 n.; landed at Drake's Bay, 128 n.
DUBAVÀ, BERNARDO, 211
DUCRUE, BENITO, S.J., 383
DUNNE, PETER M., S.J., 385 n

ECHEVERRÍA, JOSEPH, S.J., 231 n., 237, 276, 375 n., 384 n.
Ecuador, 126 n.
education, 211, 321, 370; Clavigero's, xii–xiii; of the neophytes, 372
EGUIARRETA, JUAN ANTONIO DE VIZARRÓN, 286 n.
ENGELHARDT, CHARLES ANTHONY, 86 n., 90 n., 152 n., 153 n., 156 n., 160 n., 238 n., 260 n., 353 n., 360 n., 365 n., 370 n., 381 n., 382 n., 384 n., 385 n.
England, x, 353 n.
ENRÍQUEZ, PAYO, 139 n.
Ensenada, 20 n.
ESCALANTE, FRANCISCO DE, 335
ESCOBAR, CRISTÓBAL DE, S.J., report of, 316
ESCOBAR, JOSÉ MANUEL DE, S.J., 354
Espíritu Santo, island of, 19, 26 n., 87, 240, 255; Father Taraval on, 295
Eucharist, 193, 372

fanegas, 44, 263
Favores Celestiales, 143 n.
Fehual, 265
FERDINAND VI, King of Spain, 4, 7, 317
FERRELO, BARTHOLOMÉ, 127 n.
fiscal, 146, 151, 155, 175, 178, 188, 196, 198, 231, 232, 313, 355
fish, 55, 67–72
Florida, 124, 156 n.
flying fish, 67, 70
FOCHER, FATHER JUAN, 385 n.
FONTE, BARTHOLOMÉ, 136
Franciscans, 16 n., 27 n., 28 n., 86 n., 120, 128, 139; baptizing of children, 139; colleges of, 151 n.; departure of, 386 n.; first church, 385 n.; at Loreto, 172 n.; in Lower California, 139, 382, 385 n.; in Upper California, 385 n.; sketch of, 385 n.
FRANCO, FRANCISCO JAVIER, S.J., 345, 383 n.
French and Indian Wars, 191 n.

FUENCLARA, COUNT OF, 315
Fuerte River, 149 n., 173 n., 352 n.

GALEN, CLAUDIUS, 389
GÁLVEZ, CONDESA DE, 190
GÁLVEZ, JOSÉ DE, 336 n., 381 n.
GANDÍA, DUQUESA DE, 365
GANTE, FATHER PEDRO, 385 n.
garambullo, 36
GARCÉS, FRANCISCO, S.J., 16 n.
Germany, xvi, 169
GIL DE LA SIERPE, DIEGO, 153 n.
GIL DE LA SIERPE, PEDRO, 164, 165 n.; gives boat, 153–54, 170
Gila River, 22, 179 n., 180, 201 n., 316, 319; crossed by Díaz, 125 n.
goats, 78, 84, 308, 339; killed, 190, 267
gold, 28, 29, 128 n., 132 n., 134 n., 248 n.
GOÑI, MATÍAS, S.J., 140 n.
GONZALES, THYRSO, S.J., 154 n.
Gordon Manuscript, 256 n., 292 n., 293 n., 298 n., 307 n.
GORDON, WILLIAM, S.J., 256 n., 277, 289, 293 n.
GRAHAM, ISAAC, 353 n.
grain, 43–45, 331
GRIJALVA, HERNANDO DE, 120, 126 n.
guacamote, 53
Guadalajara, 126 n., 233, 237, 280, 354
Guadaloupe, island of, 71
Guadalupe Mission, 239 n., 241, 244
Guaicuras Indians, 23, 86, 97, 105, 109, 112, 141, 142, 237, 239, 255, 258, 259, 283, 350; character of, 254; Spanish defended by, 161; embassy to, 295; enemies of Pericùes, 309; flight of, 227; hostilities of, 142; location of, 87; Missions among, 366; pleasures, 240; religion, 109: women of, 96, 97, 113
guama, 7, 8, 243, 258, 265, 270, 306; baptized, 211–12, 266, 267; bonfire, 344; confession of crime, 267; fees of, 166; death of, 212, 216, 269; dress of, 257; of the Guaicuras, 109; impostors, 115, 218, 262, 265, 269; inciting Indians, 182, 265–66; killed, 209, 282; not priests, 112; practices of, 113, 208, 306; preaching of, 115, 265; panegyrics proclaimed by, 103; promises of, 114; reprimanded, 266; selected from astute children, 112; Tomás, 266
guaribo, 47, 236, 358
Guatemala, 126, 131; Ugarte in, 152 n.
Guaymas Mission, 210, 353 n.
Guaymas, port of, 217; village of, 179 n., 192 n., 210 n., 385 n.
GÜEMES Y HORCASITAS, JUAN FRANCISCO, 317 n.
guigil, 56
GUILLEN, CLEMENTE, S.J., 234, 240, 255, 295; director of Mission, 298; explorations of, 245; journey of, 240; letters of, 289, 290, 296, 298; road opened by, 239; in Sinaloa, 200; sketch of, 219 n.; work of, 255–56, 324
Guiricatà, 358, 363; location, 360
guisache, 40
GUISI, BENITO, S.J., 219; drowned, 220
GUZMÁN, NUÑO DE, 31 n., 62; ships seized by, 121

haddock, 67
Hague Permanent Court, The, 152 n.
HELEN, EVERARD, S.J., 261 n., 264, 271; death of, 241 n.; explorations of, 246; Mission founded by, 241–42; illness, 243; success, 243–44
HERNANDEZ, FRANCISCO, 82
HERRERA, ANTONIO DE, 286; death of, 287
HEYN, PETER, 247 n.
Holland, 72 n.
HORBIGOSO, FATHER DOMINGO, 286, 287
Horcasitas, 249 n.
horses, 78, 156 n., 300
HOSTEL, LAMBERTO, S.J., 337

Huamalguà Island, 281; inhabitants of, 282
Huasinapi, *see* Guadalupe Mission

Ibò, 159, 164; first baptized, 163 idolatry, 242
INAMMA, FRANCISCO JAVIER, S.J., 370; experiments of, 389–93
Indians, viii, ix, 55, 134, 135, 208, 261; arithmetic of, 88; Aripas, 87; as sentry, 162; attack on, 342–43; attack on Mission, 193, 271; assembled at Missions, 366–68; baptized, 168, 200, 260, 261, 262, 270, 274, 282, 331, 334, 339, 362; barbarity of, 7, 90; calendar, 88–89; capture of Vaca, 124; change of name, 212 n.; children, 105, 106, 112, 115, 162, 200, 208, 211, 218, 226, 243, 259, 269, 270, 274, 385 n.; clothing of, 95–97; Chichimecas, 52; Conchò, 87, 97; conspiracy of, 166–67, 284–300, 352–54; converted, 372; customs of, 373; dances, 102; destruction of Mission, 182; deceit of, 110–11, 268–69; disease of, 90; distribution, 306; dress of, 96–98, 359; drunkenness, 91; education, 211, 370; epidemic among, 243, 264, 283, 320, 321, 346, 350, 368; exiled, 300, 307, 309; faithful, 297; festivities, 370; first baptized, 163; flight of, 227, 285, 308, 309; flogged, 307, 309, 343, 364; food of, 61, 80, 93–94, 95, 244, 258; funeral of, 113; gathering of fruit, 35; goodness of, 268; governor of Santiago, 284, 352; instruction of, 242; help to missionaries, 210; hostilities, 142, 255; household goods, 98–99; houses of, 360; idolatry among, 242; Jiménez killed by, 120; killing of, 161, 194, 255, 259, 296, 303, 307, 309, 320, 337, 342; labors of, 370; language of, 87, 88, 144, 145; at Loreto, 189; massacre, 179 n.; meals of, 94; meeting with Salvatierra, 158–59; methods of fishing, 100; most warlike, 217; nobility among, 103; old, 265; perspicacity among, 100; of Philippine Islands, 394; population, 346; punished, 274; origin of, 84–85, 89–90; outside tribes, 371; physical features, 90; pictures of, 84–85; Pimas, 217; Pomas, 55 n.; preparation for war, 272; protection of, 308–9; rattlesnake bite, 393–94; rebellion of, 284–300; 308–9; religion of, 87 n., 107–12, 265; religious services, 370–71, 379–80; shelter of, 95; repentance, 299; retreat of, 141–42; rules and regulations of, 162–63; as sailors, 247; seeking protection, 163; selection of captain, 181–82; simplicity of, 91–92; stealing of cattle, 93 n.; seeking baptism, 242; seeking food, 199; Seriès, 217, 225, 247; tranquillity of, 194; tribes, 16 n., 87, 269; uprising, 189–90; use of plants, 34, 35, 36, 37, 39, 40, 48, 49, 51, 52, 54, 55, 56; villages, 366–68; visited by Kino, 141; weapons of, 99, 100; weddings, 105; welcome to Vizcaíno, 129; with Salvatierra, 156 n.; Ugarte entreated by, 247; warfare of, 101; wives of, 103; women of, 51, 96–98, 104, 106, 162, 272, 278–79, 288, 350–51, 359; *see also* Apache, Cochimì, Coras, Guaicuras, Pericùe, Pima, Serì, *and* Uchitas Indians
insects, 58–66
Italy, xiv, xvi, 149 n., 205 n., 335 n., 336 n., 370 n.
ITAMARRA, FRANCISCO DE, 147
ITURBI, JUAN, 134

Jalisco, 19 n., 356 n.
Jesuits, 8, 26, 46, 65, 79, 102 n., 111, 139, 140, 146, 196, 210 n., 213, 304; animals imported by,

78–79; arrival in Mexico, x; business agents, 231 n.; in Canada, x; caves found by, 84; commendation of, 287; defended, 280; enemies of, 175–78, 304, 348, 354, 356; entreaties, 205; expulsion of, xiv, 151 n., 329 n., 380–85; false rumors about, 175–76; first in English colonies, x; first in Lower California, 135 n.; history of, ix, 279 n.; in Orient, ix; journey to Europe, 383 n., 384; last, 345 n.; list of, 382 n.; Missions, 136 n., 153 n.; money for, 191; nationality of, 384 n.; petitions, 154; plants introduced by, 46; praised by viceroy, 146; property of, 381 n.; proposals of, 146; provincial of, 137; records of, xv; renunciation by, 355–56; reports of, 156 n.; in South America, x; suffering of, 382 n.; at Vera Cruz, 382 n.; work of, xi; zeal of, 148
JIMÉNEZ, FORTÚN, viii, 28 n., 121, 129 n.; murdered, 120
jojoba, 40
JORDAN, DAVID STARR, 72 n.
junta, 231, 233; the nature of, 355 n.

Kadakaaman, 226, 261, 262, 263, 264, 266, 269, 270, 274, 282, 367; governor of, 272; Indians at, 280; threatened, 271
Kadakaamang, *see* San Ignacio Mission
Kansas, 125 n.
KINO, EUSEBIO FRANCISCO, S.J., xi, xviii, 3, 102 n., 154, 192 n., 235, 249; achievements of, 220–21; death of, 148 n., 221; experiments of, 144; exploration of country, 141, 180; founder of Mission, 178; Indians baptized by, 221 n.; in Lower California, 140, 220; manuscript of, 143 n.; on Red River, 23; and Salvatierra, 148–51, 179, 201 n.; sketch of,

148 n.; in Sonora, 148, 155, 220; supplies sought by, 179
KRMPOTIC, M. D., 283 n.
KROEBER, ALFRED L., 103 n.

LABAT, JEAN BAPTISTA, S. J., 71
LANZA, ANTONIO, 332 n.
La Paz Bay, 18, 19 n., 20 n., 23 n., 135, 142, 231, 239, 257, 300; Vizcaíno in, 129
La Paz, country of, 24 n., 36 n., 39 n., 320
La Paz Mission, 239 n., 283, 292 n.; Bravo at, 321; founded, 239–40; soldiers at, 286 n., 304
La Paz, town, vii, viii, 140, 173 n.
LARREA, BERNARDO RODRÍGUEZ DE (captain), 304, 326; removed, 305
LARREA, BERNARDO RODRÍGUEZ DE (son of captain), 307, 326
Las Palmas, port of, 257, 276–77
LASSEN, PETER, 365 n.
LA VERENDRYE, P. G. DE VARENNES, 131 n.
Liguig Mission, 219, 240, 255
LINK, WENCESLAO, S.J., 21 n., 240, 339, 357, 362, 363, 341; diary, 360 n.; trips of, 345–47, 358–60
LINNAEUS, CHARLES, 66, 67 n., 69, 70, 71, 72 n., 83
LISAXOAIN, IGNACIO, S.J., 353
live stock, 27 n., 172 n., 179 n., 192, 210, 264, 291, 330, 373; assembled, 326 n.; grazing for, 341; from Guadalupe Mission, 239 n.; lack of, 362; from Sinaloa, 170; Villapuente's, 191 n.
locusts, 61–66, 93; scourge of, 243
LOMBARDI, ANTONIO, xvii
Long Beach, 20 n.
LORENZO, ESTEVAN RODRÍGUEZ, 3, 205, 231; captain, 181, 201; honesty of, 325–26; quoted, 189; with Salvatierra, 156 n.; horse recovered by, 160; work of, 181, 324
Loreto, village, 24 n., 25, 158, 182, 207, 302, 321; description, 158 n.; Dominicans at, 386 n.; first Mission at, 157–59; importance of,

405

379, port of, 69, 178; population of, 160 n.; warehouse at, 195
Los Angeles County, 20 n.
Los Angeles, village of, 324; port, 21 n.; 333, 340, 341
Lower California, vii, viii, ix, xi, 336 n.; bees in, 59 n.; climate of, 21; Franciscans leaving, 385 n.; governor and judge of, 376; Indians in, 87 n.; an island, 246 n.; Jesuits leaving, 380–84; minerals in, 29; Missions in, 366–68, 386 n.; physical features of, 24–27; population of, 368; Portolá in, 381–84; poverty of, 177; reptiles in, 66; rivers of, 21; size of, 16, 368; storm in, 232
LOYOLA, SAINT IGNATIUS, ix, 46 n.
LUCENILLA, FRANCISCO, 139, 147
LUYANDO, JUAN, S.J., 31 n., 153 n.; ailments, 275; difficulties of, 269–70; founder of Mission, 261–62; preaching of, 265–66; savior of *guama*, 267; woman baptized by, 262–63; work of, 264, 268

Madrid, 316, 319
Magdalena Bay, 132 n., 245
maguey, 51
MANCERA, MARQUÉS DE, 138 n.
MANEIRO, JUAN LUIS, S.J., xvii, xviii
mangle, 49
Manila galleons, xi, 19 n., 127 n., 132 n., 315 n.; trips of, 133 n.
manta, 67, 71, 73
Manzanillo, 126 n., 127 n.
marble, 27 n.
marjoram, 46
MARTÍNEZ, PEDRO, S.J., x
Matanchel, 60, 215, 219, 229, 353, 374; Jesuits at, 384 n.; Portolá at, 382; wood from, 335
MAYORGA, GUILLERMO DE, S.J., 215, 216, 234, 306; death of, 216, 302; health of, 215
Mazatlán, island of, 219
Mazatlán, port of, 120 n., 131
MEAD, DR. RICHARD, 393 n.

medesà, 39
MEIGS, PEVERIL, 386 n.
MENDOZA, ANTONIO DE, viceroy, 126 n.
MENDOZA, ANTONIO GARCÍA, captain, 176; letters of, 176–78
MENDOZA, DIEGO HURTADO DE, 119 n., 120, 127
mescal, 51–52, 281, 282, 339
mestizos, 294
Mexico, vii, viii, ix, 49, 52, 119, 132 n.; Churches in, 138 n., 153 n., 385 n.; crossed by Marcos, 125 n.; grain in, 187; Guzmán in, 121 n.; Jesuits in, x; and the Pious Fund, 151 n.; presidios of, 201 n.; supplies from, 178
Mexico City, xvi, 12, 89 n., 120 n., 124, 125 n., 131, 133; departure of Ugarte, 180 n.; importance of, 197; Jesuits at, 381 n.
mezcal, 51 n., 53 n.
mezquitillo, 53
Michoacán, 19, 119, 131
milapà, 57, 339
MINUTULI, GERÓNIMO, S.J., 195; Lower California reached by, 192
MIRANDA, JOSÉ DE, 151, 155
missionaries, 146, 148, 168, 171, 194, 199, 215, 263, 276, 283, 287, 302, 305, 319, 350–51; advantages of, 320; called to Loreto, 193; charity, 194–95; customs, 234; direct soldiers, 169; enemies, 348; entreaties of, 352; expenses of, 375; explorations of, 245; food sought by, 189; inflamed by Kino, 148; journeys, 369; labors of, 320, 373–74; lot of, 369; neighbors, 364; obstacles encountered by, 144, 217; officials of, 368–69; orders to, 207; penetration of country by, 170–71; perils of, 209; promises, 147; provisions of, 347–48; quarters, 369; restored, 299; refuge of, 314; relation to soldiers, 203–4; renunciation of, 355–56; return to New Spain, 146; scarcity,

216, 261; shipwrecked, 219–20; smallpox among, 218; stipend for, 196, 204; uninformed, 383; wish of, 332; zeal of, 254, 357, 372
Missions, vii, ix, xii, 27 n., 122 n., 150 n., 273, 316, 349; abandoned, 366; buildings of, 330, 365; chain of, 235, 314, 316; churches, 369–70; on Colorado River, 179 n.; conditions of, 204; destruction of, 288; diseases among, 90 n.; districts, 368; Dominicans, 386 n.; extension of, 179, 180 n.; Indians at, 366–68; list of, 366–68, 382 n.; live stock, 27 n., 383 n.; location, 366–68; northern, 346; number of, 315, 317, 319 n., 366–68; officials in, 368–69; poverty at, 362; reduction of, 320; restored, 305–6; soldiers in, 286 n.; southern, 275, 320, 346–57, 358; support of, 151 n., 153, 204, 205, 206 n., 232, 315, 316, 374; visited by Salvatierra, 205
Misteca, xii, 238 n., 323
Mixton War, 126 n.
MOFRAS, DUFLOT DE, 252 n.
MOLINA, GASPAR DE, 336
Monterey (Upper California), 70 n., 132 n.; capital, 158 n.
Monterey Bay, 132 n., 326 n.; Portolá seeks, 336 n.
Moorish Idol, 68 n.
MORAGA, GABRIEL, 16 n.
MORÁN, ANTONIO, 188
mountain lion, 79–80, 83, 93, 99, 115; killed by Ugarte, 185–86
MUGAZABAL, JUAN BAUTISTA, S.J., as *alférez*, 238
Mulegè Mission, 244, 253; established, 210; first catechist in, 329
Mulegè, village, 27, 30, 207, 226, 236, 261
mulier, 72

NÀPOLI, IGNACIO MARÍA, S.J., 256, 258, 259, 277; baptism of children, 260; conspiracy against, 260; meeting with Indians, 257

Navidad, 127
Nayarit, 19 n., 353 n.
NELSON, EDWARD W., 49 n.
NEPOMUCENO, JUAN, 363; governor, 361
NEUMAYER, CARLOS, S.J., 345; death of, 344; labors of, 344–46
NEVE, FELIPE DE, 158 n.
New Mexico, 124 n.
Niparaja, 108, 112
NIZA, FATHER MARCOS DE, 125 n.
nombò, 50
nopal, 32 n., 37
Nuestra Señora de los Dolores Mission, 143 n., 192 n., 255, 297, 324, 367; a refuge, 256
Nuestra Señora de los Dolores Mission, in Sonora, founded by Kino, 148 n., 178 n.
Nuestra Señora de Guadalupe Mission, 30, 191 n., 261, 271, 340, 367
Nuestra Señora de Loreto Mission, 4, 204, 355 n., 367; destroyed, 173 n.; population of, 172 n.; services at, 379–80
Nuestra Señora del Pilar Mission, 191 n.
Nueva Galicia, 19, 52, 68, 74; magistrates of, 151

occhione, 72
OCIO, CABALLERO Y JUAN, 153, 164, 197; letter of, 166; Mission endowed by, 172 n.
OCIO, MANUEL DE, 28, 74–75; miner, 347
opuntia, see *nopal*
Oregon, 127 n., 128 n.
ORTEGA, FRANCISCO DE, 135–36
ORTEGA, JOSÉ FRANCISCO, 327 n.
OTONDO, ISIDORO DE, 139–40, 140 n., 156, 227, 247 n.; Indians welcomed by, 142; new expedition of, 147
oysters, 25, 75, 76

Palo Alto, 26 n.
palo blanco, 49

407

palo chino, 48
PALÓU, FATHER FRANCISCO, 27 n., 90 n.; story disputed by, 134 n.
Paris, 71 n., 86
PAW, M., xv, 5, 6, 7, 8, 10
pearls, 9, 19 n., 28 n., 73–76, 124, 132, 134, 136 n., 137, 138, 145, 166, 195, 376; bargain for, 326; disregard for, 175; diving for, 75–76; fishing prohibited, 376–78; Oriental, 74; report of, 120 n.
PEÑA, DOÑA ROSA DE LA, 276
PERALTA, FRANCISCO, S.J., 219
PÉREZ, JUAN, 18 n.
Pericùe Indians, 56, 86, 97, 98, 104, 106, 112, 255, 256, 260, 283, 285, 287, 289, 297, 300, 350; character of, 254; children of, 106, 107; claims of, 348–50; deceit of, 309; defeated, 303; distribution of, 320; governor of, 352; *guamas*, 114; hardships of, 354; in hiding, 302; killed, 303; Missions among, 277, 283, 366; murder of missionaries, 292 n.; plan of, 351, 352–54; rebellion of, 288–305; reduction of, 368; religion of, 108, 109; wives of, 103; women of, 96, 350
Perú, 22, 122, 125 n., 136, 137 n., 156 n., 296 n.
PHILIP II, King of Spain, 128, 133 n.
PHILIP III, King of Spain, 130
PHILIP IV, King of Spain, 137, 138
PHILIP V, King of Spain, xvii, xviii, 197, 316, 375; *cédula* of, 315; orders of, 191; quoted, 315; zeal of, 313
Philippine Islands, 6, 9, 19, 91, 127 n., 133, 196, 203, 231, 235, 247, 254, 285, 286; ships from, 204, 207, 213, 300, 348; Vizcaíno in, 128 n.
PÌCCOLO, FRANCISCO MARÍA, S.J., xviii, 3, 160, 174, 182, 194, 234, 241; absent, 197; baptism of children, 226; birth of, 155 n.; collection of provisions, 190; companion of Mugazabaı, 238; criticized, 177; death of, 275; indifference of, 198; instruction of children, 168; in Londò, 171, 190; at Loreto, 192; money obtained by, 191; at Mulegè, 210; praised, 177; report of, 156 n., 188–89; vines planted by, 6; work of, 165, 206
pigs, 78, 156 n.
Pima Indians, 217, 319 n., 353 n.; baptized, 218
pimentilla, 41
Pimería Alta, 148 n., 149 n., 192 n., 251; raids in, 316; revolts in, 353 n.
PIÑADERO, BERNARDO BERNAL DE, 138
Pious Fund, 375; beginnings of, 151 n.; support of, 153 n., 356 n.
pirates, 132 n., 134; English, 248 n.
pitahaya, 32 n., 33–34, 56, 57, 169, 189, 226, 329, 339
pitaje, *pitajo*, see *pitahaya*
PIZARRO, FRANCISCO, 125 n., 126 n.
plants, 32–58
PLINY, CAIUS, 69, 71, 81
Point Loma, 127 n.
polygamy, 104, 278, 350
porco marino, 70
porgy, 67
PORTOLÁ, GASPAR DE, 326 n., 357 n., 384 n.; governor, 382; at Loreto, 383; march of, 386 n.; sketch of life, 336 n.
Portugal, ix, 324, 336 n.
pozolli, 158, 163, 183, 208, 258, 370, 371
Prague, 321 n.
Presidio, 132 n., 135, 136 n., 193, 196, 201, 213, 238, 316, 336 n.; at Loreto, 305, 338; at Monterey, 326 n.; at Montesclaros, 352; at Nacosari, 201; new, 203, 231, 296; in northern Mexico, 201 n.; number, 376; at San José del Cabo, 304, 320; second, 366; support, 374; at Tubac, 201 n.; west coast, 204

408

PRIESTLEY, HERBERT INGRAM, 51 n., 122 n., 151 n., 335 n., 385 n.
procurators, 231 n., 237, 276, 304, 336, 352, 356, 375, 376
Puebla, city, xii, 233 n., 260 n.; college of, 151 n.
Puebla, state, 336 n.
Purísima Concepción Mission, 191 n., 228, 277, 280, 367; directed by Tamaral, 234–35; location of, 226
Purísima Concepción Mission (Colorado River), 179 n.

quadrupeds, 78–84
Quajaip, 108
Querétaro, 153; college at, 151 n.

Rahun Mission, 210
RAMUSIO, GIAMBATTISTA, 126
rattlesnakes, 20 n., 66; experiments with, 389–93
rays, 67
Red River (Colorado River), 15, 225, 247, 251, 256, 318, 332, 334, 346; Kino at, 23; Link at, 357–60; little use, 22; Missions on, 314; Salvatierra's exploration of, 180
reptiles, 66; *see also* rattlesnakes
RETZ, JORGE, S.J., 332, 339, 342; advice, 343; broken leg, 383 n.; founder of Mission, 330–31; trip of, 333
Revilla Gigedo Islands, 120 n.
RICHMAN, IRVING BERDINE, 122 n., 316 n.
Rio Grande River, 16 n.
RIVERA Y MONCADA, FERNANDO JAVIER DE, 158 n., 326, 327 n., 383 n.; murdered, 179 n.; and Portolá, 336 n.
RODEO, GASPAR, 153 n.
ROMANO, ALEXANDER, S.J., 231 n., 375 n.
roncador, 68, 70
ROTEA, JOSÉ, S.J., 85, 338
ROXAS, CARLOS, S.J., 335 n.

SAHAGÚN, FATHER BERNARDINO, 385 n.
sailors, 248, 250, 251; illness of, 252; murdered, 301; pay of, 374
SAINT FRANCIS XAVIER, ix
Salsipuedes Islands, 252
salt, 30, 31
SALVATIERRA, JUAN MARÍA, S.J., xi, xviii, 3, 8, 168, 170, 182, 190, 194, 201, 205, 206, 216, 217, 218, 225, 233, 235, 239, 249; absent, 197; affidavit of, 176; agreement of 1697, 175; appointed provincial, 177; attacked, 161; baptism of first Indians, 164; burial of, 230; cattle for, 148 n.; character of, 149–50, 218; charity, 189; collector of alms, 151, 180; criticized, 177; death of, 230; departure from Loreto, 229; departure from Mexico, 153; distress, 169, 178, 198; exploration of country, 170–71, 180, 192, 204; first sermon, 165; horse stolen, 160; illness of, 228–29; Indian liberated by, 144; instructions, 229, 231; interdict on fishing, 377–78; with Kino, 150 n.; in La Paz, 226–27; letters, 165–66, 168, 178, 198, 215; in Liguig, 199–200; main mission of, 149 n.; meeting with Kino, 179 n.; in Mexico City, 201; missionaries called by, 193, 198; at Missions, 205–7; opposition to, 175; orders, 207; permission to go to California, 150; petitions, 174, 203–4; possession of California taken in name of king, 157–62; praised, 177; quoted, 20 n., 169, 198, 239; request of, 247–48; rules and regulations of, 162–63, 180–81, 201, 305; sailing for California, 156; shot at by Indians, 200; in Sierpe's home, 153 n.; sketch of life, 101 n., 149–50; spirit, 152; in storm, 215
San Bernabé, port of, 21, 135, 286; Portolá at, 382; ships to, 286

409

San Blas, port, 247 n., 384
San Bruno, 143, 145, 146, 147, 156
San Carlos, port of, 318, 319
San Diego, city of, 326 n.
San Diego, harbor, 15, 132 n., 336 n.
San Diego Herald, xvii
San Diego Mission, 199 n., 326 n.; founded, 179 n.
San Francisco, 28 n.
San Francisco Bay, 16 n., 26 n., 28 n., 327 n.; discovered, 336 n.
San Francisco de Borja Mission, 21 n., 58, 378; endowed, 332 n.
San Francisco Javier Mission, 44, 152 n., 193, 232, 246, 275, 367; destroyed, 182; school, 211; origin, 171–72
San Gabriel Mission, 327 n.
San Ignacio de Kadakaamang Mission, 31, 74, 85 n., 244, 263, 334, 367; afflicted, 264 – 66; cotton at, 365 n.; founded, 260–61
San Javier Viggè Mission, 234
San José del Cabo Mission, 191 n., 284; founded, 277, 328, 367
San José del Cabo, village, 277 n., 366; Indians leaving, 308
San José del Comondù Mission, 191 n., 277, 367; cotton at, 365 n.; founded, 216, 302
San José, island, 19, 20 n., 87, 215, 240, 255, 326
San Juan Bautista de Londò Mission, 219 n.; founded, 170–71
San Lucas, cape, 6, 15, 17, 19, 22, 28 n., 59 n., 87, 219, 245, 277, 285, 335; pearls near, 74; rounded by Ulloa, 123 n.
San Luis Gonzaga Mission, 26, 367; founded, 256
San Marcos Island, 27
San Miguel Bay, 132 n.
San Miguel River, 148 n.
San Miguel, village, 246
San Pedro y San Pablo de Bicuñer Mission, 179 n.
San Pedro y San Pablo del Tubutama Mission, 192 n.

San Roque Island, 78
Santa Barbara, 68 n.
Santa Barbara Islands, 127 n.
Santa Catalina, island of, 20, 282
Santa Cruz, name of, viii
Santa Gertrudis Mission, 27, 191 n., 330 n.
Santa María Mission, 72, 73, 368; established, 364–65; most northerly, 86 n.
Santa María del Pòpulo Tonichi Mission, 249 n.
Santa Rosa Mission, *see* Todos Santos Mission
Santa Rosalía de Mulegè Mission, 25 n., 27 n., 31 n., 192 n.; cotton at, 365 n., 367
Santa Teresa de Caborca Mission, 192 n.
Santiago Mission, 90 n., 256 n., 260
Santiago de las Coras Mission, 191 n.
"Santo Tomás," ship, 123 n.
SARMIENTO DE SOTOMAYOR, BARCIA, 137 n.
SCHERER, HENRY, S.J., 144
SCHNITZLER, HERMAN, 77 n., 213 n.
scurvy, 286
SEDELMAYER, SANTIAGO, S.J., 357; trips of, 319
Serì Indians, 20 n., 225, 253, 353 n.; boat destroyed by, 217; and Ugarte, 247–48
SERRA, FATHER JUNÍPERO, 199 n.; founder of Mission, 132 n.; preaching of, 386 n.; wishes of, 326 n.
shaddock, 67
sharks, 73
sheep, 78, 84, 339, 373
shellfish, 68, 73
shellmounds, 25 n.
Sierra Madre Mountains, 147 n.
SIGÜENZA Y GÓNGORA, CARLOS, S.J., xii
Sinaloa, vii, x, 19, 31, 48 n., 74, 102 n., 126, 145, 155; aid from,

410

178; governor of, 137, 301, 302, 304–5; provisions from, 195
SISTIAGA, SEBASTIÁN DE, 234, 253, 261 n., 329, 334; advice of, 271; character of, 323; explorations, 246; harvest of, 263; quoted, 323; scruples, 324; sketch of, 233; *visitator*, 280
skate, 67
skunk, 79, 81
smallpox, 218, 270
snakes, 263, 389–93
soldiers, 143, 154, 156, 160, 165, 166, 170, 174, 180, 182, 192, 196, 200, 210, 240–41, 255–59, 261, 267, 271, 275, 278, 283, 295; complaints, 145; disorders, 326; discharged, 178; distribution of, 286 n., 288, 306, 378; enemies of, 203; escort of, 290; fear of, 278; guarding missionaries, 307; in South, 286 n.; illness of, 286; independence of, 304; as judges, 273–74, 378; leatherjacket, 326 n.; with Link, 357–60; murdered, 286 n., 288, 289, 294; nationality of, 129, 156 n.; number needed, 298; pay of, 374; poisoned, 213–14; with Portolá, 336 n.; to protect Mission, 190; relation to missionaries, 379; relation to viceroy, 304; repulsed, 167, 303; roads built by, 171; rumor about, 308; runaway, 189; at San José del Cabo, 304; to select captain, 180–81; subordination of, 177; support of, 198; work of, 378
SOMMERVOGEL, CARLOS, xviii, 277 n.
Sonora, vii, x, 16 n., 19, 36 n., 48 n., 260; Kino in, 148; Missions in, 180 n.; provisions from, 195; Salvatierra in, 178
South America, ix, 48 n., 126 n., 128 n.
Sparus fish, 68, 70, 72
STRAFORT, GUILLERMO, 247, 254
Strait of Anián, 130, 136 n., 254

SUÁREZ, ANTONIO, S.J., 140 n.
Supreme Council of the Indies, 196, 313, 315
swordfish, 67, 69

tajuà, 35, 36
TAMARAL, NICOLÁS, S.J., 277, 280, 284; aid refused by, 290; baptism of Indians, 278; defenseless, 290; eulogy on, 293 n.; explorations of, 45; a great spirit, 234; illness of, 289; Indians respected by, 288; letter of, 278, 290, 291; Mission moved by, 278; murdered, 294; orders of, 286; quoted, 285, 294; salute fired by, 289; sketch of life, 228 n.; warning of, 285; work of, 234–35
TAMBURINI, MIGUEL ÁNGEL, S.J., 276
tammià, 34, 35, 37
Tarahumara, 149, 275; disorders in, 147; Piccolo in, 165; tribes in, 155 n.
TARAVAL, MIGUEL, 279
TARAVAL, SIGISMUNDO, S.J., 3, 20 n., 260 n., 277, 281, 282; baptism of Indians, 283; escape from death, 295–96; manuscript of, 280; sketch of, 279–80; testimony of, 292 n.
tasajo, 56, 57
teddà, 41
tedeguà, 41
TECTO, FATHER JUAN, 385 n.
Tehuantepec, 119, 121
TEMPIS, ANTONIO, S.J., character of, 321–22.
Tepehuana, 148, 317
Tepic, Mexico, 188 n., 229, 354; description of, 353 n.
Tepocas, village, 317 n., 344 n.
Tepotzlán, xii, 260 n.
Tepotzotlán College, 151 n., 160 n., 292, 325; novitiate in, 238
Tepozcolula, 323
Texas, 125 n.
Tiburón Island, 20, 217 n.
tobacco, 46, 115

411

Todos Santos Mission, 90 n., 191 n., 277, 289, 366; established, 283-84; soldiers at, 286 n.
Todos Santos Island, 26 n.
Todos Santos, village, 214, 283, 320
Toltecs, 52 n.
TOMPES, HERNÁN FRANCISCO, S.J., 231 n., 375 n.
Topia Mission, 344 n.
Topia, province of, 317
TORTOLERO, LUIS DE, 156 n.; as *alférez*, 163; as captain, 161, 175
tezontle, 27
Tres Marías Islands, 26 n.
TRIST, NICHOLAS P., vii
Tubac, Presidio, 201 n.
Tubutama Mission, 319
Tulare County, 365 n.
Tuparàn, 108, 109, 112

Uchitas Indians, 320; location of, 255
UGARTE, JUAN DE, S.J., xviii, 3, 49 n., 154, 166, 181, 182, 184, 189, 190, 198, 216, 225, 240, 256, 257, 272, 318, 338, 375; apostle, 239; arguments of, 174-75; baptism of *guamas*, 211-12; birth, 152; boat built for, 235-36; character of, 152, 181, 183, 186; death of, 275; equipment of, 180 n.; eulogy on, 183-88; exploration of country, 213; first procurator, 231 n.; great strength of, 185-86; illness of, 247-48; in La Paz, 240-41; lion killed by, 185-86; Missions of, 211; mocked, 184, 187; and Muzagabal, 238; objections of, 198-99; physical labor of, 183-84; plans of, 235; plants vineyard, 6, 187; provisions, 170; quoted, 188, 236, 379; seeking food, 199; in Sonora, 192; in storm, 232-33; work of, 182-83, 206, 211
UGARTE, PEDRO DE, S.J., 197, 201, 210, 211, 219 n.; baptism of children, 200; escape from death, 209; health, 209; labors of, 208; Missions of, 207-8; quoted, 209; winning Indians, 208
ULLOA, FRANCISCO DE, viii, ix, 19 n., 22 n., 122, 123, 214; exploration of Gulf of California, viii, 123
United States, vii, viii, 32 n., 353 n.
University of Ingolstad, 220
University of Mexico, xiv, xv, 260 n.
Upper California, vii, 86 n., 173 n., 247 n., 314 n., 327 n.; cotton in, 365 n.; expedition to, 326 n.; Franciscans in, 385 n.; Missions of, 234 n., 239 n., 247 n., 386 n.
Uquibutama, Mission Antonio del, 192 n.

VACA, CABEZA DE, 124
VALERO, MARQUÉS DE, 229
Valladolid, college at, 151 n.
VALLEJO, DOÑA JOSEFA, 192
VALLISNIERI, ANTONIO, 394
VANIÈRE, JACQUES, S.J., 395
VÁSQUEZ, FRANCISCO PABLO, xvi
VELASCO, LUIS DE, 256
Vellicatá, village, 326, 386 n.
VENEGAS, MIGUEL, S.J., xvii, 4, 7, 18 n., 20 n., 102 n., 137 n., 138 n., 153 n., 156 n., 188 n., 219 n., 229 n., 293 n., 306 n.; history by, 3, 279 n.
VENTURA, LUCAS, S.J., 4, 44 n., 352, 383 n.; procurator, 335
Vera Cruz, viii, xii, xiv, 381, 385; Dominicans at, 386 n.; Jesuits at, 382 n.
verben, 204, 287
Vigge-Biundò, 171, 172
VILLAPUENTE, MARQUÉS DE, 30 n., 153 n., 191, 216, 260 n.; supports Missions, 151 n., 192, 237, 239, 276, 328
VILLAVIEJA, JUAN, S.J., 383 n.
VILLENA, MARQUÉS DE, 136
vineyard, 6, 42, 264
Virgen de los Dolores Mission, 197, 254-56, 324, 367
Virgen of Pilar, village, 241

Vizcaíno Desert, 23 n., 24 n.
Vizcaíno, Sebastián, 18 n., 128 n., 131 n., 245; death of, 133; proposal of, 127–28, 130–31, 133; reason for expedition, 132; voyage of, 133 n.
viznaga, 37, 56

Wagner, Javier, S.J., 306
Ward, Lester F., 359 n.
Washington, George, 289 n.
wasps, 60–61
Watson, Sereno, 2. n.
West Indies, 71 n.
whales, 67, 69, 281
White, Andrew, S.J., x
Wilbur, Marguerite Eyer, 102 n., 153 n., 307 n.
Williska, mines of, 31

xicama, 53
xocohuiztli, 131

Yaqui Indians, 217, 299, 300; daughters of, 351; good as seamen, 318
Yaqui River, 201 n., 209, 210, 213
Yeneca, 284, 285
Yucatán, 126 n.
Yuma Massacre, 179 n., 327 n.

Zacatecas, city of, 324
Zacatecas, province, 151; college in, 151 n.
Zacatula, viii
zalate, 39
Zappa, Juan Bautista, S.J., career of, 149 n.; letter of, 150
Zevallos, Francisco, S.J., xii, 355